VMware Cross-Cloud Architecture

Automate and orchestrate your Software-Defined
Data Center on AWS

Ajit Pratap Kundan

BIRMINGHAM - MUMBAI

VMware Cross-Cloud Architecture

Commissioning Editor: Vijin Boricha
Acquisition Editor: Namrata Patil
Content Development Editor: Amrita Noronha
Technical Editor: Nilesh Sawakhande
Copy Editor: Safis Editing
Project Coordinator: Shweta H Birwatkar
Proofreader: Safis Editing
Indexer: Tejal Daruwale Soni
Graphics: Jisha Chirayil
Production Coordinator: Aparna Bhagat

First published: March 2018

Production reference: 1280318

Published by Packt Publishing Ltd.
Livery Place
35 Livery Street
Birmingham
B3 2PB, UK.

ISBN 978-1-78728-343-5

www.packtpub.com

`mapt.io`

Mapt is an online digital library that gives you full access to over 5,000 books and videos, as well as industry leading tools to help you plan your personal development and advance your career. For more information, please visit our website.

Why subscribe?

- Spend less time learning and more time coding with practical eBooks and Videos from over 4,000 industry professionals

- Improve your learning with Skill Plans built especially for you

- Get a free eBook or video every month

- Mapt is fully searchable

- Copy and paste, print, and bookmark content

PacktPub.com

Did you know that Packt offers eBook versions of every book published, with PDF and ePub files available? You can upgrade to the eBook version at `www.PacktPub.com` and as a print book customer, you are entitled to a discount on the eBook copy. Get in touch with us at `service@packtpub.com` for more details.

At `www.PacktPub.com`, you can also read a collection of free technical articles, sign up for a range of free newsletters, and receive exclusive discounts and offers on Packt books and eBooks.

Contributors

About the author

Ajit Pratap Kundan is an infrastructure software consultant with 18 years' experience, having has worked with Novell, Redington, PCS, and Innodata. Currently, he is a technical consultant at VMware, Delhi and provides productive solutions for Federal Government clients, espousing the benefits of hybrid cloud with cross-cloud services. He has a graduate degree in electronics engineering from Pune University with experience in Lotus, Tivoli, PlateSpin, IDM, SUSE Linux, Sentinel, and all of the VMware products. He is an ITIL, CCNA, Lotus, SUSE, Red Hat, and VMware-certified professional.

I currently reside in New Delhi, India with my wife and two boys. I would like to thank my wife for putting up with my late-night writing sessions. I also give deep thanks and gratitude to my colleagues for their guidance and suggestions.

About the reviewer

Daniel Jonathan Valik is an industry expert in unified communications and collaboration technologies, cloud computing, and Platform as a Service (PaaS). He has worked for large software companies and start-ups in Europe, Asia (APAC), and the US. He is the founder of Hanako Consulting LLC—a strategy, product marketing, and management consulting company. He has strong expertise in areas such as IoT, DevOps, Automation, Microservices, Containerization, Virtualization, Cloud-Native Applications, Artificial Intelligence, and Contact Center Technologies.

Packt is searching for authors like you

If you're interested in becoming an author for Packt, please visit authors.packtpub.com and apply today. We have worked with thousands of developers and tech professionals, just like you, to help them share their insight with the global tech community. You can make a general application, apply for a specific hot topic that we are recruiting an author for, or submit your own idea.

Table of Contents

Preface

VMware Cross-Cloud Architecture is the most trusted platform, not only for new applications, but also for existing legacy applications. This book will introduce you to tried and tested cloud design and deployment methodologies to help you achieve your business objectives and overcome all of the challenges faced by traditional data centers. Cloud Foundation and vRealize Suite will help you to set up and integrate private clouds with public clouds such as AWS and IBM Soft Layer.

Who this book is for

This book is intended for those planning, designing, and implementing the virtualization components of the SDDC foundational infrastructure. The intended audience is core technical teams, including those responsible for product development, servers, storage, networking, security, and backup and recovery. It is assumed that the reader has knowledge of and familiarity with virtualization concepts and related topics (including storage and networking).

What this book covers

Chapter 1, *The Freedom with Cross-Cloud Architecture*, introduces different types of clouds, where we will learn about all of the cloud benefits that can help you to overcome traditional or multi-cloud challenges with Cross Cloud Architecture.

Chapter 2, *Implementing Service Architecture for Cross-Cloud Services*, makes use of VMware Cloud Foundation deployment to achieve a unified **software-defined data center** (**SDDC**) platform for the hybrid cloud, that is based on VMware compute, storage, and network virtualization, a natively integrated software stack that can be used on-premises for private cloud deployment or run as a service from the public cloud with consistent, simple operations by integrating it with VMware vRealize Suite, VMware Horizon, and VMware Integrated OpenStack to deliver a comprehensive SDDC platform.

Chapter 3, *Transforming a Data Center from Silos to Software-Defined Services*, explains how to host applications in the cloud world to provide administrators with flexibility and best control along with business values from Cross Cloud Architecture.

Chapter 4, *Designing a Mixed Cloud Model with VMware*, combines a best-in-class private cloud with leading public clouds, all powered by the ever-reliable and most flexible hybrid cloud platform offered by VMware.

Chapter 5, *Implementing Service Redundancy Across All Layers*, talks about different vCenter Server deployment topologies with redundant operations, and all of the High availability functionalities of vSphere, such as vMotion, and different Fault Tolerance options comparing their strengths and weaknesses.

Chapter 6, *Designing Software-Defined Storage Services*, discusses how to design and scale a **software defined storage service** and deep dives into reference deployment scenarios of VMware vSAN.

Chapter 7, *VMware Cloud Assess, Design, and Deploy Service*, discusses the technical analysis of all VMware Cloud components (including their design and configuration) in detail and also helps you to design correctly with best practices to follow for specific use cases and the orchestration of all cloud components.

Chapter 8, *Transforming Your Network Architecture*, provides examples of creating, provisioning, and managing networks in a software-defined way using the underlying physical network as a simple packet-forwarding backplane, and also explains how to migrate from legacy network architectures to new network virtualization techniques.

Chapter 9, *Dealing with Data Sovereignty*, explains sovereignty compliance strategies and how to use an encryption solution to secure data at all stages of the cloud journey. This chapter also shows you how to ensure that data backup and secondary data centers for data recovery/disaster recovery purposes remain local.

Chapter 10, *Designing Effective Compliance Regulations to Fix Violations*, explains design compliance regulations for multiple purposes by aligning line of business divisions with the best technology, such as VMware, to be compliant in this versatile market. Security and compliance must be a shared responsibility between IT and its cloud service provider.

Chapter 11, *Lower TCO and Greater ROI with Maximum Agility*, explains that, in order to achieve the goal of cloud, we need to extend virtualization techniques across the entire data center to lower the capital and operational expenditure, achieving maximum ROI.

Chapter 12, *VMware Pricing and Licensing for a Cross-Cloud Model*, discusses VMware Cloud Foundation pricing and licensing as well as other VMware Cloud component licensing models.

Chapter 13, *The Economics of Cross-Cloud Services*, explains a cost analysis of different cost categories and compares competitive existing solutions on the market.

To get the most out of this book

This book is intended for administrators with different levels of server, storage, and networking experience:

- All administrators can learn network design and storage scaling to manage and monitor hosts in the vSphere environment.
- Experienced VMware administrators can learn about private/hybrid cloud design and deployment in different scenarios. They can customize their designs as per customer requirements.

Download the color images

We also provide a PDF file that has color images of the screenshots/diagrams used in this book. You can download it here: http://www.packtpub.com/sites/default/files/downloads/VMwareCrossCloudArchitect ure_ColorImages.pdf.

Conventions used

There are a number of text conventions used throughout this book.

CodeInText: Indicates code words in text, database table names, folder names, filenames, file extensions, pathnames, dummy URLs, user input, and Twitter handles. Here is an example: "Open Services.msc from the run command."

Bold: Indicates a new term, an important word, or words that you see onscreen. For example, words in menus or dialog boxes appear in the text like this. Here is an example: "The syslog service can be configured on ESXi using host profiles, the VMware vSphere command line interface, or the **Advanced Configuration** options in the vSphere Web Client"

Warnings or important notes appear like this.

 Tips and tricks appear like this.

Get in touch

Feedback from our readers is always welcome.

General feedback: Email feedback@packtpub.com and mention the book title in the subject of your message. If you have questions about any aspect of this book, please email us at questions@packtpub.com.

Errata: Although we have taken every care to ensure the accuracy of our content, mistakes do happen. If you have found a mistake in this book, we would be grateful if you would report this to us. Please visit www.packtpub.com/submit-errata, selecting your book, clicking on the Errata Submission Form link, and entering the details.

Piracy: If you come across any illegal copies of our works in any form on the Internet, we would be grateful if you would provide us with the location address or website name. Please contact us at copyright@packtpub.com with a link to the material.

If you are interested in becoming an author: If there is a topic that you have expertise in and you are interested in either writing or contributing to a book, please visit authors.packtpub.com.

Reviews

Please leave a review. Once you have read and used this book, why not leave a review on the site that you purchased it from? Potential readers can then see and use your unbiased opinion to make purchase decisions, we at Packt can understand what you think about our products, and our authors can see your feedback on their book. Thank you!

For more information about Packt, please visit packtpub.com.

The Freedom with Cross-Cloud Architecture

1

This chapter briefs you on cloud service architectures. The chapter includes the following sections:

- Cloud benefits and challenges
- VMware solutions to overcome different cloud challenges
- VMware Cross-Cloud Architecture
- Overview of private, public, and hybrid clouds
- Overview of vCloud Air, AWS, and the IBM Cloud

Readers will be able to design elastic IT infra capabilities and set up a basic application hosting and DevOps environment with VMware components after going through this book. You will be able to install and configure all the building blocks to get the benefits of VMware SDDC components in an on-premises private cloud, a public cloud such as IBM or AWS, or a mix of both—a hybrid cloud.

Scaling your business with Cross-Cloud Architecture

Digital transformation is taking place in each and every market segment, including financial services, healthcare, retail, education, and government. The world is being redefined by software and data, creating new priorities for every business, and new imperatives for every IT organization. IT has to be agile enough to drive growth and extend the capabilities and services that they deliver to **lines of business (LOBs)**. IT organizations have to transform their legacy setup and extend their IT environments to public clouds to boost innovation, agility, and cost savings.

IT is playing a key role in business growth. IT organizations work as strategic partners, and business leaders are seeking better alignment with their technical teams as they evaluate go-to-market strategies and important decisions, such as mergers and acquisitions.

Organizations expect their technical teams to support them with a modern IT environment that helps them accelerate innovation and agility, so they can compete with new services and applications that will help them to grow their business rapidly. IT organizations are expected to help keep costs in line. To address these expectations, IT teams are embracing public cloud solutions.

Top IT drivers for integrating public clouds

IT leaders cite three primary drivers for integrating public clouds:

- **Disruptive approach**: In today's disrupted, accelerated, app-centric marketplace, speeding up time-to-market is critical; LOBs and developers see public clouds as the fastest option for meeting their IT platform requirements.
- **CapEx pressures**: IT teams are under considerable pressure to take advantage of potential cost savings. They are replacing on-premises infrastructures with public cloud-based hosting models or services, to increase capacity while reducing operational efforts and costs. According to a Gartner research director, *"Customers are saving 14 percent of their budgets because of public cloud adoption, which subsequently grow public cloud businesses."*
- **A cloud-first strategy**: Most senior leadership mandates a cloud-first strategy to drive reduced time to value by leveraging shared infrastructure and paying only for the resources consumed. Many enterprises are already using hybrid clouds; some mix of private and public clouds, for greater flexibility and resilience.

Businesses are strongly embracing the cloud for every challenge. Enterprises recognize the value of public cloud flexibility and agility, but still must address key challenges to integrate hybrid cloud solutions into their operations.

Cloud challenges and solutions

We have cloud options, such as a private cloud, different service provider options, and large public clouds. The best solution is possible without adding cost and complexity. The VMware Cross-Cloud Architecture helps you to choose the cloud that fulfills your business objective.

Challenge 1 – connection and security with full compliance and control

We have to manage incompatibility between different cloud models or service providers, otherwise it will create new silos and create overhead. You must avoid these silos and get a unified console to fulfill the requirements of the business objective. IT organizations are looking for ways to take advantage of the flexibility and agility that various clouds offer, even though many mission-critical and data-sensitive apps are currently running on-premises. We need to take a close look at how we can migrate applications running on-premises or in a private cloud to the public cloud, without adding any cost to their existing investments. We have to utilize the application design, SDLC processes, and maintain security and compliance best practices.

Solution: VMware overcomes this issue by extending a network to public clouds through a network virtualization technique. It interacts with public clouds and services in a secure manner by applying all governance regulatory compliance. You can maintain all on-premises network policies, even extending your applications across multiple clouds. You have all the freedom to host/publish your applications anywhere and anytime with end-to-end control and compliance.

Challenge 2 – managing/integrating across clouds

We want to host our applications and manage resources in various clouds. As organizations invest in multiple clouds, they are also creating more complex, siloed environments that don't have common management tools or enterprise-class security across their cloud infrastructure. They may even build new teams to own and operate these different silos, reducing efficiency and driving up costs. Customers are looking for a solution that can help them to manage mixed clouds from a single console.

Solution: VMware will give you the holistic view from a single console of the entire infrastructure, and also management tools to monitor and manage resources, applications, and operations across different clouds. This approach prevents you from experiencing cloud vendor lock-in, monitoring operations, and managing specific **service-level agreements** (**SLAs**). You have holistic management and your end users can connect to public clouds with confidence. A single unified management layer with automated processes delivers a fully customized cloud management platform, which gears up service delivery, enhances operations, and delivers end-user choice with control and compliance, across heterogeneous, multi-cloud environments.

VMware Cross-Cloud Architecture

The VMware Cross-Cloud Architecture provides freedom for end users and control from a service provider perspective, helping a customer to make hybrid cloud decisions, when running, managing, connecting, and securing all of their applications across any cloud in a common operating environment.

The Cross-Cloud Architecture enables uniform deployment models, security policies, visibility, and governance for all applications running on-premises and off, irrespective of the underlying cloud or hypervisor.

The following architecture consists of SDDC-based VMware Cloud Foundation with a hyper-converged software solution, a set of VMware Cross-Cloud Services, and the vRealize cloud management platform:

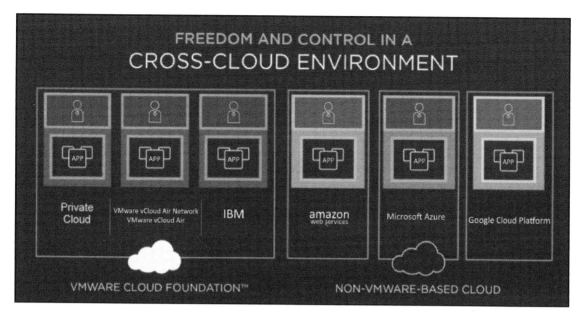

VMware Cross-Cloud Architecture

Secure connectivity across clouds

Now the question is, how can we manage and monitor resources across mixed clouds with seamless control and compliant connectivity? The answer is VMware Cross-Cloud Services, which is a set of services that will give users a common operating platform to monitor, manage, govern, and secure applications running across private and public clouds. VMware Cross-Cloud Services will provide visibility of cloud resource consumption and map it to its costs, provide dynamic on-demand networks and security policies, and automate the process of deployment (Green Field or Brown Field deployments) and migration of applications and data (new or legacy) across both VMware-based and heterogeneous clouds.

The following figure depicts multi-cloud environment operations:

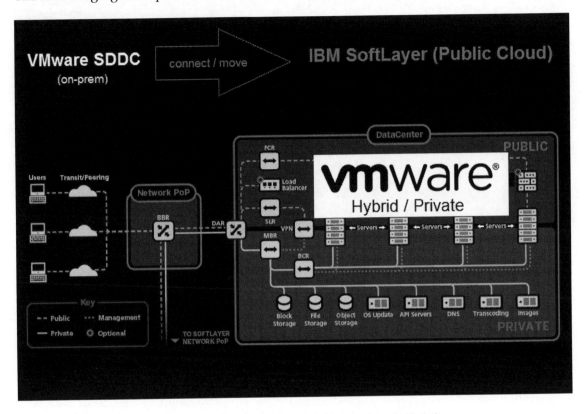

Cross-Cloud Services provides a common operating platform across private and public clouds

A single self service provisioning portal is good enough to monitor operations and manage resources of all of the customer's workloads/applications across private and public clouds.

The different customer LOBs will be able to get their specific data on demand in their customized format at any time, such as costing of specific apps or managing certain SLAs to meet business objectives.

Our goal is to provide all services across any cloud so users can consume these services without having any concern or doubts in mind.

We can achieve this by extending the same network virtualization concept that is already used in a customer's private clouds to a public cloud. Customers want to enable uniform and encrypted logical networks across all clouds, wherever their applications get hosted.

Cross-Cloud services will give unified cloud-network management, while a customer's LOBs can use public clouds as per their business demand.

Customers will get tools to secure their data and applications, as well as control their costs, by enabling developers and the business to innovate across any cloud infrastructure that fits their requirements.

The backbone of a private cloud

Customers used to say that their LOBs wanted IT resources on demand, as per their business objective. Their LOBs don't want to be dependent on the IT team, and want to consume IT services as per their need without any constraint on time and location. They want to provision apps to their end users on any device, at any time, and from any location. To achieve this, they need agile IT infrastructure that can provision them IT resources on demand from anywhere, anytime, and on any device.

For example, an Oracle database needs to be 100% available 24*7*365 days. Customers have to deliver more applications with the same resources without exceeding its TCO and at the same time, maintain the end user's demands by fulfilling all compliance parameters.

To build a robust private cloud while considering all the preceding parameters, we have to consider the following three mechanisms, which will provide customers with a resilient and flexible platform to run their businesses:

- **Virtualize all components of IT**: Customers already know the benefits of compute virtualization. VMware can extend the same concept to storage and network for optimal utilization of hardware, based on the SDDC concept.
- **Automate IT**: Virtualizing every component will drastically reduce your CapEx but you need to automate the process to reduce the Opex cost. A self service provisioning portal will help you to provision infrastructure as a service to different LOBs and this will reduce the dependency of LOBs on the IT team. It will speed up IT service delivery, which enables users to meet time to market demand and admin to monitor and manage for these services.

- **Support heterogenous environment**: Today's digital business world demands collaboration between LOBs, developers, IT Infra teams, and support for digital business transformation and innovation. VMware has a private cloud solution with open APIs, to use OpenStack (VMware Integrated OpenStack APIs) and developers can reap the benefits of containers.

We can build a private cloud integrated with all the required hardware components in a single/multiple engineered box by using the **hyper-converged infrastructure (HCI)** concept (`http://view.ceros.com/vm-ware/vmware-hci/p/1`). It has seamless, integrated, unified management, virtualized storage, network, and compute. Customers can build HCI solutions with VMware hyper-converged software (vSphere and vSAN) on any x86 (Intel/AMD processors) server or, they can buy a fully integrated solution with all the required hardware and software from any VMware partner, such as DELL, HP, Cisco, Fijitshu, Hitachi, Nutanix, Lenovo, and so on.

VMware Cloud Foundation plus the hyper-converged concept gives you SDDC in a box, which simplifies the installation, update, and software life cycle management of a private cloud, as well as reducing Opex. It brings together compute, storage, and network virtualization, enabling customers to effectively leverage virtualization technologies for efficiency, availability, performance, and scale.

It is also integrated with the vRealize cloud management platform and VMware SDDC Manager software, which helps customers to automate the deployment, configuration, and day-to-day management of a cloud across different environments. Developers get more options to innovate in the private cloud infrastructure and administrators get a single operating platform to manage private and hybrid clouds.

Extending services to public clouds

Customers can extend their VMware private clouds smoothly to vSphere-based public clouds, such as the VMware vCloud Air public cloud service, in two ways:

The following diagram explains the common operating service platform:

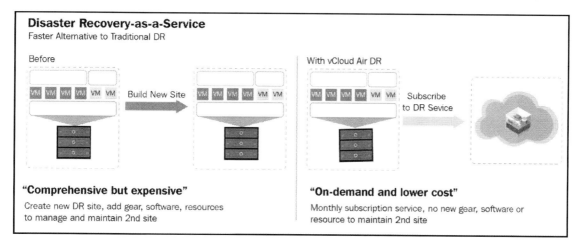

Cross-Cloud Services consumption model

The customer wants an instant way to build a disaster recovery solution or set up a test and dev environment. vCloud Air (also available from the vCloud Air Network of cloud providers) acts as a self-service **virtual machine** (**VM**) vending machine. It lowers the cost per application and utilizes existing investments with 100% compatibility, common management tools, and zero rewrites. It will also help customers with seamless app portability, which reduces time, risk, and cost. The following figure depicts minimizing risk while reducing cost and time to market:

Disaster Recovery-as-a-Service
Faster Alternative to Traditional DR

Before

Build New Site

With vCloud Air DR

Subscribe to DR Sevice

"Comprehensive but expensive"
Create new DR site, add gear, software, resources to manage and maintain 2nd site

"On-demand and lower cost"
Monthly subscription service, no new gear, software or resource to maintain 2nd site

Traditional DR versus DR hosted in public cloud

Sometimes, customers want to build a private cloud in a public cloud environment and leverage the complete VMware SDDC stack, including full management and control.

The VMware Cloud Foundation, with leading cloud service providers (IBM Cloud, Amazon Web Services, and vCloud Air), can deliver the full SDDC stack in a managed hybrid-cloud **environment as-a-service (EaaS)** option.

These options help customers with more choice and flexibility in how they build, run, and manage a private cloud and move, or extend to a public cloud. Customers can leverage their investment in technologies and in their skill sets, so they can deploy any, or all of these options using existing skills, processes, and tools.

Multi-cloud/mixed cloud use cases

A combination of public cloud services with a private cloud provides you the best possible robust and elastic cloud strategy. You get all the freedom and flexibility with no cloud vendor lock-in. You can retrieve more values with continuous innovation. VMware has transformed data centers, with freedom and control over hardware, and now VMware will provide you the same freedom and control over cloud options.

The following image shows that any app can be accessed any time, on any device in the VMware Cross-Cloud Services model:

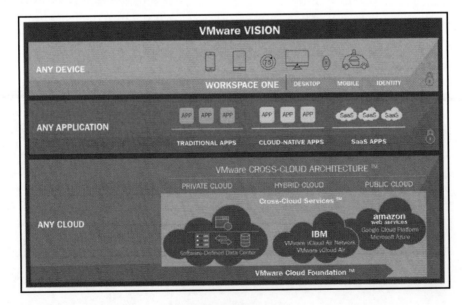

Any app on any device from any cloud

Cloud solutions supporting business objectives

The VMware Cross-Cloud Architecture and Cross-Cloud Services give customers all the options to set up their IT infra, as per their business model in different locations. It will give the customers all kinds of private, public, and hybrid cloud solutions to optimize their IT cost, as well as align with their specific business objectives.

Modernizing your data center

Customers have to adopt new applications to align with the always-changing business requirements, and they can only achieve this by leveraging cloud-native technologies available on different platforms/clouds.

Customers can avoid operational issues by integrating these new applications with existing IT operations. They can also move these existing applications to on-premises or public clouds. These applications with cloud services can be redesigned/developed to adopt new IT models. VMware solutions help customers benefit from public clouds by migrating existing applications to the public cloud.

The Cross-Cloud Architecture helps customers to build, run, connect, and secure apps across any cloud, and work in a common operating platform. Customers can build common platforms for future applications and digital business roadmaps, and avoid the bottlenecks of different cloud silos.

Customers will get more choices and interoperability with VMware Cross-Cloud Architecture and Cross-Cloud Services, in how to build, run, and manage their applications in various kinds of cloud models from different vendors. Customers have the full freedom to deploy a solution based on an SDDC-based private cloud to a VMware hybrid cloud, whichever fits with their strategy to achieve their specific business goals.

VMware hybrid clouds

VMware hybrid clouds enable customers to run their existing legacy applications and new cloud-ready applications from a common platform and get the best of both worlds. Customers can scale, consolidate, and migrate infrastructure on demand by taking advantage of existing tools, processes, and skill sets. They can extend their on-premises infrastructure to a public cloud in a different location, or can set up disaster recovery sites in different regions. It will help in data center consolidation and application migration by improving dynamic capacity capabilities for new application development.

It supports applications by providing business agility, resilience, scalability, and any choice of public cloud provider, such as VMware vCloud Air and vCloud Air network partners or, IBM Cloud and **Amazon Web Services** (**AWS**) by extending their on-premises data centers. IT teams can run any application anywhere, with complete application portability thanks to the VMware Hybrid Cloud. They can maintain operational consistency by employing a common management experience and networking constructs to maximize use of existing skill sets and tools.

Organizations seeking to reduce CapEx investment can replace on-premises data center infrastructure with VMware Cloud Foundation, a complete SDDC infrastructure platform, delivered as a service through VMware vCloudAir, VMware Cloud Foundation on IBM, and VMware Cloud on AWS. They can also take advantage of global scale and reach, with a presence in over 100 countries, vCloud Air, and 4,000+ vCloud Air network partners, including IBM and AWS.

Organizations are also exploring advanced management and automation for cloud brokering and integrating DevOps practices across multiple clouds. As needs change, they need an easy exit strategy for moving applications and virtual machines from any public cloud at any point, without vendor lock-in. VMware provides different options to customers to connect securely and manage multiple clouds with on-premises solutions or SaaS-based services.

IT organizations can take advantage of VMware's cloud management platform (VMware vRealize Suite) with advanced networking capabilities from VMware NSX together to manage different private and public clouds.

Customers can build and run applications, migrate them across multiple clouds, securely connect all clouds, and manage all workloads across networks. Advanced operations management features help to get a single unified console of the health, performance, and capacity management of virtual machines across clouds plus policy-based governance. For organizations in heavily regulated industries such as financial services and healthcare, VMware helps ensure compliance by monitoring the status of workloads, detecting drift, and automating remediation.

With cost an ever-growing issue, IT teams can also leverage VMware solutions to see and control the cost of cloud services.

VMware will help IT teams to manage any application or workload running on any cloud using Cross-Cloud Services (SaaS-based management and network services).

These planned service offerings include the on-boarding of existing cloud services and users, cloud service costing and reporting, centralized identity, access and operations management, networking, micro-segmentation, and encryption.

VMware – a partner for every cloud

It's a multi-cloud world, but it takes an integrated approach for organizations to achieve their digital transformation goals. Teaming up with VMware and standardizing on SDDC solutions that support both private and public clouds increases enterprise flexibility, security, and choice while rapidly reducing cost and risk.

Over the last two decades, VMware has been the leader in virtualization, and has held the top spot in Gartner's Magic/Leaders Quadrant for x86 Server Virtualization Infrastructure for more then seven consecutive years. VMware is positioned furthest in capability to execute and future roadmap vision in Gartner's latest report.

Customers can build a private cloud without any risk, which can extend seamlessly to compatible public clouds and run any application on any cloud.

We have to be very cautious when choosing a hybrid cloud provider compared to private or public cloud solutions. We have additional challenges such as integration, interoperability, and common operating environments in deciding a hybrid cloud provider over a public or private cloud.

We choose a private or public cloud based on customer applications and business objectives. We have to know the feasibility of applications while considering a hybrid cloud solution.

We are going to make use of a hybrid cloud for extending resources/services such as DR services from a private data center to a public cloud. We try to maintain uniform security, SLAs, and management as much as possible, so it is close to a private cloud, and achieve a common operating environment.

VMware vCloud Air

VMware's vSphere is one of the first tried and tested cloud operating platforms. vSphere hypervisor is rock solid in its performance and reliability to become a first choice for most of the cloud providers. VMware vCloud Air is a vendor agnostic public cloud platform running Microsoft, Linux, and vSphere supported operating systems and applications as per customer choice. It provides a consistent and certified platform suited to most operating systems, along with most of the applications running on x86 (32–64 bit) platforms (Intel/AMD). VMware uses the same vCloud software for both the private and public cloud deployments, along with all required APIs to keep seamless integration and management of resources.

VMware also helps in **software defined networking** (**SDN**) concepts and brings that exposure to the hybrid cloud through NSX and virtualizing both network and security components to achieve micro-segmentation.

Customers can get a hybrid cloud from VMware vCloud Air, as well as from vCloud Air partners who are certified to run VMware's vCloud Air services from different regions. Customers can optimize cost with various options to leverage VMware vCloud Air services.

AWS hybrid cloud

AWS doesn't have the privilege of providing a hybrid cloud service as compared to the other cloud providers. AWS helps customers run/host applications in their public cloud data center and utilize AWS in a hybrid environment to run their DR or extended services.

AWS is more focused on public cloud offerings and does not offer its cloud management software offsite to achieve common operating environments for both worlds. AWS leverages a direct connect service that bridges the customer's data center with a **virtual private cloud** (**VPC**) resource to get a hybrid solution. AWS has the best of the best resources and expertise to manage the hosted side of a hybrid cloud, but they don't have a roadmap for on-premises private clouds, although they are one of the best public cloud providers. Direct connect is a specific connection from a VMware or Microsoft private cloud, but is not a universal connector to integrate with other cloud providers.

The AWS GovCloud program is a hybrid cloud offering that uses AWS for on-site private clouds for the US government. AWS doesn't have this option for private customers.

AWS customers need a solution for private cloud management, and have a dependency on third-party offerings which increases Opex.

IBM Cloud for VMware solutions

IBM Cloud for VMware Solutions help customers to improve the cost per application, reduce Opex, and have the agility to extend applications/services to the IBM Cloud. You can benefit from both cloud models by expanding or migrating workloads/services using secure and seamless networking capabilities that work in heterogeneous environments, powered by VMware NSX. IBM Bluemix bare metal servers on IBM Cloud will provide you with all these services by maintaining full control and compliance.

IBM Cloud gives access to the VMware solution by managing resources as you are doing your data center. You can consume VMware software based on a pay-as-you-use model. IBM Cloud for VMware can help you with uniform management and regulatory governance for your hybrid cloud setup with a common networking and security operating model.

Solution features

The features listed are as follows:

- **Uniform management**: Self service provisioning portal, seamless access, and monitors and manages a hybrid cloud with the VMware tools and skill sets you already have
- **Pay-as-you-go-model**: Cost-effective CPU-based pricing of VMware software and pricing is per resource consumption
- **Global data centers**: IBM Cloud data centers have a footprint across North America, Europe, and Asia so you can get cloud resources in most of the places you require them
- **Network virtualization**: IBM Cloud data centers are built with robust networking infrastructure and virtualization software having the best bandwidth pipe and connectivity, which enables your applications to have the highest speed and reliability

Reference architecture

IBM Cloud for VMware Solutions is based on Cloud Foundation technology and it helps with deployment, migration, and management of these SDDC components in the IBM public cloud. You can partially deploy SDDC now to the IBM Cloud in an automated way rather than doing it manually. Deployment and configuration, which used to take several weeks, can be possible within a few hours.

This easy and simple deployment helps you to focus on other innovative works rather than putting your man hours and money into building your own environment. As you are able to create different setups on demand within a few hours, you have options to build both hybrid cloud solutions, expanding your private cloud and the IBM public cloud, as well as cloud-native solutions in the IBM public cloud. You will get disaster recovery or high-availability capabilities for your applications with the multi-cloud deployment model. The following image shows the versatile Hybrid Cloud platform:

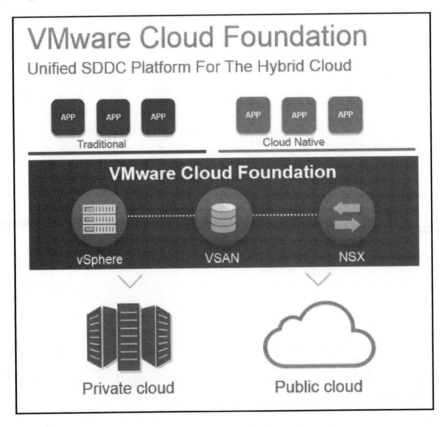

VMware SDDC on IBM Cloud

The VMware components in IBM Cloudware are:

⏱	VMware Cloud Foundation on IBM Cloud	The Cloud Foundation will automate your VMware software deployment. The VMware SDDC solution combines IBM Bluemix infrastructure with vSphere, .Virtual SAN, NSX, and SDDC Manager for a seamless hybrid cloud setup. You are able to use the same management tool to manage this setup without re-investing in resources or skill set.
🕐	VMware vCenter Server on IBM Cloud	vCenter Server on IBM Cloud helps you in on-demand, automated deployments with integrated backup, which combines IBM Bluemix bare metal servers with vSphere and vCenter solution to create, deploy, and manage your virtual machines with scale up or scale out architecture as per customer requirements.
◇	IBM Bluemix Infrastructure with VMware software	You can optimize, expand or migrate your virtual machines to high-performance, global cloud resources. You can customize your deployment in a cloud infrastructure to extend your footprint around the world on demand, and manage it all with a management control that you are already familiar with.
🔧	Cloud Professional Services	The Cloud Professional Services team helps you to plan, design, deploy, and configure VMware solutions on bare metal servers. They will help with integration, virtual machine migration, or application portability.

Choose your IBM Cloud and VMware Solution

IBM Cloud's data centers have a presence across North America, Europe, and Asia, which helps you to scale globally and also retain complete control and automation of your operations, both on-premises and in the public cloud.

IBM Cloud for VMware solutions

We will discuss high-level architecture of cloud deployment. The basic factors to start with cloud architecture and its deployment strategy are as follows:

- Cloud interfaces and formats must follow industry standards

- Information is needed to perform specific functions
- End-to-end monitoring of all resource usage by both the cloud consumer and provider
- Guarantee of reliability, availability, security, and performance
- Availability should be guaranteed at each and every layer
- Compliant identity separation to avoid leakage of data to other customers
- Full visibility and control
- Enhance productivity and rapid growth with transformation of IT setup
- Guaranteed data protection with full compliance and regulations
- Minimize manual operations with automated operations

Conceptual view

The conceptual view has three key roles—the Service Provider, Consumer, and the Cloud Broker, as depicted here:

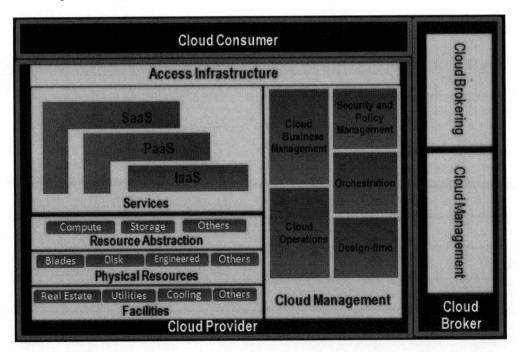

Cloud Conceptual view

The cloud provider role is the most critical among all three of them. We can't define scale for a cloud infrastructure and its specific requirements easily. You have to plan and design cloud deployment and consider all SLAs while maintaining all regulatory governance and compliance.

Cloud providers manage the costs of all factors including the cost of space, building, cooling, utilities, and rack spaces. They have to define TCO/ROI per application for specific periods of time.

Logical view

Access layers comprise two functionalities: interfaces and network, as shown here. The cloud has different interfaces to interact with the underlying services and its management capabilities. The access layer has end-user facing interfaces along with operator defined capabilities. The following figure shows natively stack with compute, storage and network pools:

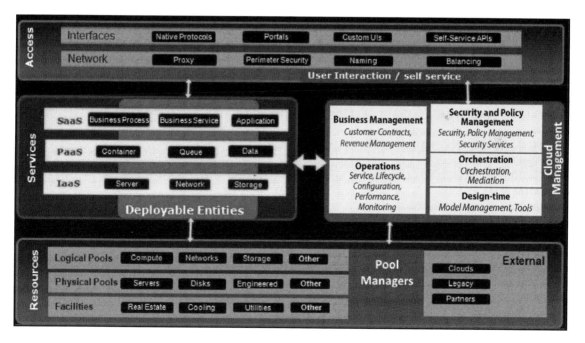

Cloud logical view

You can get the management capabilities for all types of services from a common cloud management layer. You get a holistic view and end-to-end visibility of the infrastructure through a unified management layer. The management layer is capable of supporting build time and runtime services.

Deployment view

Cloud deployment depends on the scale of deployment and the type of services. Private cloud implementations are very different compared to large scale public cloud infrastructures that support hundreds of customers.

Most public cloud deployments are big in scale and need to design mission critical infrastructure to achieve performance, availability, security, flexibility, and SLA goals.

Summary

We have learnt about VMware SDDC technology-based cloud offerings in this chapter. SDDC systems lower costs while dramatically improving ease of use. Companies can deploy on-premises, private cloud infrastructure that has the ease of use and scalability of a public cloud, with guaranteed quality of service. Cross-Cloud solutions help you to deliver the only unified SDDC platform for the hybrid cloud (AWS, IBM, and vCloud Air), with customized and well-designed on-premises cloud service deployment options.

Through an investment in VMware Cloud Foundation, companies can be assured that their data center infrastructure can be easily consumed, managed, upgraded, and enhanced to provide the best private cloud along with public cloud offerings, such as AWS and IBM, at the lowest cost. Using a modular, scale-out approach means infrastructure is added in hours, not days, and businesses can be assured that infrastructure scales linearly without any added complexity.

Choice is key: any app on any cloud at any time. Customers need a choice of where to run workloads. We shouldn't be forced into a single public cloud provider. We can choose the public cloud (such as AWS, IBM, vCloud Air, across the world) and not end up with applications trapped somewhere.

This book helps you understand why bimodal IT isn't necessarily the best path forward for the long term. We get the outcomes promised by bimodal IT without worrying about the inefficiencies that this model can introduce. Our users are far ahead of where they were a few years ago. Our infrastructure environment must reflect this fact by enabling user self service and automation, both of which are supported in an enterprise cloud scenario.

In the next chapter, we will discuss cloud services architecture and its different components, such as workload domains, racks, storage, networks, and VMware Cloud Foundation Software Design in detail.

2
Implementing Service Architecture for Cross-Cloud Services

This chapter will brief you on VMware Cloud Foundation Deployment to get a unified **software-defined data center** (**SDDC**) platform for the hybrid cloud. Based on VMware compute, storage, and network virtualization, this deployment delivers a natively integrated software stack that can be used on-premises for private cloud deployment, or run as a service from the public cloud with consistent and simple operations. It can be further integrated with VMware vRealize Suite, VMware Horizon, and VMware Integrated OpenStack to deliver a comprehensive SDDC platform.

This chapter covers the following topics:

- Architecture overview
- Workload domain logical architecture
- Rack architecture
- Storage architecture
- Network architecture
- VMware Cloud Foundation software design

Architecture overview

VMware Cloud Foundation is the unified SDDC platform for the private and public cloud. Cloud Foundation brings together compute, storage, and network virtualization into a closely integrated stack that can be deployed on-premises or run as a service from the public cloud.

The service architecture focuses on deploying it in an on-premises configuration and also as an extension to the public cloud. The Cloud Foundation architecture is shown in the following figure:

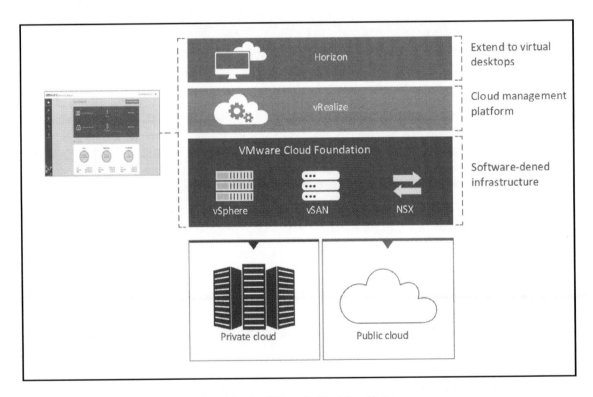

Figure 1: Overview of VMware Cloud Foundation architecture

Cloud Foundation adds several unique capabilities in addition to the core features and capabilities provided by vSphere, vSAN, NSX, and cloud management components.

Seamless integration of software-defined services

Cloud Foundation helps you to get a tightly integrated software-defined data center solution comprising of the compute, storage, and network virtualization components such as VMware vSphere, VMware vSAN, and VMware NSX, respectively, in addition to the SDDC Manager for lifecycle management automation to bring up the hardware at the initial stage. Customers have various options to upgrade individual components to higher editions or deploy and use their existing licenses.

Automating IT infrastructure

Cloud Foundation automates the installation of the entire VMware software components as the rack is installed and powered-on, and the networking is enabled. SDDC Manager leverages its knowledge of the hardware details and user-provided configuration details (such as DNS, IP address pool, and so on) to initialize the rack. This way, it saves a lot of time and prevents manual errors and repeated tasks. These activities include provisioning of workloads, automated provisioning of networks, allocation of resources based on service needs, and provisioning of end points. It helps the customer start production and the provisioning of resources for end users.

Policy-based resource containers

You can create logical entities, such as workload domains, for creating resource pools across compute, storage, and networking components. A workload domain is a customized policy-based logical entity with defined availability and performance parameters with compute, storage, and network in a single, consumable entity. You will get the required capacity with defined policies for performance, availability, and security with each logical entity. As an example, it is possible to create one logical entity for test workloads that require balanced performance and low availability, while for production workloads, which need high availability and high performance, a different entity will be defined.

SDDC Manager provides automation through its deployment workflow to map the workload domain policies into the underlying pool of hardware resources (compute, storage, and network). These logical entities (workload domains) help you follow the best practices to achieve customer operational objectives.

A logical entity (workload domain) can be customized with in definite time duration as part of the customer's time bound business objective.

Automating manual and repetitive tasks

Data center component upgrades and patch management are typically manual and repetitive tasks that are prone to configuration and implementation errors. Validation testing and dependency checking of software and hardware firmware maintains interoperability among components when one component is patched or upgraded and requires extensive testing and downtime. Customers take the difficult decision to deploy new patches before they are fully tested or defer new patches, which slows down the roll-out of new features, security, and bug fixes. Both situations increase risks for the customers.

SDDC Manager automates upgrades and patch management for the SDDC software components, which improves reliability and consistency of the IT infrastructure.

Lifecycle management is designed to be non-disruptive and helps the customer to maximize uptime for their IT services.

Unified Management Console

SDDC Manager understands the physical and virtual architecture of the SDDC and the respective products' complementing each other, so it easily monitors the system to identify potential risks, performance issues, and failures. SDDC Manager has the capability of stateful alert management to avoid notification spam on problem identification. Each notification has a brief detail of the problem and also helps in remediation steps required to recover the service. Performance issues or breakdowns are consolidated and examined for workload domains to get a detailed picture of any problem for the business service being implemented within a domain. SDDC Manager can be used to minimize the rectification time in an efficient way across every segment.

Scalability and performance

Cloud Foundation helps to deliver a private cloud instance in both green field and brown field setups. Cloud Foundation implementations can start as small as four nodes/servers and can scale out to multiple nodes/servers. It supports both scale up and scale out architectures. Cloud Foundation automatically discovers any new capacity and adds it into the existing pool of available capacities.

Workload domains

VMware Cloud Foundation creates a foundation for the SDDC by using workload domains. A workload domain is a policy-based resource container (logical architecture) with specific availability and performance attributes, and combines compute, storage, and network into a single consumable object for a specific purpose.

Cloud Foundation includes the following workload domain types:

- Management workload domain
- Virtual infrastructure workload domain
- **Virtual desktop infrastructure** (**VDI**) workload domain

This logical architecture is the foundation for the automated installation of software components, and helps to configure the appropriate services as per customer business objectives. *Figure 2* shows the logical software component design for Cloud Foundation:

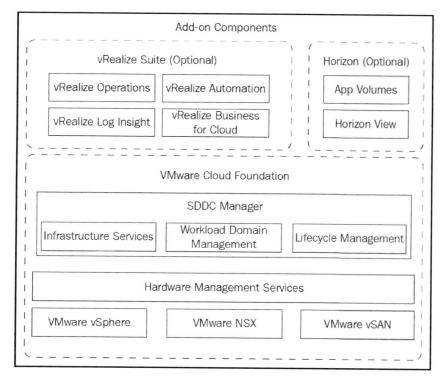

Figure 2: Software component logical design

Cloud Foundation can help with automated installation and configuration for the following components:

- SDDC Manager
- VMware ESXi hosts
- VMware Platform Services Controller
- VMware vCenter Server
- VMware NSX
- vSAN
- VMware vRealize Operations Manager
- VMware vRealize Log Insight
- VMware Horizon view
- VMware App Volumes

The following subsections brief you on how Cloud Foundation implements each of the preceding components in the specific workload domain types.

Management workload domain

During the initialization process for Cloud Foundation, the management workload domain is the first construct that is created after the imaging of the environment. The initialization process kicks off with the first login to SDDC Manager, where it defines the first four servers in each physical rack with the required parameters in the management domain. You can spread the management domain whenever you need to.

The management domain manages all of the nodes in the rack. All disk drives are claimed by vSAN for shared storage in the rack. The management domain contains the following:

- VMware vCenter Server Appliance
- NSX Manager
- NSX Controller
- vRealize Operations Manager
- vRealize Log Insight
- SDDC Manager (includes hardware and lifecycle management services)

As soon as the management workload domain is created, the initialization process is completed. The system is available to administrators from SDDC Manager, and helps to create the other types of workload domains for use.

The following figure represents the management workload domain:

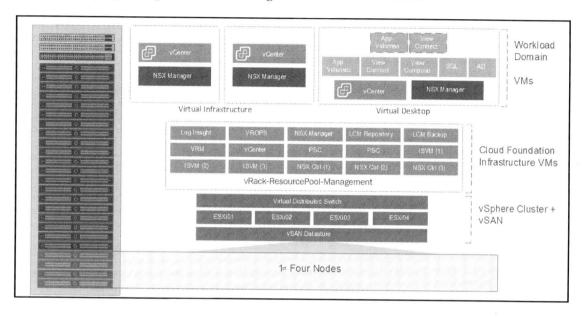

Figure 3: Management workload domain design

Workload domains

Cloud administrators can scale and customize the underlying components to meet a customer's changing business objectives. Administrators have the option to deploy all certified operating systems and application stacks from different vendors with workload domains. Administrators have monitoring rights to monitor the underlying components by using a common monitoring tool set that consolidates and relates across physical and virtual infrastructures.

During the creation of a workload domain, the workflow configures a flexible virtual data center that provides:

- The ability to deploy and configure OS instances in the form of VMs with vCPUs, memory, and storage, including networking resources
- Internet connectivity with a built-in **IP Address Management (IPAM)** solution

The following diagram represents a virtual infrastructure workload domain:

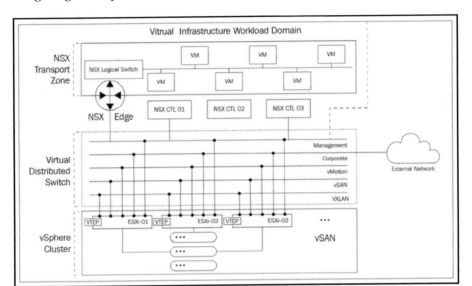

Figure 4: Workload domain design

You can opt for a modular approach to match your customers' data center capacity requirements, and you can justify better TCO/ROI to your customers with the resulting virtual infrastructure. SDDC Manager deploys the following:

- **Physical compute**: This means processing resources (CPU/RAM) with storage and network connectivity to create a resource pool by abstracting from hardware components.
- **Virtual infrastructure**: One management server should be required per workload domain (logical entity), which connects to the services controller in the management domain for required authentication and licenses. It creates logical entities as defined in a policy object by adding servers and creating storage data stores from the built-in storage (SSD/HDD) that resides in these servers. It also abstracts networking components and configures virtual switches on each server.
- **Physical networking**: SDDC Manager leverages the hardware management services to configure the **top of rack (ToR)** switches. These switches are responsible for VLAN traffic in the virtual data center, and also routes traffic for the public logical networks as defined in the policy.
- **Management**: VMware automation tools will help you monitor and manage these logical entities.

Finally, you can create as many workload domains as you have resources for. This will allow you to have separate segregated sets of resources for a variety of use cases.

VDI workload domains

You can deliver virtual or hosted desktops and applications through a single VDI platform with VMware Horizon. End users can access all of their desktops and applications through a single, unified workspace.

Cloud Foundation provisions the hardware resources in this way to deploy the required SDDC components in a fully functional environment that also auto-configures the physical infrastructure while hosting virtual desktops or applications.

The following diagram shows a VDI workload domain:

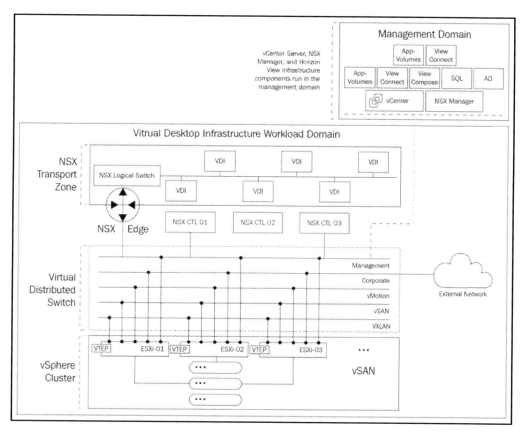

Figure 5: VDI workload domain design

SDDC Manager deploys the following for the provisioning of virtual desktops:

- **Physical compute**: This means processing resources (CPU/RAM) with storage and network connectivity to create resource pools by abstracting from hardware components.
- **Virtual infrastructure**: One management server should be required per workload domain (logical entity), which connects to the services controller in the management domain for required authentication and licenses. It creates logical entities as defined in a policy object by adding servers and creating storage data stores from the built-in storage (SSD/HDD) that resides in these servers. It also abstracts networking components and configures virtual switches on each server.
- **Physical networking**: SDDC Manager leverages the hardware management services to configure the ToR switches. These switches are responsible for VLAN traffic in the virtual data center, and also routes traffic for the public logical networks, as defined in a policy.
- **Management**: VMware automation tools will help you monitor and manage these logical entities.
- **VDI**: Cloud Foundation can be integrated with VMware Horizon and helps to automate the installation process of connection servers, security servers, app volumes, composer servers, and a DHCP relay agent as per the customer's defined policy and configuration, with full control and compliance. You can create a desktop/application pool with user/group entitlements as per the organizational policy.

VDI can facilitate the following tasks:

- Integration with LDAP/Active Directory server (for user source or creating additional users/groups with group policy) for authenticating users/groups.
- Publishing desktop/applications (persistent/floating, Windows/Linux OSes, and virtualized/legacy apps) as per the customer's business objectives on demand.
- SDDC Manager helps to create a management virtual network for the public domain so traffic can flow in and out of the logical domain and physical rack. It also helps provision VM migration between two sites or from different domains. You can deploy VM templates from a VDI infrastructure outside the one logical domain to the other virtual rack logical domains.

Hardware architecture – rack architecture

VMware Cloud Foundation is a hardware integrated solution. This means that it not only provides software configuration, but also provides automation for much of the physical hardware configuration. The following diagram depicts the standard physical rack configuration for Cloud Foundation:

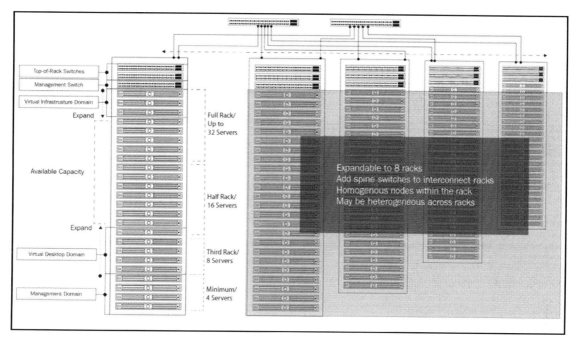

Figure 6: Cloud Foundation rack

A Cloud Foundation rack consists of the following components:

- **Spine switches**: This system comes with two spine switches that extend the network schema of the top of rack switches between racks and enables inter-rack connectivity. You can communicate between the uplink ports of the ToR switches and the spine switches. We require spine switches in multi-rack deployments, which are located in the second rack.

- **Management switch**: The management switch helps public connectivity with the baseboard management controller on each server. vSphere management, vSAN, or vMotion traffic runs on the network fabric generated by the ToR and spine switches. The management switch lacks redundancy in the physical rack. Components associated with management switches can't be customized or modified, but virtual machines/applications can be protected with maximum availability and performance.
- **Top of rack switches**: A physical rack comes bundled with two ToR switches, with 48 10GE ports and a minimum of four 40 GE uplink ports. The ToR and spine switches are capable of taking care of all network traffic (including VM network, VM management, vSAN, and vMotion traffic) from the servers with a guarantee of zero data loss and zero down time. The ToRs switches are designated for traffic to the main network through two of the uplink ports on rack 1. ToR switches are capable of providing more bandwidth with maximum availability for relentless operation. Each spine switch communicates with two Uplink ports from each ToR switch on every rack.
- **Servers**: You can scale up servers/nodes on the rack up to a maximum of 32 servers. It supports both scale up and scale out architecture. All servers/nodes should be of the same model and type within a rack. The disk size and storage configuration must be the same. Memory and CPU (per CPU core count) between servers can be different. Check the *VMware Hardware Compatibility Guide* for supported configuration.

Rack hardware

The hardware that must be used by Cloud Foundation is tightly controlled due to the hardware integration and automation. The rack has to use:

- As specific vSAN ReadyNode
- Specific physical switches for management, ToR, and spine connectivity

This allows the system to take advantage of vSAN technologies, and allows for tight integration with specific vSAN ReadyNodes. The following diagram depicts a vSAN ReadyNode and resultant disks, allowing vSAN shared storage to be used:

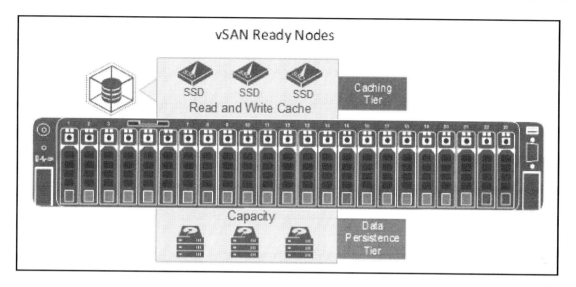

Figure 7: vSAN ReadyNodes

The VMware Cloud Foundation compatibility guide lists the supported hardware. Hardware must be on the compatibility list to be fully supported. The compatibility list can be found at

`https://www.vmware.com/resources/compatibility/vcl/cloudfoundation.php`.

Rack sizing

VMware Cloud Foundation supports up to eight racks in a single SDDC Manager instance. Each rack supports up to 32 hosts and currently has a separate management domain configured on servers in that rack. The Cloud Foundation software versions must be identical to be supported for multiple rack configurations.

Any rack that is added must have homogeneous hardware in that rack to be in a supported configuration. Hardware configuration, however, might be different between the different racks, which gives flexibility to the expansion.

For more information, visit: `https://code.vmware.com/virtual-san-design-and-sizing-guide`

Rack wiring

The wiring for the rack is very specifically defined and controlled. This allows for SDDC Manager to configure the full rack in an automated manner.

Storage architecture (software-defined storage)

The primary source of storage for Cloud Foundation is vSAN. For example, a 1U server can have eight disks in the capacity tier and two disks in the caching tier. All disks are claimed by vSAN for software-defined storage.

The amount of available physical storage in workload domains depends on the number of physical hosts. The total capacity that is usable is also dependent on the availability requirements for the workload domains that are being configured. Storage policies are configured and specific to the workload being configured.

The following diagram depicts a typical storage configuration for Cloud Foundation:

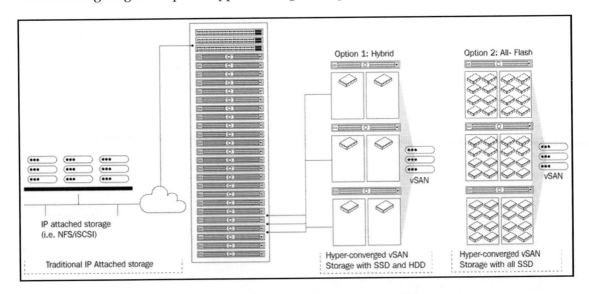

Figure 8: vSAN storage design

In this configuration, storage traffic is carried over the 10 GBPS links between the hosts and ToR switches. All vSAN members communicate over this 10 GBPS network. Best practices recommend that vSphere **Network I/O Control** (**NIOC**) should be enabled to allow network resource pools to be configured to prioritize network traffic by type.

vSAN storage policies

Cloud Foundation allows a default policy to be set as per the requirements of the workload domain. The following figure depicts the configuration of the default vSAN storage policy for the workload domain:

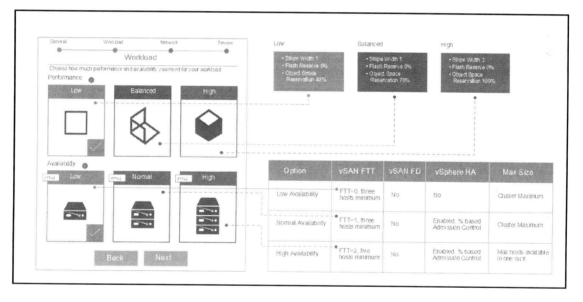

Figure 9: vSAN storage policy configuration

The default policies are defined in terms of both performance and availability. When the performance level is specified, the following settings are configured:

- **Low:** With this choice, the following vSAN parameters are used:
  - **Number of disk stripes per object**: 1
  - **Flash Read Cache reservation**: 0%
  - **Force provisioning (in spite of non-compliance)**: False
  - **Object space reservation**: 40%

- **Balanced**: With this choice, the following vSAN parameters are used:
    - **Number of disk stripes per object**: 1
    - **Flash Read Cache reservation**: 0%
    - **Force provisioning (in spite of non-compliance)**: False
    - **Object space reservation**: 70%
- **High**: The following vSAN parameters are used as per the previous dynamics:
    - **Number of disk stripes per object**: 4
    - **Flash Read Cache reservation**: 0%
    - **Force provisioning (in spite of non-compliance)**: False
    - **Object space reservation**: 100%

When the availability level is specified, the following settings are configured. Remember that the availability level determines the level of redundancy that is set for the assigned resources, and you must have enough hardware backing the workload domain to configure higher levels of availability:

- **None**: With this choice, the following vSAN parameters are used:
    - **Number of failures to tolerate**: Zero (0). Because vSAN requires a minimum of three hosts by default, three hosts are assigned to the virtual infrastructure.

- **Normal**: With this choice, the following vSAN parameters are used:
    - **Number of failures to tolerate**: One (1). Because vSAN requires a minimum of three hosts by default, three hosts are assigned to the virtual infrastructure.

- **High**: With this choice, the following vSAN parameters are used:
    - **Number of failures to tolerate**: Two (2). Because vSAN requires a minimum of five hosts by default for this setting, five hosts are assigned to the virtual infrastructure.

These settings are merely the default configuration for the workload domain, and additional policies can be defined as required from the vSphere Web Client for the cluster.

Network architecture (network virtualization or software-defined network)

The Cloud Foundation network is preconfigured to allow for simplicity of the configuration and provide the services as appropriate services for the rack. The physical configuration of the network is shown in the following diagram:

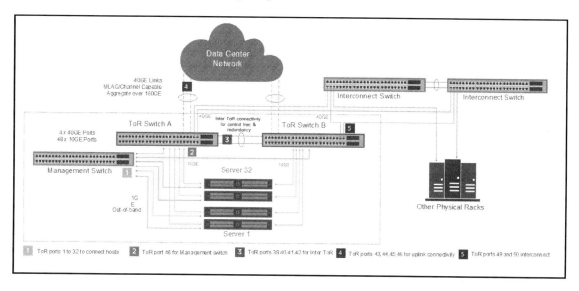

Figure 10: Physical network design

All hosts in a physical rack are connected to both ToR switches with 10 GB links. NIC port 1 is connected to ToR switch 1 and NIC port 2 is connected to ToR switch 2, with **link aggregation** (**LAG**) on each host.

The BMC is connected to the management switch over a 1G connection on each host. This connection is used for OOB management. Both ToR switches are further connected to a pair of spine switches in a dual-LAG configuration using 40G links. The spine switches are an aggregation layer for connecting multiple racks.

Cloud Foundation is designed to be resilient to certain network failures. The data path between hosts and ToR switches can tolerate a failure of one link between the host and ToR switches. The system can tolerate the failure of a ToR switch and/or spine switch between the ToR and spine switches.

All of this configuration is designed to be used with NSX to get the benefits of software-defined networking concepts.

Logical network design

In addition to the physical configuration, the virtual network configuration is also predetermined and configured from within SDDC Manager, on bring-up:

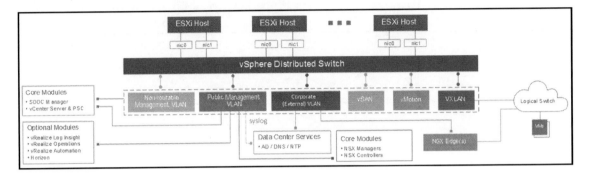

Figure 11: Logical network design

This network configuration can be added to at a later time, such as when you are configuring a new workload domain. The following diagram depicts the logical network design in the environment.

During the configuration, the following networks are configured for the rack:

- **Management network**: The workload domain's management network configuration uses the management network that was configured during the initialization process. This network is used for management functions, such as the ESXi hosts management network, vCenter Server, and the like.
- **vMotion network**: The workload domain's vSphere vMotion configuration uses the vMotion network that was configured during the initialization stage. This allows for vMotion traffic to be segregated from other traffic.
- **vSAN network**: The workload domain's vSAN configuration uses a portion of the vSAN network configuration that was configured during the initialization process, and allocates a VLAN ID from its pool. This network is used exclusively for vSAN traffic between hosts in the cluster.
- **VXLAN**: The workload domain's VXLAN configuration uses the VXLAN network that was configured during the initialization process.
- **Data center network**: Used for access to the workloads that you run in the workload domain from outside.

Specific subnets and VLANs are required during configuration for each of these networks, and generally the only modification that is required is to add additional data center networks to the configuration. This is normally done when adding additional workload domains.

VMware Cloud Foundation software design

Cloud Foundation controls the software as well as hardware in the environment using SDDC Manager. SDDC Manager is shown in the following diagram:

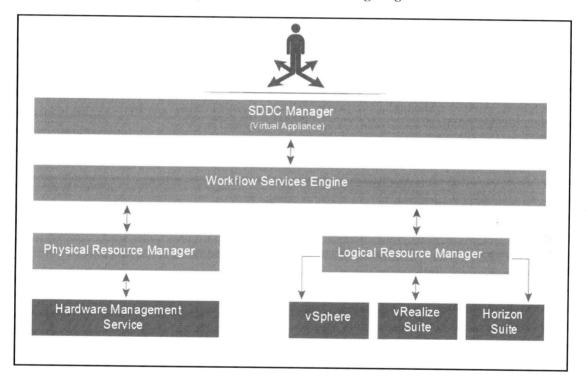

Figure 12: SDDC Manager design

SDDC Manager has three major functions, as described in the following sections.

SDDC Manager

SDDC Manager is capable of managing and monitoring the virtual, as well as physical, components of Cloud Foundation. SDDC Manager further helps you in Cloud Foundation configuration, operations, and management configurations, allowing you to do the following:

- Abstract, pool, and automate the physical components into a virtual entity.
- Scale up/down hosts or switches to the rack. Adding more racks brings scalability, performance enhancements, and easy failure management.
- Orchestrate and automate the lifecycle of logical components and management-plane components of Cloud Foundation.
- Trend analysis and proactive mapping of resources depending on their profiles, events, and operations such as vCenter Server clusters and vCenter Server cluster expansion operations.
- It has a common interface with the vCenter Server for cluster and vSAN management, hardware management services for hardware management, vRealize Operations for health monitoring, NSX Manager for network management, and VMware vRealize automation for workload management.

When you scale out infrastructure by adding physical racks, SDDC Manager helps data center administrators use the additional rack in a single pool of resources. This aggregates compute, storage, and networking components of the racks available for consumption to workloads.

SDDC Manager is comprised of the Physical Resources Manager, Logical Resources Manager, and an events engine.

Physical Resource Manager

The Physical Resources Manager manages the physical components of a physical rack and maintains a corresponding software physical rack object.

The PRM does the following:

- Defines the interfaces that access the physical resource abstractions
- Retrieves the physical hardware state by interfacing with the HMS layer
- Relays HMS events to the SDDC Manager engine

Logical Resource Manager

The Logical Resource Manager manages the logical resource state of Cloud Foundation.

LRM Controller

The LRM controller is exported as a logical managed view, which is comprised of the deployed vCenter Server and resource stats per vCenter Server.

Examples of logical resource types include the following:

- Virtual machine
- Distributed virtual switch
- Distributed virtual portgroup
- Host server
- Data store
- Total storage

LRM logical resources and LRM services

LRM builds its logical resource view of Cloud Foundation components by interfacing with vCenter Server using vSphere APIs. An example of an LRM service is the LRM alarm service, which fetches alarms from vCenter periodically.

Hardware Management Service (HMS)

The HMS allows SDDC Manager to be able to interact with the physical hardware in the rack. It is shown in the following diagram:

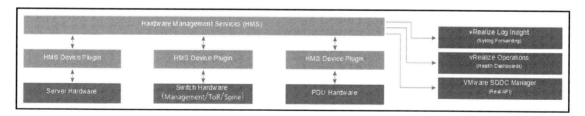

Figure 13: HMS design

The HMS enables the necessary functions required for discovering, bootstrapping, and monitoring the hardware in a physical rack in the system. The HMS out-of-band agent runs on the management switch of each physical rack.

The HMS is an abstracted software technique that manages the physical components in the racks, such as servers and network switches. SDDC Manager leverages the HMS potential (abstracting the hardware) to integrate hardware from different sources. The HMS is only visible through the SDDC Manager. We can discover, bootstrap, and monitor the hardware with an HMS solution. The HMS gets these hardware events and state changes from software plugins (such as VAAI and VASA) that hardware OEMs develop and integrate to work with their specific hardware, which enhances the overall capability of hardware and entire solutions.

Lifecycle management

The final piece of the SDDC Manager configuration is lifecycle management. **Lifecycle management (LCM)** enables you to perform automated updates on Cloud Foundation components (SDDC Manager, HMS, and LCM) as well as VMware components (vCenter Server, ESXi, and NSX).

SDDC Manager is preconfigured to communicate with the VMware software repository. The high-level update workflow is described as follows:

1. Notification/alert/defined actions of update availability
2. Download the appropriate update bundle
3. Select update targets and schedule an update by checking all dependencies
4. An update is applied to the selected targets at the scheduled time with roll back options and remediation if any fault occurs

SDDC Manager might be available while the update is installed, but VMware recommends that you schedule the update at a time when it is not being heavily used.

vSphere products

vCenter Server and Platform Services Controller are installed and configured during the primary stage and workload domain creation with Cloud Foundation. For the management domain, there is a single vCenter Server instance and two Platform Services Controllers deployed to the management domain vSAN data store that is created. For the workload domains, an additional vCenter Server instance is deployed to the management domain to manage the hosts and the vSAN cluster for that workload domain.

This design allows for separation of management and payload resources, and for isolation of workload domains for security and compliance purposes.

NSX

NSX is additionally deployed during the initial stage of the management workload domain. NSX Manager and three NSX Controllers are deployed and configured as a starting point for the networking configuration. This is expanded as the size of the environment grows.

Value-added services such as a full micro-segmentation design are not included in the default Cloud Foundation deploy service. However, they can be added as value-added services after deployment to leverage the power of NSX.

vRealize products

VMware Cloud Foundation deploys several components of the vRealize product suite during initial installation.

The following sections describe the vRealize Suite components that are installed.

vRealize Operations Manager

vRealize Operations Manager is installed as part of the initialization process for Cloud Foundation. It is a single appliance installation, configured with the appropriate content packs and dashboards for the components that are installed.

This installation is again a base configuration to provide several dashboards, adding value for the administrators in the environment. You can create customized dashboards for use as per the customer environment.

vRealize Log Insight

vRealize Log Insight is installed as a part of the initialization process for Cloud Foundation. It is a single appliance installation, which is configured with all the content packs and components of the rack sending log data to be analyzed.

This installation is a base configuration to provide a starting point for vRealize Log Insight.

vRealize Automation, VMware vRealize Business, and VMware vRealize Orchestrator

vRealize Automation, VMware vRealize Business, and VMware vRealize Orchestrator are not included in the Cloud Foundation deployment. They are perfectly compatible to be configured in workload domains to fully deliver infrastructure-as-a-service use cases. These services must be included after the initial deployment to leverage the benefits of the fully automated system.

Summary

Service architecture principles define the underlying general rules and guidelines for the use and deployment of all IT resources and assets across the customer environment. They showcase a level of understanding among the different lines of business of the customer, and form the basis for making future architecture/roadmap decisions.

The architecture is based on a design of services, which mirrors customer business objectives that comprise business processes. Service-orientation delivers business agility and a boundary-free information flow. Service representation utilizes business descriptions to provide business processes, goals, rules, policies, service interfaces, and service components, which implements services using service orchestration. Service orientation places special requirements on the infrastructure, and implementations should use open standards to get interoperability and location transparency. Implementations are customer use case specific. They are limited or enabled by customer business objectives and must be described within the final goal. Strong governance of service representation and implementation is required.

The next chapter is about strategies for hosting applications and provides freedom to end users, as well as full control to administrator/service providers. You will learn about the business value of the Cross-Cloud Architecture. We will continue with our objective to make applications accessible from anywhere, anytime, on any device. We will also learn how to transform from a silo to the cloud, and introduce DevOps for automated application release mechanisms in SDLC.

3

Transforming a Data Center from Silos to Software-Defined Services

This chapter is about strategies of how to host applications in the world of software-defined services in order to provide flexibility and control to administrators and companies. You will learn about the business value you get from a Cross-Cloud Architecture. This chapter includes the following:

- How to design a data center as per application demand
- How to handle changes in the future with a roadmap
- How to make applications accessible from anywhere, anytime, on any device by virtualizing all the components of a data center
- An introduction to DevOps and its business benefits

The data center is evolving as virtualization is directed at networks and storage platforms. This transformation means IT plays a vital role in achieving the business objectives of customers.

Need for VMware in data center transformation

Many organizations have already decided to move into the cloud (private/public/hybrid or even Cross-Cloud) by virtualizing everything in their data center, but the future roadmap is often not clear or not yet defined. Questions arise, such as the following:

- What is the current state of applications/services running in the data center?
- How do we begin to move forward considering the current state and business goals?
- What are the right technology choices/limitations in transforming our data center?
- Who can help us to achieve customer business objectives and growth plans?

These queries are still unanswered.

VMware will help customers to design customized private and public clouds across various industries/verticals in the world. VMware has extensive experience with helping customers with a complete solution that includes software products, as well as the services you need to gain the maximum benefit from cloud computing. This combination of software and expertise is unique and helps customers reap the benefits of Cross-Cloud services, as well as education/training for customers of all sizes across all industries through its large global ecosystem of partners and system integrators.

Business requirements of customers

In every project, it is important to map business requirements with available solutions in order to select the best available solution and deliver a functional infrastructure.

The following table provides a common list of customer's business requirements for the implementation of their SDDC infrastructure:

ID	Requirement
B101	Meet time-to-market deadline with better business response and improve SLA
B102	Optimal utilization of resources to boost system availability and enhance security
B103	Developers build, deploy, test, and run services with innovative ideas and designs to minimize errors and align with the line of business requirements

B104	Enhance the productivity with happy customers
B105	Optimize IT cost by adopting various options available on the market

Interoperability and integration

Interoperability is the key parameter of any system or product to work seamlessly with other systems or products without any operational overhead to the customer.

This chapter focuses on all important components that are required for a solution architecture and can provide all necessary out-of-the-box capabilities.

The interoperability between two different vendors' products/solutions depends on a past, present, and future roadmap, considering various customer requirements for their specific deployment scenarios and use cases.

Integration is a process in which separately produced components or subsystems are combined and problems in their interactions are addressed. The supported integrations between different products can vary based on changes in the past, current, and future use cases. We should review in detail any architecture design, deployment scenarios, limitations, or challenges with a customer's existing infrastructure, whether it is a physical, software-defined data center, or cloud automation solution for existing or future implementation.

VMware provides solution integrations through an ecosystem, which can be found in the *VMware Solution Exchange* (`https://solutionexchange.vmware.com/`).

An example of an integration is the Management Packs for vRealize Operations or VMware **Common Component Catalog** (**CCC**), which can provide integration with Active Directory, Infoblox, or ServiceNow.

This Orchestration Architecture Design has been developed to provide a blueprint for a customer's **software-defined data center** (**SDDC**) implementation, and is one of three architectural designs that provide the foundation layer of the SDDC infrastructure. We already discussed the Virtualization Architecture Design in the previous chapter. In this chapter, we will focus more on the architecture and design of VMware's Orchestrator product:

- Virtualization Architecture Design
- Orchestration Architecture Design
- Monitoring Architecture Design

We will discuss Orchestrator's logical and physical design considerations for performance and capacity management-related infrastructure components, including requirements, specifications, and management, along with their relationships.

The design has been laid out so that it can be replicated across sites with minimal modification.

Orchestrator content consists of:

- Workflows
- Packages
- Actions
- Configuration elements
- Resource elements

Logical design

The following illustration shows the logical design of the orchestration environment:

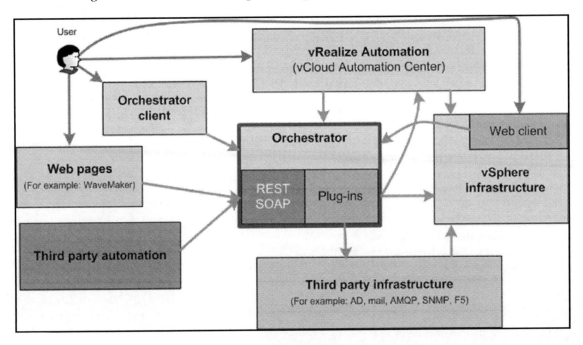

Orchestration logical design

Orchestrator topology choice

Orchestrator is a product that needs to be deployed in a single site topology with multi-node plugins.

We can also leverage the areas of package management and workflow execution, as illustrated in the following diagram. The plugins have a set of standard workflows, which can be utilized for hierarchical orchestration, management of Orchestrator instances, and scale-out of Orchestrator activities:

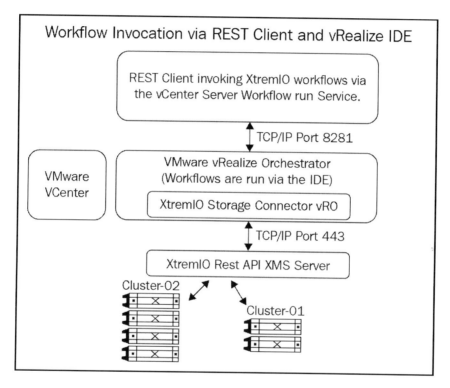

Conceptual logical design

Orchestrator server mode choice

Orchestrator runs as a single instance in standalone mode by default. We can set it to cluster mode, to get the redundancy of the Orchestrator services and start multiple Orchestrator server instances in a cluster with a shared database.

Orchestrator supports the following two server modes from a configuration perspective:

- **Standalone mode**: Run as a standalone instance by default.
- **Cluster mode**: Multiple Orchestrator server instances with identical servers. Plugins help to enable high availability with single shared databases. Clusters work in active-passive mode as only the active instance responds to client requests and runs workflows.

By exchanging heartbeats, they are able to communicate with different server instances. Each heartbeat is a time stamp that the server node writes into the cluster shared database, as per a scheduled time interval. Orchestrator cluster nodes stop responding in case of network problems, an unresponsive database, or overloading occurs. If an active Orchestrator server instance fails to send heartbeats for the failover timeout then it will become a passive instance. The equation for failover timeout is equal to the value of the heartbeat interval multiplied by the number of the failover heartbeats. This equation will help you to define the passive instance and customize the design as per available resources and consider the current and future production load.

The non-responsive node is automatically shut down, and one of the active instances takes control to resume all interrupted workflows from their last incomplete items, such as scriptable tasks, workflow invocations, and so on. We can restart the node that was shut down by using an external script based on the Orchestrator REST API.

Orchestrator does not provide a built-in tool for monitoring the cluster status and sending notifications in case of a failover. We can monitor the cluster state by using an external component, such as a load balancer. To identify node status, we can leverage the REST API of this node.

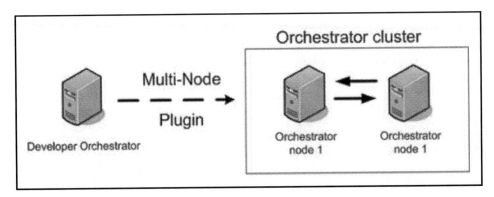

Cluster logical design

vRealize Orchestrator SDDC cluster choice

The Virtualization Architecture Design document specifies the following main cluster types within the SDDC solution: management, edge, and payload:

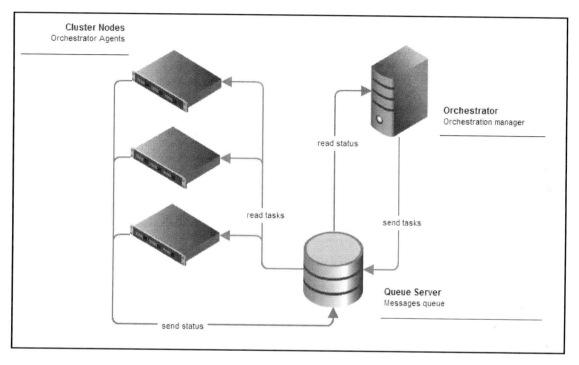

Logical management SDDC

Plugins allow you to use Orchestrator for integration with third-party technologies and applications. Exposing an external technology in an Orchestrator plugin helps you to use objects and functions in workflows that can utilize the objects and functions of third-party technology.

The third-party technologies include enterprise management tools, email systems, databases, directory services, and remote control interfaces to integrate with plugins.

Orchestrator provides a set of standard plugins that allow you to integrate technologies, such as the vCenter Server API and email capabilities, into workflows. Orchestrator open plugin architecture allows you to develop plugins to access other applications. Orchestrator implements open standards to simplify integration with external systems. You can go through the *Developing with VMware Orchestrator* (`https://www.vmware.com/support/pubs/orchestrator_pubs.html`) article to get more information about developing custom content.

All default plugins are installed together with the Orchestrator server. We have to configure plugins such as the vCenter Server plugin before using them. Plugins extend the vRealize Orchestrator scripting engine with new object types and methods. Plugins publish notification events from the external system, which triggers events in Orchestrator and the plugged-in technology. Each plugin can provide one or more packages of workflows and actions that you can run on the objects in the inventory to automate the customized objective of the integrated product.

Orchestrator has a collection of default plugins and each plugin can integrate with a third-party product API to the Orchestrator engine. Plugins provide inventory classes, extend the scripting engine with new object types, and publish notification events from the external system. Each plugin also provides a library of workflows for automating the defined use cases of the integrated product. You can see the list of available plugins on the **Plugins** page in the Orchestrator Control Center interface.

Integrated architecture design model for private and public clouds

This section provides an integrated architecture design deployment model for cloud consumer and tenant private networking and security with the ability to uplink to a cloud provider public network. This is a common deployment model that provides cloud consumer and tenant consumption of network and security capabilities for private networks, with the option to extend and uplink to external provider logical network services:

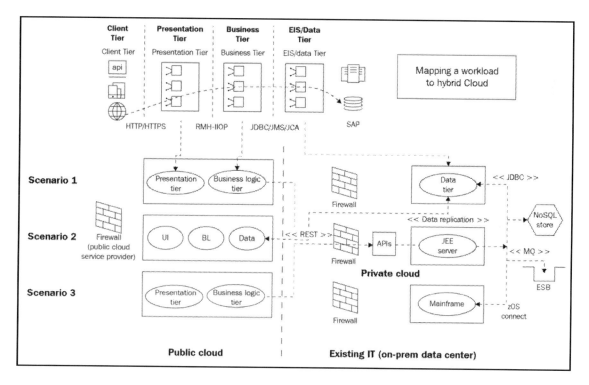

Integrated architecture design model for private and public cloud IaaS

Private cloud integrated architecture design with network and security

This section provides an integrated architecture design model for private cloud consumer deployments with a common set of deployment network service capabilities. These capabilities enable an architecture that is designed with security in mind, and provides options for either a private network security domain or a public network security domain with security segmentation. Private cloud consumers and tenants require their virtual machine and application workloads to consume external provider network services without having the risk of exposure to outside public cloud provider infrastructures:

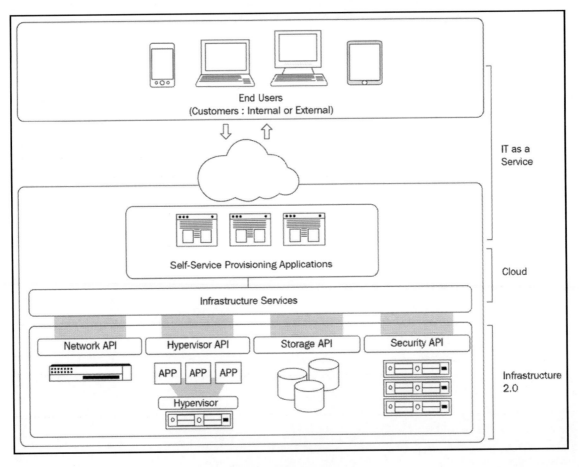

Private cloud integrated architecture design

Integrated architecture design for virtual machines and applications

This section provides an overview of the consumption components and services that are enabled in VMware NSX to allow converged blueprints to consume virtual machine and application-specific networking and security services. These diagrams can be used during the design workshop to define specific consumption requirements at the virtual machine level:

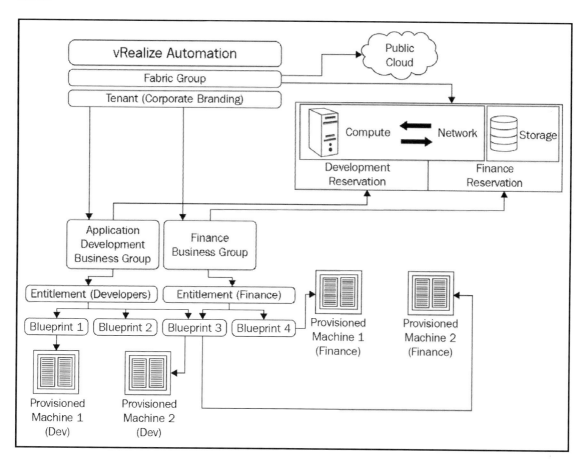

vRealize automation converged blueprint consumption model

Consumption model of network services components

The following figure explains provisioning blueprints in cloud:

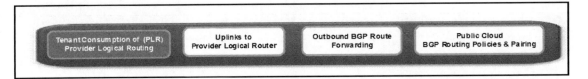

Consumption model with integrated provider network services components

Components and processes for logical switching

Logical switching is the most common network service supported out-of-the-box with NSX for vSphere. This network service enables the extension of an L2 segment/IP subnet anywhere in the fabric, independently of the physical network design. The usage of VXLAN as an overlay to the physical network enables layer 2 subnet extensions beyond a single site to a multi-site architecture.

Logical switching provides vRealize Automation cloud tenants with a very flexible, scalable, and distributed network topology for virtual machines and applications that are instantiated from the service catalogs using converged blueprints.

vRealize Automation tenants (virtual machines and applications) leverage blueprints to use network profiles that are configured to use VXLAN to enable layer 2 communications for a variety of virtual machine and application deployments with software components:

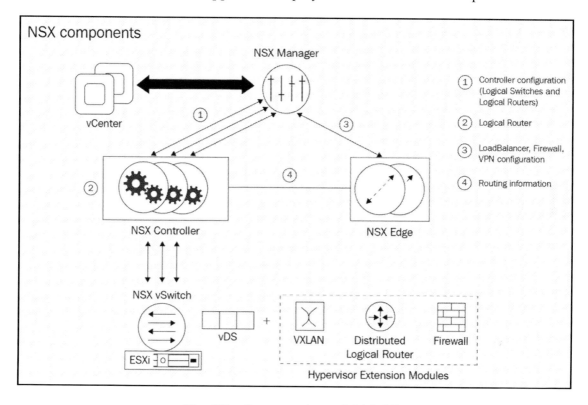

VMware NSX provider components and processes for logical switching

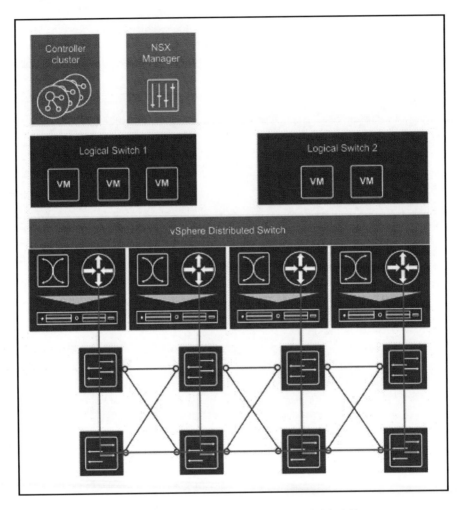

Virtual machine compute components and processes for consuming logical switching

vRealize Automation with logical switching consumption overview

A customer can achieve the following benefits:

- Preconfigured layer 2 network virtualization, which enables cloud consumers and tenants to provide VXLAN for virtual machine and application blueprints

- Layer 2 extensibility that offers virtual machines and applications instantiated out of vRealize Automation converged blueprints and service catalogs, a multi-site and multi-tenant global transport capability as an overlay to an existing customer physical network infrastructure
- Logical switching that can be implemented on top of an existing physical network infrastructure

Services	Logical switching services orientation
Logical switching service overview	The logical switching architecture is based on a design that provides cloud consumers or tenants with tenant logical switching services through dedicated or shared, privately deployed, distributed, virtual switch and port groups in conjunction with VMware NSX using VXLAN as an overlay to the physical network infrastructure.
Logical switching service rationale	Cloud consumers and tenants within vRealize Automation require an agile virtualized private network with layer 2 network capabilities that can extend the network switch topology for VLANs to multiple data center sites to overcome the boundaries of physical networks that traditionally limit layer 2 VLAN extensibility and require extensive time to provision. VMware NSX leverages VXLAN as a network overlay to the existing physical network infrastructure without having to install or replicate the same VLAN layer 2 switch topology at each site.
Logical switching service offering capabilities	Tenants can safely and securely pass traffic using VXLAN between a variety of other virtual machines and applications within a single or multi-site distributed architecture. Strong governance, service definition, and customer representation of vRealize Automation and VMware NSX integrated logical switching services are required for planning, design, and implementation.

Distributed logical switching service limitations or constraints	vRealize Automation IaaS administrators, cloud administrators, or fabric administrators are unable to deploy or custom build VMware NSX logical switches directly from within a converged blueprint and service catalog without having the transport zones preconfigured in VMware NSX. Deployments requiring advanced functionality to provision logical switching might require the implementation of vRealize Orchestrator with the required plugins enabled to develop specific workflows, depending on the deployment requirements.
Logical switching service prerequisites	The network virtualization design and deploy service must be used to plan, design, and deploy the core VMware NSX software-defined network components to implement installation and configuration prerequisites: • vSphere Distributed Switch instances must be preconfigured prior to NSX deployment • NSX Manager must be deployed and paired with vCenter Server • NSX controllers must be deployed • ESXi clusters must be prepared for NSX and configured for VXLAN VXLAN and transport zones should be designed and implemented to enable layer 2 transport services for virtual machines and applications. Validate the versions of vRealize Automation that support converged blueprint authoring to enable the drag-and-drop of VMware NSX network profiles and routing policies that will be created within converged blueprints, which can be assigned or managed by tenant business group administrators.

Introduction to DevOps and its benefits

Development and operations (DevOps) is a culture, movement, or practice that emphasizes the collaboration and communication of both software developers and other **information-technology (IT)** professionals while automating the process of software delivery and infrastructure changes. DevOps implementations use automation to accelerate IT service delivery and create a common platform of systems and processes to build, test, and run new software applications. DevOps initiatives remove the silos between various teams in the software development life cycle.

DevOps helps to deploy code more frequently and with minimum failures, which speeds up time to market for new and updated software applications and functionality, as per the business objectives of customers.

Building a data center architecture based on the SDDC with automated application provisioning transforms customer data centers for a DevOps-ready IT team.

The code stream delivers a complete application stack that has fully integrated and tested application runtime setups for development and testing engineers.

It gives various options for a developer with **application programming interface (API)** and **graphical user interface (GUI)** access to resources.

The automated solution gives you results from day one:

- Reduced provisioning time
- Increased developer productivity and output
- Improved the consistency of provisioned instances
- Reduced annual infrastructure and operating costs

A vRealize code stream is deployed to manage the delivery of dev/test application environments across a mixed cloud environment. Automated operations help to improve computing, performance, availability, right consolidation ratios, and optimized resources. Unified console and API plugins also help the team quickly reuse existing test automation scripts and integrate third-party components. IT becomes more agile by automating provisioning and testing processes. This will enhance the efficiency of data center resources and improve developer productivity while minimizing project risk and application backlog.

vRealize Automation and vRealize code streams can help the customer to enable data centers with DevOps. vRealize Automation automates the delivery of customized infrastructure, applications, and custom IT services. vRealize Automation delivers the solution to manage a heterogeneous system and hybrid cloud. A code stream automates application release delivery. vRealize Automation and vRealize code streams enable customers to deliver and manage infrastructure and applications quickly, and also maintain control as a result. End users get faster application delivery while achieving higher quality releases.

When starting a DevOps-ready initiative, consider the following points:

- Customers can maximize their efficiency by automating the release delivery process, which improves service quality and customer satisfaction. Release delivery automation can also prevent an increasing dependence on unreliable manual processes that can slow the introduction of new application functionality.
- A customer's experience with new DevOps processes leads to the following five key insights for organizations just getting started:

    1. **Choose the right proof of concept with clear objectives**: Teams seeking to enable DevOps-ready IT and increase IT agility should begin with a simple project. The POC can be a critical component, but it should be an isolated or siloed application rather than one that might negatively impact the business if things should not go as planned.
    2. **Start with a small team**: Automation involves a human and cultural change that requires support from everyone involved in the project. A smaller team (with just two or three dedicated automation engineers) will be easier to manage through process and solution transition.
    3. **Have a rollback plan**: Be sure that changes can be quickly rolled back in case of unexpected results.
    4. **Deploy any new DevOps process and a continuous delivery solution concurrently**: Modeling a new methodology in a proven solution is simpler and less time consuming than introducing a new process, and then a new solution.
    5. **Create a dashboard**: Decide what to measure and then regularly report through the solution's dashboard so that executives and other sponsors can view changes and progress.

Building, deploying, and running services in an innovative way

Innovation starts with the deployment of lightweight frameworks to enable the development of high-volume web applications, next-generation service integration, and elastic, horizontally-scalable applications. Developers leverage the power of these application frameworks to create applications that provide a rich, modern user experience across a range of platforms, browsers, and personal devices, including social media and cloud services. They can access data in a wide range of structured and unstructured formats and integrate applications using proven enterprise application integration patterns, including batch processing.

Developers can more easily support the enterprise's legacy applications and help to extend their fruitful life, and also leverage investments in software development. When business users identify required new services, developers respond faster. This shift enables developers to build innovative new applications in a familiar and productive way while retaining the choice of where (inside the data center or private, hybrid, or public clouds) to run those applications.

SDDC object life cycle

Everything, such as compute, storage, network, memory, and security, is becoming software-defined within a software-defined data center. This includes all of the policy-based management and automation tools that are used to enable a mixed cloud, including virtualized infrastructure. These tools have their own configurations that help to define and manage SDDC. These configurations have their own life cycle and this raises the question, *"What's the most effective way to manage the life cycle of these SDDC objects?"*.

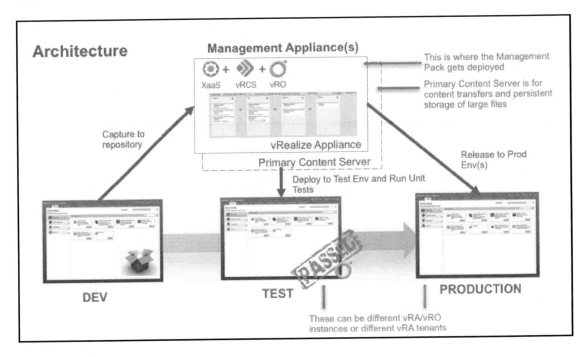

Dashboards, reports, blueprints, templates, properties, pipelines, and workflows are very important in defining how you manage your SDDC. All these objects require their own level of management. We can create something and start getting value out of the automation and abstraction that it provides at a primary stage. The need to maintain a common library of these objects, and configuration becomes critical as the number increases.

A lot of manual effort is required in order to ensure the objects within these environments are consistent with multiple clouds and tenants, while keeping a single source of truth. It also becomes very important to keep a historical record of all of the changes and updates made to these different objects and configurations. All of these tasks become easy to perform with a code stream.

vRealize code stream functionality

The vRealize code stream has the ability to capture and maintain a centralized repository of every single supported object and configuration. They can be compared, rolled back, and deployed to other projects and tenants.

It works on a model that has a centralized Gold/Master configuration or setup, which can be used to sync with other tenants and setups. Manually, effort can be made by way of a few clicks now and then, and deployments can be automatically tested prior to being deployed to production setups, and can be easily rolled back if required. vRealize tools use the same approvals engine, workflows, pipelines, and overall infrastructure and are sufficient for these activities.

Automating application release without manual intervention

Automating application deployment in a rapidly changing organization ensures quick delivery of new services/applications.

Operations teams have a major challenge when deploying new releases frequently to production after development and testing. An automatic and transparent process is required to ensure that applications are deployed successfully. We refer to this process as **Zero Touch Deployment**.

We will review two approaches to Zero Touch Deployment:

- A script-based solution
- A release automation platform

We will discuss how each can solve the key technological and organizational challenges faced by smart organizations when they are ready to implement an automatic application deployment system.

The PaaS approach delivers better benefits including lower operating expenses, fewer service outages, and simplified regulatory compliance for most applications.

The ideal setup for PaaS is the software-defined data center model for most organizations. The software-defined approach helps customers to create flexible data centers by mobilizing data center services from a hardware-defined data center. The SDDC is a new logical container that includes all the infrastructure services required to make workloads ready to use in minutes. SDDCs provide compute, network, storage, and security resources from a pool of physical hardware (servers, security devices, routers, and storage systems) by abstracting the hardware and then automating it as a resource pool for different applications to use. The SDDC approach supports both legacy enterprise applications and new services written for the cloud. This flexibility allows customers to avoid the time and cost of re-writing legacy software for the cloud, while empowering an entirely new generation of cloud-ready services to consume from day one.

Advantages of DevOps

DevOps improves collaboration between operations and development teams.

DevOps and cloud management solutions for application stack provisioning across a mixed cloud helps customer with rapid growth and cost benefits. When customers invest in DevOps, it includes an automated, continuous delivery methodology, that helps customers to cut deployment time by more than half, and deployment resources by more than three quarters.

It also doubles the speed of software releases. The elimination of manual processes also improves service quality, troubleshooting time, and end-user satisfaction levels.

Summary

This chapter is intended for readers who require an integrated cloud automation and software-defined network solution. The goal of this integration is to establish requirements for repeatability and standardized validation solutions. The primary focus is on establishing business, technical, and operational requirements for providing cloud automation, application delivery with policy-based governance using software-defined network and security integration components, capabilities, and services.

We have covered integration capabilities provided by vRealize Automation and VMware NSX, and they are consumed primarily by vRealize Orchestrator plugins, workflows, and the new converged blueprints.

VMWare's DevOps solution guides provide customers with a great curriculum on how to transform their delivery processes and activities to incorporate on-demand delivery of customer software to end users. This solution addresses the assessment, recommendation, and implementation of organizational processes, operational capabilities, and the technology necessary for customers to continuously deliver their application services in a prescriptive and consistent way, leveraging an open approach to DevOps practices.

The customer can assess current organizations, processes, patterns, and tools, and come up with a recommended strategy and roadmap for adopting DevOps practices consistent with the customer's current state and requirements, including governance and policy controls. The customer will also have recommended metrics and methods to measure returns on investment for the recommendations provided.

In the next chapter, we will cover the core elements of VMware's Cross-Cloud Architecture and services, an overview of the AWS and IBM Cloud Model, along with migration services and how to design a Cross-Cloud model to get DR as a service.

Designing a Mixed Cloud Model with VMware

4

This chapter tells you how VMware combines a best-in-class private cloud with leading public clouds, all enabled by VMware since they have the most reliable and flexible hybrid cloud strategy. VMware is delivering cloud freedom and control by providing a common operating environment for all clouds with their unique Cross-Cloud Architecture.

The core elements of VMware's Cross-Cloud Architecture are as follows:

- Migration steps across any cloud
- Designing a VMware Cross-Cloud Model with AWS Cloud
- Designing a VMware Cross-Cloud Model with IBM Cloud
- Cloud-based approaches to Disaster Recovery as a Service (DRaaS)

Core elements of VMware's Cross-Cloud Architecture

VMware Cloud Foundation helps to manage and build SDDC Clouds, and Cross-Cloud Services help customers to manage, govern, and secure applications running across various public clouds like AWS, Azure, and IBM Cloud.

VMware's Hybrid Cloud solution with VMware Cross-Cloud Architecture helps customers to run, manage, connect, and secure their applications across clouds and devices in a common operating environment. VMware has also launched the following solutions/services:

- VMware Cloud Foundation is a combination of vSphere (Compute), Virtual Storage Area Network (Storage), NSX (Network), and SDDC Manager (Management layer)
- Cross-Cloud Services enable customers to manage, govern, and secure applications running in private and public clouds (AWS, Azure, and IBM Cloud) to get the benefits of both worlds
- VMware vCloud Availability, a service to provide customers disaster recovery offerings, especially built for vCloud Air Network partners
- VMware vCloud Air Hybrid Cloud Manager to provide VMware vSphere users zero downtime during application migration to VMware vCloud Air

Cross-Cloud Services

Cross-Cloud Services are more or less like **Software as a Service (SaaS)** kind of offerings to fetch details about cloud utilization and costs, enhance regular updates in networking and security rules, and help in faster provisioning, on demand configuration, management, and migration of applications and data across both vSphere and non-vSphere private clouds and public clouds. Customers can protect data and applications with centralized locations and control costs with a uniform operating environment for both public clouds and private clouds. Developers and their customers can change freely in the clouds as per their business objectives and requirements.

The Cross-Cloud Services have:

- **Discovery and analytics**: Helps administrators in discovery, hosting, and public cloud applications compliance with regulatory governance
- **Compliance and security**: Leveraging NSX and monitoring to enhance security and compliance for applications from private to public clouds
- **Deployment and migration**: Assists developers to work across clouds, and administrators can control Cross-Cloud applications with security and compliance

Choosing suitable applications to move in the cloud

We have to build a dependency tree and segregate IT infra components to check the dependencies of each application so we can decide which of them to migrate to the cloud with minimal effort. The dependency tree consists of logical components of the website such as the database, search and indexer, login and authentication service, billing or payments, and so on for a web-based application or SaaS application, and there will be various interconnected processes like workflow systems, logging, and reporting systems for backend processing pipeline applications.

The qualified applications for the cloud are the services or components which have minimum upward and downward dependencies. We always have to start with the systems which have lesser dependencies on other services like backup, batch processing applications, log processing systems, development, testing and build systems, web-front (marketing) applications, queuing systems, content management systems, or training and PoC demo systems.

We have to choose those applications which have underutilized resources; applications which needed to scale and are running out of capacity for resources; applications with architectural flexibility; applications utilizing traditional tape drives to backup data; applications which have a global footprint like a customer-facing marketing and advertising apps; or applications used by partners are good candidates to migrate onto the cloud. We can't go for applications which require specific hardware to work like mainframe or specific encryption hardware.

We have to shortlist applications to migrate in phase-wise to:

- Maximize the benefits of the cloud in every aspect (compute, storage, network, security, availability, elasticity)
- Build support and and knowledge base with customers and showcase its impact

At this stage, the following questions that you will have are:

1. Do you map the current architecture of the qualified application to the target cloud architecture? What are the dependencies and how much effort is required to do this?

2. Is the application suitable for converting into a virtual machine and hosting on a cloud infrastructure, or does it require specific hardware and/or special access to hardware which is not possible in the cloud?

3. Does your customer have all the necessary licenses to migrate your e-qualified application with all of the third party's software into the cloud?
4. Does this application's migration require recoding or modification in the architecture in terms of a special skill set to move the application?
5. What software features are needed on premise and what are we required to have while moving to the cloud?
6. What will be the latency and bandwidth needed to host this application in the cloud?
7. What kind of identity and access authentication technique is required for this application on the cloud?

VMware Cloud on AWS

VMware Cloud on AWS is a hybrid cloud solution which provides customers with the full VMware **software-defined data center** (**SDDC**) solution on AWS Cloud to build any application across VMware vSphere-based private, public, and hybrid cloud deployments. It is an on demand scalable service which is deployed, sold, and supported by VMware. VMware Cloud on AWS will assist VMware customers to leverage their existing investments on VMware software and tools to AWS's global footprint and services like storage, databases, analytics, and other components.

Components/technologies used in VMware-AWS partnerships

This solution consists of VMware Cloud Foundation running on the AWS dedicated purpose-built infrastructure with VMware managing the full software lifecycle and service operations.

The globally available service will be optimized with a next generation bare metal AWS infrastructure. It will deliver the power of VMware's SDDC infrastructure software while providing access to the full range of advanced AWS services with integrated customer support experience. AWS will be VMware's primary public cloud infrastructure partner and VMware will be AWS's primary private cloud partner in this partnership.

VMware Cloud on AWS have a distinguished offer for the customers: to buy these cloud services using their current investments on VMware licenses. Customers can secure additional loyalty discounts for their VMware Cloud on AWS's hybrid mode.

These services will be enabled with VMware Cloud Foundation. These services will enhance the features of compute, storage, and network virtualization products (vSphere, **Virtual Storage Area Network (vSAN)**, and NSX), along with vCenter management capabilities and help it to run on next generation elastic, bare metal, AWS infrastructures.

This will help customers to rapidly deploy secure, enterprise-grade AWS cloud-based resources which are practically consistent with vSphere-based clouds. The result is a robust end-to-end service that runs seamlessly with both on-premises private clouds and advanced AWS services.

Migrating your existing applications to AWS

The process of moving applications that were originally developed to run on premises and need to be remediated for Amazon is called migration:

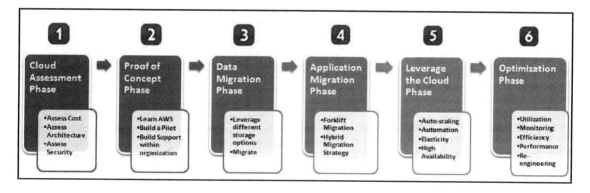

Let's look at this further to understand the phase-driven approach to cloud migration:

Phases	Benefits
Cloud evaluation: • Financial evaluation (Total cost of ownership) • Security and compliance evaluation • Technical evaluation (differentiating the application category) • Locate the applications which can be reused and the applications which need to be recoded • Move applications with valid licenses • Define the migration plan with the measured output	Business outcome for migration (like lower TCO, faster time to market, higher flexibility and agility, scalability and elasticity, better ROI) Finding out obstacles/hindrance between your current traditional legacy architecture (hardware defined) and next generation cloud architecture (software defined)
Testing scenarios with the desired results: • Get familiar with the AWS Cloud environment and its tools • Plan a pilot project to validate the solution • Test the existing application in the cloud environment with all of the used cases	Have the skillset and training on various AWS services Minimize risks by testing important tools of your proposed architecture/solution
Migrating your data: • Know about various storage types in the AWS Cloud • Move fileservers to Amazon S3 • Move commercial RDBMS to EC2 and EBS • Move MySQL to **Amazon Relational Database Service (Amazon RDS)**	Availability/redundancy, flexible storage, elastic scalable storage Automated management backup
Moving your apps: • Simple, easy to go migration strategy • Hybrid migration roadmap • Develop cloud-aware layers of code as required • Create specific AMIs for each application/software	Scaled-out service-oriented elastic architecture for all future enhancements

Utilizing the cloud: • Take the benefits of other AWS services • Automate scalability and SDLC • Hardening security and compliance • Single dashboard (GUI) to manage AWS resources • Utilizing various availability zones	Lower CapEx of IT infrastructure Adjustability and agility Automation and enhanced productivity **High Availability (HA)**
Optimization: • Optimize usage based on demand • Improve efficiency • Implement advanced monitoring and telemetry • Re-engineer your application • Decompose your relational databases	Optimized utilization and measurable impact in OpEx Single pane of glass visibility with advanced monitoring and management

The database application might be migrated between two databases of the same engine type (a homogeneous migration; for example, Oracle to Oracle, SQL Server to SQL Server, and so on) or between two databases that use different engine types (a heterogeneous migration; for example, Oracle to PostgreSQL, SQL Server to MySQL, and so on) during the migration process. We will see common migration scenarios irrespective of the database engine and look into specific issues related to certain examples of heterogeneous conversions.

Seven steps for application migration to AWS

Application migration phases with supporting tools

Application migration to AWS involves multiple steps:

1. Migration assessment analysis
2. Schema conversion to a target database environment
3. SQL statement and application code conversion

4. Data migration
5. Testing of converted database and application code
6. Replication and failover scenarios for data migration
7. Monitoring for a new production environment and go live with the target environment

Each application is different and may require changing one or more of the preceding steps. For example, a typical application contains the majority of complex data logic in database-stored procedures, functions, and so on, while other applications are heavier on logic in the application, for example, random queries to support search functionality.

Migration assessment

We have to assess the framework of the existing application and get the assessment report, which has a network diagram with all the application layers and identifies the application and database components. We have to check whether these applications will be automatically migrated or need manual migration work during migration assessment.

The database migration assessment report is the key tool in assessment analysis. This report provides important information about the conversion of the schema from your source database to your target RDS database instance.

The assessment report identifies schema objects (for example, tables, views, stored procedures, triggers, and so on) in the source database and the actions which are required to convert them (action items) to the target database (including fully automated conversion, small changes like selection of data types or attributes of tables, and rewrites of significant portions of the stored procedure). The database migration assessment report guides you with the following decisions:

- Helps you to get the compatible target engine with the source database and its attributes
- Required AWS services that can replace for missing features
- Find out unique features available in RDS which lower down customer's TCO
- Suggest re-coding or a different framework of the application for the cloud

Schema conversion

The schema conversion consists of translating the **data definition language** (DDL) for tables, partitions, and other database storage objects from the syntax and features of the source database to the target database.

Schema conversion in the AWS SCT is a two-step process:

1. Convert the schema
2. Apply the schema to the target database

Conversion of embedded SQL and application code

The next step is to address any custom scripts with embedded SQL statements (for example, ETL scripts, reports, and so on) and the application code so that they work with the new target database after you convert the database schema. This includes rewriting portions of application code written in Java, C#, C++, Perl, Python, and so on, which relate to JDBC/ODBC driver usage, establishing connections, data retrieval, and iteration. AWS SCT will scan a folder containing application code, extract embedded SQL statements, convert as many as possible automatically, and flag the remaining statements for manual conversion actions. Some applications are more reliant on database objects, such as stored procedures, while other applications use more embedded SQL for database queries.

The workflow for application code conversion is similar to the workflow for database migration:

1. An assessment report will estimate the effort to convert the application code to the target platform
2. Do code analysis to extract the embedded SQL statements
3. AWS SCT will automatically convert as much code as possible
4. The remaining conversion has to be done manually
5. Save code changes

AWS SCT uses a two-step process to convert application code:

1. Extract SQL statements from the surrounding application code
2. Convert SQL statements

An Application Conversion Project is a subset of a Database Migration Project. A Database Migration Project is a superset and includes one or more application conversion subprojects where you have a frontend GUI application conversion, an ETL application conversion, and a reporting application conversion. All three applications will be attached to the parent Database Migration Project and converted in the AWS SCT.

Data migration

It is time to migrate data from the source database to the target database after the schema and application code are successfully converted to the target database platform. We can do this by using AWS DMS. You can perform testing on the new schema and application after the data is migrated.

Note that AWS SCT and AWS DMS can be used independently. AWS DMS can be used to synchronize homogeneous databases between environments like refreshing a test environment with production data since the tools are integrated. This means that the schema conversion and data migration steps can be performed in any order.

AWS DMS is a replication server that acts as a mediator between the source and target databases. AWS DMS migrate data between source and target instances and tracks which rows have been migrated and which rows have yet to be migrated or have been left. This instance is referred to as the AWS DMS replication instance, as shown in the following figure:

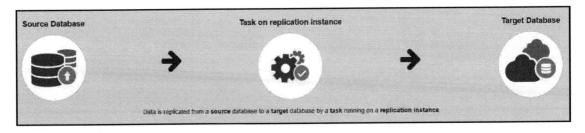

AWS DMS replication instance

AWS DMS provides a GUI to run the three steps of the data migration service to get it up and running:

1. Set up a replication instance
2. Define connections for the source and target databases
3. Define data replication tasks

AWS DMS must be able to connect to the source and target databases as well as the replication instance to execute a database migration. It will automatically create the replication instance in the specified AWS **Virtual Private Cloud** (**VPC**). When the source and target databases are also AWS resources (Amazon EC2 or Amazon RDS) in the same VPC, this is the ideal database migration.

You can migrate data in two ways:

- Full copy of existing data
- Full copy of existing data, then continuous replication of incremental data changes to the target

Initial data migration to a static database will be good for a test environment or a smaller database, but ongoing replication might be required for a larger production migration with a near-zero downtime threshold. If the application can tolerate a timeout window long enough to migrate all the data, then the full copy option is easier to set up and manage. We need to prevent users from changing data when the data is being migrated.

Testing converted code

It is time for a thorough testing of the migrated application after schema and application code has been converted and the data has been successfully migrated onto the AWS platform. The objective of this testing is to confirm the correct functional behavior of the application on the new platform.

The objective of testing will be in two stages:

- First, exercising critical functionality in the application and verifying that the converted SQL objects are functioning as required. We have to load the same test dataset into the original source database, load the converted version of the same dataset into the target database, and perform the same set of automated system tests in parallel on each system. The outcome of the tests on the converted database should be functionally equivalent to the source.

- Secondly, data rows affected by the tests should also be examined independently for accuracy. Analyzing the data independently from the application's functionality will confirm that there are no data issues hidden in the target database which are not visible in the **user interface (UI)**.

Data replication

We know that a one-time full load of existing data is comparatively simple to set up and run, but many production applications with large databases cannot tolerate a downtime window long enough to migrate all the data in a full load. AWS DMS can leverage a proprietary **Change Data Capture (CDC)** process to conduct ongoing replication from the source database to the target database for these databases. AWS DMS manages and monitors the ongoing replication process with minimal load on the source database without platform-specific technologies and components which need to be installed on either the source or target.

CDC offers two ways to implement ongoing replication:

- Migrate existing data and replicate the changes - implements ongoing replication by:
    - (Optional) Creating the target schema
    - Migrating existing data and caching changes to existing data as it is migrated
    - Applying those cached data changes until the database reaches a normal state
    - Lastly, applying current data changes to the target as soon as they are received by the replication instance
- Replicate data changes only (no schema) from a specified point in time. This option is helpful when the target schema already exists and the initial data load is already completed. For example, using native export/import tools, ETL, or snapshots might be a more efficient method of loading the bulk data in some situations. In this case, AWS DMS can be used to replicate changes from when the bulk load process started to bring and keep the source and target databases in sync.

AWS DMS takes advantage of built-in functionality of the source database platform to implement the proprietary CDC process on the replication instance. This allows AWS DMS to manage, process, and monitor data replication with minimal impact to either the source or target databases.

Deployment to AWS and Go-Live

Test the data migration of the production database to confirm that all the data can be successfully migrated during the allocated cutover window. Monitor the source and target databases to confirm that the initial data load is completed, cached transactions are applied, and that the data has reached a normal state before cutover.

Design a simple rollback plan for the unexpected event that an unrecoverable error occurs during the Go-Live window. AWS SCT and AWS DMS work together to retain the original source database and application, so the fallback plan will primarily consist of scripts to point connection strings back to the original source database.

Post-deployment monitoring

AWS DMS monitors the number of rows inserted, deleted, and updated, as well as the number of DDL statements issued per table while a task is running. You can view these statistics for the selected task on the **Table Statistics** tab:

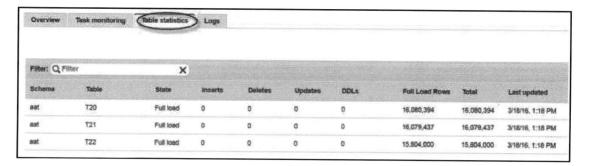

Schema	Table	State	Inserts	Deletes	Updates	DDLs	Full Load Rows	Total	Last updated
aat	T20	Full load	0	0	0	0	16,080,394	16,080,394	3/18/16, 1:18 PM
aat	T21	Full load	0	0	0	0	16,079,437	16,079,437	3/18/16, 1:18 PM
aat	T22	Full load	0	0	0	0	15,804,000	15,804,000	3/18/16, 1:18 PM

Viewing table statistics

Managing AWS with vCenter

AWS Management Portal for vCenter gives customers a simple GUI for creating and managing AWS resources from VMware vCenter.

Major advantages of this tool include:

- You can manage AWS networks, AWS resources using their infrastructure, and grant/remove access to users at the granular level
- Users can view their applications/resources if they have permission to read, create, and manage/modify EC2 instances

- AWS Connector for vCenter help users to import their virtual machines in AWS

Administrators for AWS Management Portal for vCenter are responsible for managing an AWS network, known as a VPC, creating environments, and granting users permission to access environments.

Managing administrators on the management portal

We suggest you select different users to administer the management portal. You should be an administrator for both vCenter and the management portal to create an administrator for the management portal.

Steps for adding an administrator

The steps are as follows:

1. Sign in to vCenter as an administrator, click **Home**, and then click **AWS Management Portal**
2. From the top pane, click **Admin Users**
3. Click **Add**

> When we are using the connector to authenticate users and it is in maintenance mode, we'll get the error **Unable to contact User Provider. Please contact your Administrator. We suggest you to wait for few minutes and then try again.**

4. Select the domain and one or more users, and then click **OK** in the **Select Users** dialog box

   Domains and Users are disabled if their names don't meet certain requirements. If a user is a domain user, *domain \ user* must not exceed 32 characters. If a user is a local user, *user* must not exceed 32 characters. The *domain* and *user* values must each begin with a letter and contain only the following characters: a-z, A-Z, 0-9, periods (.), underscores (_), and dashes (-).

5. Click **Save** after adding administrators

You must be an administrator for the management portal to remove an administrator from the management portal.

Steps for removing an administrator

The steps are as follows:

1. Sign in to vCenter as an administrator, click **Home**, and then click **AWS Management Portal**
2. Click **Admin Users**
3. Select the user from the list
4. Click **Remove**, and then click **Save**

VPCs and subnets management

By default, we can create up to five VPCs per region. We can create one or more subnets per VPC and one or more security groups per VPC. We should use the AWS Management Console or the AWS CLI to configure route tables, network ACLs, and other advanced VPC features.

 Each region might also have a default VPC depending on your AWS account creation time.

Steps for creating a VPC and subnets

The steps are as follows:

1. Sign in to vCenter as an administrator, click **Home**, and then click **AWS Management Portal**.
2. Click **VPC** from the top pane.
3. Select a region for the VPC. Click **Create a virtual private cloud** on the **Getting Started** tab.
4. Enter a name for the VPC in **VPC Name**.

5. Select the configuration that meets your needs, **VPC with a single public subnet** or **VPC with public and private subnets**, and then click **Next**.

   You can add additional subnets after creating the VPC. Amazon VPC console also supports additional configurations for your VPC.

6. Enter an IP address range for the VPC, in CIDR notation (for example, `192.0.0.0/16`).

7. For each subnet, enter an IP address range, in CIDR notation (for example, `192.0.0.0/24`), and select an Availability Zone.

   IP address ranges for the subnets must not overlap while creating multiple subnets in a VPC. Click Next once you are finished.

8. (Optional) Specify one or more tags for your VPC. Click **Add**, enter the tag key, and enter the tag value for each tag.

9. Click **Finish** after adding tags.

10. (Optional) To add another subnet to your VPC, select the VPC, and then click **Create a subnet** on the **Getting Started** tab. Enter a name, select an Availability Zone, and enter an IP address range for the subnet, in CIDR notation. Subnet is a public subnet by default. Click **Make this a private subnet** to create a private subnet. We can also specify one or more tags for the subnet. When you are finished, click **Finish**.

   You can only delete a non-default VPC if there are no running instances in its subnets. You can't delete a default VPC using the management portal.

Steps for deleting a VPC

The steps are as follows:

1. Sign in to vCenter as an administrator, click **Home**, and then click **AWS Management Portal**
2. Click **VPC**
3. Expand the region for the VPC, and then select the **VPC**
4. Click **Delete the virtual private cloud** on the **Getting Started** tab
5. Click **Yes** in the Delete VPC dialog box

Security groups management

A security group executes as a firewall to control the traffic for one or more EC2 instances. We can define a security group with rules to allow users to connect to EC2 instances in the VPC defined in the security group. Users have options in the template to choose one or more security groups.

Steps for creating a security group

The steps are as follows:

1. Sign in to vCenter as an administrator, click **Home**, and then click **AWS Management Portal.**
2. Click **VPC** from the top pane.
3. Expand the region for the VPC, and then select the **VPC.**
4. Click **Create a security group** on the **Getting Started** tab.
5. Enter a name and a description for the security group, and then click **Next.**
6. You must add a rule that allows inbound traffic using SSH to connect to an EC2 Linux instance:

 You can skip this step and add the rule later by selecting the security group and clicking **Add a rule** on the **Getting Started** tab.

- Click **Add.**
- Select **SSH** from the **Type** list.
- Select **Custom IP** from the **Source** list.
- Enter the IP address range in IP, in CIDR notation. For example, if your IP address is `201.0.111.29`, specify `201.0.111.29/32` to list this single IP address in CIDR notation. If your organization allocates addresses from a range, specify the entire range, such as `201.0.111.0/24`.
- Verify that **Inbound** is selected.
- Click **Add.**

7. You must add a rule that allows inbound traffic using RDP to connect to an EC2 Windows instance:

> You can skip this step and add the rule later by selecting the security group and clicking **Add a rule** on the **Getting Started** tab.

- Click **Add**.
- From the **Type** list, select **RDP**.
- Select **Custom IP** from the **Source** list.
- Enter the IP address range in IP, in CIDR notation. For example, if your IP address is `201.0.111.29`, specify `201.0.111.29/32` to list this single IP address in CIDR notation. If your organization allocates addresses from a range, specify the entire range, such as `201.0.111.0/24`.
- Verify that **Inbound** is selected.
- Click **Add**.

8. Click **Next** after adding rules.
9. (Optional) Specify one or more tags for your security group. Click **Add**, enter the tag key, and enter the tag value for each tag. Click **Next** after entering tags.
10. Review the properties for your security group. To make changes, click **Back**. Click **Finish** to create the security group.

If the security group is not currently associated with any instance, then you can delete it.

Steps for deleting a security group

The steps are as follows:

1. Sign in to vCenter as an administrator, click **Home**, and then click **AWS Management Portal**
2. Click **VPC**
3. Expand the region and the VPC for the security group, and then select the security group
4. On the **Getting Started** tab, click **Delete** the security group
5. In the **Delete Security Group** dialog box, click **Yes**

You must use the Amazon EC2 console or the AWS CLI to change the security groups for a running instance.

Environment management in AWS

Administrators use environments to organize and manage AWS resources. They give/deny permissions to users at the environment level.

You can create environments and have access to default environments as an administrator. The default environment for a region helps you manage EC2 instances created for your AWS account with region leveraging tools such as the AWS Management Console, the AWS CLI, or an AWS SDK, in place of using the management portal.

Steps for creating an environment

The steps are as follows:

1. Sign in to vCenter as an administrator, click **Home**, and then click **AWS Management Portal**.
2. Click **Dashboard** from the top pane.
3. Select a region for the environment. Click **Create an environment** on the **Getting Started** page.
4. Enter a name for the environment in **Name**.
5. Select a **VPC** from VPC.

This list includes all VPCs for the region which includes VPCs created using the Amazon VPC console and the default VPC (if it exists). You must create a VPC in this region if this list is empty.

6. Select one or more subnets from Subnets.

This list includes all subnets for the selected VPC including any default subnets. You must add a subnet to the VPC or select a different VPC if this list is empty.

7. Click **Finish**.

Once you have created an environment, you can then can create one or more templates and use these templates to launch EC2 instances into your environment. We will add a tag with the name `ws-management-portal/environment-id` and the value set to the ID of the environment once you launch an instance. You can leverage this tag to check resources by using self-explanatory billing reports (`http://docs.aws.amazon.com/awsaccountbilling/latest/aboutv2/DetailedBillingReports.html`) or EC2 utilization reports (`http://docs.aws.amazon.com/awsaccountbilling/latest/aboutv2/DetailedBillingReports.html`). Users can't modify this tag using the management portal, but users can access this to modify or delete this tag using the Amazon EC2 console, CLI, or API. If someone modifies or deletes this tag, it does not affect a users' permissions to access the instance.

Once you've deleted the environment's templates, you can delete the environment.

Steps for deleting an environment

The steps are as follows:

1. Sign in to vCenter as an administrator, click **Home**, and then click **AWS Management Portal.**
2. Click **Dashboard.**
3. Expand the region for the environment and then select the environment.
4. Right-click the environment and select **Delete.**
5. Click **Yes** in the **Delete Environment** dialog box.

Administrators can explain, start, stop, reboot, and terminate EC2 instances in the default environment for a region through the management portal.

To manage instances in the default environment:

1. Sign in to vCenter as an administrator, click **Home**, and then click **AWS Management Portal**.
2. Click **Dashboard** and expand the region.
3. To list your instances:

   - Expand **Default Environment**
   - Click **Default Environment** and then click the **Instances** tab

4. Expand **Default Environment** and select the instance to start, stop, reboot, or terminate an instance. Click the desired task under **Basic Tasks** from the **Getting Started** tab.

User permissions management

Administrators can define users' permissions to access an environment. You must be an admin for both vCenter and the management portal to provide permissions. You must be an admin for the management portal to edit or delete permissions.

The customized permissions given to a user depend on the role assigned by you to the user. The management portal briefs you with the following roles:

- **No-Access**: User doesn't have any authority to do anything
- **Read-Only**: Users can view the environment and its templates and instances
- **General**: All users have access to **Read-Only** and also can run, rename, reboot, stop, start, terminate, and import instances
- **Owner**: All users have access to **General** and also can create, delete, and rename templates to import and delete key pairs, and to create images

How to grant permissions to a user:

1. Sign in to vCenter as an administrator, click **Home**, and then click **AWS Management Portal**.
2. From the top pane, click **Dashboard**.
3. Expand the region for the environment, right-click the environment, and then click **Add Permission**.
4. Click **Add**. In the **Select Users** dialog box, select the domain and one or more users, and then click **OK**.

5. Select one or more users from **Users** and then select a role from **Assigned Role**.
6. Click **Save**. The changes are displayed in the **Permissions** tab.

To change the permissions granted to a user:

1. Sign in to vCenter as an administrator, click **Home**, and then click **AWS Management Portal**.
2. Click **Dashboard**.
3. Expand the region for the environment, and then select the environment.

4. Right-click the user and select **Properties** from the **Permissions** tab.
5. Select a different role and click **Save**. The updates are displayed in the **Permissions** tab.

To revoke the permissions granted to a user:

1. Sign in to vCenter as an administrator, click **Home**, and then click **AWS Management Portal**
2. Click **Dashboard**
3. Expand the region for the environment, and then select the environment
4. Right-click the user and select **Delete** from the **Permissions** tab
5. The updates are displayed in the **Permissions** tab after clicking **OK**

VM migration to Amazon EC2 with AWS Connector for vCenter

You can start an EC2 instance from a virtual machine which you have moved from VMware vCenter to Amazon EC2. You can leverage the AWS Connector for vCenter to migrate your virtual machines to Amazon EC2.

We have to create a migration task before starting any migration. Once the conversion task has been successfully completed, your imported virtual machine is available.

Essential components for VM Migration:

- An administrator must install and configure the connector which is part of the AWS Management Portal for vCenter.
- An administrator must create at least one environment and have permission to migrate a virtual machine into one or more environments. This is an environment other than the default environment and must be distinctly created.
- The VM must be a part of the supported operating systems and also selected supported instance types.
- Attach the VM Import Export Role For AWS Connector policy to the vmimport role which is created per the VM Import Service Role (`http://docs.aws.amazon.com/AWSEC2/latest/UserGuide/VMImportPrerequisites.html#vmimport-service-role`).
- The VM should not have a disk whose compressed size is more than 215 GB.

The following are the limitations:

- Analyzes VM Import/Export requirements with the support matrix (`http://docs.aws.amazon.com/AWSEC2/latest/UserGuide/VMImportPrerequisites.html#vmimport-limitations`).

- Amazon EC2 can do a maximum of five active migrations per region. It queues any additional migration tasks until one of the active migration tasks completes successfully or is canceled if the connector is already in the process of migrating 4 virtual machines.

The VM import authorization process

Users have no direct access to AWS. The following figure briefs you on the migration flow of a VM to Amazon EC2:

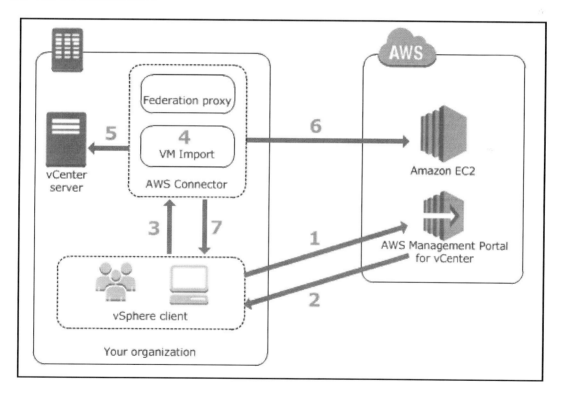

Importing a VM to AWS Cloud

1. You have to authorize the vSphere virtual machine in order to import to the EC2 environment.
2. The Management Portal checks about a user's permissions to migrate VMs to the environment by returning a token.
3. vCenter Admin sends an import request to the connector along with the token.
4. The connector validates the token.
5. The connector validates the user's permissions to export the VM.
6. The connector initiates the migration.
7. The connector sends a response to the vCenter Admin with the import task ID.

Virtual machine migration process

With the connector, vCenter can migrate a VM to Amazon EC2. The connector can migrate a maximum of four VMs concurrently.

You can't create a migration task while the connector is updating.

The following steps explain how you can migrate a virtual machine to Amazon EC2:

1. Click **Home** and then click **VMs and Templates in vCenter console**.
2. Select the virtual machine.
3. Right-click the VM, and then click **Migrate VM to EC2**. If your administrator did not give you permission to migrate VMs, then you will see a message to ask your administrator to give you permission.
4. Proceed with the aforementioned migration form as follows:

   - Select the operating system running on the VM.
   - Select the appropriate region and environment for the targeting EC2 instance. The list of environments contains only the environments which you have permission to use.
   - Select a subnet, instance type, and security group for the instance.
   - (Optional) Enter a private IP address.

- Select a security group. The list of security groups contains only the security groups associated with the environment which have been selected.
- Click **Begin migration to Amazon EC2**.
- If the connector displays a warning that there are already four active migration tasks running and that it will affect the speed of these tasks, you can either continue or cancel the migration task.

Once the migration begins, display the import task ID, even if the migration task started immediately or has been queued. Note down the task ID to monitor the migration task. Close the import window after the connector notifies you that the import task was created or queued, and the migration will continue.

5. (Optional) Monitor the migration status:
   - Click **Home** and then click **AWS Management Portal from vCenter**.
   - Expand the region for the instance, select the environment, and then click the **VM-to-EC2 Migrations** tab.
   - Find the entry with the import task ID or queued task ID which you have noted in the previous steps. The ID of the instance is shown in the Instance ID field.

6. Expand the environment, expand Imported Instances, select the instance, and then click the **Summary** tab to start the EC2 instance after the migration has completed. The ID of the instance should be the same as the instance ID that you noted from the **VM-to-EC2 Migrations** tab. On the **Getting Started** tab, click **Start instance**.

Backing up the instance

Once you start an instance, it runs until it is terminated. You can't connect to or recover the instance once your instance is terminated. You can only be sure of this if you can start a new instance with the same software as a migrated instance. Create an **Amazon Machine Image** (**AMI**) from the instance and then create a template which specifies the AMI if required.

You can use the following Amazon EC2 console or command line tools to create an AMI:

Platform	Root Volume	Topic
Linux	EBS	To create an Amazon EBS-Backed Linux AMI (`http://docs.aws.amazon.com/AWSEC2/latest/UserGuide/creating-an-ami-ebs.html`)
Linux	Instance store	To create an Instance Store-Backed Linux AMI (`http://docs.aws.amazon.com/AWSEC2/latest/UserGuide/creating-an-ami-instance-store.html`)
Windows	EBS	To create an Amazon EBS-Backed Windows AMI (`http://docs.aws.amazon.com/AWSEC2/latest/WindowsGuide/Creating_EBSbacked_WinAMI.html`)
Windows	Instance store	To create an Instance Store-Backed Windows AMI (`http://docs.aws.amazon.com/AWSEC2/latest/WindowsGuide/Creating_InstanceStoreBacked_WinAMI.html`)

You can then create a template through where you can launch instances from the AMI which have been created from your migrated instance.

Migrated EC2 instance export process

We can leverage the management portal in vCenter to export an EC2 instance which was earlier migrated from a VM. During the process for exporting an instance, create an **Open Virtualization Appliance (OVA)** file and store it in an Amazon S3 bucket in your AWS account.

If we have not previously exported an EC2 instance using vCenter, we must first specify the name which we will use for the S3 buckets that we created for instance export. AWS creates one S3 bucket in each region for this purpose, with a nomenclature which follows the form export-to-s3-name-region.

The following are the requirements:

- You must be an administrator of the management portal to export an EC2 instance.
- You can configure instance export using the AWS credentials of either an administrator or an IAM user. First verify that the user has the permissions described in *Creating the Required Accounts and Users* (http://docs.aws.amazon.com/amp/latest/userguide/install-option-connector.html#connector-accounts-fp) to allow an IAM user to complete these steps.

The following are the limitations:

- Can go for a maximum of five concurrent export tasks per region
- Can't export an instance which is currently being exported

Follow these steps to prepare for instance export:

1. Open the AWS Management Portal for the vCenter setup console (https://amp.aws.amazon.com/VCPlugin.html#setup).
2. Click **Configure Instance Export**, and then click **Create New** on the **AWS Management Portal for vCenter** page.
3. Configure the **Instance Export** page as follows:
   - As prompted, complete the bucket name in S3 bucket names
   - Click **I agree that AWS Management Portal for vCenter may do the following on my behalf**
   - Click **Create**

Follow these steps to export a migrated instance:

1. Click **Home** and then click **AWS Management Portal** from vCenter.
2. Expand the region, the environment, and the template for the instance from the dashboard.
3. Select the instance.
4. Click **Export instance to S3** on the **Getting Started** tab.
5. Enter a name for the OVA file in **S3 object file prefix** and then click **Export** in the **Export instance to S3** dialog box.

   It will show you the export task ID, and note this ID if you want to monitor the status of the export task once the export begins.

6. (Optional) Choose the environment for the instance and then click the **EC2-to-S3 Migrations** tab to monitor the status of the export process.

> This tab shows all instance export tasks from the last seven days. Find the task with the export task ID which you noted earlier. If you have to abort the export task while it is in progress, right-click the row, click **Cancel Export Task**, and click **Continue** when prompted for confirmation.

7. Access the OVA file after the export process has completed with the following steps:

- Open the Amazon S3 console at `https://console.aws.amazon.com/s3/`.
- Get the region that contains the EC2 instance which you have exported from the navigation bar. The OVA file is stored in an S3 bucket in the same region as the EC2 instance.
- Choose the bucket for your exported instances (`export-to-s3-name-region`) and then select the OVA file from the **Buckets** pane.
- Click **Actions** and then click **Download**. Follow the directions to complete the download.

You can export an EC2 instance using Amazon EC2 CLI instead of using the connector.

Troubleshooting migration

Error: Additional permissions are required to migrate multi-disk virtual machines.

You receive the error **To migrate a virtual machine with more than one disk, log into the management portal setup page and grant the additional permissions required by the VM Import/Export service** when migrating a virtual machine.

You have to follow the following process to get the necessary permissions:

1. Open the AWS Management Portal for vCenter setup console (`https://amp.aws.amazon.com/VCPlugin.html#setup`).
2. If you see an error message showing that your Import service role is missing, click **Fix Error.**
3. (Optional) Click **View Policy** to review the policy for the import service role.
4. Click **I agree that AWS Management Portal for vCenter may create the above roles on my behalf.**
5. Click **Save.**

Error: Connector is unable to reach ESX host.

While migrating a virtual machine, you will receive the following error:

Connector is unable to reach ESX host [hostname] to migrate virtual machine [name].

If the hostname mentioned in the error message is not the fully-qualified domain name of an ESXi host, use the following process to configure the DNS suffix search list so that the connector can append the suffix and resolve the ESXi hostname:

1. Locate the connector VM in the vSphere Customer, right-click it, and select Open Console.
2. Log in as an ec2-user to see Logging into the Virtual Machine Console (`http://docs.aws.amazon.com/amp/latest/userguide/manage-connector.html#access-virtual-machine-console`).
3. Run the `sudo setup.rb` command. This command shows the following menu:

   Choose one of the below options:

   1. Reset password

   2. Reconfigure network settings

   3. Restart services

   4. Factory reset

   5. Delete unused upgrade-related files

> 6. Enable/disable SSL certificate validation
>
> 7. Display connector's SSL certificate
>
> 8. Generate log bundle
>
> 9. Exit
>
> Please enter your option [1-9]:

4. Type 2, and then press **Enter**. The command displays the following menu:

    > Reconfigure your network:
    >
    > 1. Renew or get a DHCP lease
    >
    > 2. Set up a static IP
    >
    > 3. Set up a web proxy for AWS communication
    >
    > 4. Set up a DNS suffix search list
    >
    > 5. Exit
    >
    > 6. Please enter your option [1-5]:

5. Type 4, and then press **Enter**. The command displays the current DNS suffix search list. Follow the directions to update the search list to include the domain name of the ESXi host from the error message.

Validation of the certificates

By default, the connector checks the certificates of all entities which it communicates with over HTTPS, including vCenter and ESXi servers. This is required to stop vulnerabilities. The connector can't validate the certificates of the host, so the migration fails if you are migrating a virtual machine from ESX version 4.1 or earlier to Amazon EC2.

You can do one of the following to fix this issue:

- **Option 1**: Update to ESXi 5.0 or later
- **Option 2**: Disable ESX certificate validation, migrate the virtual machine, and then re-enable ESX certificate validation as follows:
    - Open the connector management console (`https://ip_address/`, where `ip_address` is the IP address of the management console) and log in using your password from your web browser
    - Click **Register the Connector**
    - Under **ESX SSL certificate** options, click **Ignore any ESX certificate errors**, and then click **Register on the Register Plugin** page

 We recommend that you keep ESX certificate validation enabled unless you are migrating virtual machines from ESX 4.1 or earlier.

- Return to the **Register Plugin** page of the connector management console, click **Trust vCenter to validate ESX certificates**, and then click **Register** once you have finished migrating the virtual machine

VMware Cross-Cloud Model with IBM Cloud

VMware's **Software Defined Data Center** (**SDDC**) on IBM Cloud enables existing VMware virtualized data center customers to extend their footprint into the IBM Cloud and includes use cases like capacity expansion into the cloud (scale up as well as scale down), migration to the cloud, disaster recovery to the cloud, backup into the cloud, and the ability to configure and provision a customized cloud environment for development, testing, training or a lab kind of setup.

We will brief you about the design of the advanced version of the VMware SDDC on IBM Cloud, which is capable of designing high levels of scalability across multiple global regions:

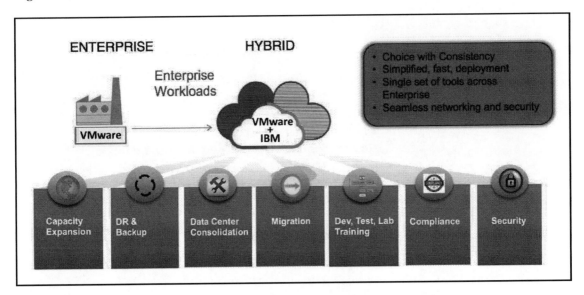

An introduction to VMware SDDC on IBM Cloud

Prerequisites

The design requires the following prerequisites:

- Customer has to acquire all needed software licenses/ keys for all products used in this design before starting implementation
- Customer has to have a SoftLayer account
- Customer has to bear for SoftLayer costs for this implementation
- Customer has to provide connectivity to any on premises environment or systems
- Customer has to provide connectivity to administrators and end users
- Customer has to get and provision the domain name

- Customer has to get hostname prefixes for the SoftLayer bare metal devices commissioned through this design
- Customer should have connection details and necessary credentials for any external systems to this design which are going to be integrated
- Customer has to bear all licensing costs of software products used in this design

When defining the VMware SDDC on IBM Cloud design as a single object, the following are the external users and systems that interface with the cloud design:

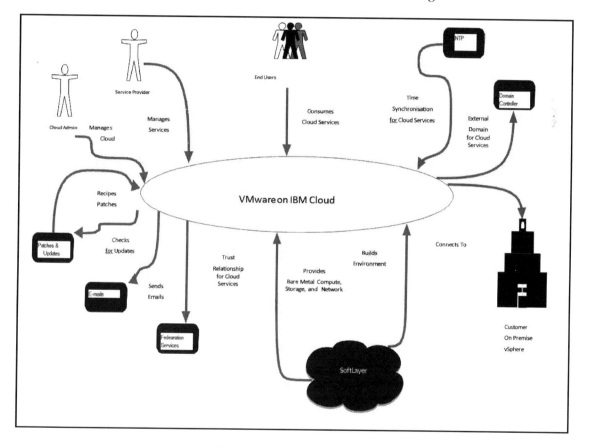

VMware SDDC on the IBM Cloud system context

The cloud users who frequently interface with this design are mentioned in the following table. It might be possible that there is no direct correlation between different users. Different users can play different roles or more than one role:

Actor	Description
Cloud admin	The cloud admin or administrator is responsible for maintaining the cloud services. This includes: • Assigning virtual resources to groups • Maintaining the Cloud Software Platform • System administrator roles
Service provider	Manages the cloud services which are provided to the customer users. This includes: • Service catalog configuration • Defining roles • Defining groups • Configuring user access • Tenant administrator roles
User	Consumes the services that the cloud admin allows access to. This typically includes: • Provisioning/de-provisioning VMs • Provisioning/de-provisioning patterns • Start/stop/restart VMs and patterns

Components/services used in this architecture

The systems that interface with the cloud design are described in the following table:

System	Description
SoftLayer	SoftLayer provides the bare metal, physical networking, and NFS storage along with automation to build a cloud design as per customer requirements
Customer on premises vSphere	Cloud design should be able to connect to an existing vSphere environment on a customer's premises to enable Hybrid Cloud capabilities
Customer SMTP relay	Cloud design connects its SMTP server to a customer's SMTP relay service to send notifications regarding the process orchestration

Customer authentication	Cloud design should be able to connect to an existing customer authentication system to establish a trust relationship which extends the customer's authentication system into the cloud
Customer DNS	Cloud design should be able to connect to a customer's **domain name service (DNS)** to extend the domain service into the cloud
NTP service	Cloud design need an external NTP service to provide time synchronization services
Patch repo	Cloud management platform applications need to connect a number of internet-based patch repositories in order to maintain the security and stability of the cloud environment

VMware Cloud services architecture on SoftLayer

VMware SDDC on IBM Cloud provides VMware automation technology on SoftLayer. This includes virtual networking, virtual storage, process orchestration, infrastructure orchestration, and software orchestration. It also provides the tools for management of these services, providing these functions. The architecture consists of at least one central cloud region built on SoftLayer, which provides the main portal for users and administration, and it can include one or more cloud regions which are managed by the central cloud and provide additional functionality for remote locations. The architecture is scaled out within a region, or by adding regions:

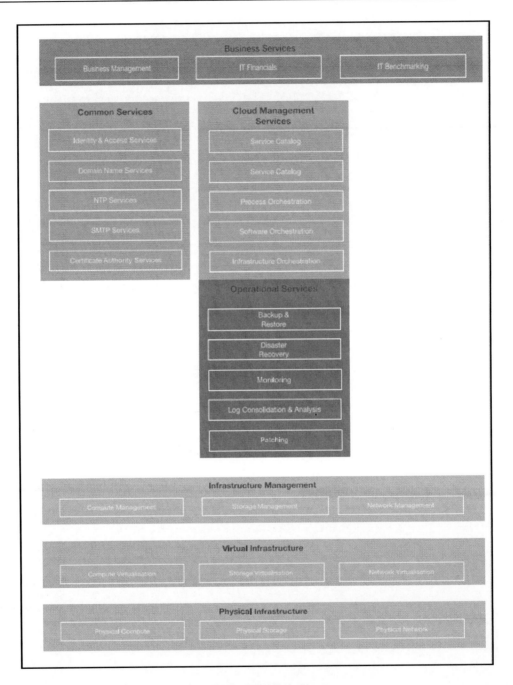

VMware SDDC on the IBM Cloud architecture

Physical infrastructure

The physical infrastructure consists of three main components: physical compute, physical network, and physical storage. The physical compute component provides the physical processing and memory leveraged by the virtualization infrastructure. The physical network component provides the network connectivity into the environment which is consumed by the network virtualization technique. The physical storage component provides the raw storage capacity.

Physical operational model

The physical operational model is explored by using the non-functional requirements to the logical operational model consumed by the virtualization infrastructure. The physical infrastructure components (hardware and software) are provided by SoftLayer bare metal, and all of the hardware and software is certified on the VMware **Hardware Compatibility Guide** (**HCG**) for cloud design:

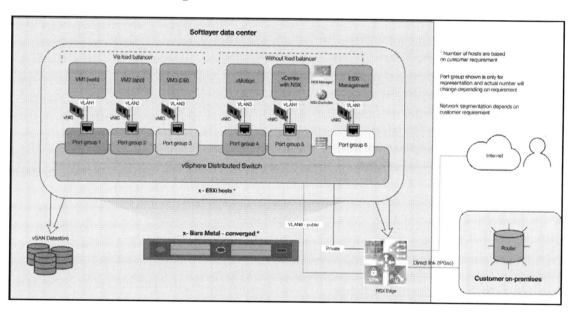

Physical operational model - virtual servers, networking, and clusters

Logical operational model

The logical operational model gives you required design components to get the functional objective:

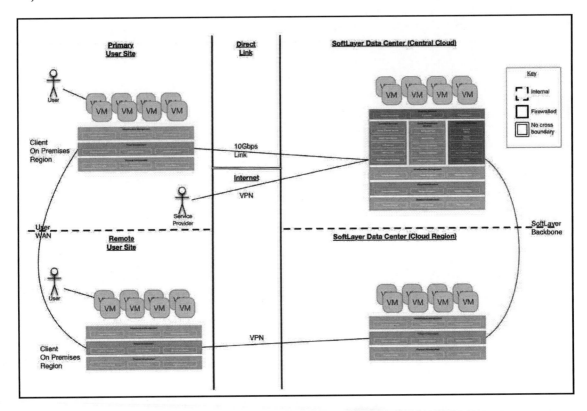

Logical structure view

Cloud design consists of two different components:

- **Central cloud**: The users and service providers are used to manage the entire cloud as well as one or more associated cloud regions through central cloud. Central cloud has the self-service portal, and additional cloud regions are added to provide remote sites. Each **cloud region** is part of the central cloud for management perspectives. vSphere environments (On premises) are connected to SoftLayer with a VPN connection over the internet or dedicated links to form additional cloud regions.

The components interact with each other within a central cloud as follows:

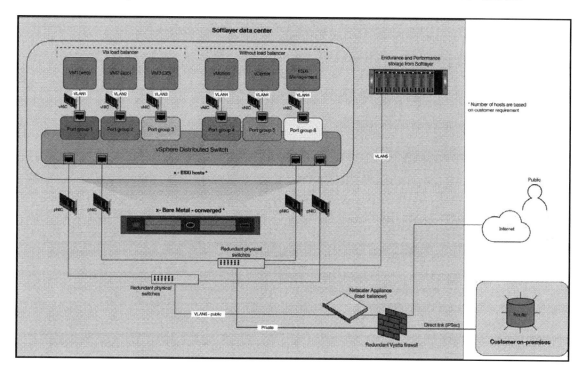

Component interaction diagram

Both the central cloud and any additional cloud regions can be built on SoftLayer.

The central cloud hosts the primary portal through which users access the cloud services. It has connections to all remote regions.

The functions map to the following software products in a central cloud is explained in detail in the following section:

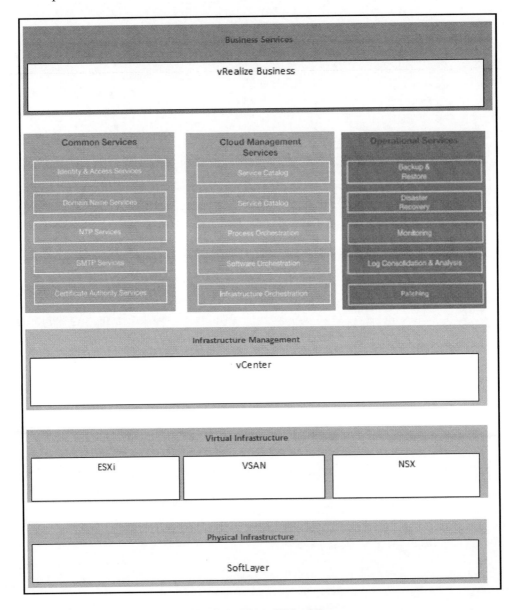

Building blocks of VMware SDDC on SoftLayer

The following figure explains abstracting physical resources as logical entities:

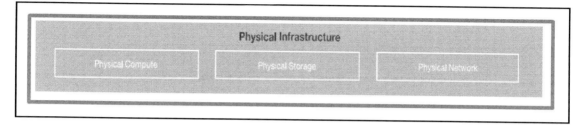

Cluster (compute, storage, and network) architecture

The physical layer breaks into clusters with the preceding design. A cluster means the pool of the compute and memory resources of all the servers in the cluster. All servers in the cluster share network and storage resources.

The following are the benefits of clusters:

- Workloads/VMs/Applications (User or Management) attached with defined hardware
- Each cluster is defined as a single object and user workloads are also defined exclusively from management workloads
- The design differentiates between the following types of clusters:
    - Compute cluster (one or more)
    - Management cluster
    - Edge cluster
    - Storage cluster

Compute clusters

Compute clusters host the VMware SDDC on IBM Cloud. Each compute cluster is built using SoftLayer bare metal. The existing infrastructure can be scaled out by adding nodes to the initial compute cluster up to the maximum number of nodes per cluster (as defined in the physical operational model). Additional compute clusters are added to the environment once the maximum has been reached:

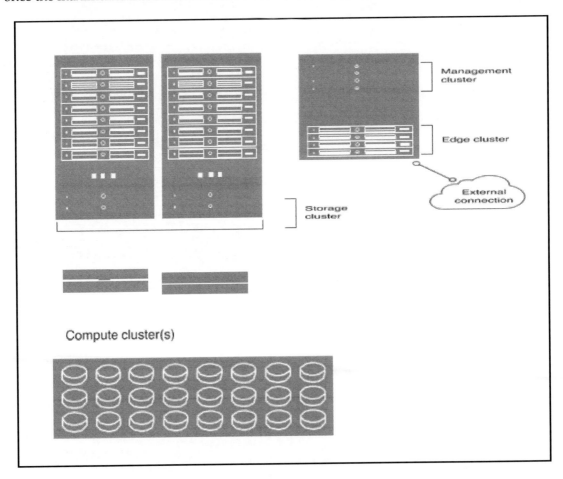

Logical cluster structure

Management cluster

The management cluster hosts the virtual machines which are responsible for managing the cloud. Both compute clusters and management clusters are created by using SoftLayer bare metal vCenter Server, NSX Manager, NSX Controller, vRealize Operations Management, vRealize Log Insight, vRealize Automation, and other shared management components which reside on these servers.

Edge cluster

Edge clusters connect the virtual networks (overlay networks) powered by NSX for vSphere and the external networks. This consists of both north-south (into the environment from outside) and east-west (between management and compute clusters) communications.

Edge clusters provide the following main functions:

- Support on-ramp and off-ramp connectivity to physical networks
- Connect to customer on premises environments

Storage cluster

A storage cluster provides network-accessible storage via NFS. This is used for backup and log archive purposes. The compute, management, and edge clusters utilize vSAN, which aggregates disks located in each host of the clusters.

Physical network provided by SoftLayer

The physical and layer 2 networking is handled by SoftLayer. The SoftLayer physical fabric provides a robust IP transport layer with the following features:

- Simplicity
- Scalability
- High bandwidth
- Fault-tolerant transport

Simplicity

The SoftLayer network is defined on three physical networks containing public, private, and out of band management (IPMI) traffic. Private and public networks are designed to go up to 20 GBPS bandwidth per physical host while the out of band management network is connected with a 1 GBPS link per host.

VLANs are configured for each of the preceding three networks while deciding network components within SoftLayer. SoftLayer will assign the new device an IP on the same VLAN if VLANs within the region have enough space for a bare metal device to be placed in the same pod. This cloud design contains SoftLayer portable subnets to provide IP addressing for virtual machines as well as IP addresses for the bare metal servers.

SoftLayer has also simplified the networking infrastructure by leveraging the best networking vendors. SoftLayer can implement and reuse automation designs to set up, configure, and monitor the network infrastructure without any issues or technical objections. APIs assist with this to get some of this automation to work and is extensively used by this cloud design to simplify management tasks.

Scalability

The SoftLayer network is configured in a multi-tier model. Each rack in a SoftLayer data center has 2 **frontend customer switches** (**FCS**) and 2 **backend customer switches** (**BCS**) connected to the public and private networks and are then connect to different, peered aggregation switches; the aggregated switches are then integrated to a pair of separate routers for L3 networking. This multi-tier design helps the network to scale across racks, rows, and pods within the SoftLayer data center.

High bandwidth

The SoftLayer data center has multiple 10 GBPS or 40 GBPS connections in all upstream network ports. Every rack is terminated with multiple 10 GBPS or 40 GBPS connections to the public internet and multiple 10 GBPS or 40 GBPS connections to the private network.

Fault-tolerant transport

You have redundancy at the server level by using 2 x 10 GBPS NICs. The backend server, frontend server, aggregation switches, and routers are redundantly connected.

Physical storage

There are two types of storage mentioned within this design, vSAN and NFS.

vSAN

VMware vSAN has a distributed storage architecture which helps the local drives on each vSphere host to be aggregated and pooled into a shared storage provided to all hosts in a vSAN cluster. The vSAN service is embedded within the physical hosts, removing the ask for external shared storage like SAN or NAS devices.

Network File System (NFS)

NFS is a protocol for file-based storage to assist a user on a customer system to access files over a network. ESXi host, which leverages NFS as a backend datastore and the storage, is provisioned by a NFS-capable external storage array existing within the same SoftLayer deployment as the central cloud or cloud region.

Storage virtualization

Storage virtualization helps with two levels of virtualization; virtualizing the storage arrays and virtualizing the block storage used by virtual machines.

VMware SDS is vSAN

vSAN abstracts a physical storage area network completely within the virtualization layer. Each host in the cluster contains local drives that are aggregated in software to act as a single disk array which is shared between all the hosts in the cluster as a shared datastore.

vSAN has the advantage of fewer components (no external drive array, fiber cabling, and so on) as there is no physical area network. It allows ease of scaling (both scale up and scale out options) while adding new compute nodes with less configurations, reducing tasks like LUN allocation. vSAN also provides high performance since the local disk is used and disk I/O is spread out across all hosts within a cluster.

Storage policies are used to define storage parameters such as performance and protection levels. The policy is set per virtual machine, allowing great options with the service levels available.

Virtual Machine Disks (VMDK)

Each virtual machine has at least one virtual machine disk VMDK file. You can have additional disks as per your application's requirements. The virtual disks are provisioned onto the datastores provided by vSAN. All virtual disks are thin provisioned to utilize maximum disks as per requirements, so unused disk space within a single virtual disk will not take up an entire datastore disk capacity assigned to specific virtual machines.

Virtual infrastructure

The virtual infrastructure layer includes the software to provide compute, network and storage virtualization. VMware products in this layer are vSphere ESXi, VMware vSAN, and VMware NSX:

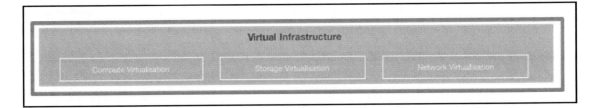

Virtual infrastructure design consists of one central cloud and can have several cloud regions which are managed by the central cloud.

Each central cloud or cloud region has the following components:

- **Management cluster**: A pool of compute resources for the management and operation of the cloud
- **Edge cluster**: Extends external connections for the system and L2-L7 services powered by VMware NSX
- **Compute cluster**: Hosts user virtual compute and storage

Compute virtualization

Compute virtualization provides the virtualization of CPU and memory which is consumed by virtual machines. This is provided by VMware vSphere ESXi and vCenter Server software.

Provisioning

You can provision new servers faster than traditional methods by virtualizing the hardware. You get flexibility to add or remove components like CPU or memory assigned to a virtual machine without any disruption or downtime.

Resource scheduling

Virtual compute is disintegrated from the physical hardware responsible for controlling the hardware where the virtual machine resides. **Distributed Resource Scheduling (DRS)** is enabled to distribute and balance the virtual machines across the cluster and help virtual machines get the necessary resources as per their demand.

Availability

You get maximum availability since the virtual machine has been decoupled from the hardware. If the hardware fails, then the operating system and applications running on it could crash in the physical infrastructure. Virtual machines can be restarted on the remaining hosts in a cluster in the event of a failure of a host, or you can create an active-active cluster for all critical virtual machines where you need zero data loss and zero downtime. You can use these features along with vMotion to take a host offline for maintenance (planned or unplanned downtime) without affecting workloads in the cluster.

Performance

vCenter controls the physical resources assigned to virtual machines and helps create resource pools. This will help you to provision resource pools depending on higher or lower priorities of the application.

vMotion and Storage vMotion

The vCenter Server allows a virtual machine to be migrated to a remote cloud region or from one cloud region to another cloud region by connecting a central cloud with one or more cloud regions. This will help to extend an on-premises cloud to a public cloud region from a single management control. This enables workloads to be migrated from customer premises into the cloud and rollback when needed without putting customers in a vendor lock in situation.

Network virtualization

Network virtualization provides a network overlay that exists within the virtual layer. It provides rapid provisioning, deployment, re-configuration, and minimizing physical devices.

Network virtualization components

The network virtualization architecture of this design leverages VMware NSX for vSphere and **vSphere Distributed Switches (vDS)** capabilities. The virtualized network is organized hierarchically with the following components from bottom to top:

- Data plane with the NSX vSwitch and additional components
- Control plane with the NSX Controller
- Management plane with the NSX Manager
- Consumption plane with a cloud management portal

Here's the NSX Architecture with all components:

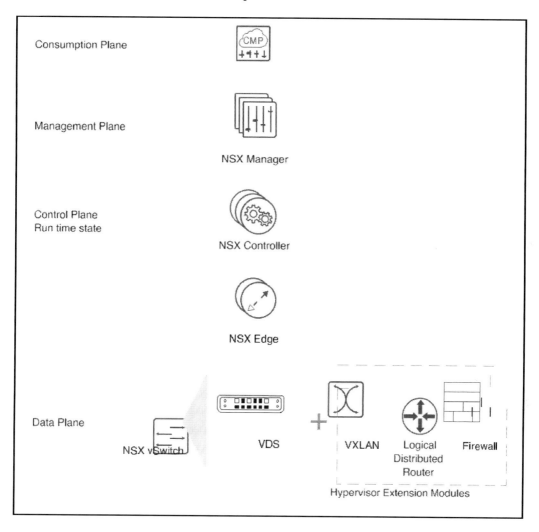

Network virtualization

Distributed virtual switches

This design implements vSphere distributed switches. vDS have many advanced features compare to standard virtual switches:

- **Centralized management**: Distributed switches are created and managed centrally on a vCenter Server so they help robust switch configuration, and are also consistent across all ESXi hosts. Centralized management saves time, reduces mistakes, give more options, and lowers operational costs.
- **Advanced features**: Distributed switches have features which are not available in standard virtual switches. These advanced features will be useful for the applications and services which are running in the customer's infrastructure like NetFlow and port mirroring which help in monitoring and troubleshooting C in the virtual infrastructure.

Distributed virtual switches can do regular health checks which helps in identifying and troubleshooting configuration errors in vSphere distributed switches.

Vulnerability assessment service helps to identify the following common configuration errors:

- VLAN trunks between a distributed switch and a physical switch and whether they are configured properly or not
- MTU settings between physical network adapters, distributed switches, and physical switch ports are compatible as required
- Virtual switch teaming policies for the physical switch port-channel settings are up to date as per the customer's objective

It monitors VLAN, MTU, and teaming policies:

- **VLANs**: Check whether the VLAN settings on the distributed switch is the same with the trunk port configuration on the connected physical switch ports
- **MTU**: Checks whether the physical access switch port MTU jumbo frame setting is the same with the distributed switch MTU setting for each VLAN
- **Teaming policies**: Validates whether the connected access ports of the physical switch participating in an Ether Channel are paired with distributed ports whose teaming policy is an IP hash

It is limited to the access switch port with which the distributed switch uplink connects to. The distributed switch allocates bandwidth for the following system traffic types with network I/O control:

- vSphere vMotion traffic
- Management traffic
- VMware vSphere Replication traffic
- NFS traffic
- VMware Virtual SAN traffic
- vSphere Data Protection backup traffic
- Virtual machine traffic
- Fault tolerance traffic
- iSCSI traffic

Network I/O control details

The bandwidth for each network resource pool is managed by setting the physical adapter shares and host limits. The bandwidth for virtual machines is managed by bandwidth reservation for an individual VM in the same way memory and CPU reservation is used.

The physical adapter assigned to a network resource pool determines the share of the total available bandwidth guaranteed to the traffic which is associated with that network resource pool. The share of transmitted bandwidth which is available to a network resource pool is determined by these factors:

- The network resource pool's shares
- Other network resource pools which are actively transmitting

Data plane

The NSX data plane has the NSX vSwitch, based on the vDS, and includes additional components. These components are comprised of kernel modules (VIBs), which execute within the ESXi kernel and provision services like **virtual distributed router** (**VDR**) and **distributed firewall** (**DFW**). The NSX kernel modules also have **Virtual Extensible LAN** (**VXLAN**) features.

The NSX vSwitch abstracts the physical network and gives access-level switching within the hypervisor. It is critical for network virtualization as it enables logical networks independent of physical constructs such as VLAN. The NSX vSwitch provides multiple benefits.

The following are four types of overlay networking capabilities:

- Creation of a flexible logical Layer 2 overlay over existing IP networks on an existing physical infrastructure
- Configures East/West and North/South communication (micro segmentations) while maintaining isolation between different tenants and workloads
- Support for application workloads and virtual machines that operate as if they were connected to a physical Layer 2 network
- Support for VXLAN and centralized network configuration

A comprehensive toolkit for traffic management, monitoring, and troubleshooting within a virtual network which includes port mirroring, NetFlow/IPFIX, configuration backup and restore, network health check, **Quality of Service (QoS)**, and LACP.

The data plane also includes gateway devices (NSX Edge gateways) which can provide Layer 2 bridging from the logical networking space (VXLAN) to the physical network (VLAN) with NSX vSwitch. NSX Edge gateway devices offer Layer 2, Layer 3, perimeter firewall, load-balancing, and other services such as **Secure Socket Layer (SSL)**, **Virtual Private Network (VPN)**, and **Dynamic Host Control Protocol (DHCP)**.

Control plane

NSX Controller is responsible for the control plane which enables unicast VXLAN and control-plane programming of components like VDR. Unicast support is important as the multicast IP range for each VLAN is limited within SoftLayer. The number of multicast or unicast IPs defines the number of VXLANs which can be provisioned.

The controller is a critical part of the control plane and will not allow any data plane traffic passing through it in any of the cases. The controller nodes are configured in a cluster per the NSX Manager instance to achieve high availability and scalability. A failure of one or all controller nodes will not affect data plane traffic.

Management plane

The NSX management plane is comprised of the NSX Manager and the REST API entry-points with the single point of configuration. NSX Manager and vCenter configure with one NSX Manager per vCenter Server.

Consumption plane

Different users interact with NSX for vSphere to access and manage the associated services in different ways:

- Cloud admin can manage the NSX environment from the vSphere Web Customer
- Users can consume the network virtualization capabilities of NSX for vSphere through the CMP (vRealize Automation) UI when deploying applications

Network virtualization services

Network virtualization services means everything gets abstracted from physical devices and creates logical switches, logical routers, logical firewall, and other components on vSphere hypervisor.

Logical switches

Cloud deployments have various applications which can be used across multiple tenants/customers. These applications and tenants/customers need isolated environments (security, fault isolation, and overlapping IP addresses) away from each other. The vSphere logical switch helps to create logical broadcast domains or segments with which an application or tenant virtual machine can be logically wired. This gives flexibility and agility while still providing all the features of a physical network's broadcast domains (VLANs) without physical Layer 2 sprawl or spanning tree issues.

A logical switch can be distributed and can span across large compute clusters. This will help in virtual machine mobility (migration with vMotion) within a region and between regions, without any complexity or foundations of the physical Layer 2 (VLAN) boundary.

Logical routers

Dynamic routing provisions the required forwarding information between Layer 2 broadcast domains, helping the cloud admin to decrease the size of Layer 2 broadcast domains and improve network efficiency and scale. NSX for vSphere extends this intelligence to where the virtual machines reside for micro segmentation, or east/west routing. This will help in more direct VM-to-VM communication without any costs to extend hops. Logical routers also help in providing north/south connectivity so that users can access public networks in secure and compliant mode.

Logical firewall

Here is the detailed understanding of NSX for vSphere Logical Firewall that helps in defining security mechanisms for dynamic virtual data centers. Following section explains distributed firewall based on five tuple rules:

- The distributed firewall part of a logical firewall assists a cloud admin to segment virtual data center objects like virtual machines depending on VM names and its parameters, the user's identity, vCenter objects like data centers and hosts, or depend on 5 tuple firewall rules (source and destination IP address and ports, Mac address).
- The edge firewall element assists a cloud admin to achieve critical perimeter security objectives like creating DMZs based on IP/VLAN constructs, tenant-to-tenant isolation in multi-tenant virtual data centers, **Network Address Translation (NAT)**, partner (extranet) VPNs, and user-based SSL VPNs.

Flow monitoring enables network activity between virtual machines at the application protocol level. The cloud admin can leverage this information to audit network traffic, define and refine firewall rules, and identify and notify threats to a customer's network.

Logical VPNs

SSL VPN-Plus assists remote users to access private corporate applications. IPsec VPN helps to get site-to-site connectivity between an NSX Edge instance and remote sites. L2 VPN assists users to extend their data center by configuring virtual machines to retain/keep network identity across regional geographies.

Logical load balancers

The NSX Edge load balancer assists with network traffic and it goes through multiple paths to a defined destination. It distributes incoming service requests evenly between multiple servers in such a way that the load distribution is visible to users. Load balancing supports getting optimized resource utilization, improving throughput, reducing response time, and preventing overload. NSX Edge load balancing helps customers up to Layer 7.

Service composer

The service composer assists in provisioning and assigning network and security services to applications in a virtual infrastructure. The service provider aligns these services to a security group, and subsequently, these services are attached to the virtual machines in the security group.

Infrastructure management

Infrastructure management helps customers in providing the logic to get the maximum advantages derived for the virtual infrastructure. These features include pooling virtual components and moving virtual resources off a node for maintenance or node failure. It decides the placement of virtual resources on nodes to balance load along with placement depending on business objectives. It is only managed by the cloud admin while others can access this component through APIs (access from other components).

Infrastructure management manages the compute, network, and storage of virtual resources provisioned by the base layer. It also helps in consolidating services to the upper layers for operational services, which are provided by VMware vCenter Server.

Compute management

VMware vCenter is employed to centralize the management of the compute resources within each ESXi host. Even the ESXi hosts can be managed individually, but putting them under vCenter control enables the following capabilities:

- Centralized control and visibility of all aspects within managed ESXi hosts and virtual machines. Provides the single pane of glass view with the vCenter web client for compute, network, and storage management.
- Proactive Optimization enables allocation and optimization of resources for maximum efficiency across the ESXi hosts.
- Extended management functions for other integrated products and services such as VMware NSX, VMware Data Protection, VMware Update Manager, and others as snap-ins extending the vCenter web interface.
- Monitoring, alerting, and scheduling. Cloud admins can view events, alerts within the vCenter web customer, and configure scheduled actions.
- VMware vCenter is the engine which performs the tasks given to it via the vSphere API web interface. VMware vRealize Automation and vRealize Orchestration are examples of applications that drive vCenter actions via the API and provide automation.

Storage management

VMware vCenter enables centralized storage management within this design, which allows for configuration and management of the following storage types:

- **Local disk storage**: Local **hard disk drives (HDD)** or **solid state drives (SDD)** that are attached to the local ESXi hosts.

- **Storage area attached storage (SAN)**: Remote block storage that is attached to the ESXi host via fiber channel or TCP/IP protocols.
- **Network attached storage (NAS)**: File-based storage that is attached to the ESXi hosts via the NFS protocol.
- **Virtual SAN storage**: Configured within the cluster object in vCenter, it enables the aggregation of local disk storage across ESXi hosts into a shared pool of storage across all ESXi hosts within a given cluster. An outage of the vCenter server does not affect the availability of vSAN storage to the cluster once it is configured.

vCenter management of storage is primarily focused on NAS and vSAN storage as SAN is not employed within this architecture. ESXi host OS and swap space are used on local non-vSAN disk storage.

NFS storage management

vCenter is responsible for configuring the mounting of NFS data stores to each ESXi host within a cluster. This confirms its access availability to any virtual machine with virtual disk files (VMDK) residing on the NFS-based data store. vMotion of the virtual machine from one ESXi host to another occurs within a cluster.

vSAN storage management

The vCenter interface or web API has the capability of configuring vSAN data stores for a particular cluster at the cluster object level within the vCenter interface. Configuring vSAN within vCenter involves the following areas of configuration:

- **Licensing:** Prior to enabling vSAN, a valid license within the vCenter licensing section is required.
- **vSAN network**: You have to configure the network which vSAN will use for its back plane network. Virtual machines have storage which is fault tolerant across a host's local disks on this network.
- **Disk group configuration**: Each ESXi host which contributes its local disks to a Virtual SAN cluster has its disks organized into disk groups. A disk group is a main unit of storage on a host. Each disk group includes one SSD and one or multiple HDDs.
- **vSAN policies**: Storage policies define the virtual machine storage characteristics. Storage characteristics specify different levels of services for different virtual machines.

Network management

vCenter Server is used to create standard and distributed virtual switches. The virtual switches connect **virtual machine** (**VM**) network interfaces to port groups, which allows communication between VMs hosted on the same host or different hosts. Virtual switches need to be connected to physical uplinks which are the network interfaces of the ESXi hosts to establish communication between hosts. VMs connected on the same virtual switch and hosted on the same host can communicate directly without the need of an external uplink.

vCenter Server enables the creation of distributed port groups for virtual machines (aggregated virtual ports with a particular set of specifications).

Common services

Common services provide the services that are consumed by the other cloud management services. It includes identity and access services, SMTP services, NTP services, domain name services, and certificates authority. This component is also the primary interface to external systems. Common services can connect to the customer's DNS for requests outside the domain managed by the cloud services. It connects to the external NTP service to synchronize its NTP service with an outside system. A trust relationship can be established between the common services and the customer's authentication service for common authentication to the cloud services:

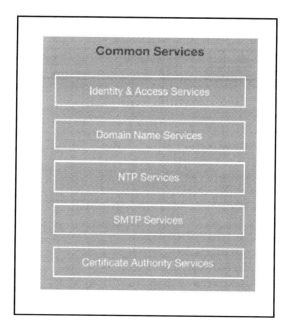

Identity and access services

Microsoft (MS) Active Directory (AD) is configured to get authentication and a directory service's backend to the VMware **Platform Service Controller (PSC)** and VMware identity appliance, as in this design.

VMware software components authenticate with the identity appliance which further authenticates with the MS AD service as per this design. AD can be scaled to different regions by adding an additional AD server to any defined region's subdomain.

DNS

DNS can be used for the cloud management and infrastructure components. DNS serves as a host name to help in IP resolution for the cloud management platform and also assists in service resolution for the AD components. DNS servers can be used as references by the on premises DNS infrastructure in addition to serving as a proxy for the customer's DNS infrastructure.

NTP services

NTP servers are an underlying layer of the SoftLayer deployment. They have to check that all other components are in timed synchronization for the authentication, replication, clustering, log synchronization, and certificate services. This will take care of both physical and virtual components.

Simple Mail Transfer Protocol (SMTP) services

SMTP is leveraged by different components for the outbound notifications. The customer's email servers can be configured for inbound email requirements (vRealize Automation, vRealize Business).

Certificate Authority (CA) services

CA, based on Microsoft CA services built into MS Windows, is deployed in this solution to change self-signed certificates for web interfaces.

Cloud management services

Cloud management services help with the primary interface for users to consume cloud services in the orchestration engines to process the additional service requests. The self-service portal is used to view the available cloud services as well as to get a view of existing cloud resources which have been deployed. The service catalog has a list of available services managed by the service provider. The service provider has to define services which are available to defined users or groups. The process orchestration engine decides the steps needed to perform a service. It has functions like getting an approval or connecting to an operational service system as part of the process. The process orchestration engine initiates the infrastructure orchestration engine to orchestrate the build of the virtual resources for a service. The software orchestration engine builds the software which is run on the virtual resources. The cloud management services have the service catalog, self-service portal, and orchestration. This is enabled by VMware vRealize Automation, vRealize Orchestrator, and **Rapid Deployment Services** (**RDS**) pattern automation.

Service catalogue

The service catalog is published with the self-service catalog and allows users to request necessary services like creating new virtual machines from templates, provisioning new deployments comprising of one or more virtual machines with software components as blueprints, or managing existing deployed resources. Advanced services are also achieved with the service catalog by initiating the orchestration component for process orchestration. The service provider can design the services available to users as well as provide other services.

Self-service portal

The self-service portal gives a single point of access for users to the VMware SDDC on IBM Cloud. Authentication to the portal is done with the AD service:

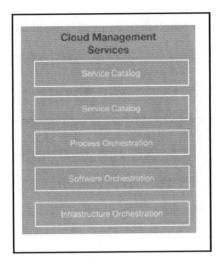

Infrastructure and process orchestration

Orchestration is configured by vRealize Orchestrator and helps automate tasks and remediation actions, including integration with third-party IT operations software.

vRealize Orchestrator has:

- A workflow designer which enables an easy-to-use drag and drop interface to design workflows. The designer supports Windows, Linux, and Mac desktops.
- A scripting designer creates or imports building blocks for the vRealize Orchestrator platform.
- An orchestration engine which runs the workflows and associated scripts.

The default deployment has a built-in workflow library with common tasks. Workflows are versioned and packaged to assist in change management.

Software orchestration

Software orchestration is provided by an RDS solution with IBM Open Patterns. RDS implements a distributed file repository and the configuration management tools to deliver IBM Open Patterns on deployed workloads. IBM Open Patterns describe the pre-defined architecture of an application for each component of the application (that is, database, web server, and so on).

The pattern/blueprint defines:

1. Pre-installation of an operating system
2. Pre-integration across components
3. Pre-configured and tuned
4. Pre-configured monitoring
5. Pre-configured security
6. Lifecycle management

Operational services

Operational services have monitoring, patching, log consolidation, log analysis, disaster recovery, and backup services for the cloud management platform. Monitoring takes care of issues with the cloud management platform and helps cloud admins with alerts on the operations dashboard as well as emails through the external SMTP relay. The patching integrates with the external patch repository to obtain updated information. Log consolidation has the logs from the cloud management platform and puts them into a central repository where the log analysis service operates to provide the cloud admin with diagnostic information. The backup service has replicas of the cloud management platform outside of the virtual infrastructure so it can be restored in the event of failure or corruption. The disaster recovery service requires at least one cloud region which is different from the central cloud. The cloud management platform is restarted at the cloud region in case of failure:

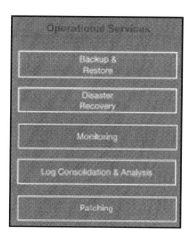

Backup and restore

The data protection service protects the infrastructure that provides virtualization, operations, security, and cloud services. It does not protect any deployed user virtual machines.

Data protection solutions provide the following functions in the design:

- Backs up and restores virtual machines and database applications
- Stores data according to organization retention policies
- Informs administrators about backup and restore activities through reports

vSphere Data Protection provides a data protection service in each region. This is separate to disaster recovery and applies even if only the central cloud exists.

The FTP server is used to back up NSX Manager. The FTP server supports SFTP and FTP protocols:

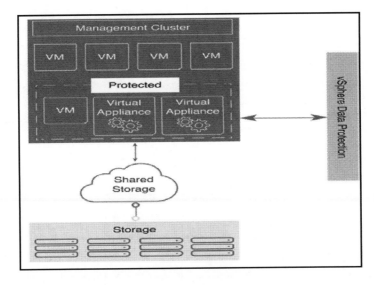

Data protection architecture

Disaster recovery

The disaster recovery service included in the data protection service is implemented by securing the management services in the complete site failure scenario. It is an optional service to give additional protection. It is only valid where a central cloud and minimum one cloud region are to be included.

VMware **Site Recovery Manager** (**SRM**) and vSphere Replication are configured to provide this service by keeping the same IP address of the cloud management services at both sites.

 Each central cloud or cloud region in this design is equivalent to the site construct in Site Recovery Manager.

Since the central cloud contains the portal and manages the services in all the regions, the following applications are in scope of disaster recovery protection:

- vRealize Automation together with the VMware vRealize Orchestrator
- Analytics cluster of the vRealize Operations Manager

The services that support the services at each site do not require disaster recovery protection. This includes:

- vSphere, NSX, and vCenter services which manage the services at the local site only
- Authentication, DNS, and NTP which is distributed to the cloud regions anyway
- vRealize Log Insight and Software Orchestration which is replicated to all cloud regions:

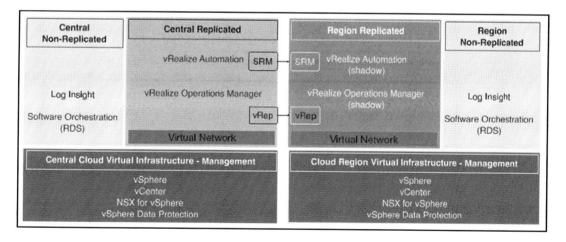

Disaster recovery architecture

Monitoring

vRealize Operations Manager is required to track and analyze the operations of multiple data sources within the design by using specialized patented analytics algorithms. These algorithms enable vRealize Operations Manager to learn and predict the behavior of every object it monitors. Users access this information by using views, reports, and dashboards.

vRealize Operations Manager has functional elements that collaborate for data analysis and storage, and supports creating clusters of servers with different roles:

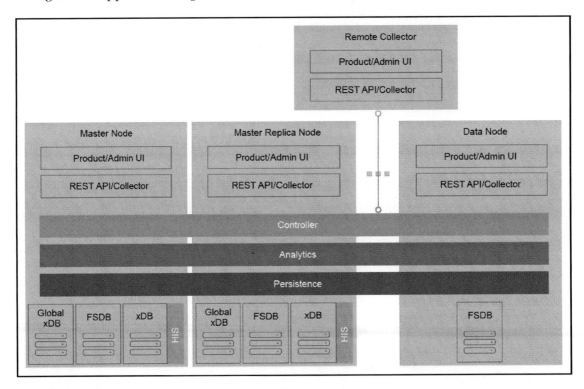

vRealize Operations Manager architecture

Several vRealize Operations Manager instances are deployed in the management cluster for high availability and scalability, where they have the following roles:

- **Master node**: Initial node in the cluster. The master node manages all other nodes in large-scale environments. The master node is the single standalone vRealize Operations Manager node in small-scale environments.
- **Master replica node**: Enables high availability of the master node.
- **Data nodes**: Enables scale-out of vRealize Operations Manager in larger environments. Data nodes have adapters installed to perform collection and analysis. Data nodes can also host vRealize Operations Manager management packs.
- **Remote collector node**: Enables navigation through firewalls, interfaces with a remote data source, reduces bandwidth across regions, or reduces the load on the vRealize Operations Manager analytics cluster. Remote collector nodes only fetch objects for the inventory and forward collected data to the data nodes. Remote collector nodes do not keep data or perform analysis. They can be installed on a different operating system than the rest of the cluster nodes.

The master and master replica nodes are data nodes with extended capabilities.

vRealize Operations Manager can have two kinds of clusters, according to the nodes that participate in a cluster:

- **Analytics clusters**: Tracks, analyzes, and forecasts the operation of monitored systems. Comprised of a master node, data nodes, and a master replica node.
- **Remote collectors cluster**: It only collects diagnostics data without storage or analysis. Comprised only of remote collector nodes.

The functional components of a vRealize Operations Manager instance interact to provide analysis of diagnostics data from the data center and visualize the result in the web user interface:

Architecture component diagram	Description
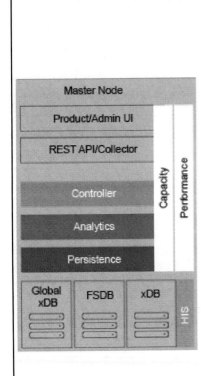	**Admin/Product UI server**: The UI server is a web application which works as both the user and administration interface. **REST API/Collector**: The Collector retrieves data from all components in the data center. **Controller**: The Controller is responsible for the data flow of the UI server, Collector, and the analytics engine. **Analytics**: The analytics engine creates all associations and correlations between different data sets, takes care of all super metric calculations, helps in all capacity planning functions, and is responsible for triggering alerts. **Persistence:** The persistence layer takes care of the read and write operations in the underlying databases across all nodes. **The File System Database (FSDB)**: FSDB keeps the collected metrics in raw format. FSDB is available in all nodes. **xDB Historical Inventory Service (HIS)**: The xDB keeps data from HIS. This component is available only on the master and master replica nodes. **Global xDB**: Global xDB keeps user preferences, alerts, and alarms, and customization which is connected to the vRealize Operations Manager. This component is available only on the master and master replica nodes.

Log consolidation and analysis

Log consolidation and analysis gives consolidation of the logs produced by each of the cloud services together with complete analysis. VRealize Log Insight is responsible for this. It also helps in real-time log management and log analysis with machine learning-based intelligent grouping, high-performance searching, and troubleshooting across physical, virtual, and cloud environments.

It fetches data from ESXi hosts using the syslog protocol and connects to vCenter Server to get events, tasks, and alarms data, and integrates with vRealize Operations Manager to send notification events and enable launches in context.

Patching

VMware Update Manager takes care of patching all VMware software components including the VMware ESXi hosts, virtual appliances, and management tools. It connects to the internet to get the latest vulnerability patches and automatically executes user-defined patches with the specific components to remove vulnerabilities.

Business services

The business services component helps the service provider with analytics on IT financials, business management, and benchmarking data of the cloud. The IT financials have the details of TCO/ROI. The business management helps in metering and chargeback functionalities for the service provider. Benchmarking capabilities have the features for service providers to analyze IT spending for the cloud along with the future roadmap and suggestions for improvement.

Business services are services which have business functionalities including business management, IT financials, and IT benchmarking. **vRealize Business** (**VRB**) is designed to give financial information, reporting, and modeling. VRB integrates with vRealize Automation.

Business management

vRealize Business provides the following business management capabilities:

- Automatic private cloud metering
- Costing and pricing

IT financials

vRealize Business provides the following capabilities for financial management:

- Automatic service catalog pricing (integrated with vRealize automation)
- Private cloud consumption analysis
- Out-of-the-box reporting (exportable data set)

IT benchmarking

Additionally, vRealize Business can assist in modeling cost projections across cloud environments.

The private cloud and public cloud cost comparison matrix will help in decision-making to keep applications in a private, public, or hybrid cloud.

Cloud-based approaches for Disaster Recovery as a Service (DRaaS) solutions

Disasters do not only define natural occurrences such as hurricanes, blizzards, and earthquakes, but also manual errors like data breaches and cyber-attacks and even downtime, which can occur because of simple human error. All of these can have the same impact as natural occurrences.

Most customers don't have a proper disaster recovery plan and capabilities to execute disaster recovery testing or a routine DR drill task. You have so many replication technologies on the market, but the difficulties of creating and testing these tasks along with the expense of operating expenses of a secondary site can put a critical application at risk.

vCloud Availability supports customers' vSphere environments by leveraging native vSphere replication and providing the simplest way to secure critical applications. It also helps with native integration with on-premises systems without any third-party agents being loaded, meaning that you are just reducing both complexity and cost. It also assists customers with picking and choosing which applications to protect.

Our objective is to manage applications deployed on-premises and off-premises. You can leverage the ecosystem of partners who are responsible for customized and differentiated managed services from infrastructure to applications. The VMware vCloud Air Network has cloud provider partners who provide these services across the geography and are compatible with VMware-based clouds.

The VMware large partner ecosystem gives customers flexibility, scalability, geolocation, compliance, and security. vCloud Air Network partners help customers manage the difficulties of their IT operations by utilizing VMware technologies to migrate and manage their applications including old and new ones.

Partners are utilizing vCloud Availability to provide DRaaS and help customers with various options which will be best suited for their requirements and business needs. Customers can take these benefits as they help partners to provision a reliable disaster recovery solution, tightly integrated with existing VMware solutions, and do not need any additional software.

It is well-designed and configured to be connected to the cloud management interface. VMware has all the core modules and technical support for cloud service providers to develop the new service, which is very helpful from a time-to-market perspective.

Summary

You have learned how to define priorities for applications migration, calculate the effort required to migrate them, understand the one-time operating expenses involved and predict the timeline by documenting the dependencies, create a dependency tree (workflow), and select the tools which you need to build or customize. You have learned how to build a cloud migration roadmap. Most customers leave this step and quickly jump to the next phase of building a pilot project as it gives them a better understanding of the technologies and tools, and also builds confidence to move ahead.

In this chapter, we have learned how VMware Cloud on AWS benefits customers with the best of both worlds from a single unified platform. This new cross cloud service will make it easier for customers to retain their investment in existing applications and processes while taking advantage of the global presence, advanced capabilities, and scale of the AWS public cloud. Customers will be able to leverage their existing investment in VMware licenses through customer loyalty programs.

We have also learned how IBM and VMware jointly build a solution to simplify the cloud provisioning process. This solution brings together the IBM Bluemix infrastructure with VMware VSphere, Virtual SAN, NSX, and SDDC Manager so you can easily extend your VMware workloads from your on-premises environment to the IBM Cloud. Configuration takes hours, not weeks, and you can manage your workloads just as you used to do on premises. Customers can choose from more than 50 IBM Cloud data centers around the globe to meet their needs, allowing them to expand into a new region or look for physical redundancy or disaster recovery options.

Disaster recovery as a service (DRaaS) is the replication and hosting of physical or virtual servers provided by a public cloud service provider to avail failover in the event of a man-made or natural disaster. VCloud Air Network and its partner ecosystem will help you design your DRaaS as per customer requirements across any geography.

In the next chapter, we will learn about various features to get service redundancy across all layers of a data centre, including compute, storage, and network with SLA management to get the defined QoS. We will also touch on how to move to Green IT while making our data centers ready for the current market.

5
Implementing Service Redundancy Across All Layers

The following chapter provides an overview and a set of guidelines regarding vCenter server deployment topologies and their corresponding High Availability options. We will discuss the different options and compare their strengths and weaknesses. In this chapter, we will cover the following topics:

- vSphere vMotion, Storage vMotion, DRS, and DPM
- vSphere fault tolerance and High Availability and CPU/memory reservations
- vSphere Metro Storage Cluster and VM-to-VM affinity rules
- vSphere replication and vSphere data protection for backup
- VMware DC migration/relocation plan (pre-migration activity and checklist)

vSphere virtualization software

vSphere provides a powerful solution to address customers' business continuity/disaster recovery requirements, High Availability (HA), and SLAs for mission-critical applications. The consolidation, automation, HA, and security benefits of vSphere also help to simplify IT operations:

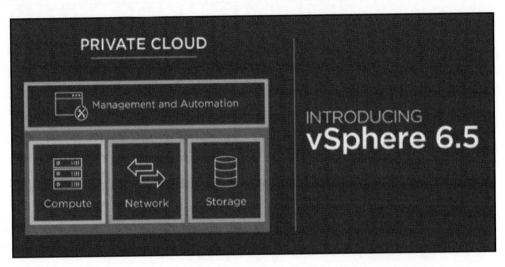

vSphere 6.5: A platform for a private cloud

VMware helps to accommodate customer requirements using an appropriate VMware architecture with the design qualities shown in the following table:

Design Quality	Description
Scalability	Refers to the ability of vSphere-as well as the related network, storage, and security elements-to handle a growing volume of work in a capable manner, or its ability to be enlarged to accommodate that growth.
Extensibility	Refers to how well the system is designed to include hooks and mechanisms for expanding and enhancing the system with anticipated capabilities, without having to make major changes to system infrastructure.
Availability	Refers to the ability of vSphere and its related infrastructure to achieve highly available operations.

Manageability	Refers to the flexibility of the vSphere environment and the ease of operations related to its management. Manageability can include both scalability and flexibility.
Performance	Refers to the performance of the vSphere environment and its related computing environments. This does not necessarily reflect the impact of other technologies within the infrastructure.
Security	Refers to whether a design choice has a positive or negative impact on overall infrastructure security. This term also refers to whether a quality has an impact on the ability of a business to demonstrate or achieve compliance with certain regulatory policies.
Recoverability	Refers to the ability to restore the vSphere environment to the point at which a failure occurred.

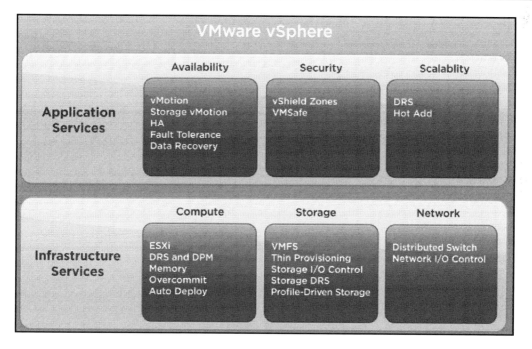

vSphere services and functionalities

VMware vCenter Management Server

vCenter provides centralized visibility, proactive management, and extensibility for VMware vSphere, all from a single console. vCenter provides centralized control and visibility, as well as the following features:

- **vSphere Web Client**: This manages the essential functions of vSphere from any browser anywhere in the world.
- **vCenter Single Sign-On**: This feature allows users to log in once and access all instances of the vCenter Server and vCloud components, without the need for further authentication.
- **Custom roles and permissions**: These features restrict access to the entire inventory of virtual machines, resource pools, and servers by assigning users to custom roles. Users with appropriate privileges can create these custom roles, such as night-shift operator or backup administrator.
- **Inventory search**: With this feature, users can explore the entire vCenter inventory-including virtual machines, hosts, datastores, and networks-from anywhere within vCenter.

The VMware vSphere Update Manager automates patch management and eliminates the manual tracking and patching of vSphere hosts and virtual machines. It compares the state of vSphere hosts with their baselines, then updates and patches to enforce compliance. As well as this, the update manager has many other features, such as the following:

- It helps you to monitor patch status across the virtual infrastructure, using its patch-compliance dashboard
- It stages and schedules patching for remote sites
- It stores snapshots for a user-defined period so administrators can roll back the virtual machine, if necessary
- It securely patches offline virtual machines without exposing them to the network, reducing the risk of non-compliant virtual machines
- It makes sure that the most current version of a patch is applied, notifying the user with an automatic notification service. It also automatically migrates virtual machines to other hosts during patching
- It migrates virtual machines back after patching

The following diagram depicts vCenter Server with redundancy:

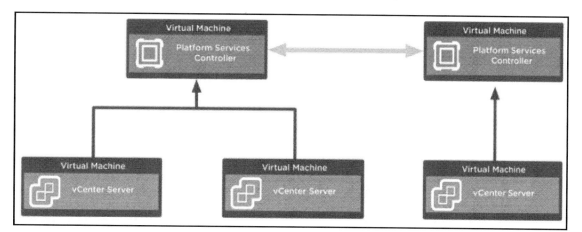

vCenter Server - basic terminology and components

vCenter main components

This section is a short introduction to the main components of a vCenter installation. The vCenter Server is the central management platform for administering and automating the vSphere infrastructure, consisting of basic virtual machines and ESXi hosts.

- **A vSphere domain**: Sometimes referred to as an SSO domain, the vSphere domain basically provides a common VMware directory service, which encompasses the vCenter SSO LDAP directory (the SSO users and groups) and references to external directories (for example) and, typically, Active Directory. With vSphere, this domain name can be configured as something other than the default domain name, but should not be named identically to other; externally connected directory services, such as Active Directory. Apart from this, vCenter servers and other solutions (such as vRealize Automation) are registered within a vSphere domain. The scalability limit is currently 10 vCenter servers per vSphere domain. The information shared within a vSphere domain is not limited to LDAP directory information.

  The following information is replicated between the Platform Services Controllers of a vSphere domain, and is therefore shared within a vSphere domain:

  - Licenses
  - Roles and permissions

- Tags
- Certificate information through the use of the new **VMware Certificate Authority (VMCA)**

As a vSphere domain forms a security boundary, it is also a boundary for certain enhanced vSphere 6.0 features. For example, the new feature of Cross-vCenter vMotion-at least when its execution is UI-based, via the vSphere web client—is only possible between vCenter servers of the same vSphere domain. The feature, however, is executable via an API call without both the source vCenter server and the target vCenter server needing to be in the same vSphere domain. In the case of vCenter servers that are in separate vSphere domains, the API call has to provide two user account credentials-one for each vCenter server.

Environment preparation

Before starting the implementation of vCenter Single Sign-On, it's important to ensure that certain elements of the environment are in place and fully functional.

In order to establish a working, highly available vCenter Single Sign-On solution, the following must be in place:

- SSO/Web Client server nodes must be created as virtual machines
- SSO/ Web Client server nodes must be registered within a DNS service
- The VMware SSL Update tool must be installed on both nodes
- The external load balancer must be configured

It's also worth making a note of the key configuration information that is needed throughout the implementation. The following table should be used to capture these environmental specifics, which will be used during the installation procedures:

Component	Hostname	FQDN	IP address
SSO node1			
SSO node2			
SSO load balancer address			
Web Client server node1			
Web Client server node2			
Web Client server load balancer address			

Certificate for the vSphere Web Client and the Log Browser

After the certificate has been created, follow these steps to complete the installation and configuration of the certificate for the Web Client:

Task ID	Task description	Screenshot
1.	Log in to the vSphere Web Client server mode1.	
2.	Open `Services.msc` from the `run` command. Stop the VMware vSphere Web Client service from the service control manager. Stop the VMware Log Browser service from the service control manager.	
3.	Back up the current certificates (`rui.crt`, `rui.key`, `rui.pfx`) for the vSphere Web Client. By default, the certificates are located at `C:Program FilesVMwareInfrastructurevSphereWebClientlogbrowserconf.`	
4.	Copy the new certificate files (`rui.crt`, `rui.key`, `rui.pfx`) to this directory. If you are following this resolution path, the certificates are located at `C:certslogbrowser.`	
5.	From the Command Prompt, run the following command: `set JAVA_HOME=C:Program FilesCommon FilesVMwareVMware vCenter Server – Java Components`	
6.	Navigate to the `SsoRegTool` directory. By default, this directory is located at `C:Program FilesVMwareInfrastructurevSphereWebClientSsoRegTool.`	

1. Create the Log Browser certificate-authority-signed certificates.
2. Update the certificates on Web Client server node 1.
3. Update the certificates on Web Client server node 2.
4. Configure the Load Balancer for the Web Client server VIP.

Verify that the environment is working properly

Now that the whole environment has been updated, check to ensure that the web client is working properly:

1. Log into the Web Client on the load-balanced URL as Administrator@vsphere.local
2. Ensure that the SSO configuration is correct
3. Log out of the Web Client and log back in with an account that can manage the vCenters
4. Ensure that you can manage the vCenters

To test HA and ensure that there is no dependence on the primary SSO node, perform the following steps:

1. Shut down the primary SSO node
2. Wait for one minute after the VM is shut down (it takes the Cisco ACE a minute to detect that the nodes are offline)
3. Open the Web Client and ensure that everything is still accessible
4. Power up the VM and ensure that, when you connect to it, you can still manage the vCenter(s)

Comparison of the vCenter deployment topologies

The different deployment topologies of vCenter have already been discussed in detail and compared with each other. In this chapter, the differences are presented again in a summarized and highlighted form using a tabular presentation. The evaluation of the criterion of HA assumes that all deployment topologies are implemented with vSphere HA, following common best practices for that feature. The evaluation furthermore assumes that the database is always embedded with vCenter Server, except for these topologies, where the vCenter server is clustered using Windows failover clustering. Data consistency in the following comparison evaluates the differences in backup data consistency resulting from the fact that some deployment topologies are highly distributed, and are therefore harder to back up in a consistent way across all systems. It does not evaluate the general fact that the backup data consistency in the Windows edition of vCenter Server is generally considered superior compared to that used by the VCSA. The following figure shows vCenter Server Deployment Models comparison:

Comparison Criterion / Deployment Topology	High Availability	Backup and Recovery		Architectural Flexibility	Operational Complexity
		Operation	Data Consistency		
Basic Embedded Deployment	O	++ (Operation) ++	+	--	++
Single Site with PSC HA Mode	+	O / --	O	+	O
Single Site with vCenter Windows Failover Clustering and PSC HA Mode	++	---- / NA	NA	+	----
Multi-Site with PSC HA Mode	+	O / --	O	++	--
Multi-Site with PSC HA Mode and vCenter Windows Failover Clustering	++	---- / NA	NA	++	----

vCenter deployment topologies—comparison

Centralized virtual network management: With vSphere's distributed virtual switch, you can simplify the provisioning and administration of virtual networking through a centralized interface. You can create and manage a single distributed switch with distributed virtual port groups that span a datacenter-wide array of ESX/ESXi hosts. With a simplified setup and monitoring of private VLANs, network traffic is segmented easily into shared environments that retain network runtime states centrally as virtual machines live-migrate from server to server in shared DRS clusters, simplifying network troubleshooting and monitoring by enabling users to do the following:

- Repurpose older storage at the protection site
- Use different storage technologies at opposite sites (SAN to NAS, FC to iSCSI)
- Use secondary storage only for protected virtual machines, not for all
- Integrate automatically with Microsoft's **Volume Shadow Copy Service** (**VSS**) to ensure consistent recovery copies
- Leverage flexible RPOs of 15 minutes to 24 hours

- Control virtual machine replication via VMware vCenter Server
- Scale to hundreds of virtual machines per cluster
- Use multiple point-in-time snapshots to revert to previous known states

The features that vSphere can provide to efficiently manage your environment, giving you all the benefits of virtualization and more are as follows:

- **Bare-metal architecture**: VMware ESX and ESXi insert a robust virtualization layer directly on the server hardware for near-native virtual machine performance, reliability, and scalability.
- **Small footprint**: VMware ESXi is a compact, 200 MB form factor of the production-proven VMware ESXi hypervisor. It is a fraction of the size of a general purpose operating system for unparalleled security and reliability.

vSphere HA/redundancy features

Apart from the HA discussions led for the various deployment topologies there are several HA technologies available in the vSphere stack. These technologies are described in the following sections. The following image gives an overview of the technologies that we will be looking at:

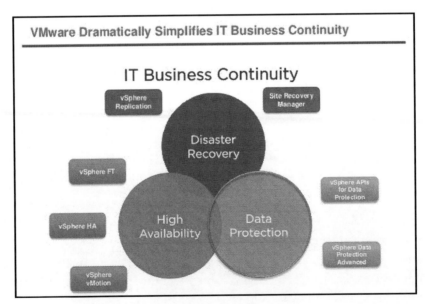

vSphere's unique High Availability functionalities

vSphere HA

vSphere HA is a robust feature, which has been on the market for many years now, and that almost every IT department administering a vSphere environment knows and actively uses. As a result, this feature is not described in detail here; only its basic principles will be discussed.

From its basic principles, vSphere HA is a feature that is active in a vSphere cluster. A vSphere cluster is a group of ESXi hosts sharing a common configuration. Within this vSphere cluster, each ESXi host monitors all other hosts in the cluster, and exchanges and communicates the status of the cluster with each other over a specially configured network interface and selected shared datastores. With the introduction of vSphere 5, a master/slave model has been introduced with vSphere HA. That means that there is only one master in a vSphere HA-enabled vSphere cluster. The ESXi host with the master role basically goes through the following steps to search for failed hosts:

1. Determine an ESXi host failure within the cluster
2. Determine which VMs have been running on that failed host and have to be restarted
3. For each failed VM that has to be restarted, select a host within the cluster that fulfills all necessary requirements and initiate the restart of the failed VM on the selected host

The following is a basic diagram illustrating the function of vSphere HA:

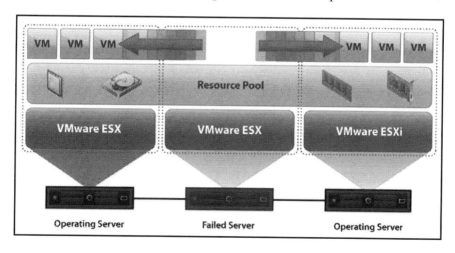

vSphere HA

Additionally, vSphere HA can monitor the state of the guest OS within a VM via VMware Tools, and may restart VMs whose guest OS does not answer anymore, perhaps because of a blue screen in a Windows guest OS.

vSphere HA is a mainstream feature within the vSphere stack, and-as a rule of thumb-should always be enabled within a vSphere cluster to provide added value, in terms of HA, to all kinds of virtual machines.

It is also recommended that you enable vSphere HA Admission Control in a cluster and define a minimum amount of spare capacity within the cluster. Here, a percentage value should be specified in order to not be affected by the well-known side effects of the HA slot size.

vSphere vMotion details

vSphere vMotion allows for the live migration of running virtual machines from one physical server to another with continuous service availability and complete transaction integrity, and with no downtime.

Using vSphere vMotion, you can provide many of the benefits of virtualizing an infrastructure. It allows you to perform maintenance on running hardware without impacting the physical server that it is running on in maintenance mode, as well as use proactive features such as vSphere DRS.

EVC feature details

vSphere vMotion requires that the CPUs in each host are similar to verify that live migrations can be performed successfully. EVC verifies that all hosts in a cluster present the same CPU feature set to virtual machines, even if the actual CPUs on the hosts differ. Using EVC prevents migrations performed with vSphere vMotion from failing because of incompatible CPUs.

By setting EVC on the cluster during its initial design, hosts with newer CPUs can be added at a later date, without disruption. EVC can also be used to perform a rolling upgrade of all hardware with zero downtime. Set EVC to the highest level possible with the CPUs that are currently in use.

vSphere DRS feature details

vSphere DRS provides load balancing of the cluster by using vSphere vMotion to migrate workloads from heavily-loaded hosts to less-utilized hosts in the cluster. It can be set up to operate in the following modes:

- **Manual**: Recommendations are made but not acted upon unless an administrator initiates the migration.
- **Partially automated**: Recommendations are made but not acted upon unless an administrator initiates the migration, but initial power-on placements are made automatically.
- **Fully automated**: Initial power-on placement is automatic and all recommendations are acted upon automatically by the system.

How aggressively vSphere DRS operates depends on the migration threshold value that is set. The threshold value has five different levels, ranging from conservative to aggressive. The lower the setting, the less likely a migration is to occur, unless certain criteria happen, such as the system entering maintenance mode or if there is a significant projected performance gain as a result of the migration. The highest threshold level accepts any migration request generated by the system, regardless of how big the performance gain might be. The third level provides the best compromise between load balancing and reducing the number of vSphere vMotion events.

VMware vSphere Distributed Power Management

As a feature of vSphere DRS, VMware vSphere Distributed Power Management is also provided. This feature allows vSphere DRS to provide power savings, by powering down hosts that are not needed, to provide resources during periods of inactivity.

The vSphere DPM feature is enabled by having vSphere DRS migrate the current workloads to other hosts and place the hosts in standby mode. Once demand increases in the cluster, the standby hosts will be powered back on.

vSphere DPM, much like vSphere DRS, has different modes of operation, which are independent of the vSphere DRS settings. The different modes available are as follows:

- **Off**: vSphere DPM will not be used.
- **Manual**: vSphere DPM will recommend that certain hosts should power-off, but actual powering them off must be manually initiated by an administrator.

- **Automatic**: vSphere DPM recommends that certain hosts should be shut down. Restarts will be triggered automatically.

The migration threshold also exists for vSphere DPM, allowing you to set vSphere DPM's behavior, ranging from conservative to aggressive. This functions in exactly the same way as vSphere DRS.

Resource pools feature details

A resource pool is a logical abstraction that allows you to flexibly manage resources. Resource pools can be grouped into hierarchies and used to partition available CPU and memory resources. As a general practice, a resource pool with limit and reservation settings is necessary only for virtual machine workloads that require dedicated and isolated resources.

The following is a list of the ways in which resource pools can help you:

- They allow CPU and memory resources to be assigned in a flexible way. Reservations can be statically assigned or dynamically expandable to account for growth or other free resources becoming available.
- They allow resources to be isolated to prevent unfair resource utilization between resource pools.
- They allow for a limit to be set to prevent the overutilization of resources.
- They allow shares to be set for priority access to a pool of resources, rather than being individually assigned.
- They create another layer that must be monitored.

vSphere Fault Tolerance

vSphere **Fault Tolerance** (**FT**) is a feature originally introduced in vSphere 4.0, which provides continuous availability for VMs and their applications. This is achieved by creating a live shadow instance of a VM that is always up to date with the primary VM. The market share of vSphere customers productively deploying this feature has been very small in the past because of some strong extra requirements on the server hardware infrastructure and some severe scalability limits, requiring that the VMs should be protected with FT itself, as well as for the ESXi hosts running FT-protected VMs.

The basic architecture of vSphere TS in vSphere is depicted as follows:

vSphere Fault Tolerance

As depicted in the preceding image, FT works in the following way:

1. When FT is enabled on a VM, a secondary/shadow VM gets cloned from the primary VM.
2. After the secondary VM is deployed, a mutual heartbeat/monitoring channel is established using vLockstep technology. Every action occurring on the primary VM is executed on the secondary VM as well.
3. After a failure of the primary VM or the ESXi host hosting the primary VM, an almost immediate activation of the secondary VM is executed.
4. Split-brain situations are avoided using a few small so-called tie-breaker files using atomic locking.

FT technology has received the following new features, described in keywords:

*   An increase in the vCPU limit of an FT-protected VM from 1 to 4 (the limit of 64 GB RAM per FT-protected VM remains).
*   FT does not rely on VMDK disks that are shared between the primary and secondary VM anymore. Instead, each VM of an FT-protected VM pair uses its own VMDK files independently.

- Replication of the execution state between both VMs is achieved with an ongoing process that is comparable to a never-ending vMotion process with fast checkpointing.
- The introduction of support for the following features:
  - VADP-based backups
  - H/W assisted MMU virtualization
  - Paravirtual devices

Relevance of vSphere Fault Tolerance for vCenter HA

Both PSCs and vCenter servers may be protected with FT. However, given the FT-induced vCPU maximum of four per VM, the protection of a vCenter VM with FT is only supported up to an environment of 100 ESXi hosts and 1,000 VMs.

VM Component Protection (VMCP)

VMCP is a new extension of the vSphere HA stack, introduced with vSphere. It basically reacts to certain failure scenarios of the shared storage connectivity by powering off and restarting the affected VMs on healthy hosts. According to the failure scenarios, two cases are distinguished:

1. **All paths down (APD)**: APD is a storage-device state where the connectivity to a storage device (for example, a LUN) is broken, and the ESXi host does not know whether or when the device will be back online.
2. **Permanent device loss (PDL)**: PDL is a storage-device state where the ESXi host knows that the device has been permanently removed and will never come back.

The ESXi hosts distinguish between APD and PDL by means of SCSI return codes, which a storage array might return to the ESXi host. VMCP can be customized to react to APD and PDL in different ways, depending on the requirements. Note that the availability of this feature is not limited to a certain storage protocol. On the contrary, it is available for all storage protocols, including NFS.

vSphere Metro Storage Cluster (vMSC)

vMSC is a specific vSphere storage configuration that is certified within the VMware HCL. Concerning its use case, such a configuration is targeted for environments where disaster and downtime avoidance is a key requirement. Its main functional principle is to extend the benefits of vSphere HA-which are typically limited to a single geographic site/datacenter-to two datacenters/geographical locations. In order to achieve this, it is not only necessary to spread the ESXi hosts of a vSphere cluster across two sites/datacenters, but also the storage representation of the datastores, which are accessed by the ESXi hosts. Different vendors have certified their solutions with VMware. A vMSC configuration is possible with all kinds of storage connectivity protocols (FC, FCoE, iSCSI, NFS), depending on the vMSC product of a certain storage vendor. The architecture of those vMSC solutions might differ in various aspects. The following graphic, therefore, represents only one possible vMSC configuration:

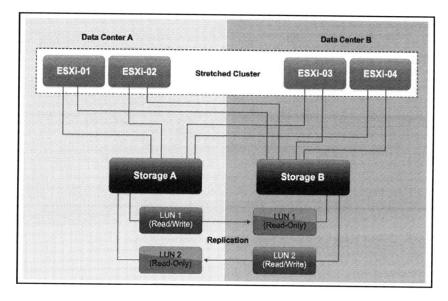

vSphere Metro Storage Cluster

All four ESXi hosts depicted in the preceding graphic belong to one single vSphere HA cluster that spans two datacenters. HA failover after an ESXi host or storage failure is seamlessly possible, even across both datacenters. The limitation concerning the geographical distance between the two datacenters depends on the concrete storage vendor product certified with VMware for vMSC, but can be up to 100-300 km.

Furthermore, a typical infrastructure requirement for a vMSC implementation is to have a stretched layer 2 network established across both datacenters, with all VLANs transparently available at both datacenters. The applications/VMs that typically benefit from such a setup are those that do not already provide redundancy on their application layer, but which have an intrinsic SPOF. For example, a vCenter server without Windows Failover Clustering is a typical candidate for placement in a vMSC-enabled vSphere cluster in order to minimize the downtime for vCenter in the case of a datacenter failure.

vSphere Replication

vSphere Replication is built into the vSphere stack, and leverages a network-based replication mechanism to create redundant copies of virtual machines for disaster recovery. The replication traffic is copied via dedicated vmkernel networks of involved ESXi hosts. While a variety of vSphere Replication topologies are possible, a detailed discussion of these is clearly beyond the scope of this book. Nevertheless, a common topology (replication between two sites/vCenter instances) is depicted as follows, in order to get an impression of how vSphere Replication works:

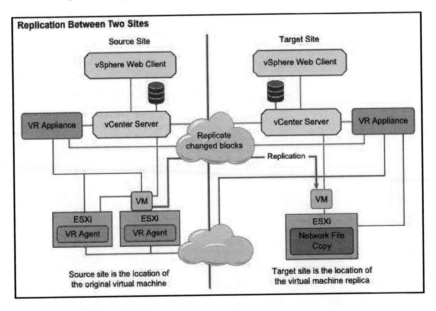

vSphere Replication

While vSphere Replication provides many valid use cases for adding disaster recoverability to certain business-critical VMs, the use case to protect a vCenter server or a PSC itself by means of vSphere Replication does not seem to be the most obvious, and this option has some disadvantages, or at least inherent complexities:

- To recover VMs with vSphere Replication requires the availability of the target site vCenter Server system and the corresponding vSphere Web Client and vSphere Replication Appliance.
- This means that a vCenter Server system, in order to be protected by vSphere Replication, must either be just a normal VM managed by another vCenter Server system, or must not be the vCenter Server system of the target site.

vCenter Watchdog

The vCenter Watchdog is a process that monitors a subset of vCenter services and tries to restart them in case of a failure. The protected services are as follows:

- **HTTP Reverse Proxy**
- **vCenter Web Services (vws)**
- **vCenter Server Service (vpxd)**

The vCenter Watchdog process is enabled by default on the Windows edition of vCenter Server, as well as within the appliance. Two attempts are made to restart the monitored services. If the restart fails both times, the whole VM gets rebooted. The restart of the whole VM can be disabled, as described in the KB article found at `http://kb.vmware.com/kb/2127930`.

vCenter database clustering

A few valid facts about the database clustering of the vCenter DB are as follows:

- The vCenter database is the most important data source of configuration and inventory data within a vCenter system. Clustering this component can increase the availability of the vCenter system to cover additional maintenance and failure scenarios. Almost all vCenter deployment topologies can benefit from clustering the vCenter database. In deployment topologies, where the vCenter server itself gets clustered, the clustering of the vCenter database is a logical design decision.

- vCenter database clustering is only supported with the Windows version of vCenter Server, and is only supported when choosing Microsoft SQL Server as the backend database for vCenter Server. For more information, see the VMware KB article at `http://kb.vmware.com/kb/1024051`.

Memory reservations

Memory reservations are not a direct availability feature of the vSphere stack, but are an efficient measure to guarantee service levels for performance and RAM resource availability to VMs, especially in the case of a failure of one or more ESXi hosts, where vSphere HA has to kick in to restart failed VMs. Without any reservations, the restarted VMs would not be guaranteed to receive any physical RAM resources at all (with the exception of overhead RAM, which the hypervisor needs to run a VM in the first place, and which has to run in physical RAM). RAM reservations are required, for example, in order to receive vendor support for running certain applications on a virtual platform (such as SAP).

For a vCenter Server environment, it is also recommended, or at least is seen as good practice, that you define a certain amount of RAM of the configured RAM of the vCenter Server VMs (including the PSCs) as a reserve in order to achieve a minimum-service level of available physical RAM resources, which is available to the vCenter VMs at all times.

Maximizing memory performance

To maximize virtual machine memory performance, keep the virtual machine's active memory in physical RAM. Additional recommendations include the following:

- Limit host memory over commitment or configure virtual machine reservations, or do both.
- If reservations are configured, set them slightly above the virtual machine's average active memory size. Monitoring tools can provide information about the active memory.
- Virtual machine reservations increase administrative overhead, so it might be better to design a consolidation ratio that does not overcommit active memory.

CPU and memory shares, reservations, and limits

CPU and memory configurations for virtual machines are highly configurable in ESXi. This gives the flexibility to configure the following:

- **Shares**: These allow an administrator to set a relative priority to a virtual machine's access to CPU or memory. When there is contention on the system, higher-priority workloads have a higher chance of using the resource.
- **Reservations**: These allow an administrator to guarantee CPU or memory to a virtual machine. In this case, no other resource will be able to utilize the assigned resources.
- **Limits**: These allow an administrator to limit the amount of physical resources that a virtual machine can consume. This can be useful in simulating contention or in preventing a resource from fully consuming CPU or memory resources.

To simplify configuration and administration, avoid using these parameters unless you have a clear reason to make changes. For example, if there is a critical application that must continue to receive resources, even during periods of resource contention, a reservation allows the resources to be available, and shares can be used to set relative priorities.

Virtual machine disks

When designing the virtual machine configuration, structure the disks in a way that suits the environment. In many cases, deploying a system disk and a separate application data disk is desirable in order to simplify backup procedures. However, this might not be ideal for every backup solution or environment. It all depends on business policy. Consider the following when making decisions about a virtual machine's configuration:

- A separate application data disk can easily be increased in size, if necessary.
- Separate disks help to distribute I/O load.
- Do not place all system disks on one single datastore and all data disks on another. Place a virtual machine's system and data disks on the same datastore, unless they have widely varying I/O characteristics.
- Configure one partition per virtual disk. If there are multiple partitions, extend the last partition only if the size of the disk is increased.
- Consider thin-provisioned disks if data growth is slow or static.

Depending on how the operating system initially formats its disks, the benefits of thin provisioning can be negated. If the formatting operation writes zeroes to all sectors, the disk will be prematurely inflated. Use the operating system vendor's documentation to find formatting options that do not write zeroes to all disk sectors during formatting operations.

- As of vSphere 6.0, the maximum VMDK size is 62 TB. This makes planning possible for virtual machines with larger storage capacity requirements (mailboxes, file servers, databases), and provides a more attractive option for virtualization. Not all functions of vSphere are supported with large capacity disks.

Multiple virtual disks

If a virtual machine has multiple disks, keep them on the same datastore, if possible, to simplify configuration and administration. For example, when planning the replication of a virtual machine's files to another logical unit number (LUN) or data center, replicating a single LUN replicates all the virtual machine's files. This configuration simplifies the configuration and administration of products such as Site Recovery Manager.

There are good reasons to sometimes place a virtual machine's disks on separate LUNs. If the virtual disks have different I/O characteristics, they might be placed on separate LUNs that accommodate those characteristics. Another reason might be that a data disk is exceptionally large. Such a large disk might be kept on another datastore or on another LUN that is accessed using raw device mapping.

Virtual disk location

In most cases, storing virtual machine disks together on shared storage, rather than on local storage, is recommended. Many of the benefits of vSphere, such as virtual machine migration and availability, depend on shared storage.

In rare cases, local storage might also be required. For example, local storage might be less expensive and may be used by smaller organizations to run parts of their workload. In addition, vSAN uses local storage (SSD and HDDs) to create its datastore.

Swap file location

Swap files are created whenever a virtual machine is powered on. The size of the swap file depends on the amount of RAM and reservations that have been configured. By default, they are stored in the same directory as the rest of the virtual machine configuration. However, this can be changed. There are two main alternatives for the swap file location:

- Local storage, with the virtual machine files on shared storage
- Dedicated shared storage, but not with the virtual machine files

The location depends on the business requirements of the organization. Relocating the virtual machine swap file can have an impact on the following:

- **vSphere vMotion performance**: If the swap file is not on a shared volume, it will need to be recreated, which can affect performance of vSphere vMotion.
- **Ease of administration and provisioning**: If the swap file is relocated, it is more difficult to administer than if everything is located in a single directory.
- **Datastore replication performance**: Replicating swap data does not make sense. Thus, configuring the swap file outside of replicated traffic might be an attractive option for reducing bandwidth requirements.

Virtual SCSI HBA type

The adapter used by virtual machines can affect the features or performance. Consider the following alternatives:

- Use the default choice unless it does not support a required feature. For example, Microsoft Windows Server 2008 cluster services require a serial-attached SCSI device (paravirtual SCSI or PVSCSI HBA).
- If there is a need to configure a non-default choice, create a template to simplify virtual machine provisioning.

Virtual NICs

Virtual NICs are important for maintaining the network performance of virtual machines. Consider the following:

- Specify the operating system correctly when creating a virtual machine. The default drivers are recommended in most cases.

- Install VMware Tools on the virtual machine. The tools contain driver updates for VMware-specific devices, including network drivers.
- Use VMXNET3 adapters for enhanced performance and their feature set.

Virtual GPUs

Depending on the use cases for the virtual machines and the software they are running, it might be necessary to add support for hardware-accelerated 3D graphics to the virtual machines. This impacts the supportability of features, given the hardware requirements of the physical hosts. Consider the following:

- vSphere 6.0 and above supports NVIDIA- and AMD-based GPUs.
- Select the appropriate rendering mode for the virtual machine's needs. Automatic, hardware, and software are the supported modes.
- vSphere vMotion is available as long as the physical hardware exists on the destination host.
- Various versions of Windows and Linux are supported. Validate supportability in the guest OS compatibility guide.

VMware vSphere Flash Read Cache

VMware vSphere Flash Read Cache is a write-through cache mode that enhances virtual machine performance without modifying the applications and operating system. Flash Read Cache virtualizes server-side flash, providing a high-performance read cache layer that dramatically lowers application latency.

Flash Read Cache software is natively built into the core ESXi hypervisor. However, virtual machines cannot detect Flash Read Cache, and therefore cannot see the performance impact or allocation of the flash resource.

The performance enhancements are based on the placement of the Flash Read Cache directly in the virtual machine's disk data path, enhancing read-intensive workloads. Depending on the workload, this might be an attractive solution to enhance the performance of these virtual machines.

Guest operating system considerations

vSphere allows for a large number of different guest operating systems to be run at the same time, but on different virtual machines. The following list provides some basic guidelines for running virtual machines with different guest operating systems:

- Keep the variations minimal for each guest operating system. This approach simplifies administration and troubleshooting.
- Use standardized templates for the installation of each key application and guest operating system.
- Use standard sizing for virtual machines. This approach simplifies administration, troubleshooting, and chargeback.

VMware Tools

VMware recommends that you use only supported guest operating systems that also include VMware Tools. The benefits of VMware Tools include the following:

- Efficient memory management using `vmmemctl`
- Better console display and mouse operation
- Graceful virtual machine shutdown from the vSphere Web Client menu
- Time synchronization, if required

Templates

Templates allow for common configurations to be easily replicated when deploying virtual machines. They can also speed up the amount of time required to deploy a large number of virtual machines.

From vSphere 6.0, a content library has been introduced to allow for simplified management of templates, whether they are individual VMs, OVFs, or vApps. It can even store other files, such as ISOs. This prevents virtual machine and template sprawl, and allows for a single source for the storage of these items that can be shared among multiple vCenter Server instances.

Consider the following when designing your environment:

- Use templates to provision virtual machines because they are faster, less error prone, and decrease administrative overhead.
- Configure a template for each operating system and each key application. Refer to the architecture design for PaaS and IaaS to build an optimized catalog.
- Create at least one content library to store templates and associated media. The content library can be stored on the local vCenter server filesystem, on an NFS share, or on a VMFS datastore.
- Create the content library using less-expensive storage. In most cases, provisioning virtual machines does not require the highest-performing storage technology.

Templates and multiple sites

A content library can be shared externally from the vCenter Server instance. In this way, it can be used to share templates and media across separate sites. To do this, a content library is created on one vCenter Server instance and then subscribed to by other vCenter Server instances. When configured, a subscribed library can either download all content immediately or on demand as items are used. In addition, a subscribed library can be configured to synchronize with the original vCenter server system to allow updates to be downloaded.

Using content libraries allows for simplification of the administration of the template infrastructure used to deploy environments.

Snapshot management

A VMware snapshot represents the state of a virtual machine at the particular time it was taken. It includes the files and memory state of a virtual machine's guest operating system, as well as the settings and configuration of the virtual machine and its virtual hardware. Snapshots allow you to restore a VM to a particular state at a specific point in time, so that you can, for example, use a snapshot for troubleshooting. Snapshots are also a useful tool that you can use to back out of changes that you have made, such as when you are applying patches to an operating system or application. You might also use a snapshot to perform testing prior to committing the changes. Do not use virtual machine snapshots as a backup solution. For backup and recovery, use a backup and recovery utility, such as vSphere Data Protection.

Although virtual machine snapshots are useful in some situations, snapshots do not come without a price. There may be an issue with the performance of a virtual machine with multiple snapshots. Multiple snapshots are of more concern in production environments than in test and development environments.

Consider enacting a management policy regarding snapshots. Different environments require different policies. A production environment requires a different policy than a development and testing environment. For example, a production environment policy might allow only a single snapshot and only for a short time, perhaps to diagnose an issue. A test and development policy, however, might allow multiple snapshots for a longer period of time.

Consider making virtual machine snapshots a part of the change management procedures, at least in production environments. With a change management policy, creating a snapshot would require management approval and would not be the decision of a single administrator.

Virtual machine security considerations

Virtual machines are the containers in which applications and guest operating systems run. By design, all VMware virtual machines are isolated from one another. This isolation enables multiple virtual machines to run securely while sharing hardware resources (CPU, memory, I/O), and provides their ability to both access hardware and to maintain uninterrupted performance.

Even a user with system administrator privileges on a virtual machine's guest operating system cannot breach this layer of isolation to access another virtual machine without privileges explicitly granted by the ESXi system administrator. As a result of virtual machine isolation, if a guest operating system running in a virtual machine fails, other virtual machines on the same host continue to run. The guest operating system failure of one virtual machine has no effect on the following:

- The ability of users to access other virtual machines
- The ability of other operational virtual machines to access the resources they need
- The performance of other virtual machines

Virtual machines are similar to physical machines in that they are vulnerable to attack, primarily through their network interfaces. To secure virtual machines, software should also be installed to protect the virtual machines from network vulnerabilities. Consider the following measures that can be taken to protect virtual machines from attacks:

- Confirm that antivirus, antispyware, intrusion detection, and firewalls are enabled for every virtual machine in the virtual infrastructure.
- Keep all security measures up to date; make sure that you apply the latest security patches.
- Use a patch management tool to keep the virtual machine software and applications up to date.
- If the data center requires it, use smart card readers to access virtual machines with the vSphere Web Client remote console.
- Use vCenter Server's system roles to limit access to the virtual machine console windows.
- Create virtual machines from virtual machine templates that have been secured.
- Virtual machines can be further protected by setting up resource reservations and limits on the host. For example, through the detailed resource controls available in ESXi, a virtual machine can be configured so that it always receives at least 10% of the host's CPU resources.
- Resource reservations and limits protect virtual machines from performance degradation that would occur if another virtual machine consumed excessive shared hardware resources. For example, if one of the virtual machines on a host is incapacitated by a denial-of-service (DoS) attack, a resource limit on that machine will prevent the attack from taking up so much of the hardware resources that the other virtual machines are also affected. Similarly, a resource reservation on each of the virtual machines ensures that, in the event of high resource demands by the virtual machine targeted by the DoS attack, all the other virtual machines will still have enough resources to operate.

Encryption and security certificates

ESXi and vCenter Server use and support standard X.509 version 3 certificates to encrypt session information between components. In vSphere 6.0, the VMware Certificate Authority (CA) provisions vCenter Server components and ESXi hosts with signed certificates, by default.

The following certificates are in use, by default, for VMware virtual infrastructure:

- **ESXi certificates**: These are used for SSL communication to and from the ESXi host. These certificates are provisioned by VMware CA by default, and stored locally on each ESXi host.

- **Machine SSL certificates**: These are used for communicating to and from vCenter Server instances and Platform Service Controller instances. Unlike previous versions of vCenter Server, all communication goes through the reverse proxy and therefore, generally, a single certificate can be used. These certificates are provisioned by the VMware CA and stored in the VMware Endpoint Certificate Store (ECS).

- **Solution User certificates**: These are used by all solutions and services added to vCenter Single Sign-On for inter-component communication. These certificates are provisioned by the VMware CA and stored in VMware ECS as well.

- **vCenter Single Sign-On signing certificates**: These are root certificates that are used to sign all certificates provisioned by VMware CA. This is provisioned during the installation of the Platform Services Controller and is stored on the host filesystem. This can be changed, but it must be managed by the vSphere Web Client.

Signed certificates are now used for the entire infrastructure, and are automatically regenerated as needed for all solutions and for vCenter Server systems (where they are added to the Platform Services Controller domain). This solves many of the challenges that existed in previous releases. Note, however, that certificate operations are currently only administered through the command line.

If signed certificates are required, the vCenter Single Sign-On signing certificate can be replaced with an equivalent subordinate CA certificate from an external CA to allow it to function as a member of the certificate hierarchy in the environment.

Monitoring and management design practices

Design the monitoring and management infrastructure to support the solution architecture which you are implementing. The following are VMware components that provide options for monitoring and managing vSphere virtual infrastructure:

- vSphere Web Client (installed with vCenter Server deployment), and optionally the VMware Host Client, which both provide graphical user interface tools for the management of virtual infrastructure. The vSphere client (C#) is no longer being developed, and is not included in the vSphere 6.5 release.

- VMware vSphere Command-Line Interface (CLI) provides a set of commands that can be used to manage, configure, and automate administrative activities for ESXi and your vSphere virtual environment.
- VMware vSphere PowerCLI provides a Windows PowerShell interface to manage and run scripts in the vSphere environment.
- VMware vRealize Orchestrator provides an interface to automate operations management with workflows, as configured by an administrator.

Time synchronization

Time synchronization between virtual infrastructure components is important in order to prevent errors from occurring with Kerberos security, for auditing environmental access, and to gather accurate and useful performance and logging data.

Any logging or performance data cannot be accurately interpreted if the timestamp information on the data is not synchronized between the managed and management components. For example, the vSphere Client performance graphs are not displayed if the time is not synchronized to within a few minutes between the vCenter Server system, ESXi hosts, and virtual machines.

Time synchronization can also affect applications. For example, database transactions might not be processed correctly if a time synchronization problem exists between multi-tiered applications running on separate virtual machines.

VMware recommends using Network Time Protocol (NTP) or Active Directory to synchronize all the management and host components to a common time source. (Servers added to Active Directory are automatically synced using Windows Time Services.) An NTP best practice is to synchronize with multiple NTP time sources to improve time accuracy and service availability. Larger organizations might consider creating internal NTP servers to which they can synchronize. Creating internal NTP servers prevents large numbers of internal hosts and virtual machines from directly accessing (and overloading) an external NTP server.

If NTP or Active Directory time synchronization is not available, VMware Tools time synchronization can be used within a VM so that times are synchronized.

Syslog logging

The syslog service provides support for system logging, network logging, and collecting logs from hosts. You can use the syslog service to redirect and store ESXi messages to a server on the network.

This is most useful where there is no local storage, or if an environment has a policy that requires logs to be retained from ESXi hosts.

From vSphere 6.0 onward, syslog services are installed with vCenter Server, and only need to be configured to be used.

In addition, vRealize Log Insight is an attractive solution that allows for the centralized collection, storage, and analytics of log data from the infrastructure.

Performance monitoring

Use vSphere best practices, along with the organization's SLAs, to determine what to monitor. In addition, use vSphere best practices, SLAs, and SME interviews to determine the performance thresholds that you want for CPU, memory, storage, and network resources.

Beyond normal vSphere monitoring, if there are any other specific services or applications that require specific monitoring, you should automate performance monitoring whenever possible and create alarms for notification when performance thresholds are exceeded.

Virtual machine backup and restore

Virtual machines should be backed up in accordance with established environmental backup procedures. Generally, there are two ways of backing up the virtual machines:

- **Full virtual machine backups**: These take up significant amounts of space, but are easily restored to the exact state that the virtual machine was in when the backup took place.
- **In-guest backups**: These use less space, but are more difficult to back up and restore, as the underlying operating system must usually be up and running prior to recovery. vSphere Data Protection provides an effective solution for the backup and restoration of virtual machines. Details of its operation are covered in the BCDR architecture design.

The following are general system backup design considerations:

- When determining backup requirements and solutions, refer to the SLAs in place to help assess the suitability of the design.
- Downtime is defined as time when a server is not available to its users. Backup time is the amount of time it takes to make a backup. Ideally, backup does not require that a server also not be available-your users would hope that they can use a server while it is being backed up. In addition, most businesses find having scheduled downtimes for backups too restrictive, and demand a very short time window in which systems are not available.
- The **recovery point objective (RPO)** specifies the point in time to which data must be restored, and, therefore, the amount of acceptable data loss, measured in elapsed time. The RPO starts counting time since the last backup. It helps to clarify the frequency of when backups are required.
- The **recovery time objective (RTO)** specifies the service level and the duration of time agreed upon by which a business process must be restored after a disaster. The RTO starts counting downtime and specifies a maximum amount of time it takes for recovery. The RTO helps clarify the order in which VMs need to be recovered.
- Running backups inside guests in VMs might be feasible, except that, in the virtual world, many workloads are consolidated onto one server. Having backups made of all VMs on the same host, running concurrently, can magnify resource demands to unacceptable performance levels, and the loads can tax CPU and network resources considerably.
- Balance cost compared to need. Having a backup agent in every VM might facilitate the ease of restore operations, but the additional licensing fees might not be justifiable under tight IT budgets.
- Backup types can affect recovery time. Full backups can take longer than a file backup and restore. Restores from incremental backups can require a full backup as a starting point.
- The frequency of backups can impact the ability to meet recovery point and recovery time objectives. With more frequent backups, data is more current.

VM-to-VM affinity rules

As we already stated for memory reservations, VM-to-VM affinity rules are also not a direct availability feature, but are a very important configuration detail when configuring application redundancy for VMs. For example, if you have multiple PSCs in a redundant configuration, it is important that you ensure that all PSC VMs belonging to such a redundant configuration are kept on separate hosts within the same cluster (provided that the PSC VMs of such a configuration are placed within the same vSphere cluster).

Backup and recovery - embedded deployment model

The basic principle of the backup and recovery procedure is the usage of an image-level backup/restore method, leveraging the **vSphere API for Data Protection** (**VADP**). The recommended way to backup and restore vCenter Server is by means of the **vSphere Data Protection** (**VDP**) appliance, which is the VMware implementation of a VADP-enabled backup solution. Other VADP-based backup solutions from third-party vendors should be suitable as well.

The requirements needed for a vCenter VM to be backed up via a VADP-based backup solution are listed in the aforementioned documentation, and are briefly listed here for convenience:

- The VM must have VMware Tools installed and running. This is a requirement because VMware Tools allows the quiescing of the filesystem, which is mandatory when taking image-level backups of a vCenter VM.
- The VM must use a **fully qualified domain name** (**FQDN**) with the correct DNS resolution, or must be configured with a static IP address.
- VDP and other VADP-enabled backup solutions create a quiesced VMware snapshot of the VM, so the infrastructure or vSphere implementation, as well as the VM configuration, must support this.

Backup and recovery - external deployment model

For an external deployment model, where the PSC and the management node are separately installed and where multiple PSCs within a vSphere domain can coexist in federation, replicating with each other either in separate sites or within the same site behind a load balancer, things become a little bit more complicated in terms of backup and recovery procedures.

Migration architecture design

Migration architecture design provides a blueprint enabling the delivery of VMware's IaaS Migration Portal toolset in the customer's environment. The customer will leverage this portal to deliver **Physical to virtual (P2V)** and V2V migrations for the migration project.

This section provides the conceptual, logical, and physical design needed to deliver the **Cloud Migration Portal (CMP)** and VMware Converter solution, and details the various strategies and considerations needed to perform the migrations.

The design incorporates VMware best practices within the project's technical and business constraints, and the specific requirements identified. Technical, organizational, procedural, and policy-related requirements have been considered. The following is a list of modules that support the migration architecture:

- **SDDC Infrastructure**: This module provides a foundational approach to building a software-defined data center architecture delivered in a single physical data center. It consists of compute, storage, and network virtualization capabilities, and provides a design that considers scalability and availability of management components, utilizing the underlying virtualization platform. In addition, it provides layer 2 and layer 3 logical connectivity between virtual machines, and layer 3 connectivity between overlay networks and external networks using VMware NSX Edge routing functionality (static or dynamic). Finally, it provides virtual storage capabilities to the management stack.

- **SDDC Operations**: This module provides comprehensive monitoring for the software-defined data center. The foundational monitoring platform delivers performance and capacity-management dashboards for management components. It also provides optimized, consolidated, and operationalized process definition for monitoring, performance, and capacity management for the SDDC infrastructure. Additionally, it provides enhanced role, responsibility, and skill set enablement guidance.

- **SDDC Automation**: This module expands the software-defined data center with cloud computing capabilities. It provides enterprise-ready architecture for the delivery of **infrastructure as a service (IaaS)**, and provides a self-service portal for consumers to request and manage IaaS services. It also provides a service catalog with automation and approval workflows, an optimized service life cycle (service definition, design, development, release), governance processes, and supporting materials based on VMware best practices. Additionally, it provides a service-/tenant-focused role, responsibility, and skill set enablement guidance, and enables application service offerings for application consumption.

- **Business Continuity/Disaster Recovery**: This module delivers comprehensive business continuity. It enables the recovery of business applications if a site failure occurs using VMware Site Recovery Manager. It also enables the backup and recovery of data stored within a virtual machine, or the whole virtual machine, using VMware vSphere Data Protection.

Migration process flow

To achieve successful migrations, both the processes and tools need to be implemented and adhered to. This will ensure that the migration process flows smoothly, with risks managed as required. The following represents the overall workflow design for the migrations:

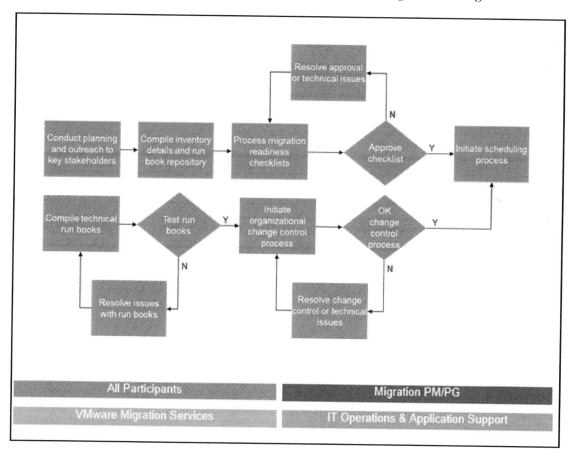

High-level migration workflow

Migration scheduling

Once the preparation is complete, the migration scheduling can occur. This process can integrate into an externally-approved workflow, approval can be within the CMP tool itself, or all migrations can be pre-approved. As the **customer** is filling the migration pipeline, any servers submitted to be scheduled are assumed to have been approved by the **customer's** change process. Once the migration schedule is complete, it is handed over to the migration team to execute:

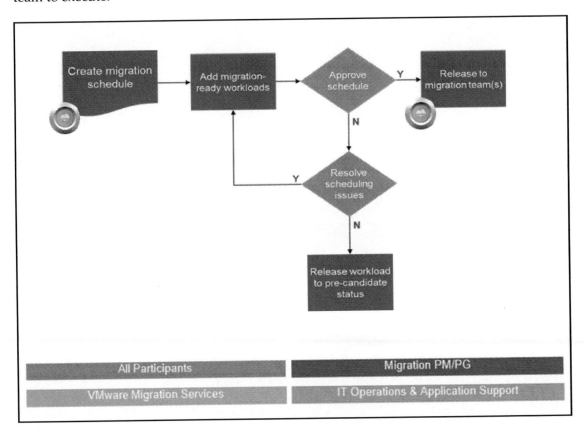

Migration flowchart

Migration execution

VMware's Cloud Migration Services team will take the allocated migration schedule and execute the plan conforming to the agreed-upon run book accompanying this architecture design. At a high level, the following tasks will be performed during the migration execution stage:

1. Validate the workload information
2. Validate vSphere vCenter and ESX(i) connectivity from CMP and Converter
3. Ensure the schedule/window is achievable
4. Perform pre-migration steps, as per the run book
5. Perform migration, as per the run book
6. Perform post-migration steps, as per the run book
7. Perform rollback steps as required, and as documented in the run book

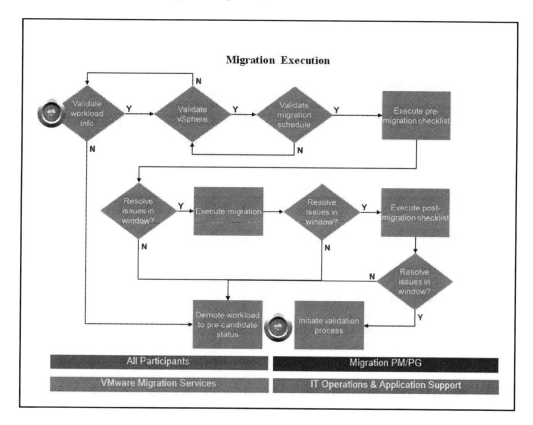

Migration execution

Migration validation

Once the pre-migration, migration, and post-migration steps are complete, the Cloud Migration Services team hands the server back to the customer application team for migration validation. This process ensures that once the migration is complete, all applications are validated and the migration can be signed off:

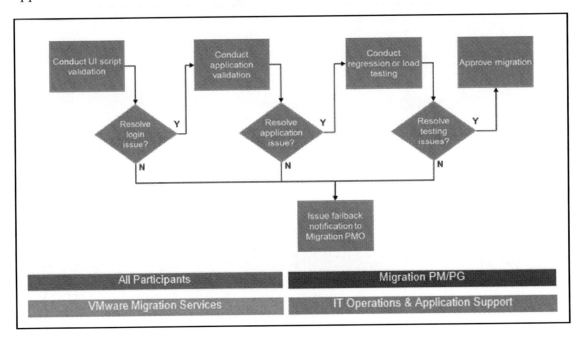

Migration validation

This section will provide you with a blueprint enabling the delivery of VMware's IaaS Migration Portal toolset in the customer's environment. VMware's Cloud Migration Factory will leverage this portal to deliver P2V and V2V migrations for the customer's migration project.

This chapter provides the conceptual, logical, and physical design to deliver the **Cloud Migration Portal** (**CMP**) and VMware Converter solution, and details the various strategies and considerations to perform the migrations.

The design incorporates VMware best practices within the project's technical and business constraints and the specific customer's requirements. Technical, organizational, procedural, and policy-related requirements have to be considered.

The customer has built a new virtualization platform to house the virtual and physical source machines as part of a data center relocation project.

The customer has to design a solution that provides the following:

- A migration workflow
- A migration toolset
- Migration scheduling and batching

Customer business objectives

The following table provides a list of success criteria to customers for the migration of physical and virtual workloads:

Title	Description
Assess workloads in scope for migration	Assess and plan for migration workloads, based on application workshops and collected performance data.
Install and configure IaaS migration portal, as per design	Installation and configuration of the CMP tool will allow the VMware Migration Factory to complete migrations of virtual and physical workloads to the destination data center.
Complete physical and virtual migrations	Successfully migrate physical and virtual machines to a new virtual platform, as per the design.
VM hardware upgrade	The VMs should be upgraded to the highest level of hardware supported by the hosts on the target platform.
Virtual hardware standardization	The migration of the VMs should, as far as possible, facilitate the standardization of the VM hardware, including the VMXNET version and SCSI adapter.

Migrated virtual machine framework

When migrating a physical machine to a virtual machine, the best practice is to standardize the configuration for the virtual environment. The following framework will be applied as a baseline for the virtual machine configuration:

- CPU, RAM, and storage specifications will be based on average utilization and a mutually agreed growth percentage (15%)
- The virtual network adapter will be configured to VMXNET 3 where possible
- The virtual SCSI adapter will be LSI Logic SAS where possible
- Disks will be thin-provisioned where possible

An analysis of the environment has been undertaken during the virtualization phase, to determine the resource requirements for each server. After the migration to a virtual machine has been completed, it is recommended that a review be undertaken using vRealize Operations Manager, over a period of up to 30 days, to ensure that there has not been a service impact. If quantifiable service degradation is noted, an in-depth analysis of the virtual machine may be required by the customer's operations staff in conjunction with the application's owners.

Responsibility matrix

The following table illustrates the pre-requisites and roles for Virtualization Migration Project in detail:

Task	Customer's Operations	Customer's Network	Customer's Storage	VMware
Audit physical/virtual servers	R/A			I
Communications execution	R/A	I	I	I
Identify P2V and P2NV candidates and priorities	R/A			C
Identify V2V and V2NV candidates and priorities	R/A			C
Determine outage windows	R/A			I
Schedule P2Vs	R/A	C	C	I
Schedule V2Vs	R/A	C	C	I

Task	Customer's Operations	Customer's Network	Customer's Storage	VMware
UAT testing	R/A			I
Conduct pre-migration testing	R/A			I
Perform P2Vs	C/A	A	A	R/A
Perform V2Vs	C/A	A	A	R/A
Conduct post-migration testing	R/A	I	I	R/A
Conduct UAT	R/A	I	I	I
Identify hardware for repurposing	R/A	I	I	
Decommission redundant physical infrastructure	R/A	I	I	

Customer requirements will be discussed and recorded as baseline requirements in the functional requirements. In conjunction with identifying the requirements, a number of constraints, risks, and assumptions will also be considered.

Constraints for the migration activities are listed in the following table. Constraints are restrictions that could affect the performance of the project. The most significant constraint is the outage window, which may limit when migration activities can be scheduled.

Design risks

The risks for the upgrade project are listed. Risks are factors that may impact the successful delivery of the VMware Migration Portal or in-scope migrations. Risks can negatively impact the reliability of the design. The solution supporting the migration of the workloads onto VMware vSphere contains various components that must be integrated for the tool to function as expected. The two core software solutions used by the VMware Migration Service are as follows:

- VMware CMP
- VMware vCenter Converter Standalone

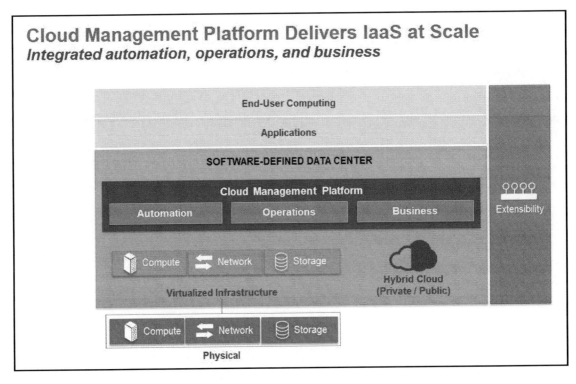

IaaS portal conceptual design

These components will be required to interact with the source and target infrastructure components, such as the physical servers (source) and vCenter servers (target), and therefore VMware recommends that you locate these components to have maximum accessibility.

After all migration activity has been completed, both CMP and Converter can be decommissioned and the resources/licenses can be returned to the resource pool.

VMware vCenter Converter standalone has a limit of 10 concurrent P2V/V2V jobs. Should there be a need to migrate more than 10 machines concurrently, additional instances of Converter should be set up, configured, and tested prior to any migration activity. Currently, customers have a targeted upper limit of 40 concurrent machines in a batch. VMware's recommendation is to provision 1 CMP server and 8 Converter servers for the best migration performance.

IaaS migration portal logical design

The following figure provides an overview of the network architecture and information flow between the various components/participants/roles in the migrations. These components are installed on virtual machines, and therefore can easily be relocated to another network segment, if there is a need to do so during or after the initial pilot:

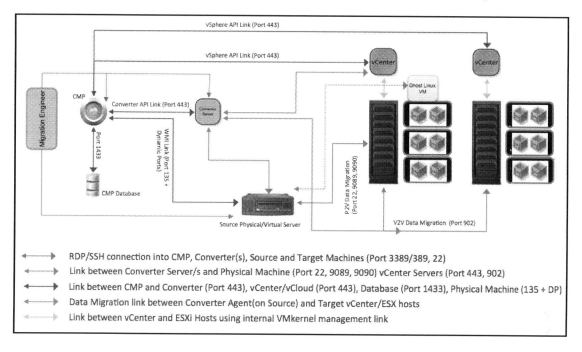

IaaS migration portal logical design

VMware CMP physical design

CMP is a proprietary VMware tool available to VMware Professional Services, used to schedule and orchestrate server migration life cycles. Being a web-based tool, CMP can be accessed both externally by the CMS team via a VPN, and also internally by VMware and customers staff. This software has been specifically designed to integrate with both the open and proprietary VMware APIs with relation to VMware Converter, VMware vCenter, and VMware ESX(i) to ensure a scalable and secure working model.

CMP sits above and adds to the functionality of VMware Converter, enabling job scheduling, job allocation, and reporting. Within the customer's migration project, CMP will be installed in the customer's target private cloud environment, which is within the same facility as the source data center.

Supported guest operating systems that can be converted by VMware Converter 5.5 Standalone are as follows:

- Windows XP Professional SP3 (32 bit and 64 bit)
- Windows Server 2003 R2 SP2 (32 bit and 64 bit)
- Windows Vista SP2 (32 bit and 64 bit)
- Windows Server 2008 SP2 (32 bit and 64 bit)
- Windows Server 2008 R2 (64 bit)
- Windows 7 (32 bit and 64 bit)
- Windows 8 (32 bit and 64 bit)
- Windows Server 2012 (64 bit)
- Red Hat Enterprise Linux 3.x (32 bit and 64 bit)
- Red Hat Enterprise Linux 4.x (32 bit and 64 bit)
- Red Hat Enterprise Linux 5.x (32 bit and 64 bit)
- Red Hat Enterprise Linux 6.x (32 bit and 64 bit)
- SUSE Linux Enterprise Server 9.x (32bit and 64 bit)
- SUSE Linux Enterprise Server 10.x (32 bit and 64 bit)
- SUSE Linux Enterprise Server 11.x (32 bit and 64 bit)
- Ubuntu 10.04 LTS (32 bit and 64 bit)
- Ubuntu 12.x (32 bit and 64 bit)
- Ubuntu 13.04 (32 bit and 64 bit)

VMware Converter Linux migration process

The customer has requested details on the standard process that the VMware Migration Factory normally follows to migrate Linux servers from the source to the destination using VMware Converter.

The following figure depicts this process flow as it is delivered by the VMware Migration Factory:

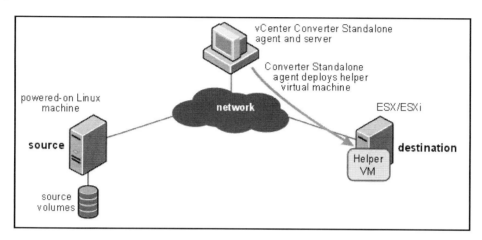

VMware Converter Linux migration process

The following figure depicts the Migrating Linux server with P2V Converter tool:

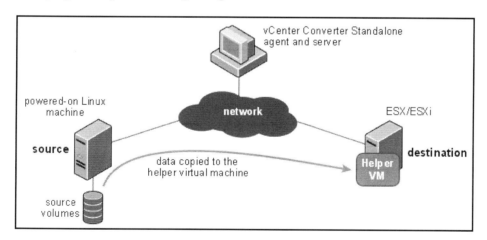

vCenter Converter workflow

The data transfer from the source machine to the Helper VM occurs using SCP. The end-to-end process is as follows:

1. Converter connects to the source machine through SSH, and runs the vmware-sysinfo binary to collect hardware and OS configuration (CPUs, memory, networks, storage).
2. Converter creates the destination VM on the vCenter server (an empty VM).
3. Converter powers on the destination VM from an ISO image (CD-ROM boot).
4. A Helper service auto starts in the destination VM.
5. The Helper service connects to the source (through SSH) and transfers the data from all volumes configured for cloning through the tar command. Data is written to the local disks (from Helper's point of view, these are the destination VM virtual disks).
6. After the cloning and reconfiguration phases, the target VM is powered off, the ISO image is disconnected from the CD-ROM device, and, after a reboot, the destination starts from the cloned OS.

For the second part, all of the code in the helper VM is run as root; however, it is not visible outside of the Helper VM. On the source, Converter runs, as root, the following code fragments:

- vmware-sysinfo binary (collecting the source server configuration) and some commands related to that process-that includes mkdir, unzip, uname, lvm, and so on.
- tar on each individual file system scheduled for conversion. It is possible for you to use the sudo command (and it is mentioned in the User's Guide on page 46). The account used should be able to execute commands without being prompted for a password (otherwise the conversion would fail).

A log bundle of a successful conversion can be exported and examined from individual log files. The commands that the Converter server runs are in converter-worker.log files. The commands that the Helper service runs are in the converter-helper.log file. The commands that the vmware-sysinfo binary uses are available in the public source code, as required.

This method was not adopted by the customer, and they requested that all Linux migration be done as *cold* V2V migrations in Converter as the customer's Linux machines use LVM partitions. When LVM partitions are used, each partition can only be created as new disks when doing *hot* migrations.

VMware Converter agent

VMware Converter requires an agent to be installed on the source server. This agent allows VMware Converter to scan and monitor the disks, hardware, and application services.

The agent is installed remotely, and does not require a reboot except for Windows NT 4.0 and Windows 2000 servers. This reboot requirement does not impact the customer's migration project, as there are no NT4 or Windows 2000 workloads in scope.

Network/security changes

All migrated machines will be configured to maintain their existing network configuration, including VLAN and IP settings. Any DHCP reservations (if used) should be changed to use the host name instead of the MAC address for the reservation.

Port requirements

The following table outlines the ports (bi-directional) that have to be opened for migration data traffic to flow:

Source	Destination	Ports (TCP)	Application ID
Remote access	CMP	3389	Ms-rdp
CMP	vCenter (source and target)	443, 902	Ssl, VMware
CMP	Physical	135, 1024-65000	Active-directory, ms-virtualserver-6500
CMP	Converter	443	Ssl
CMP	ESX	443, 902	Ssl, VMware
Converter	Source	22, 135, 137-139, 443, 445, 9089, 9090	Ssh, active-directory, ms-netlogon, ssl, swyx-cds, symantec-endpoint-manager
Converter	ESX	443, 902, 903	Ssl, VMware, kazaa
Converter	vCenter (source and target)	443	Ssl
Source server	ESX	443, 902, 903	Ssl, VMware, kazaa

Source	Destination	Ports (TCP)	Application ID
Linux Helper VM	Source Linux Machine	22	Ssh

The preceding mentioned ports are to be opened on firewall for migration activity.

 ICMP must be available between the IaaS Migration Portal Components (CMP, Converter) and vCenter/source machines.

Operational readiness for migration

- Local administrator access to the source server
- Access to create and manipulate VMs with vCenter
- Availability of computing services staff to provide application testing
- Business/application owner approval for an outage
- Application owner availability for testing pre- and post-conversion
- Storage allocation for the migrated VM

Pre-migration activities

VMware will track readiness with the VMware team and with the nominated customer teams directly, and escalate any concerns to the customer project manager to ensure readiness for migration. The following are pre-migration activities, put into motion two weeks before migration:

1. Confirmation of candidates for the migration window a minimum of two weeks prior to the migration window. The focus will be on ensuring a consistent pipeline, a gradual ramping up to accommodate increasing migration size and complexity, and grouping workloads within move groups.
2. Change approvals submitted and changes approved for migration. Content from the IaaS Migration Run book can be leveraged here as technical inputs (for example, activity sequencing and infrastructure rollback approaches).

3. Resource planning (VMware will request and the customer will secure resources for the customer migration tasks, and VMware will plan its own internal resourcing).

4. Resource coordination (VMware will coordinate VMware and customer resources according to the plan, and will escalate to the customer in the event that customer resources are unavailable for the customer's migration tasks).

5. Confirmation that the source infrastructure remains operational and fit for purpose. Customer operational teams have the best understanding of the operation of the source infrastructure. If performance, stability, or capacity issues arise, customers are to advise VMware so that a joint determination of whether to proceed with the migration batch can be made.

6. Confirmation that the destination infrastructure is ready for the workloads in the migration batch from a performance, capacity, and stability perspective.

7. Confirmation that application contingency plans are in place, including rollback. The customer will provide contingency plans for the applications, databases, and related operating system services. These plans may simply adopt the infrastructure contingency plans in many cases, with or without additional plans at the application level. VMware will validate the existence of the plans.

8. Confirmation that application dependency smoke tests are provided and tested. These tests will be used by VMware to perform initial testing prior to handing over to the application teams, and will cover the startup of critical services, presence of critical files, and up to 10 simple steps with no specific application knowledge required. These tests are intended to help ensure a clean handover to the business application teams, while not unnecessarily slowing down the migration process. If the steps are unclear or exceptions are encountered, VMware will triage and determine the next steps together with customer.

P2V migration options

When migrating servers from a physical infrastructure to virtual machines, there are two distinct methods that can be used:

- **P2NV (P2 new V) rebuild**: Build a new virtual machine and transfer the data from the physical server
- **P2V conversion**: Convert the physical server, as-is, to a virtual machine

A P2NV/rebuild operation is the cleanest method, whereby a fresh operating system is deployed and the application is installed onto it. Data is then migrated from the existing physical server to the new virtual machine and then the physical server is decommissioned. This method is lengthy in comparison to the P2V method. In the case of this project, VMware will P2V the server first; the customer will build a new virtual machine and migrate the application at a later date.

A P2V operation copies the data from the existing physical server into a virtual machine. This method is generally far quicker than rebuilding the server; however, if the operating system on the existing physical server is not in a healthy state, the process of converting the server to virtual may render the operating system non-functional, requiring a rollback to the physical server. If the root cause can be determined, then a second P2V attempt may occur. However, if this fails, it may be more efficient to rebuild the server as a VM rather than P2V.

There are a couple of methods for the P2V conversions that may be used:

- **Hot clone**: Full outage
- **Hot clone**: Post synchronization

Hot clone - full outage

A hot clone - full outage uses the VMware CMP to convert the server to a virtual machine. The operating system remains running during the cloning window; however, the application services are stopped as a full copy of the machine is migrated onto the target. Any changes made to the data on the server after the cloning has begun will be lost.

The prerequisites for hot clone migration are as follows:

Title	Description
Supported operating system	The operating system must be supported as documented in this design.
CMP platform	The CMP platform must be deployed to deliver the migration service with the VMware Migration Factory.
Network connectivity	The source hosts/vCenter, destination hosts/vCenter, and the CMP platform all require connectivity on the ports specified in this design.
VLANs	The VLANs used by the source VMs should be provisioned on the new hosts to prevent the need for changing IP addresses, which may introduce additional complexity.

Title	Description
Capacity	There must be sufficient capacity at the destination for compute and storage resources.

The hot clone – full outage benefits are as follows:

Title	Description
Data integrity	The application services are disabled during the entire conversion, maintaining data integrity.
Disk resize	Disks can be shrunk or enlarged during the conversion.
Drivers	Utilizes OS-based drivers, which maximizes hardware compatibility.

The hot clone – full outage drawbacks are as follows:

Title	Description
Downtime	The application server will be unavailable during the entire conversion process.
Converter agent	As part of the installation, a converter agent is installed into the guest operating system.
Dynamic disks	Dynamic disks are converted to basic disks on the target.
Disk layout	Linux machines that use LVM partitions will be created as new disks On Windows machines; if a partition is moved to a new disk, it will create it as an extended partition

The hot clone – full outage risks are as follows:

Title	Description	Mitigation
Migration failure	If there is a network interruption during migration, the migration will fail.	The source VM stays in place and can be powered on or the migration restarted.

Title	Description	Mitigation
Application does not run	The application does not run on the new platform.	Proper planning to identify VLANs and other requirements, such as hardware dongles. If the application does not run after migration, the server can be rolled back to the original until the problem can be rectified.
Application tied to a MAC address	Some applications use a MAC address for licensing. This MAC address will change when migrated to the new platform.	Attempt to identify any applications tied to MAC addresses and the process to update the license for a new MAC address. Only servers migrated from vSphere can retain their MAC addresses. (vSphere VMs have a unique set of MAC addresses).

Hot clone – post-synchronisation

A hot clone—pre-clone with synchronization uses the VMware Cloud Migration Portal and Converter to migrate the server to virtual; however, instead of stopping application services during the entire conversion window, VSS is used to track changes made to the disks. At the end of the conversion process, specified services are stopped and the changed blocks are synchronized with the target virtual machine. CMP can also shut down the physical server and power on the virtual machine, greatly reducing the outage window. This is not applicable to Linux migrations as SSH is used in a file-level copy. Additionally, any migrations resizing FAT volumes or shrinking NTFS will be unable to utilize this feature.

The prerequisites for post synchronisation migration are as follows:

Title	Description
Supported operating system	The operating system must be supported as listed in this design.
CMP/Converter platform	The CMP/Converter platform must be deployed to deliver the migration service with the VMware Migration Factory.
Network connectivity	The source hosts and vCenter, destination hosts and vCenter, and the CMP/Converter platform all require connectivity to each other.

Title	Description
VLANs	The VLANs used by the source VMs should be provisioned on the new hosts to prevent the need for changing IP addresses, which may introduce additional issues.
Capacity	There must be sufficient capacity at the destination for computing and storage resources.
VSS Support	The application must be **Volume Shadow Copy Service** (**VSS**) aware.
Free space	The application must have enough free space for the VSS snapshots.

The hot clone – postsynchronisation migration benefits are as follows:

Title	Description
Outage window	The outage window for an incremental data copy is far smaller than that for a full data copy.
Drivers	Utilizes OS-based drivers, maximizing hardware compatibility.
Scheduling cutover	The synchronization and cutover can be scheduled for a specific time.

The hot clone – postsynchronisation migration drawbacks are as follows:

Title	Description
Data integrity	All application services must be stopped for postsynchronization to occur correctly and must be VSS aware.
Converter agent	As part of the installation, a converter agent is installed into the guest operating system.
Dynamic disks	Dynamic disks are converted to basic disks on the target.

The migration risks in post synchronisation scenarios are as follows:

Title	Description	Mitigation
Migration failure	If there is a network interruption during migration, the migration will fail.	The source VM stays in place and can be powered on or the migration restarted.
Application does not run	The application does not run on the new platform	Proper planning to identify VLANs and other requirements, such as hardware dongles. If the application does not run after migration, the server can be rolled back to physical until the problem can be rectified.
Application tied to MAC address	Some applications use a MAC address for licensing. This MAC address will change when migrated to the new platform.	Attempt to identify any applications tied to MAC addresses and the process to update the license for a new MAC address.
Data integrity	Because the server will be running the application during migration, data will change and be synchronized at the end of the P2V window. This will need to be verified on a case-by-case basis.	Verify that applications are VSS aware. Determine all application services in scope. Conduct thorough testing after P2V to ensure postsynchronization was successful.
Cutover scheduling	If there is not enough time for the initial copy to complete, then the cutover schedule may be missed.	Allow enough time for the initial copy to complete.
Size of deltas	If a high rate of data change is experienced between the initial copy and final synchronization, the delta copy may take some time to complete.	Validate the change rate on the server before using this method.

V2V migration options

When migrating servers from virtual infrastructure to virtual machines, there are three distinct methods that can be used:

- **V2 new V (V2NV) rebuild**: Build a new virtual machine and transfer the data from the virtual server.
- **V2V conversion (hot)**: Migrate the virtual server as-is to the destination vCenter using the P2V method.
- **V2V conversion (cold)**: Migrate the virtual server as-is to the destination vCenter.

A V2NV/rebuild operation is the cleanest method, whereby a fresh operating system is deployed and the application is installed onto it. Data is then migrated from the existing virtual server to the new virtual machine, and then the virtual server is decommissioned. This method is lengthy in comparison to the hot or cold V2V method. In the case of this project, VMware will V2V the server first, and then the customer will build a new virtual machine and migrate the application at a later date. This method will be deployed based on the time constraints for V2NV servers.

A V2V operation migrates the data from the existing virtual server to the destination. This method is generally far quicker than rebuilding the server; however, if the operating system on the existing virtual server is not in a healthy state, the process of migrating the server to a new destination may bring with it errors from the source. If there are errors in the source, it may be more efficient to rebuild the server as a VM rather than V2V.

The migration of virtual machines between vSphere platforms has several options, each with benefits and drawbacks. Some of the options have less downtime; however, they may require more preparation and will potentially incur more risk. For this project, the following approaches are possible:

- V2V conversion (cold)
- Enhanced vMotion

V2V conversion

A V2V migration copies the virtual machine from one virtual platform to another virtual platform. The source platform and destination platform can be different, provided that the conversion software supports both platforms. VMware CMP/Converter can be used to migrate the VMs from the existing environment to the new environment. Converter 5.5 is compatible with vSphere 4 and 5. The customer currently has one source vCenter running on vSphere 5 and later in scope.

V2V requirements

The prerequisites for V2V migration are listed in the table:

Title	Description
vCenter versions	The current vCenter versions are supported.
CMP/Converter platform	The CMP/Converter platform must be deployed to deliver the migration service with the VMware Migration Factory.
Network connectivity	The source hosts and vCenter, destination hosts and vCenter, and the CMP/Converter platform all require connectivity to each other.
VLANs	The VLANs used by the source VMs should be provisioned on the new hosts to prevent the need for changing IP addresses, which may introduce additional issues.
Capacity	There must be sufficient capacity at the destination for compute and storage resources.

CMP migration process

The migration process using VMware CMP/Converter is a non-destructive process that generates a clone of the physical/virtual machine data in the virtual environment.

VMware CMP is managed through a simple, task-based user interface, enabling VMware Migration Factory to convert physical machines to VMware virtual machines using the following steps:

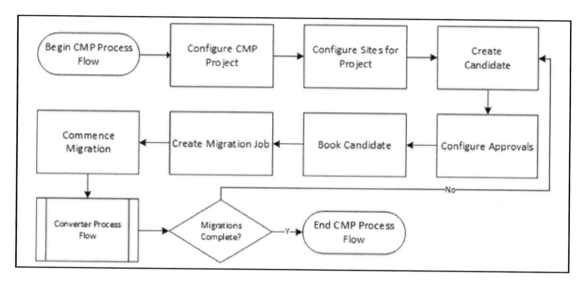

VMware CMP migration process

VMware CMP communicates with the guest OS running on the source machine for the activity. To prevent potential data synchronization issues, application services will be stopped during the final/cutover migration.

Timing estimate (P2V/V2V timing)

Using the P2V/V2V Conversion method recommended, the data of the source server will pass over the network fabric. It is assumed that the slowest link between the source and destination hosts will be 1 GBPS. Given that there will be other network traffic to compete with, it is assumed that migrations can achieve approximately 20 MB per second (field-based experience).

Assuming that there is 200 GB of disk per server for the calculations, we can also assume that the 200 GB will be about 60% utilized. The V2V process does not transfer whitespace, so this free space will be factored into the calculations:

Average Disk x Disk Utilisation = Total Amount of Data to Transfer per VM

200 GB * 0.6 = 120 GB of Data to Transfer

Data To Transfer per VM	= Time Required
Expected Throughput	
(120 GB x 1024) = 122,880 MB	= 4096 seconds / 3600 = 1.71 hours
20 MBPS	

Actual throughput will be captured during pilot migrations. Actual disk capacity to be transferred will be collected from VMware Capacity Planner.

Post-migration activities

Postmigration activities involve the final testing and validation of the correct workload operation prior to resuming delivery of normal application services. The specific activities include the following:

- Application startup for testing. This may be a limited release to ensure that the application is not inadvertently used by end users while testing is undertaken and prior to the formal resumption of application services.
- Application test plan execution.
- Resumption of application services.
- Open the service to end users.
- Resume normal application monitoring.
- Track next backup results and confirm backup success.

VMware will provide management over the postmigration activities:

- Track status of VMware and customer activities and report.
- Review migration and apply any lessons learned to the next migration event.
- Track any failed migrations, track issues to resolution, and reschedule failed migrations.

Summary

As with most IT products and architectures, there is no single solution that perfectly fits in every scenario. Just looking at vCenter Server, we have seen that there are quite a few deployment topologies available to us, ranging from the basic embedded deployment, with its unmatched ease of operation-but which lacks some advanced availability options and architectural flexibility-to the multi-site with PSC HA mode and vCenter Windows Failover Clustering, providing the most advanced option for HA and architectural flexibility while at the same time lacking basic functionality, such as a supported backup procedure and being quite complex in daily operations.

So the decision as to which deployment topology to choose will always be a compromise depending on the concrete requirements and priorities that have been defined for a concrete environment. A final design decision for a concrete vSphere environment may depend on whether a higher priority is granted to ease of operation while maintaining quite good high-availability qualities with vSphere HA, or Watchdog protection.

You can minimize downtime with uniform, cost-effective failover protection against hardware and operating system outages within your virtualized environment with vSphere HA features such as vMotion, HA, FT, DRS, and DPM. You can also monitor hosts and virtual machines, and automatically restart virtual machines on other hosts in the cluster when an outage is detected. HA provides uniform, automated protection for all applications without modifications to the application or guest operating system. vSphere vMotion allows you to move an entire running virtual machine from one physical server to another, without downtime. The virtual machine retains its network identity and connections, ensuring a seamless migration process. You can transfer the virtual machine's active memory and precise execution state over a high-speed network, allowing the virtual machine to switch from running on the source vSphere host to the destination vSphere host. This entire process takes less than two seconds on a gigabit Ethernet network. This is possible over virtual switches, vCenter servers, and even long distances, and helps you to achieve 99.99999% uptime with zero data loss and zero downtime.

Migration tasks, such as moving physical servers between data centers and across locations, are simplified with virtualization. P2V conversions are the fastest and easiest way to migrate physical machines from one location to another. VMware's Converter installs a small footprint on the physical host, then copies the entire machine to a virtual file. That flat file is then easily copied to a new location or sent via FTP across different locations. We only need to bring the VM online, take down the physical machine, and ship it to the new location. Hardware maintenance is made easy with virtualization. VMware's vMotion enables you to move guests off their underlying physical hardware to another host seamlessly, with no interruption to service. A production server can be moved off a host while the host undergoes maintenance or hardware upgrades, and then be migrated back, all while powered on and serving clients. Centralized management of the data center is the ultimate administration tool, and with virtualization the entire data center is managed through one console. Individual servers are managed through the same console that is used for disaster recovery. Operating system upgrades and updates are handled through the same console that is used for provisioning RAM and adding processors. VMware's vCenter provides the single pane of glass to get a holistic view of the entire virtual infrastructure across different locations.

In the next chapter, we will learn about how to design and deploy VMware VSAN, how to size servers to get the correct storage capacity with the desired IOPS—as per application demand, and how to lower TCO and get better ROI with VMware VSAN. We will also discuss one customer case study regarding the challenges to managing legacy storage and business value with software-defined storage.

6
Designing Software-Defined Storage Services

In this chapter, we will learn more about how to design a software-defined storage service. In order to dive into this topic, we will cover the following topics and look at reference deployment scenarios:

- The ability to design and deploy VMware **Virtual SAN (vSAN)**
- How to size servers to get the correct storage capacity with desired IOPS
- Defining VMware software-defined storage and its business value
- A software-defined storage checklist and architecture design
- A software-defined storage configuration with all features

Software-defined storage overview

The software-defined storage module expands the power of virtualization by adding VMware vSAN, fully integrated, hypervisor-converged, storage software, to an environment. Virtual SAN creates a cluster of server hard disks and solid-state drives that present a flash-optimized, highly resilient, shared-storage datastore to the environment. This allows for on-demand policies to be specified for virtual machines, which enable the administrator to control the capacity, performance, and availability attributes.

Software-defined storage is a key technology in the **software-defined data center** (SDDC) methodology. This module helps customers on their SDDC journey, so that they realize the benefits of compute-style policies for their storage infrastructure.

Purpose and applicability to the SDDC solution

The software-defined storage module extends the SDDC architecture through the delivery of software-based storage solutions powered by VMware technology. The module provides a validated solution based on VMware recommended practices in a practical design. The technical materials align to Virtual SAN 6.2, included with VMware vSphere® 6.0, Update 2.

The next figure illustrates the following:

- A conceptual overview of the solution with software-defined storage included in the environment
- How software-defined storage is implemented

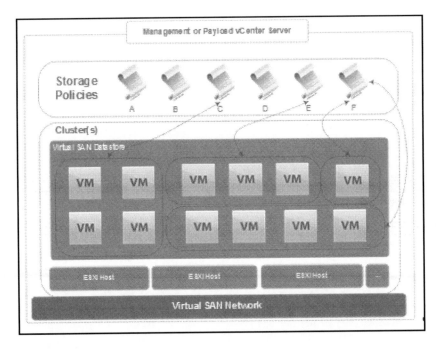

Software-defined storage module conceptual overview

Business requirements

The following bullet points list a customer's business requirements for the implementation of the software-defined storage infrastructure:

- To reduce the cost of proprietary enterprise storage
- To eliminate the need to ramp up skills to manage enterprise storage
- To have better management of storage policies so that the usage of storage can be tiered to the requirements of the business

Requirements and dependencies

The software-defined storage module has the following requirements:

- A minimum of three VMware ESXi hosts providing storage resources to the Virtual SAN cluster are required for regular use cases.
- vSphere components (ESXi hosts and VMware vCenter Server) must be using version 5.5 Update 1 or later. This content assumes that VMware vSphere 6.0 Update 1 and Virtual SAN 6.1 are being used to access all features and functionality provided.
- Each ESXi host providing storage resources to the cluster must:
    - Have a minimum of one SSD or PCIe flash device for the caching storage tier as specified in the *VMware Compatibility Guide for Virtual SAN* (http://www.vmware.com/resources/compatibility/ search.php?deviceCategory=vsan)

 VMware vSphere Flash Read Cache must not use any of the flash devices reserved for vSAN.

    - Have a minimum of one traditional spindle HDD or one SSD for the capacity tier as specified in the *VMware Compatibility Guide for Virtual SAN* (https://www.vmware.com/resources/ compatibility/search.php?deviceCategory=vsan)

- Have a storage controller as specified in the *VMware Compatibility Guide*

 Just a Bunch of Disks (JBOD) is supported by Virtual SAN 6.0 and later for use in blade server environments.

- VMware recommends having a minimum of 32 GB of RAM in each ESXi host, which will accommodate the maximum number of disk groups.
- All ESXi hosts participating in the Virtual SAN cluster should have a 10 GB network for Virtual SAN traffic.

 A 1 GB network can be used for smaller environments that are using hybrid mode ONLY. However, the performance of high-traffic operations, such as cloning a disk, will be impacted. A 10 GB network is highly recommended for these environments and required for all-flash Virtual SAN environments.

- Virtual SAN All-Flash is required if deduplication and compression are being used.
- The VMware vSphere High Availability isolation response setting should be set to power off virtual machines so that there is no possibility of split brain conditions if there is an isolation or network partition.

Architecture overview

Let's look at the architecture in detail in the following sections.

Conceptual design

The following figure illustrates the design at a high level for the customer:

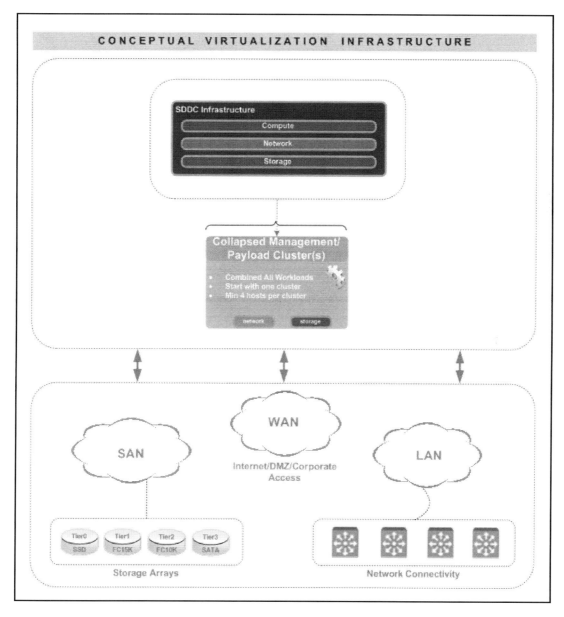

Conceptual design (for DC)

Logical design

Software-defined storage logically extends the abilities that exist with compute resources to the storage infrastructure. Rather than using CPU or RAM reservations, limits, and shares, with software-defined storage, the administrator defines policies that are assigned to virtual machines and allows the characteristics of the storage to be defined and changed as business requirements change. Software-designed storage logical design is illustrated here:

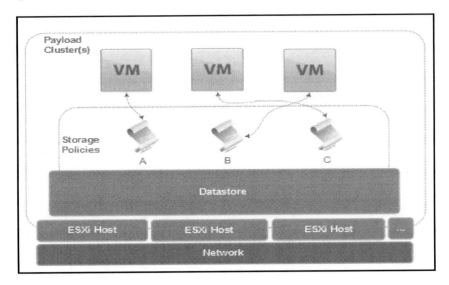

Software-defined storage logical design

The software-defined storage architecture design addresses all the functional components of a solution that have an impact on the resulting logical designs in the environment.

Virtual SAN (vSAN)

vSphere has an embedded software-defined storage solution called vSAN in its hypervisor footprint. vSAN leverages the local storage of ESXi hosts to use it as a shared storage for virtual machines. We can configure vSAN in the vCenter Server interface, which basically aggregates server disks, including solid-state flash disks and magnetic hard disk drives to create a simple, fast, agile, and robust shared storage volume. Virtual SAN is designed for virtual machines and enables a tiered storage infrastructure based on the different use cases.

vSAN design workflow

Designing a vSAN environment can be more easily understood by breaking the design into components. The following are the main points that must be addressed:

- Is vSAN going to benefit this environment?
- Is hardware required?
- How is the vSAN volume provisioned?
- Assessment of the application policy requirements.
- Is monitoring required?
- Is basic performance testing of the hardware required?
- Is basic failure testing of the hardware required?

The following figure shows the Virtual SAN workflow:

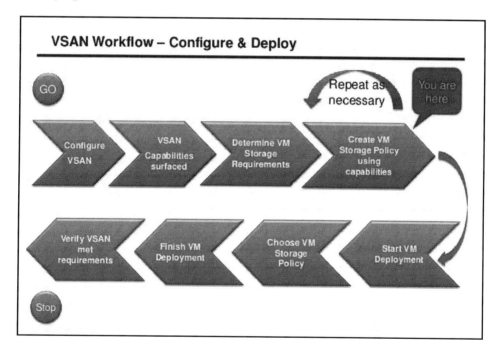

Virtual SAN workflow diagram

Use case-specific information is not contained in this workflow. Configuration for specific use cases is based on the hardware and policy configurations, as described in the following section.

Design parameters/considerations for vSAN

The design recommendations in this section are contextually based on best practices when used in the context of software-defined storage technical materials.

The major areas and decision points in this section are as follows:

- Hardware considerations
- Network design
- vSAN datastore characteristics
- vSAN sizing
- vSAN design assumptions vSAN design assumptions and constraints

These recommendations are based on generalized best practices that fit into the *VMware SDDC assess, design*, and *deploy service.*

Hardware considerations

The choice of physical hardware to be used in a vSAN environment is important to the configuration. See the *VMware Compatibility Guide* for information on the following components:

- **Solid state disks (SSDs)** or PCIe flash devices
- Magnetic **hard drives (HDDs)**
- I/O controllers

Many vendor solutions include vSAN. If not using a pre-built solution, you can:

- Build your own servers with supported hardware
- Select a third-party option for a vSAN ReadyNode as listed in the *VMware vSAN Compatibility Guide*

 VMware Engineering and VMware Technical Support provide support only for environments with hardware listed in the *VMware Compatibility Guide.*
It is important that the underlying hardware chosen for the solution is appropriate.

Comparing hybrid and all-flash designs

vSAN has two configuration options, a hybrid configuration containing both flash disks and magnetic disks, and all flash disks.

Hybrid configurations use a flash disk to enable the caching tier and magnetic disks for capacity and persistent data. Flash disks can be utilized for both the caching and capacity tiers in an all-flash configuration; 10 GB networking is compulsory, along with the flash disks for an all-flash configuration.

All-flash vSAN configuration gives efficient/high throughputs, advanced features, and consistent performance, irrespective of applications as compared to hybrid configurations.

Both hybrid clusters and all flash clusters have a basic prerequisite of 10% of consumed capacity for the flash cache layer.

Consider the following parameters about drives (flash or magnetic):

- **Compatibility**: The make/model of the PCIe or SSD devices must be certified in the vSAN listings (*vSAN Ready Nodes Guide*) of the *VMware Compatibility Guide*
- **Performance**: PCIe devices have an edge over SSD devices in performance
- **Capacity**: The maximum capacity for PCIe devices is always better than the maximum capacity listed for SSD devices for vSAN in the *VMware Compatibility Guide*
- **Write endurance**: The write endurance of the PCIe or SSD devices must meet the demand of both capacity and cache in all-flash configurations, as well as cache in hybrid configurations
- **Cost**: PCIe devices are costlier compared to SSD devices

We have to take the following into consideration when using all-flash configurations:

- vSAN with vSphere 6.1 or higher version
- 10 GB network for better performance
- Maximum number of all-flash servers is 64
- Flash Read Cache reservation should be not used
- All drives must be defined/notified as flash
- Drive endurance should be as per the requirement

SSDs

All reads and writes go to the SSD first, so the SSD is critical for any vSAN solution. The SSD is critical in hybrid configurations for speed. SSDs can be used for both the caching layer and capacity tier for all-flash configurations.

The configuration of the SSD is divided between a non-volatile write cache, approximately 30%, and a read buffer, 70%. The endurance and the number of I/O operations per second for the SSD are critical factors in the performance of the solution. The cache is set to 100% writes as read performance is not a factor for an all-flash.

The SSD endurance classes are as follows:

Endurance class	Terabytes written in 5 years (TBW)
Class A	>=365 TBW
Class B	>=1,825 TBW
Class C	>=3,650 TBW
Class D	>=7,300 TBW+

The following table lists the VMware recommendations for the endurance class based on the SSD tier as described in the *VMware vSAN Design and Sizing Guide*, other than the general classes.

The SSD endurance classes by tier classes are as follows:

Endurance class	SSD tier	TB writes per day	Terabyte writes in 5 years
Class A	All-flash— Capacity	0.2	365
Class B	Hybrid—Caching	1	1,825
Class C	All-flash—Caching (medium workload)	2	3,650
Class D	All-flash—Caching (high workload)	4	7,300

Select a higher performance class of SSD for optimal performance of vSAN. VMware recommends classes of performance in the *VMware Compatibility Guide* as per the following table:

The SSD performance classes are as follows:

Performance class	Writes per second
Class A	2,500 – 5,000
Class B	5,000 – 10,000
Class C	10,000 – 20,000
Class D	20,000 – 30,000
Class E	30,000 – 100,000
Class F	100,000+

There is a direct dependency between the SSD performance class and the vSAN performance ratios. The highest-performing hardware supports optimal performance of the solution. Cost is the major factor and might make a lower class of hardware more attractive, even though the performance or capacity might not be good for the solution.

Best practices always recommend choosing an SSD size that is a minimum of 10% of the expected size of the consumed HDD storage capacity, before **failures to tolerate (FTT)** is defined.

If 1 TB of HDD storage is consumed in a 2 TB disk group then the SSD size should be 100 GB (minimum).

First, decide on disk groups, sizing, and expected future growth before selecting a drive size. We can use endurance class B and performance class E SSDs to get the best performance from the Virtual SAN volume with optimized cost.

Magnetic hard disk drives

The HDDs (SAS/SATA/NL-SAS) in vSAN hybrid configurations are used for data storage capacity. They are also a critical and determining factor in the available stripe width for VM storage policies. To get a defined stripe width, we must ensure that a particular stripe width should be available across all servers in the cluster to achieve the objective. If the VM has a high failure to tolerate setting then we need additional HDDs, as each component must be replicated to meet the requirement.

VMware supports the following three types of magnetic disk:

- **Serial Attached SCSI (SAS)**
- **Near Line Serial Attached SCSI (NL-SAS)**
- **Serial Advanced Technology Attachment (SATA)**

NL-SAS are enterprise SATA drives with a SWAS interface. We can achieve the best results with SAS and NL-SAS drives. SATA magnetic disks can be used in capacity-centric requirements where performance is not the critical factor.

The speed of the HDDs should be selected to meet the solution/application objective for which the cluster is designed. VMware defines HDD characteristics and speed in the following table.

The vSAN HDD environmental characteristics are as follows:

Characteristic	Revolutions per minute
Capacity	7,200
Performance	10,000
Additional Performance	15,000

VMware best practices suggest using an SAS HDD configuration that fits the objectives of the solution being designed. A lower cost disk will enable a higher number of failures to be tolerated if performance is not a critical factor. If there are no high-performance requirements, then selecting 10,000 RPM drives gives a balance between cost and performance.

VMware will not recommend mixing and matching HDD speeds to get a blend of various parameters in the solution, as there will only be a single volume in the vSAN datastore.

The best practice is to select one kind of HDD per cluster. Create a separate vSAN cluster for a higher performing configuration and if the solution needs different characteristics.

I/O controllers

The I/O controllers are very important to a vSAN configuration for the selection of disk drives. vSAN supports SAS, SATA, and SCSI adapters in either pass-through or RAID 0 modes. Only these two modes are supported. Most storage adapters support both modes. Performance is mostly dependent on the I/O controller.

When selecting a storage adapter, we have to consider the following points:

- Which modes does the I/O controller support? (RAID 0, pass-through, or both).
  - SSD performance should be reviewed in RAID 0 mode
  - RAID 0 mode has an operational overhead, which can impact performance
- Storage controller interface speed.
- Number of devices certified for the controller.
- Number of controllers to be utilized. Multiple controllers can minimize the failure domain and improve speed with increased cost.
- Controller queue depth is critical for performance. You should choose a queue depth of 256 or higher generally, as it is a very important, determining factor for the performance of vSAN.
- vSAN needs complete control over the drives irrespective of the choice made. Performance of pass-through and RAID 0 modes is normally very similar for most interfaces.

VMware best practices suggest using I/O controllers suited to the design parameters of the solution, such as:

- Model of the SSDs
- Model of the HDDs
- Queue depth of the controller
- Number of disks (and corresponding disk groups) to be configured

Host memory requirements

vSAN memory requirements are defined based on the number of disk groups and disks that the hypervisor manages. To support the maximum number of disk groups, 32 GB of RAM is required. The recommended configuration for the software-defined storage module is to use 256 GB of RAM for the ESXi hosts. This is enough memory to support the largest disk group configuration allowed.

> A best practice is to assign a consistent amount of RAM to each host in the cluster.
>
> If there are separate hardware configurations with disparate amounts of RAM in the hosts, create multiple vSAN clusters. vSphere DRS will help to balance the load among hosts.

Host CPU overhead

vSAN does not have specific CPU requirements because it introduces less than 10% CPU overhead. This impacts available resources in high consolidation ratio workloads and CPU-intensive applications.

When designing and sizing the environment, take the projected resource requirements for the environment into account so that performance does not suffer due to a lack of resources or overcommitment of resources.

Hardware design decisions

The following table lists design decisions for hardware choices in the environment.

The hardware design decisions are as follows:

Design decision	Design justification	Design implication
A hybrid vSAN configuration will be used.	Hardware has already been purchased before the design workshop.	
The SSDs to be used in the configuration are: 1 x 400 GB SSD	SSDs from performance class E are used to achieve a high level of performance and scalability from the vSAN configuration.	
The HDDs (capacity tier) to be used in the configuration are: 3 x 1 TB NL SAS 7.2K	Hardware has already been purchased before the design workshop.	NL SAS HDDs are not suitable for I/O intensive applications
We can use I/O controllers in the configuration with the following characteristics: 12 GBPS modular SAS HBA	I/O controllers having a high queue depth and more drives give a good balance between performance and availability for the vSAN configuration.	
The ESXi hosts will have 256 GB of RAM.	This will support the maximum configuration for vSAN and the virtual machine memory requirements in the environment.	

Network design

vSAN uses the network to transport all information, including communication between the cluster nodes and VM I/O operations. Transport is done by a specially created VM kernel port group, which must be configured on all hosts in the cluster even though the hosts are not giving storage resources to the cluster.

We have to design the network considering how much replication and communication traffic is running between hosts. The amount of traffic directly correlates to the number of VMs that are running in the cluster, how write-intensive the I/O is for the applications running, and whether an all-flash configuration is being used.

This traffic should be isolated on its own layer 2 network segment such as vMotion. You can configure this with dedicated switches or ports, or by using a VLAN, as shown in the following figure:

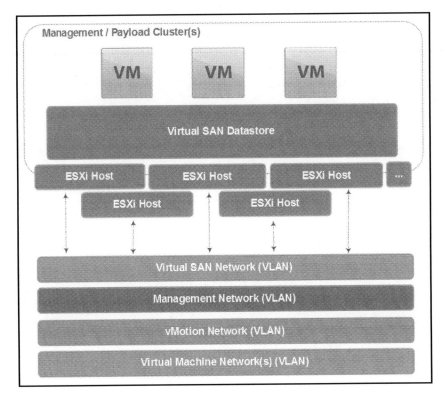

Conceptual network diagram

The following are the major decision points discussed in this section:

- vSAN network configuration:
    - Network speed requirements
    - Type of virtual switch to be used
    - Jumbo frames
- Multicast requirements
- BCDR and teaming considerations

vSAN network port group

vSAN needs a VMkernel network configuration for synchronization and replication activities. This port group should normally be dedicated and isolated to vSAN traffic. If a 10 GB network interface is being used then it can be shared. 1 GB networks need a dedicated NIC defined to the port group.

VMware suggests using a dedicated port group, network card, and an isolated network for vSAN traffic. This enhances security and stops other traffic from affecting the performance of vSAN.

Network speed requirements

vSAN supports the following configurations:

- Hybrid vSAN configurations have options for 1 GB or 10 GB Ethernet for network uplinks. The amount of activity on the vSAN might consume a 1 GB network, and could be the constraint in an I/O-intensive setup as follows:
  - Rebuild, replication, and synchronization operations
  - Critical and intensive real-time disk operations, such as cloning a VM
  - Large environments with more VMs
- All-flash vSAN configurations are supported only with 10 GB Ethernet network uplinks. An all-flash configuration consumes good network bandwidth because of the increased speed of the disks in the configuration with improved performance.

A 10 GB network is needed to get the best performance (IOPS). A massive decrease in array performance can be expected without it. VMware always suggests a 10 GB Ethernet connection for use with vSAN in all configurations.

Type of virtual switch

vSAN supports use the of vSphere standard virtual switch configurations or VMware vSphere Distributed Switch configurations. The benefit of using vSphere Distributed Switch configurations is that they allow **Network I/O Control** (**NIOC**) to be used, which allows for prioritization of bandwidth when there is contention in an environment.

vSphere Distributed Switch using NIOC is an attractive option for environments that have a limited number of ESXi host network ports. It allows the interface to be shared and prioritizes performance levels in contention scenarios.

VMware recommends using a vSphere Distributed Switch for the vSAN port group. Priority can be assigned using NIOC to separate and reserve the bandwidth for vSAN traffic in the environment.

Jumbo frames

vSAN supports using jumbo frames for vSAN network transmissions. The environment is supported fully, whether or not jumbo frames are used. The performance gains are often not significant enough to justify the underlying configuration necessary to enable jumbo frames properly on the network.

VMware recommends using jumbo frames for vSAN only if the physical environment is already configured to support them, they are part of the existing design, or if the underlying configuration does not create a significant amount of added complexity to the design.

VLANs

VMware recommends isolating vSAN traffic on its own VLAN. When multiple vSAN clusters are designed then each cluster must get a dedicated VLAN or segment for their own traffic. This will help to stop interference between clusters and aid in troubleshooting cluster configuration.

Multicast requirements

vSAN prerequisites advise you to always enable IP multicast on the physical switches and routers, which handle vSAN traffic along with the layer 2 path and the layer 3 path (optionally). It is used mostly for intra-cluster communication for heartbeats and exchange of metadata between the ESXi hosts participating in the cluster. Multicast traffic can be designed for named port groups, by using IGMP (v3) snooping. VMware best practices advise you to not implement multicast flooding across all ports.

Multicast communication is not configured on most switches. There is no IGMP snooper setup so traffic will not pass. Design an IGMP snooper so traffic can pass, or explicitly disable IGMP snooping on the port to be sure that multicast traffic is passed.

VMware best practices tell you to enable multicast only on the segments or ports that are being used for Virtual SAN.

Networking failover, load balancing, and teaming considerations

Business continuity and disaster recovery (BCDR) is major factor for any design or setup in a network failure scenario. vSAN works with teaming configurations for network cards, for better availability and redundancy of the network.

 vSAN does not currently use the teaming of network adapters for bandwidth aggregation.

VMware always suggests the use of multiple network adapters configured with the following teaming algorithms for assured performance:

- Route based on starting virtual port—active/passive failover configuration of adapters in the team
- Route based on IP hash—active/active failover configuration with:
  - Static EtherChannel for standard switches
  - **Link Aggregation Control Protocol (LACP)** port channel for vSphere distributed switches

We can make use of NIOC and QoS for sharing the NIC between traffic types, such as if a 10 GB network card will be used for all traffic on a blade system.

Network design decisions

The following table lists the design decisions for the network choices in the environment:

Design decision	Design justification	Design implication
A dedicated port group will be used for vSAN network traffic and configuration.	vSAN traffic has to be shared with other network traffic because an ESXi host only has a single 10 GB dual-ported network card. Hardware has been purchased before a design workshop.	Single point of failure as there is only a single 10 GB dual-ported NIC.
10 GB networking will be used for the vSAN network so that performance is optimal.	Increased throughput available to provide peak performance of the environment.	None.
vSphere Distributed Switches will be used for the configuration to verify that the interfaces can be shared, but traffic for vSAN is still prioritized as appropriate during contention scenarios.	vSphere Distributed Switches provide NIOC and enhance the performance in an environment.	None.
Jumbo frames will not be used in this environment.	The performance gains are not significant enough to justify the underlying configuration necessary to enable jumbo frames properly on the network.	None.
Dedicated VLAN will be used for vSAN traffic.	VLANs segregate traffic to verify that traffic is isolated and secure.	None.
IP multicast is set up only to be available on the vSAN network ports.	Prevent traffic from flooding networks that are not needed.	None.
NIOC is used for QoS for the network traffic.	This will help prevent degradation of performance for network traffic caused by another traffic type.	None.

vSAN cluster and datastore design

vSAN simplifies the storage configuration because there is only a single datastore for VMs. vSAN uses the concept of objects and components for storage of virtual machine data. An object consists of multiple components that are distributed across a vSAN cluster, based on the assigned policy for the object.

There are currently four different types of objects:

- **VM home namespace**: Location for VM configuration and log files
- **VM swap object**: Created for the VM swap file (only created when the VM is powered on)
- **VMDK**: Stores the data that is on a disk
- **Snapshot delta VMDKs**: Created for use when a VM has a snapshot created on it
- **Memory object**: Created when the snapshot memory option is selected when creating or suspending a virtual machine

Each object can be a maximum of 255 GB in size, and if they are larger, split into multiple components. Currently, vSAN 6.2 has a maximum of 9,000 components per host, which can be a limiting factor as to how far it can be scaled. More components are required for larger and more redundant VMs.

For example, one VM with a 500 GB disk (and no snapshots) will always consume the following components:

- Two for VM home namespace (failures to tolerate is always one)
- Two for VM swap objects (assuming that there is less than 255 GB of RAM in the machine)
- Two for the VMDKs (assuming no mirroring and no failures to tolerate)

As a result, sizing the environment appropriately means that limits on the configuration can be avoided.

The following sections discuss how to size the datastore and describe the different considerations that you must consider:

- vSAN disk format
- Disk groups
- Failures to tolerate policy

- Fault domains
- Hosts per cluster
- Datastore sizing

vSAN disk format

In vSAN for vSphere 6.0 and later, the disk format has been upgraded. The following configurations are available:

vSAN version	Format type	On-disk version	Overhead	Supported hosts
5.5/6.0	VMFS-L	v1	750 MB per disk	ESXi 5.5 U1+
6.0	VirstoFS	v2	1% of physical disk capacity	ESXi 6.0+
6.2	VirstoFS	v3	1% of physical disk capacity	ESXi 6.0 U2 +

Newer, on-disk versions are not supported on older ESXi hosts. For example, with vSAN 5.5 v2, on-disk versioning is unsupported.

As a part of the software-defined storage technical materials, the recommendation is to use the VirstoFS (v3) format unless there are backward compatibility concerns for the cluster. This configuration provides the broadest set of features available with vSAN.

Disk groups

We have to take decisions about the number of disk groups and the flash-to-magnetic disk or flash-to-flash ratio in vSAN. vSAN support is limited as follows:

- Hybrid configuration has a minimum of one flash device for cache and a maximum of seven magnetic disks for capacity per disk group
- All-flash configuration has one flash device for the cache and a maximum of seven flash devices for capacity per disk group
- Hosts can have a maximum of five disk groups/host

As the number of disks rises in configuration, the more cache is required and large capacity will be available for virtual machines. This will increase costs due to the limitation of the disk group. Multiple disk groups need one flash device per group for the cache and at least one device for capacity.

Disk group sizing is critical when designing the volume. We have to consider the following aspects while designing the number of disk groups per host:

- Available/usable space on the vSAN datastore
- Number of failures to tolerate in the cluster

The number of disk groups should be balanced between hardware and space requirements for the vSAN datastore. More disk groups give more space and provide redundancy in the system. Adding more disk groups can be expensive. The total usable space in the configuration can be good enough depending on the number of disks configured in the hosts.

Failures to tolerate policy

The number of **failures to tolerate** (**FTT**) policy settings is one of the core availability mechanisms with vSAN. The policy defines the number of replicas (mirrors) of virtual machine components. This policy can be defined to all virtual machines or specific VMDKs. This policy is critical while designing and sizing storage capacity, as it directly affects the consumption by the virtual machine of the storage.

There is an equation for FTT, where n FTT, $n+1$ copies of the data are required, and $2n+1$ servers contributing storage are needed. As an example, if the number of FTT is equal to 1, the VM or disk has two replica mirror copies of components generated across the cluster. If the number is equal to 2, three mirror copies are generated, and so on. The mirrors take over if there is a failure.

This will help in a better storage utilization than has been designed, because of the replicas generated. They also need additional components. This design must be configured depending on the availability design of the virtual machine or disk. These configurations are mentioned in a storage policy and attached to the respective workloads. By default, FTT is set to 1 even if the policy is changed to be another value. The maximum number of FTT is 3.

We must keep the default value of 1 for FTT and will change it only if we require a higher level of fault tolerance. This policy must be used extensively with higher priority virtual machines.

Fault domains

With vSAN on vSphere 6.0, fault domains allow for tolerance of environmental failures (such as a full rack failure) rather than just a single host.

An example of using fault domains is shown in the following figure:

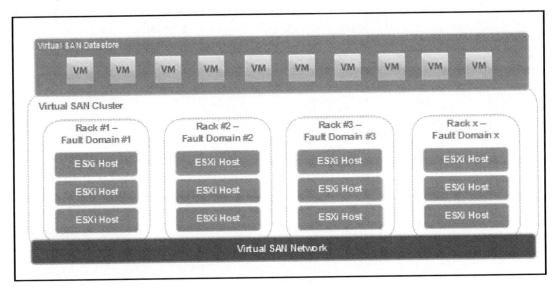

Fault domains

If a system has to tolerate n number of failures, we need $2n+1$ hosts, or $2n+1$ fault domains required. This enables replica data to expand out across the domains to hosts, and improves the ability to handle a better than single host failure. You need a minimum of three fault domains, while VMware suggests four or more to achieve redundancy. VMware also recommends having six hosts (two per fault domain) for a minimum level of redundancy.

We can leverage fault domains to protect the environment from failure considering there are many hosts to support the configuration.

Hosts per cluster

Decide the number of hosts for a cluster depending on the following points:

- Usable space required on the vSAN datastore
- Number of failures to tolerate in the cluster

We have to decide the number of hosts considering a balance between hardware and space:

- A higher number of ESXi hosts and/or disk groups transferred into more hardware costs
- Fewer ESXi hosts and/or disk groups can limit resource availability and compromise performance

For example, if the vSAN cluster is designed with only three ESXi hosts then only a single failure can be protected. We need more than three hosts to protect more than one failure.

 VMware best practices suggest configuration with four hosts per cluster while a maximum of 64 hosts per cluster is supported with a vSAN configuration.

Deduplication, compression, and RAID 5/RAID 6 erasure coding

Space efficiency mechanisms such as deduplication and compression can be configured to reduce the size of space used for storing data. vSAN can do block-level deduplication and compression to increase usable space. Redundant data within each disk group will be reduced by enabling deduplication and compression on a vSAN all-flash cluster.

Deduplication erases redundant data blocks while compression reduces additional redundant data within each data block. With these techniques, we can reduce the amount of space needed to store the data. vSAN sequentially runs deduplication and then compression tools, as data moves from the cache tier to the capacity tier.

Deduplication and compression is configured in cluster configuration but is attached to a disk group level. As soon as deduplication and compression is enabled, then redundant data within a specific disk group gets reduced to a single copy. vSAN does a rolling reformat of every disk group on every host to achieve this. This whole process will take time based on the data stored on the vSAN datastore. Whenever deduplication and compression is disabled in the future, then there should be sufficient physical capacity available to accumulate the data that has been released by the feature.

Disk groups can be ready to use RAID 5 or RAID 6 erasure coding for the disks to guarantee that the data is still protected and using less storage space, compared to the default RAID 1 mirroring.

Datastore sizing

vSAN volume sizing can be done in various ways based on the critical factors for customers. Policy configurations can affect the usable space in the cluster. The final sizing might require more hardware and disk groups to be configured properly.

VMware helps you with the VMware Virtual SAN TCO and Sizing Tool (`https://vsantco.vmware.com/`) to minimize complexities while doing the sizing of the vSAN datastore clusters. Just enter the various parameters as input in this tool and the calculator will give you the optimal configuration as output.

Virtual SAN TCO and Sizing Calculator

VMware suggests using the Virtual SAN Sizing Tool for the actual number of hosts and storage sizing for the cluster from compute, storage, and network perspectives. We should use eight or more hosts in the cluster to support the configured fault domains for proper availability and recovery. The actual datastore size and number of hosts is based on the applications/virtual machines being hosted on vSAN datastore. For more information on VSAN sizing and design tool you can refer to the link `https://vsansizer.vmware.com/vsansizing/html/dcScaleDeploymentsOptions.html`.

vSAN cluster and datastore design decisions

The following table lists the design decisions for the vSAN cluster and datastore design in the environment:

Design decision	Design justification	Design implication
The vSAN on-disk format will be the v3 - VirstoFS file system.	Newest format supports enhanced features of vSAN.	None.
One disk group will be configured. 1 SSD HD for cache tier and 3 NL SAS HDDs for capacity tier.	This will meet the needs for availability and performance.	None.
FTT setting will be, by default, set to 1, and a separate policy will be configured for higher levels of availability where needed.	All VMs are protected against a single failure. High priority virtual machines can be protected with additional levels of availability as needed.	None.

Fault domains will not be used in this design.	Number of hosts in a default design is too small to make proper use of fault domains.	None.
Collapsed management/payload clusters for DC and DR.	Most applicable use of the servers that were already purchased without using a witness appliance (if 2 node cluster is used).	None.
Deduplication and compression is not enabled in this design.	Deduplication and compression is not available for hybrid configuration.	None.

vSAN design assumptions

Delivering the software-defined storage design as part of the *VMware Virtualization Deploy Service* assumes the following:

- Hardware will be in place before engagement delivery
- 10 GB networking is in place
- The customer has personnel with vSphere and storage experience
- All hardware is certified and listed in the *VMware Compatibility Guide*
- The customer has suitable experience configuring vSphere and with storage technologies

vSAN policy design

vSAN policy application has features to configure policies on demand, and to change policies of running virtual machines.

We will discuss the following topics:

- vSAN policy options
- General policy design recommendations

vSAN gives you options to configure various policy attributes/parameters in a storage policy. These attributes/parameters can be used alone or combined to enable different service levels. Understand the policies and the objects before any design decisions are applied. The policy options are given in the following table:

Capability	Use case	Value	Comments
Number of disk stripes per object	Performance	Default 1 Maximum 12	Standard RAID 0 stripe configuration used to improve performance for a virtual machine disk. This will tell you about the number of HDDs on which each replica of a storage object is striped. If the value is > 1, it will enhance the performance and improve the overall system.
Flash read cache reservation (%)	Performance	Default 0 Maximum 100%	Flash capacity reserved as read cache for the storage = % of the logical object size which will be reserved for that object. We can use this setting only for workloads that must have read performance issues addressed. The flipside of this feature is that other objects cannot use a reserved cache. VMware best practices suggest not using these reservations unless it is needed as unreserved flash is shared uniformly between all objects.

Number of failures to tolerate	Availability	Default 1 Maximum 3 **Note**: Maximum value is 1 if disk size is > 16 TB.	Determines the number of host, disk, or network failures a storage object can tolerate. The higher the value, the more failures can be tolerated. If the fault tolerance method is mirroring then for n failures tolerated, $n+1$ copies of the disk are created, and $2n+1$ hosts or fault domains participating storage are required. The higher the n value then the more replica virtual machines are created, which can consume more disk space. If the fault tolerance method is erasure coding then to tolerate one failure, four hosts (or fault domains contributing storage) are needed and to tolerate two failures, six hosts or fault domains are needed.
Failure tolerance method (Available with all-flash vSAN)	Performance or capacity	Default: RAID 1 (Mirroring)	Defines the mechanisms used to tolerate failures. RAID 5/6 is only supported on all-flash Virtual SAN clusters where the number of FTT is = 1 or 2. FTT =1 indicates a RAID 5 configuration and FTT=2 indicates RAID 6 configuration.
IOPS limit for object	Performance	Default: 0	Determines IOPS limit for a disk IOPS calculated. Base size of 32 KB is by default. Read and write are regarded as equivalent and cache hit ratio or sequence are not taken into account while calculating IOPS. No limit is applied if the limit is set to 0.

Disable object checksum	Override policy	Default: No	vSAN does a complete checksum to guarantee the integrity of data by ensuring that each copy of a file is the same as the source file. The system checks the authenticity of the data during read/write operations, and if an error is found, vSAN repairs the data or reports the error.
Force provisioning	Override policy	Default: No	This is good for a planned expansion of the vSAN cluster, and provisioning of VMs should go on as vSAN will automatically bring the object into compliance as resources become available.
Object space reservation (%)	Thick provisioning	Default 0 Maximum 100%	The percentage of the storage objects that will be thick provisioned during VM creation. The rest of the storage objects will be thin provisioned.

Policies are designed based on the application demands as they are configured differently based on the object. The following table lists the default policy options configured to the different objects in vSAN.

The following table lists object policy defaults:

Object	Policy	Comments
Virtual machine namespace	1 FTT	Configurable but changes are not recommended.
Swap	1 FTT	Configurable but changes are not recommended.
Virtual disks	User-configured storage policy	Can be any storage policy configured on the system.
Virtual disk snapshots	Uses virtual disk policy	Same as virtual disk policy by default. Changes are not recommended.

Application demand assessment

Policy design is kick started with an assessment of business needs and application demands. Policies help any configuration to be customized as required.

Start by assessing the following various application demands:

- I/O requirement and profile of applications on a per-virtual-disk basis
- Types of applications
- Scalability from a compute and storage perspective
- Follow application best practice guidelines (block size)

We have to configure vSAN policies for availability and performance in a traditional manner to balance the space consumed and recoverability options. The default system policy is good enough and no additional policies are needed in most of the cases until/unless there are specific application demands for performance or availability.

Policy design decisions

The following table lists the design decisions for the vSAN policy design in the environment:

Design decision	Design justification	Design implication
Number of FTT policy will be set to 1.	Limited by number of ESXi hosts in the cluster. The customer may decide to increase the number of FTT to 2 for DC cluster in the future for business critical VMs.	None.
Disable object checksum policy set to No.	Object checksum feature is avoiding data integrity issues and it consumes a small overhead.	None.
IOPS limit for object policy set to 0.	No existing use cases are identified to limit IOPS for a virtual machine.	None.
Force provisioning policy will be enabled.	Allows the provisioning of virtual machines with a policy that cannot be met by the current vSAN cluster resources.	None.

Number of disk stripes per object policy will be set to 1.	In general, the default stripe width of 1 should meet most of workload types.	None.
Flash Read Cache reservation policy will be set to 0.	Simplify management and troubleshooting. All virtual machines equally share the read cache of an SSD.	None.
Failure Tolerance Method policy configured as RAID-1 (Mirroring).	For a hybrid model, only RAID-1 is supported.	None.
Object space reservation policy will be set to 100%.	All virtual machines will be created with full allocated disk space up front (thick). Simplify management and troubleshooting.	None.

vSAN monitoring design

Monitoring the vSAN environment is critical to deployment success. This section describes considerations for monitoring design and best practices (if included in the engagement):

- General monitoring practices
- Virtual SAN Health Check Plug-in
- Virtual SAN Observer
- VMware vRealize Operations Manager monitoring
- Monitoring design

General monitoring practices

vSAN supports amazing monitoring capabilities. vSAN can be monitored from the VMware vSphere Web Client for normal monitoring of the datastores.

Monitoring can happen on different objects in the vSphere Web Client along with clusters and datastores. Hosts who are part of a vSAN cluster can be monitored in the same fashion as every other vCenter managed host.

You can monitor the hosts' physical disks and virtual disks that are participating with vSAN from the cluster level. Capacity, operational status, health status, policy information, and compliance status can all be seen for each host, VM, and disk on the vSAN datastore from the cluster level review.

You can view the standard performance information, state of the disks, status of the volume, and partition group information from the vSAN datastore level. There is also a capacity monitoring page available in vSAN, as shown here:

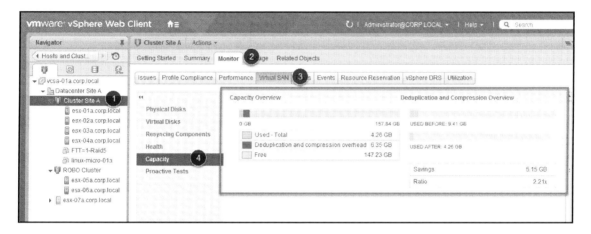

Capacity overview interface

Virtual SAN Health Check Plug-in

In vSphere 6.0, VMware introduced the Virtual SAN Health Check Plug-in as a simple way to check the health of the vSAN cluster. As of vSAN 6.1, it is included by default.

The plugin provides details on the following:

- Whether the vSAN configuration is fully supported, functional, and operational
- The root cause in the event of a failure with instant notifications and helps in speedy remediation
- Testing various aspects of the configuration

The following figure shows an example of the Virtual SAN Health Check Plug-in. VMware recommends using the Virtual SAN Health Check Plug-in to allow for easy monitoring of the vSAN clusters:

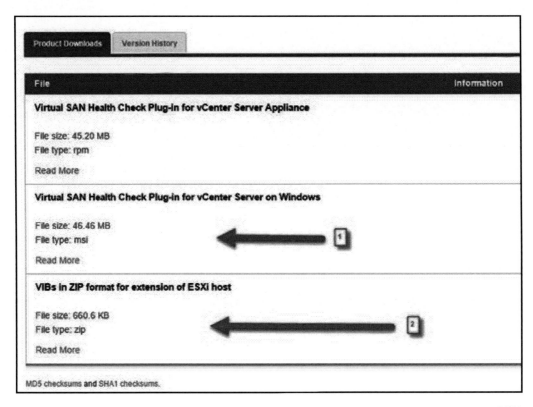

Virtual SAN Health Check Plug-in

Virtual SAN Observer

For information on how vSAN is operating, you can use Virtual SAN Observer, a tool that provides visibility into vSAN performance metrics and counters. This tool is included with vSphere 6.0. As a part of this release, the **Ruby vSphere Console (RVC)** provides an interactive command interface that can be used to manage, monitor, and troubleshoot. RVC includes functions for the following:

- vSAN configuration
- vSAN health monitoring
- vSAN disks statistics

- vSAN performance statistics
- Observer

You can use Observer to monitor information on vSAN. Observer is a GUI tool that shows vSAN-related statistics. It can be utilized for vSAN performance outputs and for analysis.

 The Observer is primarily a troubleshooting tool. VMware does not recommend running it continuously.

The Observer user interface displays performance information for the following:

- Statistics of the physical disk layer
- Extensive physical disks group details
- CPU usage statistics
- Consumption of vSAN memory pools
- Physical and in-memory object distribution across vSAN clusters

An example of the interface is shown in the following figure:

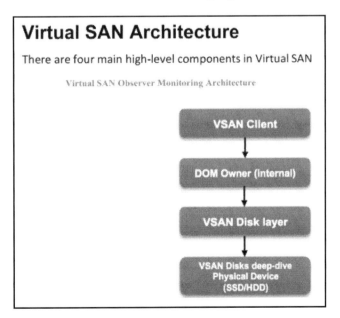

Virtual SAN Observer architecture

vRealize Operations Manager monitoring

vRealize Operations Manager management pack for storage devices helps you collect data from vSAN. The management pack can also integrate with any storage device that has a VASA plugins or APIs.

vRealize Operations Manager helps you monitor operations by creating dashboards and alerts as needed for a vSAN setup.

VMware suggests vSAN with vRealize Operations Manager should be designed and deployed for end-to-end monitoring.

Monitoring design

The following table lists the design decisions for the vSAN policy design in the environment:

Design decision	Design justification	Design implication
Virtual SAN Health Check Plug-in and the Web Client interface will be used.	vSphere Web Client will be the main interface for configuration, management and troubleshooting.	None.
vRealize Operations Manager console with the storage management pack 6.0.5 will be installed (if in the environment), and Observer to provide a comprehensive view of the vSAN environment.	The vRealize Operations Management Pack for Storage Devices 6.0.5 provides visibility into vSAN 6.0 storage environment. Predefined dashboards allow the customer to follow the path from a VM to the vSAN and identify any problem that may exist along that path.	vRealize Operations Manager 6.x must be used in the environment and the software edition must be supported for the installation of storage management packs.

Scalability limits of vSAN

Requirements for vSAN scalability are shown in the following table. Always validate these limits with the latest updates to the *vSphere Configuration Maximums Guide* (https://www.vmware.com/pdf/vsphere6/r60/vsphere-60-configuration-maximums.pdf).

The vSAN scalability limitations are as follows:

Option	Limit
vSAN ESXi host	
vSAN disk groups per host	5
Magnetic disks per disk group	7
SSD disks per disk group	1
Spinning disks in all disk groups per host	35
Components per vSAN host	9000
vSAN cluster	
Number of vSAN nodes in a cluster	64
Number of datastores per cluster	1
vSAN virtual machines	
Virtual machines per host	200
Virtual machines per cluster	6400
Virtual machine virtual disk size	62 TB
Virtual SAN VM Storage Policy	
Disk stripes per object	12
Percentage of Flash Read Cache reservation	100
FTT	3 if VM disk is <= 16 TB 1 if VM disk is > 16 TB
Percentage of object space reservation	100
Virtual networking	
vSAN networks or physical network	2

Product documentation and tools

VMware provides tools and documentation that aid in the configuration of its products. This section describes the documentation and tools used in the compilation of this kit.

VMware product documentation

VMware installation and administration guides are available at `www.vmware.com`. The guides include the information necessary to install and administer the products included within this module. These guides are the primary source of deployment information. The information in this document provides additional installation and configuration guidance.

This document covers the products listed in the following table.

The software-defined storage software versions are as follows:

Item	Version
VMware vCenter Server Appliance VMware vCenter Server for Windows	6.0 Update 2
VMware ESXi server	6.0 Update 2

Although most information contained within this document is specific to the versions listed in the preceding table, some also applies to prior versions. See the vSAN documentation from the *vSphere Storage* guide in the *VMware vSphere Documentation* (`https://www.vmware.com/support/pubs/vsphere-esxi-vcenter-server-pubs.html`) for more information.

Supporting documentation

The following reference material has aided in the development of this kit:

- *VMware Virtual SAN Design and Sizing Guide* (`https://storagehub.vmware.com/export_to_pdf/vmware-r-virtual-san-tm-design-and-sizing-guide`)
- *VMware Virtual SAN Health Check Plug-in Guide* (`http://www.vmware.com/files/pdf/products/vsan/VMW-GDL-VSAN-Health-Check.pdf`)
- *vSphere 6.0 Configuration Maximums Guide* (`https://www.vmware.com/pdf/vsphere6/r60/vsphere-60-configuration-maximums.pdf`)

Tools

The VMware Virtual SAN TCO and Sizing Calculator (`http://vsantco.vmware.com/`) tool was used in the creation of this kit.

Summary

We have gone through the software-defined storage concept with VMware vSAN, which consolidates conservative IT infrastructure silos for industry-standard vSAN-ready servers. The internal storage of servers gets virtualized with vSAN to help the customers transform their data centers without risk, reducing **total cost of ownership** (TCO), improving ROI, and scale for future application demand. vSAN consists of a single, integrated platform for storage, compute, memory, and networking, and builds on the foundation of VMware vSphere and VMware vSAN, the software-defined enterprise storage solution natively integrated with vSphere.

VMware solutions make vSAN the ideal storage platform for business-critical applications, disaster recovery sites, **remote office and branch office** (ROBO) implementation, test and development environments, management clusters, security zones, and **virtual desktop infrastructure** (VDI). We can trust vSAN to run most critical applications. vSAN helps customers modernize their infrastructure by enhancing three key areas of today's IT needs: higher security, lower cost, and faster performance. You learn to design a redundant control plane that is built-in to minimize risk without compromising flash storage output. vSAN lowers TCO by providing more highly available, efficient, and cost-effective stretched clusters compared to legacy storage solutions. Operational costs are also reduced with intelligent operations that bring 1-click hardware updates for assured hardware experiences and pro-active health checks for custom, real-time support. vSAN is designed to scale for future IT demands by optimizing flash performance for traditional and next-generation applications. This enables customers to get the benefits of vSAN for all the applications and infrastructure.

In the next chapter, we will learn more about the technical analysis of all VMware cloud components, as well as compute, storage, network, memory, Orchestrator, security, monitoring, and management with their design and configuration, in detail. We will also learn about the design and deploy configuration of vRealize Business, vRealize Hyperic, and Navigator in the next chapter.

7
VMware Cloud Assess, Design, and Deploy Services

In this chapter, we will learn about the technical analysis of all VMware cloud components and their design and configuration in detail. This chapter will help you create the correct design with best practices for specific use cases. We will go through the following topics:

- Compute, storage, and network virtualization design overview
- Infrastructure as a Service with Orchestration
- Cost visibility and metering of all components
- Monitoring components and integration with VMware products
- Application release automation with Zero Touch Deployment

We will start with compute, storage, and network virtualization design and will give more focus on all cloud components of the vRealize family, such as vRealize Automation, vRealize Operations, vRealize Orchestrator, vRealize Hyperic, vRealize Log Insight, vRealize Business, and vRealize Infrastructure Navigator, along with their integration with each other in this chapter. This chapter outlines the services VMware will provide to deliver the **Infrastructure as a Service (IaaS)** solution.

VMware can help customers to accelerate their **Software-Defined Data Center (SDDC)**/cloud initiative to deliver an IaaS solution including governance, people, processes, and technology that will enable a customer to stand up a private cloud using the vRealize Suite, which is scalable and operational. This IaaS solution incorporates the core components that a customer needs when creating a private cloud and runs it as quickly and efficiently as possible.

VMware will make recommendations to close any high priority gaps in readiness. Closing the gaps identified during this assessment will decrease project risk and increase the probability of success when operating a VMware SDDC/cloud solution in a sustained manner. This service facilitates implementation of a production deployment of cloud computing services through proactive analysis and remediation recommendations.

VMware Cloud (SDDC) assessment, design, and deploy service solution overview

The solution provides customers the flexibility to select additional capabilities to complement the base core components which easily interlock with the target platform.

The VMware Virtualization Design and Deploy Service is built for a customer who is adopting or expanding their virtualization infrastructure deployment. The service provides a comprehensive design of the virtual infrastructure, followed by the deployment and validation of the solution using the capabilities provided by vSphere.

The primary objective of this service is to design and deploy a virtualization solution using vSphere according to a documented architecture that can be successfully implemented and validated in the customer's environment. This includes utilization of vSAN if appropriate for the environment.

Secondary objectives include the following:

- To provide a virtualization solution overview and knowledge transfer so that customers can effectively participate in subsequent design and deployment activities
- To conduct a current state analysis on the existing physical or virtual environment to prepare for the design activities

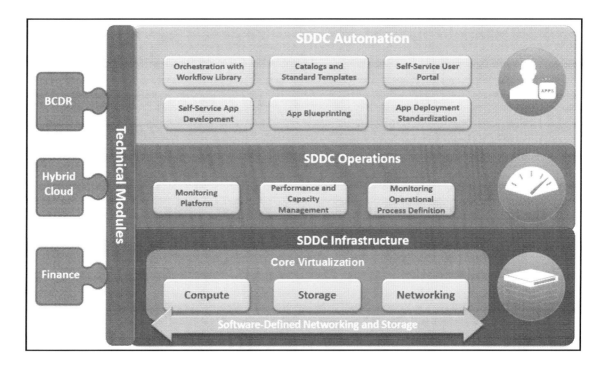

Virtualization conceptual design

The following diagram illustrates the conceptual design of the environment for the virtualization infrastructure.

Select the appropriate diagram for the service being deployed or configure the diagram appropriately based on the layers of the virtualization architecture diagrams document.

This diagram depicts the default design for a virtualization deployment service and the base design that the virtualization design service is customized from. This design has a collapsed edge/payload cluster. Replace as appropriate to your end design if performing the virtualization design service:

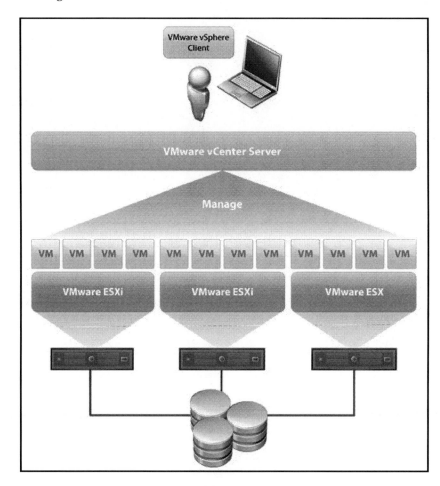

Virtualization deploy service conceptual design

This diagram depicts a vSAN Deploy Service with a single cluster. Replace as appropriate for the end design. You cam remove this if you're not doing a vSAN Deploy Service:

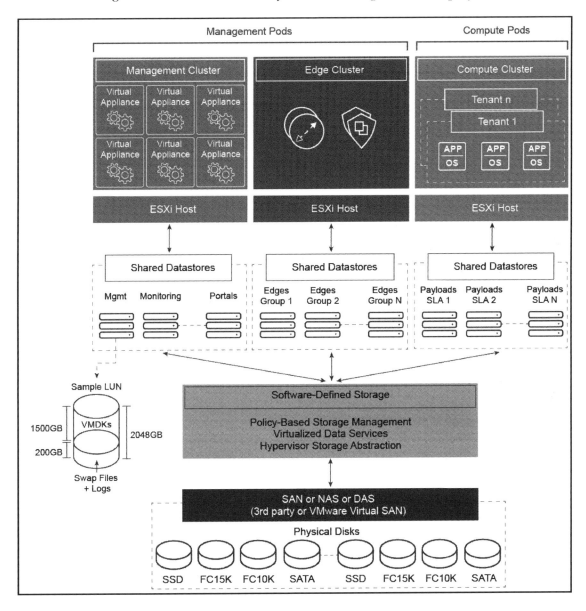

VSAN deploy service conceptual design

Logical design

This section describes the logical design for the engagement. The logical design is meant to show more granular detail about how the solution is being configured.

Virtualization logical design

The following diagram shows the logical design of the virtualization infrastructure.

This depicts the default design for a virtualization deploy service and the base design that the virtualization design service has customized. This design has a collapsed edge/payload cluster. Replace as appropriate for the end design if performing the virtualization design service:

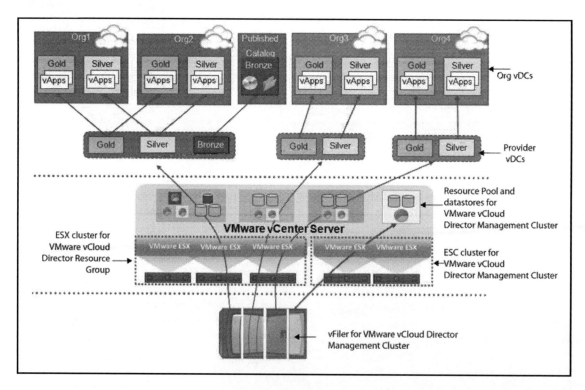

Virtualization deploy service logical design

This diagram depicts a vSAN Deploy Service with a single cluster. Replace as appropriate for the end design.

Remove if not doing a vSAN Deploy Service.

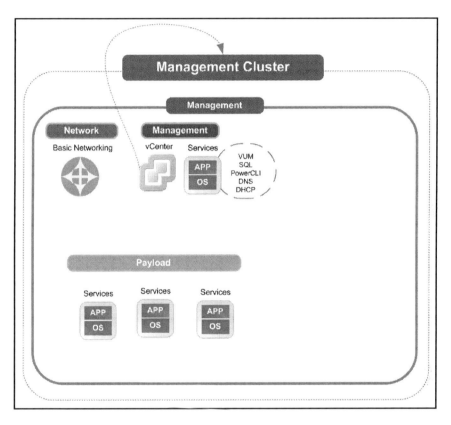

Storage virtualization: vSAN Deploy Service logical design

This chapter details the recommended implementation of the infrastructure service architecture and is based on VMware best practices with customer-specific requirements and business goals discussed during the assessment phase. This chapter provides logical and physical design considerations, which encompass all VMware vRealize Automation-related infrastructure components, including requirements and specifications for distributed deployment and scaling considerations. The design can be duplicated across sites and locations with minimum modification. You can use this chapter to implement the solution using different hardware vendors, assuming that requirements do not change.

A customer wants to provide faster and more streamlined end-to-end lifecycle management, self-servicing, just-in-time provisioning of virtual machines, and automated delivery of services to its end users' business units.

Customers also want to empower their operations teams to extend the out-of-the-box capabilities to meet their current and future needs, while being sufficiently flexible to meet the requirements of business functions to provide rapid time to market response and agile scalability options.

It outlines the conceptual, logical, and physical design considerations for vRealize Automation core functionality, distributed execution, and integration components.

The following infrastructure elements are included in this design document:

- VMware vRealize Orchestrator (embedded in the vRealize Automation appliance):
    - Workflow interacts with customer's active directory during virtual machine provisioning, to add virtual machines to organization units
- The vRealize Automation self-service portal
- Approval workflows
- Automated IaaS provisioning with service catalog and single virtual machine blueprints
- Role-based access control
- NSX integration

Cloud tenant design

A tenant is an organizational unit which is part of vRealize Automation design and can represent a business unit within a company who consumes cloud services from a service provider. Each tenant has its own unique configuration while little system-level configuration is uniform across tenants.

Comparison of single tenant and multi-tenant deployments

vRealize Automation supports both models, either a single tenant or multiple tenants. The configuration changes depending on the number of tenants.

We can configure system-wide configuration such as branding and notifications on default tenants and can attach to one or more tenants. Infrastructure configuration can be configured in any tenant and is uniform among all tenants. The infrastructure resources, such as cloud, virtual compute resources, or physical machines, can be shared into fabric groups managed by fabric administrators, and the resources in each fabric group can be attached to business groups within each tenant by using reservations.

Single tenant deployment

All configurations can apply to the default tenant in a single machine design setup. Tenant administrators are responsible for managing users and groups, and configuring tenant-specific branding, notifications, business policies, and catalog offerings. All users log in to the same portal at the same URL with the functionalities given to them, defined by their roles:

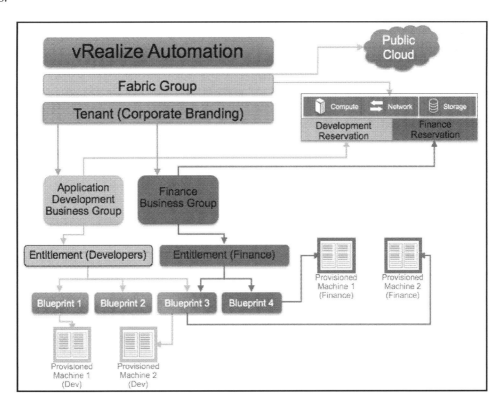

vRealize Automation default (single) tenant

Multitenant deployment

The administrator used to create new tenants for each organization using the same vRealize Automation instance. Tenant users log in to the portal console at a URL specific to their tenant. Tenant-level configuration is differentiated from other tenants and the default tenant while users with super user roles can see and manage rules across multiple tenants.

The following table briefs you on the various options for designing a multi-tenant deployment:

Characteristic	Description
Manage only in the default tenant infrastructure configuration	All infrastructures are managed by IaaS and fabric administrators from a single console in the default tenant. The shared infrastructure resources are aligned to the users in each tenant by using reservations.
Manage each tenant for infrastructure configuration	Each tenant is responsible for its own infrastructure and has its own IaaS administrators and fabric administrators. Each tenant can use its own infrastructure sources or share a common infrastructure. Fabric administrators only manage reservations for the tenant users.

The following diagram shows a multi-tenant deployment with a centrally-managed infrastructure. The IaaS administrator in the default tenant is responsible for all policy settings of all infrastructures available for all tenants:

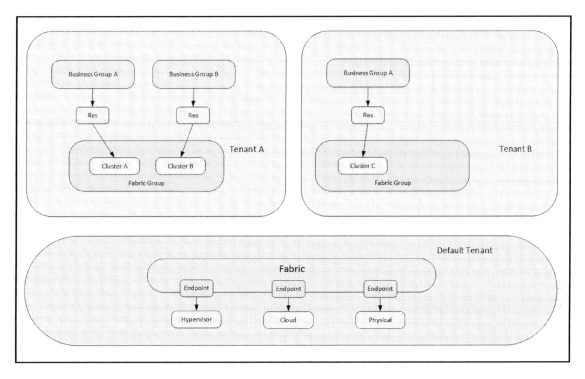

Multi-tenant example with infrastructure configuration only in the default tenant

The IaaS administrator can segment the infrastructure into fabric groups depending on their type and purpose for use.

A fabric group may have all virtual resources or all tier 1 resources. The fabric administrator of each group can assign resources from their fabric groups while the fabric administrators exist only in the default tenant who can assign resources to business groups of any tenant.

The following figure shows a multi-tenant deployment where each tenant takes care of its own infrastructure. The system administrator is the only user who logs in to the default tenant to manage system-wide configuration and create new tenants:

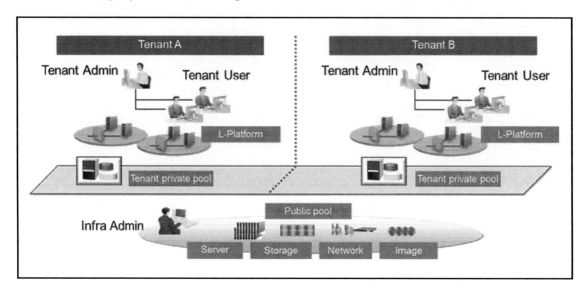

Multi-tenant example with infrastructure configuration in each tenant

Each tenant has an IaaS administrator who can create fabric groups and appoint fabric administrators with their respective tenants. Although fabric administrators can create reservations for business groups in any tenant, in this scenario, they typically create and manage reservations within their own tenants. If the same identity store is configured in multiple tenants, the same users can be designated as IaaS administrators or fabric administrators in each tenant.

Cloud automation IaaS design

The following figure shows the conceptual design of the vRealize Automation groups and vSphere resources:

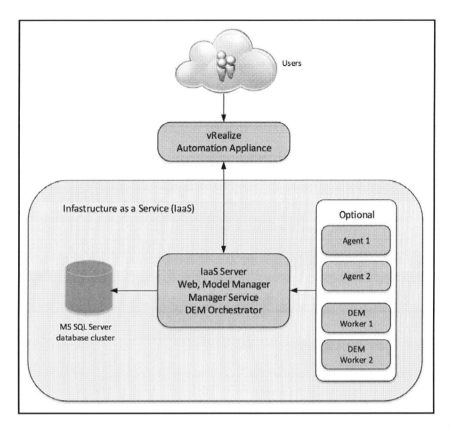

vRealize Automation conceptual design

The following table lists the key constructs of vRealize Automation integrated with the vSphere infrastructure.

The VMware vSphere's main components are as follows:

Components	Details
vSphere (vCenter) endpoint	Provides the information required by vRealize Automation IaaS to access vSphere compute resources. It requires the appropriate permissions for the vSphere proxy agent to manage the VMware vCenter Server instance.

Compute resource	A virtual object within the vRealize Automation representing a vSphere cluster or resource pool and datastores or datastore clusters. The virtual machines requested by business group members are provisioned on the compute resource.
Fabric groups	vRealize Automation IaaS organizes the compute resources into fabric groups.
Fabric administrators	Compute resources that are organized into fabric groups are managed by fabric administrators.
Compute reservation	A share of compute (vSphere cluster, resource pool, datastores, or datastore clusters) resources, such as CPU and memory reserved for use by a particular business group for provisioning virtual machines.
Storage reservation	Similar to compute reservations, pertaining only to a share of the available storage resources.
Business groups	A collection of machine consumers usually corresponding to an organization's business units or departments. Only users configured in the business group can request virtual machines.
Reservation policy	Used by vRealize Automation IaaS to determine the virtual reservation from which a particular virtual machine is provisioned. Each virtual reservation can be added to one reservation policy.
Blueprint	The complete specification for a virtual machine, determining the machine attributes, the manner in which it is provisioned, and its policy and management settings. The blueprint allows the users of a business group to create virtual machines on a virtual reservation (compute resource) based on the reservation policy and used platform and cloning types. It also allows specifying or adding machine resources.

vSphere infrastructure

The following figure shows the logical design constructs discussed in the previous section as they would apply to a deployment of vRealize Automation integrated with vSphere:

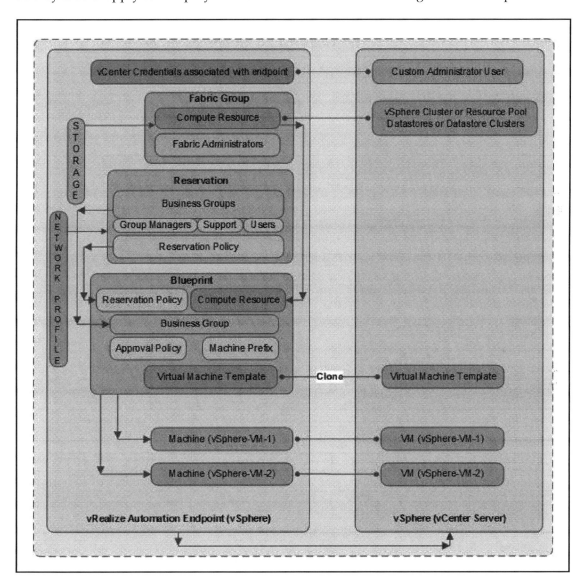

vRealize Automation integration with vSphere endpoint

Infrastructure source endpoints

An infrastructure source endpoint is a connection to the infrastructure that can provide a set (or multiple sets) of resources, which can then be made available for consumption by end users. vRealize Automation IaaS regularly collects information about known endpoint resources and the virtual resources provisioned therein. Endpoint resources are also referred to as compute resources in many contexts and the terms are often used interchangeably. The method in which data is collected is through the proxy agents that manage and communicate with these endpoint resources.

The compute resources and agent managers can be defined in an endpoint during the installation of the vRealize Automation IaaS components or, the agent can be configured for the compute resources on an individual basis after installation.

The endpoint decisions are as follows:

Design decision	Design justification	Design implication
Two vSphere endpoints will be created for all communication between vRealize Automation and the vSphere platform. The endpoints will use domain-based service account credentials for communication.	Two physical data center locations	To access the required vSphere resources, the credentials will need appropriate permissions for the vSphere Proxy Agent to manage the vSphere instance
One endpoint will be created specifically for the IPAM integration with Infoblox.	Allow vRA to assign an IP address provided by IPAM	Nil

This chapter details the recommended implementation of monitoring with performance and capacity management architecture and is based on VMware best practices, customer-specific requirements, and business goals discussed during the assessment phase. It includes logical and physical design considerations for performance and capacity management-related infrastructure components, including requirements, specifications, management, and their relationships. The design has been laid out so that it can be replicated across sites with minimum modification.

The following is an overview of the cloud implementation:

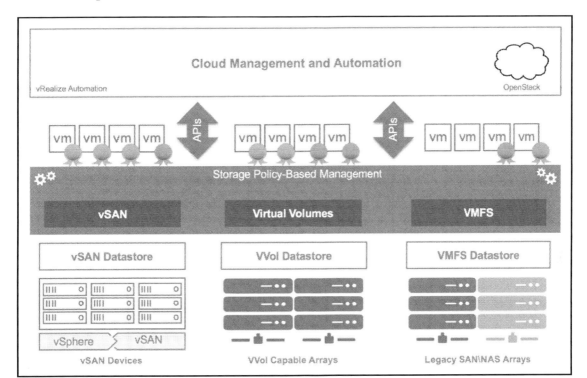

A customer will use vRealize Operations Manager to provide predictive performance analysis, capacity demand planning, and automated log management within the SDDC infrastructure. This is achieved through the use of the following VMware products:

- vRealize Operations Manager
- vRealize Infrastructure Navigator
- vRealize Hyperic server
- vRealize Log Insight

vRealize Operations Manager provides patented analysis of infrastructure components within the SDDC infrastructure. Static and dynamic analytic-driven and customer-defined alerts are provided. Predefined dashboards are presented for the VMware vSphere environment. Custom dashboards can be created to customize the display of analytic data. Adapters are available to allow vRealize Operations Manager to consume data from non-native data sources.

vRealize Infrastructure Navigator is used to discover application services, visualize relationships, and map dependencies of applications on virtualized compute, storage, and network resources. This relationship data is used by vSphere and vRealize Operations Manager to aid in the creation and display of *n*-tier applications and primary network services within the virtual environment.

vRealize Hyperic is used to monitor operating systems, middleware, and applications running in physical, virtual, and cloud environments. Collected infrastructure and application data is consumed by vRealize Operations Manager, extending the scope of performance and capacity monitoring insight available with vRealize Operations Manager.

 Although the instance of the vRealize Hyperic server installed in this core element is configured to monitor only standard infrastructure counters within the SDDC infrastructure, it is also available for application monitoring. The instance will require additional configuration and sizing modifications to accommodate application monitoring.

vRealize Log Insight is used to deliver automated log management through aggregation, analytics, and searches, enabling operational intelligence and enterprise-wide visibility in dynamic hybrid cloud environments.

The SDDC monitoring core element includes two main views (or dashboards) that are available - one within vRealize Operations Manager and one within vRealize Log Insight. Data from vRealize Infrastructure Navigator and vRealize Hyperic is consumed by vRealize Operations Manager.

vRealize Operations Manager

vRealize Operations Manager 6.0 is installed in the form of a **virtual appliance (vApp)** encapsulating a VMware virtual machine. Each instance of the vApp can be configured to perform one of the following roles within the complete vRealize Operations Manager instance/cluster. These building block roles are:

- **Master node**: Mandatory first node in the cluster, or single standalone node in smaller deployments
- **Master Replica node (optional)**: Used to provide high availability to the master node role
- **Data node**: Used for scalability
- **Remote collector node**: Used to overcome data collection issues, such as limited/poor network performance across the enterprise network

vRealize Operations Manager 6.0 is available in two different deployment models, and is deployed as either a preconfigured vApp or as a Windows or Linux installation package. To align with the VMware product roadmap, and for ease of deployment and long-term supportability, the customer deployment will employ the vApp model.

Application architecture overview

The following table shows the vRealize Operations Manager logical node architecture with functional descriptions of the architecture components:

Architecture component diagram	Description
  Master Node (Data Node 1) HTTP Service Collector Transaction Locator Transaction Service Analytics Common DBs Resource DB	**HTTP Service**: Main product **user interface** (**UI**). Supports the main product UI, admin UI, and Suite API. **Collector**: Process responsible for collecting inventory and metric data from the configured sources. **Transaction Locator**: Process responsible for coordinating activities between the master, master replica, and remote collector nodes. **Transaction Service**: Process responsible for caching, processing, and retrieving metrics for the analytics process. **Analytics**: The analytics process is responsible for processing all incoming data as well as generating SMTP and SNMP alerts on the master and master replica nodes. **Common DBs**: Collection of database processes that perform the following: • Store all collected metric data • Store user content, metric key mappings, and role privileges • Manage cluster administration data • Stores all resource, collector, adapter, collector group, and relationships • Stores all alerts and alarms data as well as root cause and object historical properties/versions **Resource DB**: Stores all resources, collectors, adapters, collector groups, and relationships

vRealize Operations Manager logical node architecture (master and master replica nodes)

The following figure shows the vRealize Operations Manager logical cluster architecture:

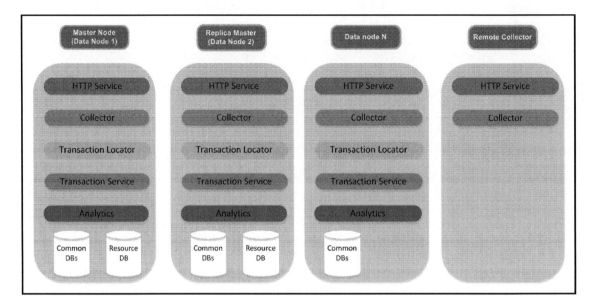

vRealize Operations Manager logical cluster architecture

vRealize Infrastructure Navigator

vRealize Infrastructure Navigator is installed on a vApp consisting of one virtual machine. The virtual machine contains a database and web server.

vRealize Infrastructure Navigator performs the following high-level functions:

- It maps virtual infrastructure resources, such as virtual machines, web servers, mail servers, database servers, application servers, cache servers, messaging servers, application management servers, and virtualization management servers.
- It displays relationships between virtual machines and external machines through services.

- It allows you to take advantage of integration with other VMware products, such as vCenter Server, VMware vCenter Site Recovery Manager, and vRealize Operations Manager.
- It allows you to define a multi-tier application pattern and then discover all instances of this pattern in the vCenter Server. You can then view these application instance maps.
- It allows you to create or define manual applications that in turn allow you to track a group of virtual machines.
- It allows you to create or define roles that you can use to find instances of the applications in your environment.

Application architecture overview

The logical application architecture for vRealize Infrastructure Navigator is described in the following table, showing interactions between vRealize Infrastructure Navigator components and external technologies.

The vRealize Infrastructure Navigator application components are as follows:

Component	Description
Server in vRealize Infrastructure Navigator virtual machine	The server component reconciles the data from Active Discovery and transfers the data to the database component.
Database in vRealize Infrastructure Navigator virtual machine	The database component stores the data received from the server component. The database component also stores vRealize Infrastructure Navigator configurations. vRealize Infrastructure Navigator does not support the storing of data in an external database.
vRealize Infrastructure Navigator plug-in in the VMware vSphere web client	The vRealize Infrastructure Navigator plugin in the vSphere web client provides a graphical user interface that you use to view and analyze dependencies.
Inventory service	The inventory service is a vSphere component to which vRealize Infrastructure Navigator exports its data.

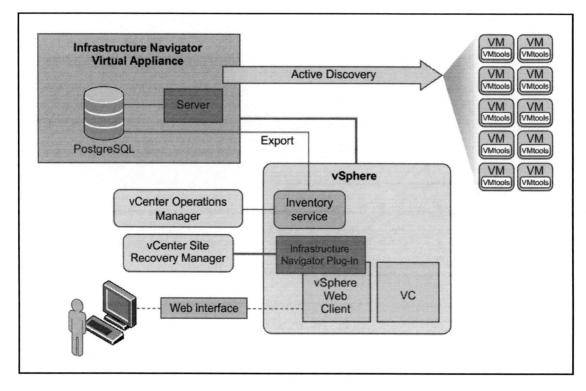

vRealize Infrastructure Navigator architecture

The vRealize Infrastructure's minimum requirements are as follows:

Component	Minimum requirement
CPU	2 vCPU
Memory	4 GB
Disk size	24 GB
Network	1 GBPS

Security

The security model of vRealize Infrastructure Navigator can be broken down into two areas—*Authentication* and *Communication*.

Authentication

You must log in to the vSphere web client as an administrator to use the services offered by vRealize Infrastructure Navigator.

An administrator is a user who is assigned the administrator role on the vCenter Server, or a user in a group that is assigned the administrator's role on the vCenter Server. A user or group must be assigned the administrator role on the vCenter root folder (vCenter Server top-level object) and all the child objects that propagate from the root folder.

Communication

The following table provides a list of ports that vRealize Infrastructure Navigator uses for communication:

vRealize Infrastructure Navigator communication ports	
Port number	**Description**
From your PC to vRealize Infrastructure Navigator (configure vRealize Infrastructure Navigator)	
5480	For appliance web console.
5489	To communicate with VMware vSphere Update Manager. This port is only used in the environment where vSphere Update Manager is installed.
22	To enable SSH access to the vRealize Infrastructure Navigator virtual appliance.
vCenter Server to vRealize Infrastructure Navigator	
2868	For plugin download. This download happens as part of the registration process.
6969	For connectivity from vSphere web client to vRealize Infrastructure Navigator.
vRealize Infrastructure Navigator to vCenter Server	
443	To access the vSphere web service API.
80	To access the vSphere web service API.
10109	To access vSphere Inventory Service.

vRealize Infrastructure Navigator to target hosts	
443	For VIX protocol on target hosts to perform discovery.
902	For VIX protocol on target hosts to perform discovery.

Licensing

If you deploy the vRealize Infrastructure Navigator virtual appliance on the vCenter Server, the virtual appliance is deployed without a license key. As a result, application discovery is disabled. You must enter a valid license key to start the application discovery process.

After you enter a valid license key, vRealize Infrastructure Navigator monitors the number of virtual machines it discovers with regard to the number of virtual machines allowed. You can acquire a license depending on the number of virtual machines and applications running in your environment.

The vRealize Infrastructure Navigator licensing design decision is as follows:

Design decision	Design justification	Design implication
The license used will be the vRealize Operations Manager Enterprise license.	Provided as part of the customer's enterprise license agreement.	None.

vRealize Hyperic

vRealize Hyperic is installed as a virtual application consisting of two virtual machines - vRealize Hyperic services/web server and the PostgreSQL database.

Application architecture overview

The following figure shows the logical and physical application architecture for vRealize Hyperic with interactions between the vRealize Hyperic components and external technologies:

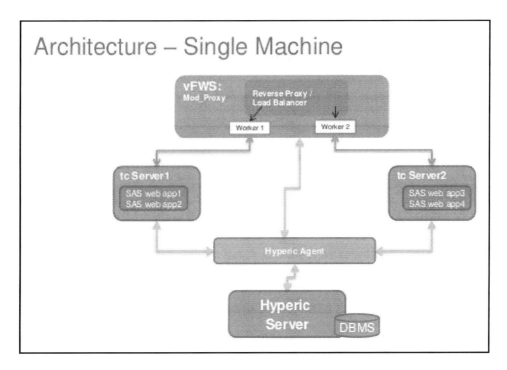

Hyperic architecture

Notice the following key components:

- **Server in vRealize Hyperic virtual machine**: Reconciles the data collected from the agents deployed on other systems, and transfers the data to the database component
- **Database in vRealize Hyperic virtual machine**: Stores the data received from the server component, and also stores vRealize Hyperic configurations

 vRealize Hyperic supports the use of external databases, but only with the standalone installation (non-virtual appliance), which is not included in this SDDC solution.

vRealize Log Insight

vRealize Log Insight delivers real-time log management and log analysis with machine learning-based intelligent grouping, high-performance searching, and troubleshooting across physical, virtual, and cloud environments.

vRealize Log Insight collects data from ESXi hosts using the syslog protocol. It can connect to vCenter Server to collect events, tasks, and alarms data, and can integrate with vRealize Operations Manager to send notification events and enable launch in context. It also functions as a collection and analysis point for any system capable of sending syslog data.

Application architecture overview

vRealize Log Insight is installed through the deployment of a virtual appliance and has the form factor configurations listed in the table after the following figure:

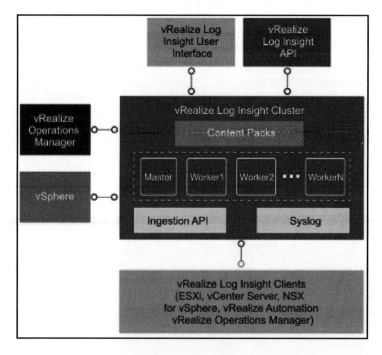

vRealize Log Insight architecture

The vRealize Log Insight form factor configuration is:

Form factor	CPUs	RAM	IOPS	GB/day	Msg/sec	Environment size
Extra small	2	2 GB	75 IOPS	3 GB/day	200	Up to 20 hosts
Small	4	8 GB	500 IOPS	15 GB/day	1,000	Up to 100 hosts
Medium	8	16 GB	1,000 IOPS	38 GB/day	2,500	Up to 250 hosts
Large	16	32 GB	1,500 IOPS	113 GB/day	7,500	Up to 750 hosts

Deployment architecture

vRealize Log Insight is typically deployed using one of the following deployment scenarios:

- **Directly to vRealize Log Insight over syslog**: Deploying directly to vRealize Log Insight is the most straightforward deployment for smaller implementations or proof of concept. In this configuration, restarting vRealize Log Insight causes older versions of ESXi to stop sending logs to the appliance. The source and host name fields in the incoming syslog messages point to the source of the log.
- **Using a syslog-ng/rsyslog relay**: Using a `syslog-ng/rsyslog` relay requires managing another syslog server. This option is more flexible because `syslog-ng` can split the logs into multiple destinations. For example, one log to syslog, and another to a local disk.

For larger installations, this option can be more scalable because you can have multiple levels of rollups. For example, one for each payload cluster or data center.

The vRealize Log Insight architecture design decision is as follows:

Design decision	Design justification	Design implication
For this design, a customer has to make the decisions listed in this table.		
vRealize Log Insight will be deployed so that systems will be configured to send their log data directly to the vRealize Log Insight server.	This approach simplifies the implementation and allows direct integration with the vSphere infrastructure and vRealize Operations Manager.	See the section *Scalability* for more information on scalability design considerations.

Scalability

By default, vRealize Log Insight is deployed using a single virtual machine with no clustering. To scale up, increase resources such as the amount of CPU, memory, or IOPS available to consume. IOPS is typically the limiting factor, depending on the number of queries.

If your installation is too big for a single instance, distribute data across multiple vRealize Log Insight instances, dividing data according to the following:

- Data center
- Role
- Tag, host, or IP address range

You can also use a `syslog-ng` or `rsyslog` system to split a single feed of data.

The vRealize Log Insight scalability design decision is as follows:

Design decision	Design justification	Design implication
For this design, a customer has to make the decisions listed in this table.		
An additional vRealize Log Insight appliance will be deployed as needed for scalability and is assigned based on groupings.	Provides the ability to scale with the underlying infrastructure.	None

Security and authentication

Authentication to vRealize Log Insight is maintained through the use of local account authentication or Active Directory authentication.

When assigning access control, use the types of roles described in the following table.

The vRealize Log Insight user roles are as follows:

Role	Description
Normal user	Access the full functionality of vRealize Log Insight to view log events, run queries to search and filter logs, import content packs into their own user space, add alert queries, and manage their own user accounts to change the password or email address. These users do not have access to the administration options, cannot share content with other users, cannot modify the accounts of other users, and cannot install a content pack as a content pack.
Admin	Access the full functionality of Log Insight, administer Log Insight, and manage the accounts of all other users.

The vRealize Log Insight authentication design decision is:

Design decision	Design justification	Design implication
Access control will be performed through the use of Active Directory authentication and assigned to users through the use of Active Directory group membership.	Using Active Directory group membership allows customers to easily administer the assignment and remove control through existing Active Directory policies and procedures.	None

Communication

vRealize Log Insight uses the firewall ports listed in the following table:

Source	Destination	Port	Protocol	Service description
Admin workstation	Log Insight appliance	22 (SSH)	TCP	Secure shell connectivity
Admin workstation	Log Insight appliance	80 (HTTP)	TCP	Web interface
Admin workstation	Log Insight appliance	443 (HTTPS)	TCP	Web interface
System sending logs	Log Insight appliance	514 (syslog)	UDP/TCP	Syslog data

System sending logs	Log Insight appliance	1514 (syslog)	TCP	Syslog data
Log Insight appliance web service	Log Insight appliance Tomcat service	9006-9007 (Tomcat)	TCP	Tomcat service
System sending logs	Log Insight appliance	9240 (vAPI)	TCP	Log Insight application programming interface
Log Insight appliance	System sending logs	111 (rpcbind)	UDP/ TCP	Service that converts RPC program numbers into universal addresses
Log Insight appliance	System sending logs	736 (rpcbind)	UDP	Service that converts RPC program numbers into universal addresses
Log Insight appliance	NTP server	123 (NTPD)	UDP	Provides NTP time synchronization
Log Insight appliance	Log Insight appliance	16520-16580 (loginsight)	TCP	Log Insight service
Log Insight appliance	Email server	25 (SMTP)	TCP	Email notifications
Log Insight appliance	Email server	465 (SMTP)	TCP	Email notifications
Log Insight appliance	Log Insight appliance	12543 (Postgre)	TCP	Database traffic

Integration with different cloud components

Integration is a process in which separately produced components or subsystems are combined and problems with their interactions are addressed.

VMware provides solution integrations through an ecosystem, which can be found at the *VMware Solution Exchange* website (https://solutionexchange.vmware.com/).

vSphere integration

vRealize Log Insight can be configured to pull data for tasks, events, and alarms that occur in one or more vCenter server instances. vRealize Log Insight uses the vSphere API to connect to vCenter Server systems and collect data.

You can also configure ESXi hosts to forward syslog data to vRealize Log Insight.

The support for vSphere products is as follows:

Type of integration	Supported product versions
Tasks, events, and alarms data collection	vCenter Server 5.1 and later
Syslog feeds	ESXi 4.1 and later

The vSphere Integration design decision is as follows:

Design decision	Design justification	Design implication
All vCenter Servers and ESXi hosts will be configured to send their tasks, events, and alarm data to the vCenter.	Enables the ability to centrally review logs.	None.

vRealize Operations Manager integration

vRealize Log Insight and vRealize Operations Manager can be integrated in either of the following ways:

- Log Insight can send notification events to vRealize Operations Manager
- The launch of the in-context menu of vRealize Operations Manager can display actions related to vRealize Log Insight

The vRealize Operations Manager integration design decision is as follows:

Design decision	Design dustification	Design implication
vRealize Log Insight will be integrated with vRealize Operations Manager.	Enables the ability to centrally review logs.	None.

VMware vRealize Business Manager

VMware SDDC services cost management expands the SDDC solution by providing cloud operations admin visibility into the financial aspects of their infrastructure and enables them to optimize and improve these operations.

This package is based on VMware vRealize Business Standard. This suite provides information about the cost of a virtual machine and utilization of shared resources to help better manage demand, budget, **capital expenditure (CapEx)**, and **operational expenditure (OpEx)**. This capability drives accountability over cloud resources to lower the **total cost of ownership (TCO)**, and optimizes costs and sourcing across internal virtual infrastructures and private and public clouds.

This section discusses the recommended implementation of VMware vRealize Business Standard and is based on VMware best practices, customer-specific requirements, and business goals. It provides both logical and physical design considerations that encompass all related configurations. These configurations include requirements and specifications for all the SDDC platform-related costs. The design can be replicated across sites and different hardware with minimum modification.

Conceptual design

The complete vRealize business suite provides the following key capabilities:

- **Business management for the cloud**: Drives accountability over cloud resources and helps optimize costs and sourcing across internal virtual infrastructures and private and public clouds.
- **IT Financial Management**: Enables the organization to manage and optimize the cost of delivery. IT financial management requires vRealize Business Advanced, which is not covered in this cost management module.

- **IT benchmarking**: Integration with IT financial management verifies that IT leadership has full visibility into their cost efficiencies compared with their peers and service competitors. IT benchmarking requires vRealize Business Enterprise, which is not covered in this cost management module.
- **Service quality management**: Confirms that IT is delivering the agreed upon service. Service quality management requires vRealize Business, which is not covered in this cost management module.

This cost management module focuses on vRealize Business, which covers business management for private/public cloud capabilities:

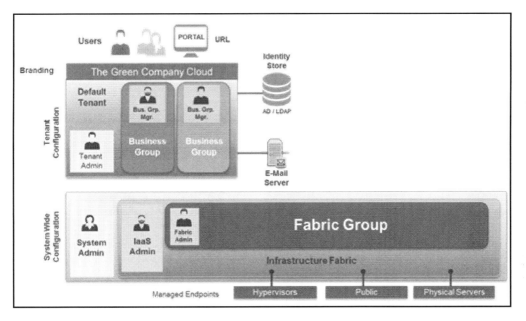

vRealize Business conceptual design

vRealize Business Standard architecture

vRealize Business Standard architecture is a web application built on a set of components and services: the server, FactsRepo inventory service, Data Transformation Service, data collection services, and Reference Database (Reference Library).

The following figure illustrates the main components of vRealize Business Standard:

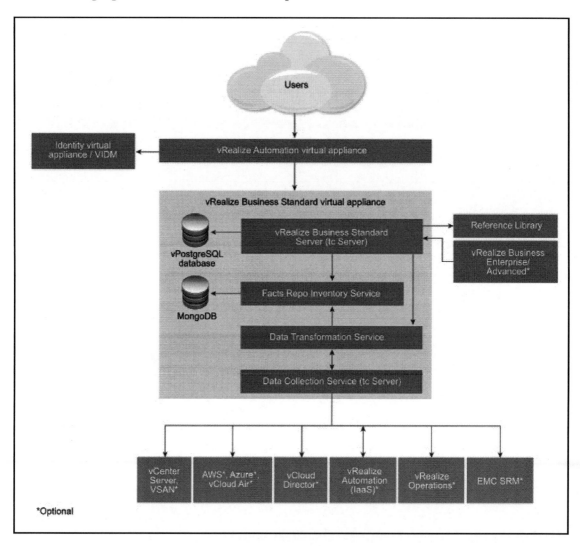

vRealize Business Standard architecture

Data collection service

Data collection services collect inventory information (servers, virtual machines, clusters, storage devices, and associations between them) and usage statistics (CPU and memory) from infrastructure endpoints such as VMware vCenter Server, VMware vCloud Director, and public clouds (**Amazon Web Services** (**AWS**), Microsoft Azure, and VMware vCloud Air). Data collection services include a set of independent services for collecting data from each endpoint. By default, data collection intervals are configured to suit target endpoints and are adjustable by way of a configuration file, as you can see from the following table:

Endpoints	Dataset	Interval
VMware vCenter	Inventory	10 minutes
	Tags	10 minutes
	VMware vRealize Operations Manager	30 minutes
	Storage	12 hours (720 minutes)
	Usage statistics	24 hours (1,440 Minutes)
vRealize Automation		60 Minutes
vCloud Director		120 Minutes
VMware vCloud Air		24 Hours
Amazon AWS		24 Hours

Data Transformation Service

The Data Transformation Service converts the source-specific data received from data collection services into the structures consumable by FactsRepo. The Data Transformation Service is a single point of aggregation of data from all data collectors.

FactsRepo inventory service

FactsRepo is an inventory service built on MongoDB to store the raw data received from the Data Transformation Service. vRealize Business Standard Server uses the FactsRepo data for the cost computation.

Server

vRealize Business Standard Server is a web application that runs on Pivotal tc Server. The server consists of business logics, financial configuration, cost calculation formulas, the cost model, and the components described in the following tables. vRealize business administrators can manipulate these components through the web UI and API interfaces, and can create reports. The server uses a VMware vFabric Postgres database as a persistent store to keep the computed cost data, reports, and configuration data.

The server components are as follows:

Component	Description
Expenses	Calculates cost for expenses such as server, storage, operating system, maintenance, labor, network, and facilities. The module has a user interface that lets you configure various cost calculation parameters.
Cost allocation	Calculates the cost of a virtual machine according to uptime and usage. You can also configure some allocation parameters.
Consumer allocation	Allocates costs according to tags of the virtual machine or according to a mapping provided by the user or mapping as defined in Realize Automation.
Cloud comparison	Calculates the expected cost of the existing inventory from Amazon and Azure.
Public cloud	Provides you with a summary of the infrastructure that is deployed with a public cloud provider (such as Amazon, Azure, or vCloud Air).
Reports	Generates reports with cost details for vCenter Server, vCloud Director, vRealize Automation, and the public cloud.
Reference database	Holds known configurations and default costs for each configuration, vendor, and geography.

Reference database

VMware hosts an external reference library portal that provides reference costs for most infrastructure components. The reference library includes industry wide pricing and utilization benchmark data. The reference library can be accessed on `https://vrb-hub.vmware.com` using port `443` and `SaasFTP.digitalfuel.com` on port `22`.

The vRealize Business Standard reference database component is responsible for providing default, out-of-the-box costs for each of the supported cost drivers. The reference database is a compressed and encrypted file that users can download. They can import the data into vRealize Business Standard manually or use automatic updates. If the auto update process fails to run on port `22` (FTP), the process starts on port `443` (HTTPS). The new values affect cost calculation. The reference data used depends on the currency you select during installation. Currency details are provided in this document in the following sections.

External interfaces

The following interfaces (APIs) are published to external applications:

Component	Description
vRealize Automation	Calls vRealize Business Standard to get the cost profiles.
vRealize Business Advanced and Enterprise	Can receive inventory information, which is used as a basis for cost model creation. A special HTTPS API is designated for vRealize Business Advanced and Enterprise.

The system collects data continually from the external sources and updates the tables hourly, daily, or monthly, as scheduled. The collected data can be viewed on the dashboard or can be used to generate reports. This update occurs daily. However, the update might trigger when there are changes in the user interface and when there are major changes in the inventory, such as initialization of the system or the addition of a new server connection or account.

When a job starts, it collects inventory, usage information, and user changes to cost formulas that were made before starting the job, and the most current defaults from the reference database. The job then invokes a series of calculation steps on the data, without interfering with the ongoing inventory or user changes. When the calculation is finished, the costs are updated.

vRealize Business Standard appliance role

vRealize Business Standard server appliances can be set up to function as a dedicated data collection server. You must select the enable data collector role during vRealize Business' initial setup and disable the server role. In a large distributed environment, data collector appliances are installed closer to the target endpoints as with a remote data center. The data collector retrieves raw data from endpoints and sends the data to a vRealize Business Standard server for cost calculations.

Supported product integrations

vRealize Business Standard integrates with various products and lets you use the information directly from the integration without having to manually enter the information.

VMware vSphere

vRealize Business Standard allows the addition of one or more vCenter Server machines to get the complete inventory list. The inventory list contains information related to virtual machines configuration, VMware ESXi host capacity, cluster capacity, storage policies, storage capacity, attributes, and tags.

VMware vCloud Director

vRealize Business Standard integration with vCloud Director lets you view the organizational constructs from vCloud Director. vRealize Business Standard supports organization, organization **virtual data center** (**VDC**), virtual machines, and vApp constructs.

VMware vRealize Business Advanced and Enterprise

vRealize Business Standard exposes APIs to let third-party systems extract data in a CSV format. The information includes object properties, along with costs and allocations for virtual machines, physical servers, data stores, and the public cloud. vRealize Business Advanced and Enterprise use these APIs to collect private and public cloud information for cost models and reports.

VMware vRealize Operations Manager

vRealize Business Standard can integrate with vRealize Operations Manager in two ways. For vRealize Operations Manager 5.x , vRealize Business Standard connects through a vRealize Business Standard internally. For vRealize Operations Manager 6.x, you log in to vRealize Operations Manager by using the credentials.

In an environment where vRealize Operations Manager 5.x is installed, vRealize Business Standard gets the expected CPU and memory utilization for each ESXi host from vRealize Operations Manager. For vRealize Operations Manager 6.x, you can set the expected CPU and memory utilization for the host by using the system defined value (computed using historical averages), by defining a global value, or by defining a value at each cluster level. This value is used for calculating the virtual machine cost allocation.

VMware vRealize Automation

vRealize Business Standard is closely integrated with vRealize Automation. vRealize Business Standard appears in the **Business Management** tab in the vRealize Automation user interface. vRealize Business Standard uses vRealize Automation services such as single sign-on authentication and authorization. vRealize Automation provides cost profiles to compute daily virtual machine costs and reports. The IaaS component of vRealize Automation consumes the base rate APIs of vRealize Business Standard to compute blueprint prices of virtual machines. vRealize Business Standard data is integrated with the IaaS component of vRealize Automation. You can define rules and categorize according to the vRealize Automation hierarchy. For more information, see the Consumption Analysis description in the *vRealize Business Standard User's Guide*
(https://www.vmware.com/support/pubs/vrealize-business-standard-pubs.html).

Integrating vRealize Business with public clouds

vRealize Business Standard can integrate with public cloud platforms such as AWS, vCloud Air, and Microsoft Azure, which enable your organization to dynamically scale its IT infrastructure. vRealize Business Standard provides its users an overview of how their investments are spread across the public cloud.

Solution logical design

The following diagram shows the logical design of a customer's vRealize business solution:

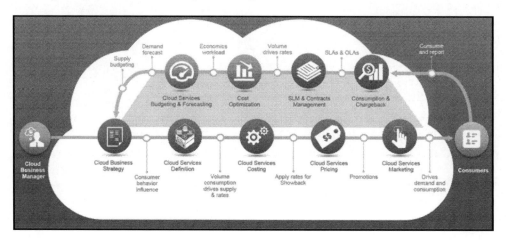

vRealize business solution logical design

The design has a single vRealize Business appliance that serves all roles (server, FactsRepo inventory services, Data Transformation Services, data collector service), and includes an external reference database. The vRealize Business Standard appliance is integrated with the standalone or IaaS instance of vRealize Automation. The user interface is provided by the vRealize Automation appliance (CAFE), and user authentication/authorization is provided by the VMware Identity Manager or VMware Identity virtual appliance.

vRealize Business Standard is configured with the following endpoint products to deliver cost management, analysis, and comparison functions:

The private cloud:

- VMware vCenter Server
- VMware vCenter Server with VMware vSAN
- VMware vRealize Automation
- VMware vRealize Operations
- VMware vCloud Director

Public cloud:

- VMware vCloud Air
- Amazon AWS

This monitoring integration architecture design provides a blueprint for describing the integration and interoperability of specific solutions for a customer's environment as a part of a monitoring implementation.

This chapter details the recommended architecture for interoperability and integration between other VMware or third-party solutions based on VMware best practices and customer-specific requirements and business goals discussed during the assessment phase. It provides both consumer and provider interface details on what service components are required. The specific configuration of these components can be found in the accompanying monitoring configuration workbook.

Service orientation principle

Architecture principles define the underlying general rules and guidelines for the use and deployment of all IT resources and assets across the enterprise. They reflect a level of consensus among the various elements of the enterprise, and form the basis for making future architecture decisions.

The architecture principle definitions are as follows:

Principle	Service orientation
Statement	The architecture is based on a design of services, which mirror real-world business activities comprising the enterprise (or inter-enterprise) business processes.
Rationale	Service orientation delivers enterprise agility and a boundary-free information flow.
Implications	Service representation uses business descriptions to provide context (that is, business process, goal, rule, policy, service interface, and service components) and implements services using service orchestration. Service orientation places unique requirements on the infrastructure, and implementations should use open standards to realize interoperability and location transparency. Implementations are environment-specific. They are constrained or enabled by context and must be described within that context. Strong governance of service representation and implementation is required.

The following are terms used to define the type of interactions between products and components within the monitoring solution area.

Interoperability

Interoperability is the ability of a system or a product to work with other systems or products without special effort.

VMware provides product interoperability matrices. See *VMware Product Interoperability Matrixes* (`http://partnerweb.vmware.com/comp_guide2/sim/interop_matrix.php`).

The following section outlines interoperability between the VMware products within the monitoring solution area.

VMware vRealize Operations Manager

VMware vRealize Operations Manager does not have any native interoperability with other VMware products. All interactions with other VMware products require product-specific management packs. These management packs allow vRealize Operations Manager to integrate with other VMware products.

Business scenario

Insert the customer-specific business scenario that triggered the requirements for the interoperability.

The following headings can be deleted because vRealize Operations Manager is integrated through management packs instead of interoperability. The headings are for your use as needed.

Interoperability requirements

Using the definitions within this chapter, all vRealize Operations Manager management packs are *integration* points, not points of interoperability. Modify this section if documenting specific interoperability. Otherwise, you can delete this section.

Consultant: Insert the environment requirements and architecture impacts, if any.

Relevant contents could include:

- Firewall rules
- Specific configuration in place
- Specific objects to be created and consumed

Integration with vRealize Operations Manager

Integration is a process in which separately produced components or subsystems are combined and problems in their interactions are addressed.

This section describes the interfaces provided by products within the monitoring solution area that interact with external systems including the consumer and provider interfaces and the business process behind the scenarios that the customer wants to address.

VMware and the customer have agreed to extend the out-of-the-box functionality of vRealize Operations Manager by configuring the following VMware products as data sources within the vRealize Operations Manager environment. These data sources are enabled through VMware management packs and additional out-of-the-box dashboards:

- VMware NSX
- VMware vRealize Automation
- Select storage devices
- Supported storage devices are listed in the VMware Solution Exchange (`https://solutionexchange.vmware.com/store/products/management-pack-for-storage-devices`)

The following figure is a summary graph that shows the reference architecture:

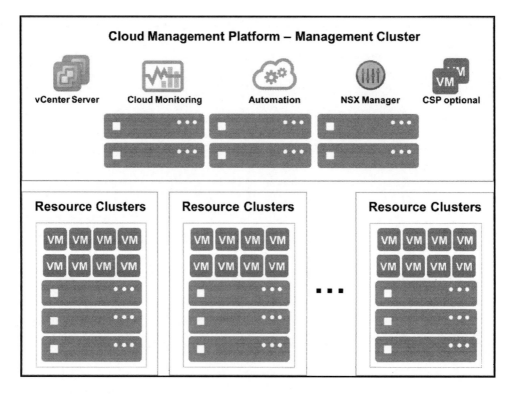

Consumers and providers architecture

Integration between vRealize Operations Manager and vRealize Automation

VMware and customers have agreed to extend the out-of-the-box functionality of vRealize Operations Manager by installing the following VMware products as data sources within vRealize Operations Manager.

The customer is implementing vRealize Operations Manager as part of their monitoring management solution. The monitoring management solution will be integrated with one or more instances of the VMware cloud automation product, vRealize Automation.

Business objective

Customers get extensive visibility into the performance, health, and risk capacity of the tenant's business groups with this management and monitoring tool supported by the underlying cloud infrastructure. The cloud dashboard (self service provisioning portal) suggests action points for the problem alerts at every layer of the entire infrastructure. A vRealize Operations Manager customized dashboard helps administrators to get granular visibility into each layer of the Cloud.

Cloud administrators get the growth trends of resource usage across tenant business groups by using an Operations dashboard and take corrective actions. It helps them in further capacity planning and to identify under-utilized and over-utilized workloads to avoid capacity risk. It also predicts capacity shortfall by creating what-if capacity scenarios based on customer requirements.

It minimizes the time to troubleshoot a tenant's workload, correlating with infrastructure issues by facilitating line-of-sight visibility into performance, health, and capacity risk issues for business groups in any cloud layer.

vRealize Operations Manager integration with vRealize Automation enables the following:

- Customized dashboards developed for vRealize Automation to provide a quick overview of vRealize tenants, business groups, reservations, and reservation policies supported by cloud stack.
- Correlation between vRealize Automation cloud objects (tenants, business groups, reservations, reservation policies, and so on) and virtualization objects (VMs, clusters, data stores, and so on) with extensive visibility.
- Management packs built on vRealize Operations analytics leveraging capacity and performance analytics coupled with smart alerts to provide population alerts and instructions to simplify a cloud infrastructure's day-to-day operations.

Insert the customer-specific business use cases that triggered the requirements for the integration.

Integration requirements

The following sections list the minimum requirements for the integration of vRealize Operations Manager with vRealize Automation using the management pack for vRealize Automation.

Additional information is available from the VMware Solution Exchange site (`https://solutionexchange.vmware.com/store/products/management-pack-for-vrealize-automation`). Refer to the release notes and user guide for more information.

Insert the environment requirements and architecture impacts, if any.

Credentials

Each instance of the management pack must be configured with a target user account with privileges to read data from the target system. For the VMware vRealize Automation management pack, this means a vRealize Automation user account able to read vRealize Automation objects.

Firewall rules

The following information summarizes the network exchange flows required for proper interaction of the management pack for vRealize Automation.

The following are the vRealize Automation management pack port requirements:

Port	Number	Protocol	Source	Target	Description
vRealize Automation API port	443	TCP	vRealize Operations Manager virtual appliance (all nodes within a cluster)	vRealize Automation appliance	General API port
vRealize Automation API port	443	TCP	vRealize Operations Manager virtual appliance (all nodes within a cluster)	vRealize Automation IAAS machine	General API port

VMware vCenter Single sign-on server	443	TCP	vRealize Operations Manager virtual appliance (all nodes within a cluster)	vCenter Single sign-on server	Single sign-on service over HTTPS

Specific configuration with specific objects to be created and consumed

Integration between vRealize Operations Manager and vRealize Automation using the management pack is compatible with the following product versions:

These requirements depend on the management pack used for integration. Consult the readme file and user guide for the latest version and requirements information (`https://solutionexchange.vmware.com/store/products/management-pack-for-vrealize-automation`):

- vRealize Operations Manager 6.0 or later
- VMware vCloud Automation Center 6.1 or later
- vRealize Automation 6.2 or later
- At least one configured and functioning instance of the VMware vCenter adapter within vRealize Operations Manager for each VMware NSX management pack instance is required

Installation of the vRealize Automation management pack will provide additional dashboards to aid with the monitoring of one or more vRealize Automation instances. These additional dashboards are:

- vRealize Automation Cloud Infrastructure Monitoring
- vRealize Automation Top-N
- vRealize Automation Tenant Overview

The management pack allows visibility into various vRealize Automation parameters. All of the available objects are documented in the user guide of the management pack (`https://solutionexchange.vmware.com/store/products/management-pack-for-vrealize-automation`):

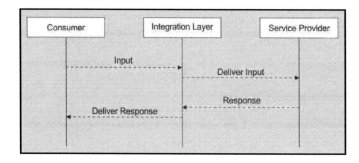

Component relationships for vRealize Automation

Application release automation with Zero Touch Deployment

Success rewards enterprises who adopt digital solutions and automation to accelerate innovation. Recognizing the opportunity to increase IT agility and be a better partner to lines of business, the customer has begun a transformation to DevOps-Ready IT that will improve the way the team updates existing applications and releases new internal and external services. While representing a change in IT culture, DevOps acts as a bridge between operations and development teams.

DevOps enables automation to fasten IT service delivery and help in the standardization of systems and processes required to build, test, and run new software applications. DevOps removes the silos between different teams in the software development lifecycle. DevOps enhance the deployment of code on demand with less failures, which speeds time to market for new and updated software applications with more features.

Once an IT team starts building a cloud infra based on the SDDC that automates application provisioning, then they are good to go with DevOps.

You can deliver a complete application stack that is fully integrated and tested, application platforms for development and testing, and with engineers supporting a developer's choice of **application programming interface (API)** and **graphical user interface (GUI)**. The automated solution gives instant and impressive results:

- Reduced provisioning time from a week to hours
- Enhanced developer productivity
- Stable consistency of provisioned instances
- Minimized annual infrastructure (CapEx) and OpEx costs

Customers use vRealize Suite as part of the automation process to manage the delivery of dev/test application platforms across a hybrid cloud environment as intelligent operations improve computing performance and availability, precise consolidation ratios, and optimized resources. They can reuse existing test automation scripts and integrate third-party components by utilizing unified views. Customers become more agile by automating the end-to-end process. The team improves the efficiency of data center resources and better developer productivity while minimizing project risk.

Customers define application releases with application quality on committed time and a customer will realize the importance of release automation to improve its DevOps practices and application release delivery. A customer can advance the innovation journey by adding continuous delivery capabilities to get increased consistency across the software development lifecycle, which will further accelerate application delivery and improve code when meeting deadlines. Businesses expect development and deployment tasks to be completed within **service-level agreements (SLAs)** and with operations agreed, but without consistency in software configuration, processes, and testing across all teams involved in the software development lifecycle, new releases continue to take a long time to reach production-level quality. Customers need to ensure standard configurations as the software progresses from development, testing, staging, and into production. Customers also have to automate testing at each phase and give better status tracking till delivery. Operations and development engineers find it hard to collaborate throughout the service lifecycle from design and development processes to production support.

Summary

The VMware Cloud assess, design, and deploy service delivers a SDDC that expands the power of virtualization and automation to data center services. This service provides integrated SDDC infrastructure for the enterprise that includes VMware best practices in a practical and scalable design that is holistic, cohesive, and modular. This chapter summarized the following:

- **Cloud infrastructure**: This module provides a foundational approach to building a software-defined data center architecture delivered in a single physical data center. It consists of compute, storage, and network virtualization capabilities and provides a design that considers scalability and availability of management components, utilizing the underlying virtualization platform.
- **Cloud operations**: This module provides comprehensive monitoring for the software-defined data center. The foundational monitoring platform delivers performance and capacity management dashboards for management components.
- **Cloud automation**: This module expands the software-defined data center with Cloud computing capabilities. It provides enterprise-ready architecture for the delivery of IaaS and provides a self-service portal for consumers to request and manage IaaS services.
- **Cloud business management**: This module provides infrastructure cost visibility to the provided services using VMware vRealize Business for Cloud.

In the next chapter we will learn about the network and security component of the cloud model and how network virtualization makes it possible to programmatically create, provision, and manage networks with software, using the underlying physical network as a simple packet-forwarding backplane. We will also learn about the basics of network virtualization and highlight the benefits of this new approach.

8
Transforming Your Network Architecture

This chapter is focused on the network and security components of a cloud model. Network virtualization makes it possible to programmatically create, provision, and manage networks in a software-defined way, using the underlying physical network as a simple packet-forwarding backplane. Network and security services in a software stage are distributed to hypervisors and *attached* to individual **virtual machines (VMs)** in accordance with networking and security policies defined for each connected application. In this chapter, we are going to cover how to migrate from legacy network architectures to a new network virtualization technique, network virtualization versus software-defined networking, and securing the data center by limiting lateral movement within the data center:

- Network virtualization and highlighting the benefits of this new approach
- Outlining key characteristics/key functionality of a virtualized network
- Introducing the technologies for network virtualization
- Enhancing data center security and automating IT processes
- Securing the data center by limiting lateral movement within the data center

Specific terminology described in the following table is used to refer to different components of the VMware Network Virtualization services in this chapter. This chapter is providing directions on micro-segmentation and related NSX components.

The VMware Network Virtualization service terminology is as follows:

Term	Description
VMware NSX Manager	NSX Manager is the centralized network management component of VMware NSX, which is installed as a virtual appliance on any VMware ESXi host in your VMware vCenter server environment. It provides an aggregated system view, a single point of configuration, and REST API entry points.
Distributed firewall	The NSX for vSphere distributed firewall is a hypervisor kernel-embedded firewall at the virtual NIC level that provides visibility and control for virtualized workloads and networks.
VMware NSX Virtual Switch	NSX Virtual Switch is the software that operates in server hypervisors to create a software abstraction layer between servers and the physical network.
VMware NSX Controller	NSX Controller is an advanced distributed state management system that controls virtual networks, and overlays transport tunnels.
VMware NSX Edge	NSX Edge provides network edge security and gateway services to isolate a virtualized network. NSX Edge offers a perimeter firewall, load-balancing, and other services, such as SSL VPN and DHCP Relay.
Distributed logical router	NSX for vSphere distributed logical router provides an optimal data path for routing traffic within the virtual infrastructure. It routes east-west traffic in a distributed fashion to provide better throughput and performance.
VXLAN	Virtual eXtensible LAN uses a VLAN-like encapsulation technique to encapsulate MAC-based OSI Layer 2 Ethernet frames within Layer 4 UDP packets. This is used in virtual networking to increase the scalability of the platform.

Assumptions, risks, constraints, and use cases

During initial design workshops, baseline requirements were defined and recorded in the solution requirements document. The overall structure of this document is to describe various aspects of the solution designed to meet customer requirements. Throughout this document, key points of particular importance are highlighted and identified with one of the following icons.

The interpreting information about design requirements and decisions is as follows:

Icon	Label	Definition
	Design Decision	Identifies a design decision that has been made
	Constraint	Identifies constraints that have influenced design choices
	Assumption	Identifies where an assumption has been made in the absence of factual data
	Design Consideration	Identifies an area that requires further discussion with architecture and operations teams
	Instruction	Used to convey special information or instructions
	Risk	Identifies any risks with the solution design or deployment

Design guidelines

The following guidelines were followed during the creation of this distributed firewall design:

- The solution design must meet the diverse requirements of the organization. These requirements include network zones design, existing physical and virtual platforms, applications, services, operating procedures, cloud management platform integration, and performance, as comprehensively described in the solution requirement document.
- The solution design should contribute to reducing operational effort by lowering the number of firewall rules to manage.
- The solution design should dramatically improve (or at least not hinder) performance. Improving or maintaining performance is achieved by providing inline rate rule processing, which reduces contention and latency by providing linear scalability.
- The solution design should grant availability. Availability is typically achieved by providing hypervisor redundancy.
- The solution design should provide an acceptable level of security. Security can be achieved through controlled access (where required), and isolation (where necessary).
- The solution design should enhance the functionality of the infrastructure.
- The solution design should facilitate the adoption of the VXLAN network virtualization solution based on Vmware NSX.
- The network should be designed to support vSphere features such as VMware vSphere vMotion®, VMware vSphere High Availability, and VMware vSphere Fault Tolerance.

Networking and distributed firewalling best practices

The following VMware networking best practices were considered during the creation of this design:

- Create rulesets, placing application-specific rules before general services rules.
- Define the last rule in the last DFW section as a catch-all rule, with a block action for traffic not processed by the proceeding set of rules.

- Leverage NSX service composer's security policies for general rules.
- Leverage NSX security groups with dynamic membership for automatic rules generation and integration with existing CMP automation tasks.
- Group scope-related rules in sections within the DFW to streamline operations.
- Reduce firewall rules creation across the organization, by processing rules on DFW for traffic involving external NSX trusted zones.
- Increase performance by reducing the rule table's size on ESXi hosts, limiting DFW rules to specific clusters rather than all clusters.
- Network adapters from a standard or vSphere Distributed Switch can be added or removed without affecting the virtual machines or the network service that is running behind that switch. If all the running hardware is removed, the virtual machines can still communicate among themselves within the same ESXi host. If one network adapter is left intact, all the virtual machines can still connect with the physical network.
- For best performance, use VMXNET3 virtual NICs.
- For future VXLAN adoption, identify and configure network ports with 1600 MTU.
- When creating a distributed port group, do not use dynamic binding.

Network virtualization

Management of networks is one of the most time-consuming tasks in the process of provisioning workloads. Physical infrastructure takes more time for the provisioning of networks as well as verifying that the network changes will not affect other devices using the same networking infrastructure.

You can define the policy for the provisioning of physical networks to allow instant creation of virtual networks and rapid attachment of virtual machines to the virtual network. If the host has required a virtual network, then the virtual machine will work properly; otherwise, you must find a host with the available network, and provide the capacity to run your virtual machine. We need policy-based pre-configured networks for cloud deployments where speed, agility, and flexibility are critical requirements.

We can only get rid of these bottlenecks by decoupling virtual networks from their respective physical setup. For this, we need the capability of programmatically recreating all physical networking attributes, needed by virtual machines, in the cloud environment. Network virtualization helps in instant network provisioning with the creation of virtual networks without any change in the physical network infrastructure:

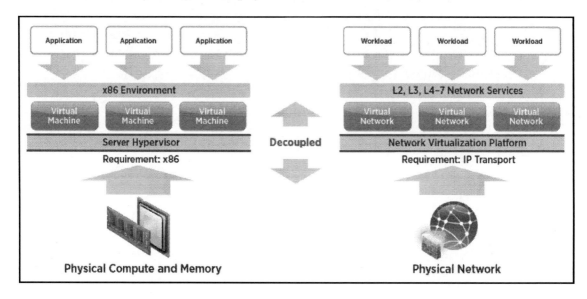

Network virtualization architecture overview

As a major feature of network virtualization, distributing firewalls brings the benefits of decoupling virtual network functions from the physical infrastructure, providing a critical capability for managing highly automated enterprise cloud environments, and thanks to its provisioning model, providing an extremely flexible mechanism to scale according to the organization's volume.

NSX for vSphere components

The following sections describe the components in detail, and how they are relevant in network virtualization design. It is important to remember that the solution will provide distributed firewall capabilities only. A full featured adoption of the NSX platform will be the subject of evaluation and adoption by the customer in the future, and so a brief description of the solution's components is being provided in this chapter.

NSX for vSphere platform

NSX for vSphere creates a network virtualization layer on top of which all virtual networks are created. This layer is an abstraction between the physical and virtual networks. The components required to create this network virtualization layer are as follows:

- vCenter Server
- NSX Manager
- NSX Controller
- NSX Virtual Switch
- NSX for vSphere API

These components are separated into the following planes to create communication boundaries and provide isolation for workload data from system control messages:

- Data plane
- Control plane
- Management plane

VM data is limited completely within the data plane. Different virtual machine data is differentiated from other virtual machines, because it is on different logical switches. The data is carried over defined transport networks in the physical network. The data plane also consists of NSX Virtual Switch, distributed routing, and the distributed firewall.

The control plane has network virtualization control messages. Control plane communication must be carried out on secure physical networks (VLANs) which are segregated from the transport networks of the data plane. Control messages are used to define networking attributes/parameters on NSX Virtual Switch instances, and also to configure and manage disaster recovery and distributed firewall components on each ESXi host.

The management plane is responsible for the network virtualization orchestration. Cloud management platforms like VMware vRealize Automation will be used to request, consume, and destroy networking resources for virtual machines. Communication is managed from the cloud management platform to the VMware vCenter Server to create and configure virtual machines, and to NSX Manager to consume networking resources.

The different planes are well-connected through the APIs, including REST, VMware vSphere, and VMware VIX APIs. The API's utilization depends on the component being controlled by vCenter and the cloud management platform.

NSX Manager

NSX Manager provides the centralized management plane for the NSX for vSphere architecture and has a one-to-one mapping with vCenter Server for workloads. NSX Manager performs the following functions:

- Provides a single point of configuration, and the REST API entry points in a vSphere environment configured for NSX for vSphere.
- Responsible for deploying NSX Controller clusters, NSX Edge distributed routers, NSX Edge services gateways (in the form of OVF format appliances), guest introspection services, and so on.
- Responsible for preparing ESXi hosts for NSX for vSphere by installing VXLAN, distributed routing, and firewall kernel modules, as well as the **User World Agent (UWA)**.
- Communicates with NSX Controller clusters through REST, and hosts through the Pivotal RabbitMQ message bus. Note that this is an internal message bus specific to NSX for vSphere, and does not require any additional services to be set up.
- Generates certificates for the NSX Controller nodes and ESXi hosts to secure control plane communications with mutual authentication.

VMware NSX can link with multiple vCenter and VMware NSX deployments by managing them from a designated single primary NSX Manager.

There will be both an NSX Manager primary instance and one or more secondary instances in a cross-vCenter NSX scenario. The primary NSX Manager instance is linked to the primary vCenter Server instance, and enables the creation and management of universal logical switches, universal logical (distributed) routers, and universal firewall policies. Secondary NSX Manager instances are utilized to manage networking services local to itself. A maximum of seven secondary NSX Manager instances can be attached with the primary NSX Manager in a cross-vCenter NSX environment. The configuration of network services on all NSX Manager instances can be configured from one central interface.

 There is still a one-to-one relationship between an NSX Manager and a vCenter Server.

To manage all NSX Manager instances from the primary NSX Manager in a Cross-vCenter VMware NSX deployment, the vCenter Server instances must be connected with VMware Platform Services Controllers in Enhanced Linked Mode.

Distributed firewall

NSX for vSphere distributed firewall is a hypervisor, kernel-embedded firewall providing visibility and control for virtualized applications and networks. Access control rules will depend on VMware vCenter objects, like data centers, clusters, and virtual machine names, network constructs (like IP, or IP set addresses), VLAN/DVS port-groups, VXLAN/logical switches, and security groups, consisting of a user group identity from the Active Directory. Security enforcement is executed at the kernel and virtual NIC levels also help with scalable firewall policy enforcement without any change or trouble to the physical infrastructure. The distributed firewall reduces CPU overhead and executes at line rate.

The distributed firewall with flow monitoring function shows network activity between virtual machines at the application protocol level used to audit network traffic, define and refine firewall policies, and identify botnets.

Service composer

The service composer bundled with NSX for vSphere defines a model for utilizing network and security services. Customers can attach and apply firewall rules and security services in real time to applications running on virtual infrastructures through the service composer. Security policies are applied to VMs groups, and the rule is automatically attached with all new virtual machines that are a part of this group:

- A **security group** can have a dynamic and static inclusion of objects in a container. This container can be used as a source or destination field for a distributed firewall security policy.
- A **security policy** comprises of security services and/or firewall rules.

The service composer implements security policy definition and enforcement by detaching the assets that need to be secured with the policies that define how to secure them.

NSX for vSphere system requirements

The following table details the system requirements for all components in the NSX for vSphere solution.

Requirements for NSX Edge services gateway sizing varies based on individual workload requirements, so all the various options are listed in the following table.

The following are the NSX for vSphere specifications:

VM	vCPU	Memory	Storage	Quantity
NSX Manager	4	16 GB	60 GB	1
NSX Controller	4	4 GB	20 GB	3
NSX Edge services gateway**	1 (compact) 2 (large) 4 (quad-large) 6 (x-large)	512 MB (compact) 1 GB (large) 1 GB (quad-large) 8 GB (x-large)	512 MB 512 MB 512 MB 4.5 GB (with 4 GB Swap)	Varies with use case
Distributed Logical Router Control VM	1	512 MB	512 MB	Typically 2 in HA pair
Guest Introspection	2	1 GB	4 GB	1 per ESXi
NSX Data Security	1	512 MB	6 GB	1 per ESXi
NSX Controller	4	4 GB	20 GB	3

As a general guideline, if the VMware NSX managed environment contains more than 256 hypervisors, VMware recommends increasing NSX Manager resources to 8 vCPU and 24 GB of memory.

Micro-segmentation conceptual design

The micro segmentation solution contains various components that must be integrated to make them work well together. These components range from networking devices and infrastructure services, to storage area network devices and applications. Each of these components has a large number of potentially valid configurations, but only a few of these configurations result in an integrated, functional system that meets the specified business and technical requirements of a solution.

The key components in the conceptual design are described in the following sections:

- **Internal project networks**: These networks represent the main project's workloads; these workloads can be virtual cloud-based, or legacy physical and virtual-based. The VTS-Unicredit network security model allows systems of any type to reside in alternative networks classified in multiple zones: Intranet (ISZ), and Secured (Margherita). Standard rules of this network security model allow for VMs in Margherita zones to communicate among them, but only if members of the same project, and for VMs in the ISZ zone, communicate among different projects. NSX DFW will grant that this rule be enforced.
- **External non-trusted networks**: These networks are external to the VTS-Unicredit managed network zones. Connectivity to and from external networks is through standard firewalls. The networks falling in this category include the internet and other networks used to interconnect the cloud to third-party provided services.
- **Internal non-projects networks**: This category is currently represented by a single management network that is accessed by a dedicated network interface, and it is mainly used and targeted at the backup process.
- **Perimeter firewalls**: This category includes the physical firewalls, which exist at the perimeter of the data centers. Traffic internal to projects, whatever the network zone they are into, won't be enforced by perimeter firewalls. Only traffic with external, non-trusted network-based services will.

The micro segmentation logical view is as follows:

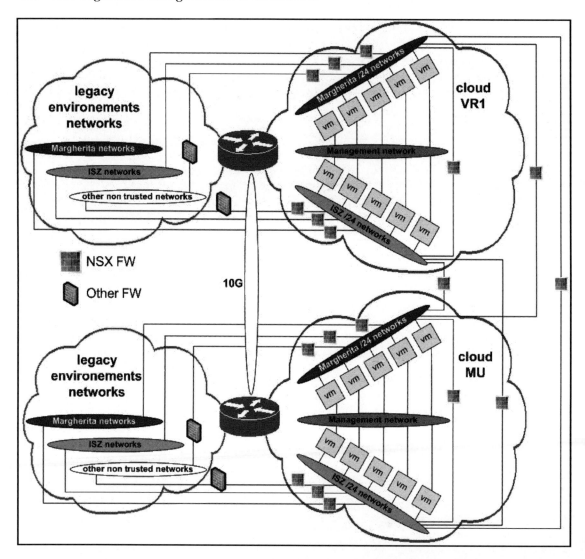

Micro segmentation logical view

vSphere infrastructure in each site hosts 2 vCenter servers: one instance dedicated to the cloud management plane components, and one vCenter for the workload resources, with dedicated clusters for production, Q&A, and test environments.

The three types of clusters are as follows:

- **Payload cluster(s)**: Which will host all of the VMs provisioned for customers
- **Edge cluster**: Which will host all edge service gateways and NSX Controller appliances
- **Management cluster**: Which has all management VMs, such as the NSX Manager instances, the vCenter Server, and any other management VMs that are needed

Network virtualization logical design

The NSX DFW solution will be deployed over an existing VMware vSphere virtualization infrastructure, coupled with an existing cloud consumption management platform. The solution has two independent deployment target data centers.

Within this deployment, the construct of the cloud tenant has been declined by the customer in the project entity, which is identified as a group of VMs characterized by the same customer, application, reference environment, and network zone. The tenant and project are considered as the same entity in the following descriptions.

NSX for vSphere architecture will consist of the following clusters, as per VMware best practices:

- A set of management clusters (one for the smaller site, two for the second site) containing the NSX Manager instance, the vCenter Server instances, and any other management VMs that are needed by the cloud and IAAS manager. The clusters don't have the underlying hosts prepared for NSX for vSphere to protect the management components from unintentional lockout.
- A set of payload clusters that contain the workloads and have the underlying hosts prepared for NSX for vSphere.

Each set of clusters is managed by an independent vCenter instance: two instances in one site and one instance in the second site.

The DFW is loaded as an ESXi kernel module, and provides line-speed firewalling services, with no dependence from the underlying network design. Consequently, when limiting NSX deployment to a distributed firewall feature, design choices are not stringent. Yet this design will simplify the network configuration by eliminating the need to trunk a large number of VLANs to all hosts if and when VXLAN is adopted.

Actually, with no overlay in place, VLAN trunks are configured on TOR switches, and resources external to the cloud are accessed by a routing layer providing the proper firewall, and NAT services according to the traffic patterns. The **distributed firewall (DFW)** manages security, and ensures projects are kept separated and unable to access other projects' VMs on the network when needed.

The NSX distributed firewall will be servicing two different cloud infrastructures:

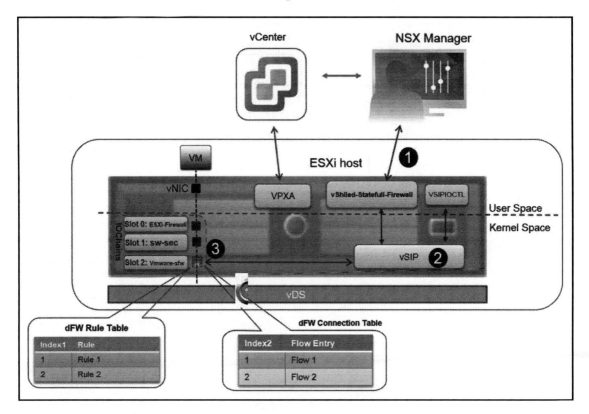

Distributed firewall architecture

The vSphere Cluster design decisions are as follows:

Design decision	Design justification	Design implication
For this design, the administrator has made the following decisions.		

The customer has organized the workloads in multiple vSphere clusters, distributed under multiple vCenter management boundaries. vSphere clusters host management and payload workloads separately. In absence of the overlay network, there is no option to evaluate edge cluster deployment.	This design choice offers better separation in terms of security, management, and resources.	NSX Manager has to register with the vCenter Server instance that is managing the hosts that provide payload compute resources (and edge compute resources, when this is the case). Multiple vCenter servers require multiple NSX Manager instances and multiple NSX controller clusters for any future network overlay adoption.

NSX for vSphere component placement

We are using two vCenter server instances to manage the environment for each site: vCenter Server for the management components, and vCenter Server for the payload clusters.

For future adoption of VXLAN, an additional cluster with three hosts as a minimum for hosting the logical switches and the distributed logical router control plane components (NSX Controller nodes, ESG VMs, DLR control VMs) will be deployed under the payload vCenter server instance:

Design decision	Design decision (placement)	Design implication
Admin has made the following placement decisions for this design:		
NSX Manager instance	Management Cluster	None
NSX Controller nodes to be deployed	NSX Edge Cluster	None
NSX Edge services gateways	NSX Edge Cluster	None
NSX for vSphere Logical Router Control VMs	NSX Edge Cluster	None

NSX for vSphere component placement

The following diagram depicts the logical organization of vSphere Clusters, and where the deployed NSX for vSphere components will run.

The cluster layout for NSX for vSphere is as follows:

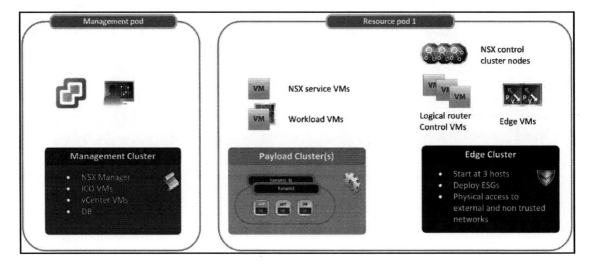

Managing with two vCenters per site

High Availability of NSX for vSphere components

NSX logical firewall objects and configurations are entirely saved into the NSX Manager database. The NSX Manager will be deployed in the management vSphere Cluster, where it is protected by VMware vSphere High Availability. This will ensure that NSX Manager is restarted on a different host in the event of the primary host failing.

In a future VXLAN scenario, the NSX Controller nodes will run on the NSX Edge cluster, and vSphere DRS rules will be set to make sure that different controller nodes are not located on the same host at any time.

Scalability of NSX for vSphere Components

NSX Manager and vCenter Server instances map one-to-one with each other, so if the environment crosses the limits supported by a single vCenter Server, then a new NSX Manager server must be deployed with respect to a new vCenter Server. The new NSX Manager instance can be configured in a cross-vCenter configuration for VMware NSX, while the vCenter Servers are configured in Enhanced Linked Mode.

NSX logical firewall scalability is simply granted by adding ESXi hosts, as the workloads have a demand for an increasing amount of computing resources.

Firewall logical design

The key logical design decisions regarding firewalls involve determining where the various types of rules will be applied within a typical project environment, and the role that the distributed firewall will fulfill. Firewalls can operate in two main layers:

- **(Physical) external firewalls**: Traditional firewalls are the entry point to the cloud environment from external environments such as legacy virtual environments, non/trusted networks, and the internet, if applicable. This represents the first level of filtering on traffic from the external environment.
- **NSX for vSphere distributed firewalls**: The NSX for a vSphere distributed firewall is distributed across the NSX prepared ESXi hypervisors. Projects commonly use granular east-west firewalling for the network zone internal to the project, and north-south firewalling for traffic with external networks behind legacy firewalls. The NSX distributed firewall operates at the VM vNIC level, meaning that a VM is always protected irrespective of the way it is connected to the logical network.

The following table details design decisions that were made regarding the firewall hierarchy:

Design decision	Design justification	Design implication
Admin has made the following decisions for this design:		
External traffic filtering from non-trusted networks will be handled outside of NSX at the perimeter firewall. The rules will be defined by the customer at both the perimeter firewall and at the distributed firewall.	Some networks fall in the untrusted category, which means the perimeter firewall management ownership and responsibility are detained by a subject different, and a full trust policy cannot be applied.	Services generating this kind of traffic will need firewall rules set both at the perimeter firewall and at the distribution firewall, with the collaboration and coordination of both parties.

External traffic filtering from legacy-trusted networks will be handled at the NSX distributed firewall. The rules will be defined by the customer at both the perimeter firewall and at the distributed firewall. The perimeter firewall will be configured to trust any ingress and egress traffic with the cloud workloads, and the distributed firewall will be used for granularity.	Moving the granular firewalling under the management of NSX for vSphere provides the benefits of orchestration and agility around the potentially rapid creation of tenant networks. It also leverages dynamic security group memberships based on vCenter inventory objects.	The customer will decide which generic firewall rules to use for the physical perimeter. The rules will reflect a general trust relationship, and are outside of the scope of this design. The goal of this solution is to ensure that granular firewalling requirements (after initial filtering) can be met using the distributed firewall.
After DFW deployment and projects onboarding, the existing routing functions will be moved from the legacy firewalls to the data centers distribution routers, which will also provide network separation.	No more need to maintain intercommunication rules at the original firewall, which acted as a workload default gateway. The distribution router can take over the function.	None.

NSX for vSphere firewall decisions

The following table represents the network traffic enforcement points derived from the application of the aforementioned defined design decisions:

Traffic	1 side	2 side	Enforcement point
East-West	VR cloud ISZ	VR cloud ISZ	Traffic permitted in VR DFW
East-West	MU cloud ISZ	MU cloud ISZ	Traffic permitted in MU DFW
North-South	VR cloud ISZ	MU cloud ISZ	Traffic permitted in both DFW
North-South	VR cloud ISZ	MU cloud MARG	Traffic controlled in MU DFW
North-South	MU cloud ISZ	VR cloud MARG	Traffic controlled in VR DFW
North-South	VR cloud MARG	MU cloud MARG	Traffic controlled in master DFW

North-South	VR cloud	Legacy MARG (VR or MU)	Traffic controlled in VR DFW
North-South	MU cloud	Legacy MARG (VR or MU)	Traffic controlled in MU DFW
North-South	VR cloud ISZ	Legacy ISZ (VR or MU)	Traffic permitted in VR DFW

Distributed firewall

The vShield-Stateful-Firewall service demon runs constantly on the ESXi host and performs multiple tasks:

- Interacts with the NSX Manager to retrieve DFW policy rules
- Gathers DFW statistics information and sends it to the NSX Manager
- Sends audit log information to the NSX Manager
- Receives configurations from the NSX manager to create/delete DLR Control VM, and create/ delete ESG
- Parts of the host preparation process, including SSL-related tasks from NSX Manager

The distributed firewall supports security rules at the Layer 2 and Layer 3 levels. Layer 2 rules are meant for actions that happen at Layer 2 (such as ARP), whereas layer 3 policies define rules to manage traditional traffic between virtual machines.

Distributed firewall rules can be logically separated into sections, which can be useful to partition rules that are dedicated to different needs; for example, (for different departments).

The following table details a constraint regarding the need for the selective application of firewall rules:

 NSX for vSphere Distributed Firewall Scope:

Currently, the NSX for vSphere distributed firewall does not natively provide a multitenant model, so a filtering mechanism is required using the `Applied To` function, so that the scope of rule application is restricted.

Security administrators can specify which virtual machine (and therefore, which vNICs) receives the rule by using the `Applied To` function. It defines the scope at which the rule is applicable; that is, where the rules are enforced. Different types of objects can be specified for this setting, such as a data center, a cluster, a distributed port group, a network, a logical switch, and so on.

NSX Manager and NSX Service VMs running in a cluster that is protected by a distributed firewall are automatically excluded from firewall protection by default. Other virtual machines can be manually added to the exclusion list.

The NSX for vSphere distributed firewall decisions are as follows:

Design decision	Design justification	Design implication
For this design, **Error! Unknown document property name.** has made the following decisions:		
Distributed firewall rules will be organized into different sections to match the different logical entities (cloud infrastructure services, management services, ad-hoc application rules, ISZ roles and service composer roles).	Sections help to segregate firewall rules between different logical entities, and therefore improve readability.	The security administrator should be organized to keep the rules into their respective sections.
Whenever possible and appropriate, distributed firewall rules will be applied to specific security groups in the environment.	Applied to define the scope at which the rule is applicable. This will reduce the number of rules per host, and will improve efficiency because the distributed firewall will have fewer rules to evaluate for every new session.	The security administrator will have to modify the default configuration where rules are applied to all VMs regardless of their location.
Generic cloud management infrastructure rules section will be created in the distributed firewall.	Workloads are only protected at the distributed firewall level. Generic infrastructure services must also be enforced at the same level.	Network information for the various infrastructure elements must be known.

Different NSX firewall sections will be created for common network and OS services, system management services and PaaS services. Rules scope will be the relevant security groups.	Creating separated firewall sections grouping same-nature services, providing better operations and problem analysis support.	Network information for the various infrastructure elements must be known.
The NSX for vSphere distributed firewall will be used to firewall traffic to and from VMs based on security policies for all the cases where project workloads, cloud and non-cloud, run in a Margherita network zone.	As described previously, generic filtering of external traffic and network separation is occurring at higher-level tiers, so the best place to offer granular firewalling for virtual machines is at the hypervisor layer using the distributed firewall. This provides micro-segmentation of workloads with independence from the originating subnets. Multiple different applications will be deployed single or multiple "network zones", so the filtering must be granular at the lowest level, for flexibility.	Distributed firewalls will be configured on all NSX for vSphere prepared hosts in the payload clusters. This will allow configuration of firewall filtering based on security groups and security policies. Security policies will provide the best level of automation in creating rulesets when applications are frequently added or removed.
For the test and QA environment, the vCenter VM will be added in the exclusion list.	In the QA and test environment, the vCenter environment will be the same for the management and for the payload clusters. The DFW will not be installed in the management cluster, but to avoid any control loop, the vCenter VM will be excluded. The production environment is not necessary, because the vCenter VM is located in another vCenter environment not connected to NSX.	After the installation of the NSX Manager, it will be necessary to populate the exclusion list. The vCenter will not be filtered by the DFW.

If there are plans to integrate additional cluster in the NSX environment (brownfield migration), there will be a rule in the default section to allow any traffic applied only to this cluster.	This design allows to prepare the cluster without impacting the current workload. Once the network rules are completely replicated in the NSX environment, the rule can be removed.	It is necessary to identify all clusters outside of the cloud in the same vCenter that can be imported in the distributed firewall.

The following table represents the NSX firewall according to the aforementioned defined design decisions:

N	Label	Notes
1	Cloud services	Static rules allowing communication between Cloud Orchestrator and provisioned VMs
2	Common services	Static rules allowing other common services, networks, and OS specifics
3	Management tools	Static rules allowing execution of management services on all VMs
4	PaaS services	Static rules for well-known standard services for PAAS integration
5	Application rules	Dynamic-specific application rules requested by the application owner
6	ISZ projects	Dynamic rules allowing traffic inside ISZ projects
7	Service Composer rules	Service composer section, with dynamic rules allowing traffic inside projects
8	Default rule	Default policy blocking all traffic

Security groups and policies

Security groups are logical groupings that can be used to determine what needs to be protected by the NSX for vSphere distributed firewall. It allows static or dynamic grouping based on inclusion and exclusion of objects such as virtual machines, vNICs, vSphere clusters, logical switches, and so on.

Security group considerations:

- Security groups can have multiple security policies assigned to them
- A virtual machine can belong to multiple security groups at the same time
- Security groups can be nested inside other security groups
- You can include and exclude objects from security groups
- Security group membership can change dynamically
- If a virtual machine belongs to multiple security groups, the services applied to it depend on the precedence of the security policy mapped to the security groups

If the vCenter VM's objects are used within a security group, VMware NSX still needs to know the IP address of those virtual machines. Indeed, the underlying firewall rules configured within the kernel are IP-based, despite being abstracted as objects at the configuration layer. NSX for vSphere requires VMware Tools running in all virtual machines so their properties can be reported into vCenter. NSX for vSphere has enhanced IP detection to deliver better security enforcement for virtual machines, even in scenarios where a VM might not have VMware Tools running. The following table lists the assumptions that have been made regarding the installation of VMware Tools on virtual machines.

The VMware Tools are used in the cloud for:

Design assumption	Design justification	Design implication
Admin has made the following assumptions for this design:		
VMware tools are expected to run in cloud VMs in order to avoid reduced management functionality. All pre-defined operating system images will begin with VMware Tools installed.	The NSX for vSphere distributed firewall requires up-to-date IP address information from virtual machines to be reported into VMware vCenter for management using security groups.	Any objects that cannot be categorized, for example, when the IP address for a VM cannot be determined due to the lack of VMware Tools, will trigger the default firewall policy. In this example, the policy blocks traffic.

Security policies define how content is going to be protected. In this solution, the policies take the form of firewall rules that are applied to one or more security groups. For the **"Error! Unknown document property name"** solution design, a security policy will be created to enforce traffic among VMs within projects in the Margherita network zone. Each project will have its firewall rules categorized under the *Service Composer* section in the distributed firewall configuration. It will then be necessary to orchestrate the enforcement of any rules for a specific project in the *Service Composer* section without applying all rules to all projects. This requires an approach of applying the security policy to the lowest common object denominator that defines the scope of the project, that is, the project security group. The following table lists decisions that were made regarding the primary approach to security grouping.

The security grouping decisions are as follows:

Design decision	Design justification	Design implication
Admin has made the following decisions for this design:		
Security groups will be used to dynamically apply firewall rules. Security tags and IP-sets will define group membership for VMs of different projects, OSs, PaaS categories, and networks.	It is necessary to find a way to apply firewall rules at a level that captures all objects within a workload that needs to be in scope for filtering.	Specific firewall groupings and rules will vary with projects and other VMs attributes. The process of setting such VM tracts is applied outside NSX at the orchestration level, but flexibility is offered by configuring all ESXi hosts in the payload clusters to use the distributed firewall. The logical constructs and application of security rules can then be handled as part of the onboarding process, and as orchestrated service requests are up and running. At this point, no specific designs are required regarding the distributed firewall other than availability.

Testing the distributed firewall rule application:

It will be necessary to plan for and perform extensive testing on the NSX for vSphere distributed firewall rule application in the multitenant setup to verify that tenant filtering occurs successfully. The impact of applying firewall rules outside of their intended scope is high.

This solution is essentially a Greenfield deployment from the point of view of NSX for vSphere. The following table details a decision made regarding the default firewall rule to use with the distributed firewall; that is, what rule should be applied to any traffic that is not explicitly dealt with in its own individual rule.

The default distributed firewall policy decisions are as follows:

Design decision	Design justification	Design implication
Admin has made the following decisions for this design:		
The default policy for the NSX for vSphere distributed firewall will be set to Deny.	A default *distributed firewall deny policy* can be straightforwardly recommended for Greenfield deployments, because there are no existing communication between applications to consider other privileges. This recommendation provides the most secure solution, because traffic will be blocked unless it is specifically allowed (as opposed to allowing all traffic through and blocking exceptions).	This decision simplifies the distributed firewall design. Only setting the default deny policy at the point of deployment is required. **Error! Unknown document property name.** knows the firewall requirements upfront, additional policy requirements can be configured by the customer at the point of project onboarding. Alternatively, firewall rules can be created by monitoring blocked traffic flows using NSX for vSphere Manager and opening the respective ports required for protocols.

NSX Manager design

The following section details the design of NSX Manager that will be deployed consistently across all sites.

The NSX Manager logical design is shown as follows:

Attribute	Specification
Vendor and model	VMware Virtual Hardware Version 8
Processor type	VMware Vcpu
NIC vendor and model Number of ports/NIC x speed Network	VMXNET3 1x Gigabit Ethernet <DPG>
Local disk RAID level	N/A

Network virtualization platform management

The process through which new and existing firewall rules change has been designed from the **Cloud Orchestrator (CO)** consumption and orchestration platform. The process covers the lifecycle for establishing firewall rules in the cloud setup:

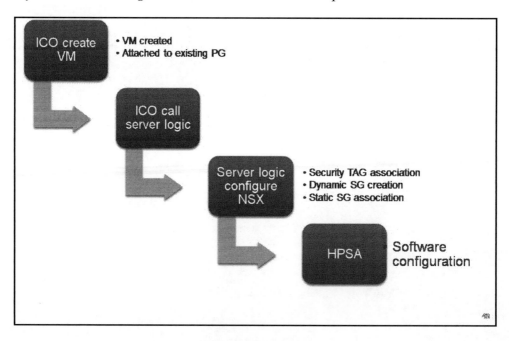

Firewall configuration process

Message Bus Client: The NSX Manager connected with the ESXi host with a secure protocol called AMQP. The **Advanced Message Queuing Protocol** (**AMQP**) is an open standard application layer protocol for message-oriented middleware. The defining functionalities of AMQP are message orientation, queuing, and routing, including the point-to-point and publish-and-subscribe model (`http://en.wikipedia.org/wiki/Publish%E2%80%93subscribe`).

The vShield-Stateful-Firewall works as a RabbitMQ Client in the ESXi. It is a user space service daemon, and uses a TCP/5671 connection to the RabbitMQ server in the NSX manager. NSX Manager used the message bus to send different information to the ESXi hosts:

The policy for the DFW module, controller nodes IP addresses, and the private key and host certificate to authenticate the communication between the host and controller, and requests to create/delete DLR instances.

vSIP: The VMware Internetworking Service-Insertion Platform is the distributed firewall kernel space module. The vSIP gets firewall rules from the NSX manager through vShield-Stateful-Firewall, and downloads them to each VMVMware-sfw.

The VMware Internetworking Service-Insertion Platform is also a framework that has the capability to dynamically involve third-party software, and VMware's own virtual as well as physical security and networking services into the VMware virtual network.

VPXA: It is a vCenter agent, installed on the ESXi host to communicate with the ESXi host for the first time. vCenter manages the ESXi host for vSphere-related tasks with VPXA. It is not a direct part of the DFW architecture, but the VPXA is being utilized to report the VM IP address with VMtools:

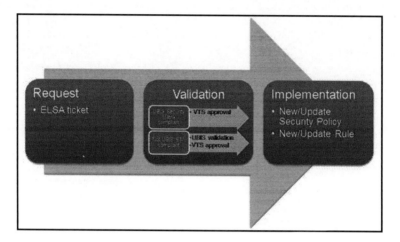

Firewall rule lifecycle process

Consumption layer

NSX for vSphere virtual networks and associated constructs can be accessed or consumed through cloud management platforms, the NSX for vSphere REST API, or the VMware vSphere Web Client:

- **Consumption through cloud management platforms**: Cloud management platforms like vRealize Automation help to get self-service provisioning of virtual networks and respective features from a service portal.
- **Consumption through API**: NSX for vSphere integrates with a powerful management interface through its REST API. A client can read an object by using an HTTP GET request to the object's resource URL. A client can create an object with an HTTP PUT or POST request, which includes a new or modified XML body document for the object. Lastly, a client can delete an object with an HTTP DELETE request.
- **Consumption through the vSphere Web Client**: The NSX Manager component integrates with the vSphere Web Client, and provides a networking and security plug-in that allows consumption directly from NSX Manager for users with the necessary privileges.

The consumption method design assumptions are as follows:

Design assumption	Design justification	Design implication
This table contains all assumptions related to consumption method design:		
It is assumed that, for projects, consumption of NSX for vSphere resources will be through Cloud Orchestrator integrated with OpenStack for IaaS services (with a custom Rest service broker) and the VMware vSphere Web Client Networking and Security plugin will potentially be used by customers' staff during project onboarding and any administrative configurations. The orchestration and automation layer will handle NSX dynamic objects lifecycle tasks.	The Networking and Security plugin is an interface for manually consuming NSX for vSphere resources. It offers low-level configuration for those cases where the Rest service broker can't be leveraged, and troubleshooting options that are more aligned to the roles that customer's technical staff will take when managing the environment than is typically offered to a customer.	Both consumption methods will be available by default, but the NSX for vSphere access model will assume that customers will not typically be given privileges to administer NSX for vSphere directly through the vSphere Web Client. The option to do this is still available, at the customer's discretion; however, there is no multitenancy at the vSphere Web Client Networking and Security plug-in level. If someone is granted elevated privileges, they can access the entire environment.

NSX for vSphere logging environment

All NSX components including NSX Manager, NSX Controller, NSX Virtual Switch, and NSX Edge, which give you full network visibility and data. NSX for vSphere has centralized reporting and monitoring, distributed performance and scaling, and can be deployed/configured with automation. NSX for vSphere is based on a REST API provisioned by NSX Manager, and all operations can be executed programmatically by scripting, or higher-level languages.

ESXi hosts has a syslog service (`vmsyslogd`) that enables a standard technique for logging messages from the VMkernel and other components. ESXi is configured to send the logs across the network to a syslog server. There are multiple levels of logging, which can be enabled as per requirement.

The syslog service can be configured on ESXi using host profiles, the VMware vSphere command line interface, or the **Advanced Configuration** options in the vSphere Web Client.

NSX for vSphere management layer

The NSX for vSphere management layer comprises the NSX Manager and NSX Controller cluster. In this instance, each NSX Manager instance will send syslog data to a collector in its local data center.

The NSX Manager syslog decisions are as follows:

Design decision	Design justification	Design implication
Admin has made the following syslog decisions for this design:		
Syslog information will be exported on a per-site basis for NSX Manager and ESXi hosts, leveraging an existing centralized syslog solution based on Splunk.	All of the administrative events relating to operations performed on the NSX Manager will be logged to a centralized location for troubleshooting purposes.	Syslog server information will be provided by **Error! Unknown document property name.** and requires that each NSX Manager and each ESXi host prepared for NSX be directed to the collector on the relevant server address and port.

 NSX Manager cannot forward messages to multiple or alternate loggers based on the result of sorting.

NSX for vSphere deployed components

Another type of logging to consider is for components that exist outside of the management plane (such as the distributed firewall). The components are logged centrally, but the logging is slightly different, as described in the following sections.

Distributed firewall logs

Log entries generated by the distributed firewalls can be viewed and sorted using the vCenter web user interface. The distributed firewall operations are run from the ESXi hosts. Therefore, to review and identify the actual firewall operations, you must check the ESXi log.

Distributed firewall monitoring

If the distributed firewall does not have enough memory, it will start dropping traffic. The distributed firewall administrator is notified of the lack of available memory by the following actions:

- Receiving an alert when a new rule could not be configured due to the shortage.
- A syslog message that states the distributed firewall cannot create new connections due to the shortage. If a rule relating to the flow creation also has logging turned on, a second message is generated to indicate that the packet was also dropped.

The firewall administrator can resolve the issue by freeing memory on a host; for example, by moving a guest to another host.

If the distributed firewall vCPUs are over-utilized or maxed out, packets can also be dropped. If logging is enabled for the related flow, a log message is generated for dropped packets.

In an *All Failure* scenario, packets are discarded and the distributed firewall operates in a Fail Closed mode until the failure is remedied. Please go through the table for more understanding on distributed firewall design policy with benefits:

Design decision	Design justification	Design implication
Admin has made the following decisions for this design:		
The VMkernel log on all hosts prepared for NSX for vSphere will be sent to syslog collectors to analyze and troubleshoot the flows interacting with the distributed firewall, and the NSX Edge services gateway virtual machines will syslog directly.	Host logs will contain the details of any distributed firewall-related actions, because they are kernel-level operations. The `vmkernel.log` file will capture all firewall events relating to any virtual machines on specific hosts. NSX Edge services gateways are virtual machines that can generate syslog messages directly so pinpointing a particular instance will be possible; for example, by searching on an IP address or related information.	Host-level syslog messages are controlled by advanced settings on the individual ESXi servers on a per VM basis. These settings will be captured as part of both the ESXi host design and NSX Edge services gateway provisioning workflows respectively. Regular expression matching on NSX for vSphere specific terms can be performed in the VMware vRealize Log Insight tool.

Backup and recovery – backing up the NSX Manager data

It is critical that NSX Manager is backed up on a regular basis. Backup system configuration is provided by the NSX Manager appliance interface. Backups can be scheduled on an hourly, daily, or weekly basis, down to the minute. The backup file is saved to a remote location that the NSX Manager can access through the FTP or SFTP protocol. It is possible to exclude logs and flow data from backups.

 FTP and SFTP are currently the only available options for backup of the NSX Manager. SFTP is recommended for increased security.

The following table details design decisions made regarding NSX Manager backups:

Design decision	Design justification	Design implication
Admin has made the following decisions for this design:		
NSX Manager backups will be created using the internal backup utility.	The VMware recommended approach for achieving a consistent backup state, encapsulating all relevant NSX Manager data, is to use the internal backup mechanisms compared with an image-level snapshot backup. This ensures that all relevant data is reinstated upon a restore.	The NSX Manager backup will be handled separately from the other virtual machines in the management cluster.
NSX Manager backups are stored in the share `<share name>` that is hosted on `<filer name>`.	The internal backup solution is configured to store backups on specific volumes. `<ABCD>` volume has been selected for redundancy and available space to store backups infinitely.	NSX Manager backups will be stored infinitely, or until manually removed.

Backup jobs are configured to run at `<HH:MM>` Central European Time every calendar day.	Based on analysis performed on traffic volumes, `<HH:MM>` Central European Time is suitable for backing up the NSX Manager data. It has been decided that backups will be run every calendar day for consistency and granularity.	Backups are run every `<nn>` hours. Therefore, if any data changes in-between backups, those changes will be lost after a successful restore.
In conjunction with the scheduled backup, it Is possible to run an on-demand backup job using the API POST `https://NSX-Manager-IP-Address/api/1.0/appliance-management/backuprestore/backup.`	This API allows to pro-actively backup the NSX Manager database during the configuration from the automation layer.	This approach will significantly increase the amount of backup storage required on the destination FTP server. It will be necessary to take care of the purge of the old files.

A backup can only be restored into a new NSX Manager instance, not on an existing appliance that has been previously configured.

Backing up the vSphere Distributed Switch

The vSphere Distributed Switch configuration is stored in the vCenter database. In addition, the configuration of a vSphere Distributed Switch instance can be exported from the vSphere Web Client, or by using VMware CLI for re-import and recovery.

Monitoring and troubleshooting

Now, we will learn about different monitoring and troubleshooting components of the NSX for vSphere solution.

Flow monitoring

NSX for vSphere provides the capability to monitor, in detail, the traffic being exchanged between protected VMs, and to gain visibility into the applications running on different hosts and VMs. For each flow, you can view the source, destination, application, and ports in use. The number of sessions and packets transmitted per session are also captured, and those details can be used to directly configure firewall allow and block rules.

It is only possible to view flow information for machines that are running on hosts within clusters that have been prepared for NSX for vSphere, and have the distributed firewall enabled.

The vSphere Web Client Live Flow option enables viewing of both TCP and UDP connections to a virtual NIC for a particular virtual machine.

It is discussed that this type of tool could offer benefits regarding monitoring and troubleshooting of potential future network configurations.

Activity monitoring

Activity monitoring provides a way to ensure that security policies are enforced correctly. After data collection is enabled for activity monitoring, you can view data, such as which virtual machines are accessed by users and machine resource utilization. Activity monitoring also enables viewing the interactions between inventory containers and groups that accessed VMs.

vSphere Distributed Switch monitoring

The NSX Virtual Switch is built from the vSphere Distributed Switch, so the native functionality provided by the vSphere Distributed Switch can be leveraged for monitoring and troubleshooting purposes. Features such as NetFlow/IPFIX, RSPAN/ERSPAN, and port mirroring are all supported for monitoring and troubleshooting purposes.

Port mirroring

Users can leverage RSPAN and ERSPAN features when they like to centrally monitor network traffic, and they can take advantage of a sniffer or network analyzer device connected multiple hops away from monitored traffic.

Port mirroring helps in mirroring a distributed port's traffic to other distributed ports or defined physical switch ports. Port mirroring features can be leveraged to centrally monitor network traffic, and by using a sniffer or network analyzer device, connect multiple hops away from monitored traffic. Distributed switches give five options for the port mirroring features, as mentioned in the following table.

The port mirroring options are as follows:

Port mirroring session type	Cisco equivalent	Description
Distributed Port Mirroring	SPAN	Mirror network traffic from a set of distributed ports to other distributed ports (from the same vSphere Distributed Switch instance) on the same host. No physical switch configuration required.
Remote Mirroring Source	RSPAN	Mirror network traffic from a set of distributed ports to specific uplink ports. Physical switch configuration required.
Remote Mirroring Destination	RSPAN	Mirror network traffic from a set of VLANs to distributed ports. Physical switch configuration required.
Encapsulated Remote Mirroring (L3) Source	ERSPAN	Mirror network traffic from a set of distributed ports to a remote agent's IP address, to use when the source and destination are running on different L3 networks. No physical switch configuration required.
Distributed Port Mirroring (legacy)	SPAN	Mirror network traffic from a set of distributed ports to a set of distributed ports or uplink ports.

vSphere Distributed Switch alerts

NSX Virtual Switch alarms provide alerts regarding events related to the vSphere Distributed Switch. Some of the available preconfigured triggers include health status, reconfiguration, port blocked, port deleted, link down, and host removal:

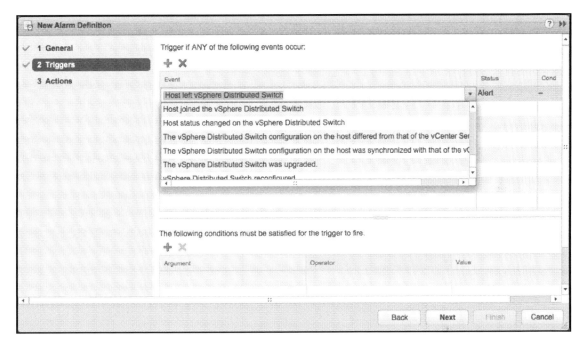

NSX Virtual Switch alerts

For more detail on the ESXi host level events and alarms, refer to the VMware vSphere monitoring and performance guide available at the following location:

```
http://pubs.vmware.com/vsphere-60/topic/com.vmware.ICbase/PDF/vsphere-esxi-
vcenter-server-60-monitoring-performance-guide.pdf
```

vSphere Distributed Switch network health check

The vSphere network health check tool helps to catch common configuration errors such as:

- Unmatched VLAN trunks between a virtual switch and a physical switch

- Unmatched MTU configurations between Virtual NIC, the virtual switch, the physical adapter, and physical switch ports
- Unmatched teaming configurations

vSphere administrators help to transfer failure data to network administrators to sort out problem resolutions. The vSphere health check utilizes the Layer 2 echo protocol to transmit Ethernet broadcast frames to the physical switch. If reply packets are not reached, warnings are shown in the vSphere Web Client:

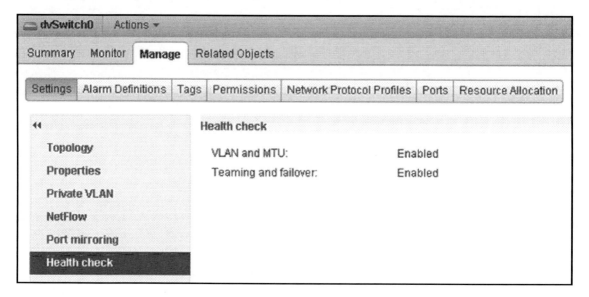

Check that the number of MAC addresses generated by the network health check will be less than the size of the physical switches MAC table. The network health check for vSphere Distributed Switch instances generates one MAC address for each uplink per instance, for each VLAN, multiplied by the number of hosts in the instance to be added to the upstream physical switch MAC table.

SNMP

ESXi hosts give all of the support for SNMP agents to run on the ESXi host, and all NSX Virtual Switch instances or vSphere Distributed Switch instances. SNMP network MIBs give standards-based visibility into NSX Virtual Switch objects.

SNMP network monitoring has been advanced to give support for SNMPv3, support for IEEE/IETF networking MIBs for standard Layer 2 information monitoring, and Layer 3 and higher protocol (TCP/UDP) MIB support. The following are some key parameters regarding virtual switches that are available through standard MIBs:

- Port state (up or down) per virtual switch (vSphere standard switch, vSphere Distributed Switch)
- Traffic counters per port, per VLAN
- LAG data for network adapter teaming details
- LLDP information for the Layer 2 topology discovery

Using this enhanced MIB support, network administrators can collect important virtual network data that can help in the monitoring and troubleshooting of network issues.

 For more information about the notifications generated from the ESXi host's SNMP agent, refer to the KB article determining the MIB module listing, name, and type of an SNMP OID (2054359) at: `http://kb.vmware.com/kb/2054359`.

NetFlow/Internet Protocol Flow Information Export (IPFIX)

While ESXi has supported NetFlow Traffic Analyzer for a long time, support for IPFIX was introduced in vSphere 5.1. IPFIX is a more advanced and flexible protocol that allows users to define the flow records that can be collected from the vSphere Distributed Switch and sent to a collector. The following are some key attributes of the IPFIX protocol:

- Users can employ IPFIX templates to define records
- Template descriptions are sent by vSphere Distributed Switch to the collector engine
- IPv6, MPLS, and VXLAN flows can be exported
- The VMware vRealize Network Insight will help you address centralized solutions for the centralized flow collector.

Performance and scalability

Moving the firewall functionality from physical devices to a kernel module inside the hypervisor will increase the overhead of the ESXi operating system. The amount of overhead is subject to several aspects like the physical server, the workloads, and the number of rules.

On NSX, it is possible to configure a threshold for the overhead. If this threshold is crossed, the NSX Manager will generate a warning event.

The configurable values are:

- **CPU percentage**: Refers to the CPU used by the firewall module over the total CPU capacity of the hypervisor
- **RAM percentage**: Refers to the RAM used over the allocated heap memory for the firewall module
- **CPS**: Refers to the connection per second value

The Firewall Threshold design is as follows:

Design decision	Design justification	Design implication
Admin has made the following decisions for this design:		
CPU percentage will be configured at 10%.	This value allows to track any spiker related to the distributed firewall. A low value is useful in the initial phase to better identify the resource usage trending and patterns, and can be eventually raised.	A central syslog server is mandatory to collect the alarm event from the environment.
The RAM percentage will be configured at 50%.	This value allows to track any spiker related to the distributed firewall.	A central syslog server is mandatory to collect the alarm event from the environment.
Connection per second 50000.	This value allows to track any spiker related to the distributed firewall.	A central syslog server is mandatory to collect the alarm event from the environment.

Scalability considerations

The number of rules tested on a single NSX Manager is 100,000.

In addition to the previous number, a single vNIC is tested by up to 3,500 rules. To control the number of rules applied to a single vNIC, it is necessary to use the `Apply-To` function.

The following are some important recommendations based on the cloud design:

Design decision	Design justification	Design implication
For this design, **Error! Unknown document property name.** has made the following decisions.		
Every time it is necessary to open a rule from a security group to another security group, add both groups in the `Apply-To` field.	This configuration will enforce the rules only on the required VMs (source and destination).	In the operating procedure, it is necessary to add this step.
Reduce as much as possible the usage of global rules. In case of general rules that have to be configured on all VMs, leave the "Distributed firewall" value in the Apply-To field.	Each general rule will be enforced an all VMs.	Each general rule will be part of the maximum rules per vNIC (3,500).

VXLAN

The introduction of a network virtualization brings several benefits:

Scalability:

- VXLAN uses a 24-bit network identifier that allows you to use up to 16 million Layer 2 segments
- Reduces the number of MAC addresses on the physical devices, increasing the consolidation ratio from a network prospective
- Allows you to create a logical Layer 2 domain across physical servers located on different physical L2 domains

Performance:

- With the VXLAN, the broadcast traffic is controlled using the multicast protocol, reducing the storm effect on the physical network devices. It has also introduced an ARP suppression system with NSX that allows you to reduce the ARP traffic on the network.
- In conjunction with the VXLAN, it is possible to use the distributed router. This technology allows you to use the hypervisor to route traffic between logical segments.

Automation:

- With the VXLAN, it is possible to use a REST API call to add new networks without interacting with the physical devices

MTU on the transport network

When leveraging encapsulation technologies, it is important to increase the MTU supported both on ESXi hosts, as well as on all interfaces of the devices deployed in the physical network. VXLAN adds 50 bytes to each original frame, leading to the recommendation to increase the MTU size to at least 1,600 bytes. The MTU on the ESXi server, both for the internal logical switch and for the VDS uplinks, is automatically tuned to 1,600 bytes when provisioning VXLAN to hosts from the NSX Manager UI.

NSX Controller

The Controller cluster in the NSX platform is the control plane component responsible for managing the hypervisor switching and routing modules. The controller cluster consists of three controller nodes that manage specific logical switches. The use of the controller cluster in managing VXLAN-based logical switches eliminates the need for multicast configuration at the physical layer for the VXLAN overlay.

The controller nodes are VM-based, and must be deployed in the vCenter, paired with the NSX Manager. This means that in the production environment, the three controllers cannot be deployed in the management cluster, because it is connected to a dedicated management vCenter. The controller VMs can be implemented in the Edge cluster for the production environment.

IGMP usage

VMware NSX doesn't requires a multicast on the physical network; however, it is possible to use the IGMP Snooping functionality on physical switches to reduce the traffic on the network interface of the ESXi servers.

In the unicast replication mode, the Broadcast, Unknown unicast, and Multicast (BUM) traffic inside a VXLAN will be converted into unicast traffic. In case of a large implementation being a problem, the traffic will be multiplied for the number of hypervisors connected to a logical switch.

Using a hybrid replication mode, the BUM traffic is converted into multicast traffic inside the same L2 domain. The traffic is replicated using unicast traffic across different Layer 2 domains:

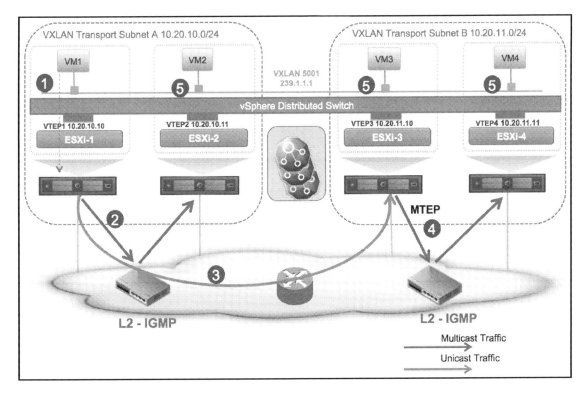

IGMP usage in hybrid mode

Hybrid mode

The hybrid mode doesn't require multicast routing (PIM). It only requires the IGMP Snooping querier on the transport network.

Brownfield migration

In this section, a possible migration strategy to bring the legacy network inside is described.

Migration inside the same hardware infrastructure

One of the procedures to bring the legacy environment inside a VXLAN overlay is to use the same physical infrastructure and leverage the L2 bridging functionality to connect the VXLAN to a traditional VLAN.

The bridge allows you to move the VMs from a VLAN to a VXLAN with minimal impact:

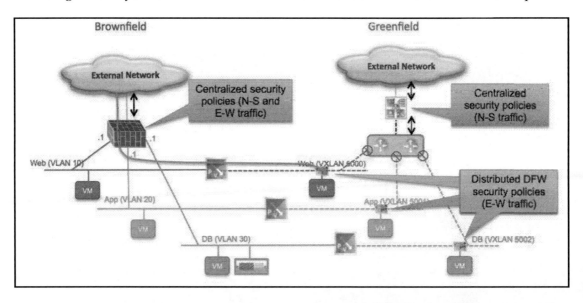

The next step consists of migrating the L3 interface from the physical firewall (Margherita) to the distributed router. This step is disruptive, but it is possible to reduce the impact using dynamic routing between the legacy environment and the VXLAN environment.

Migration to a new hardware infrastructure

Another migration scenario could be the usage of a new physical infrastructure. In this case, there are some advantages and some constraints.

The advantage is the greenfield approach, with the renewal of the hardware and the limited interaction with the legacy hardware (no host preparation on the old ESXi).

The main disadvantage is related to the migration of the workloads, especially if the SSO domain is different; the VM must be migrated with downtime.

From a network prospective, the procedure is the same as in the previous section. For bridging the legacy VLAN to the new infrastructure, it is possible to use two ESXi hosts in the legacy environment, connected and controlled to the greenfield infrastructure. In this way, it is possible to bridge the legacy network to the logical switches:

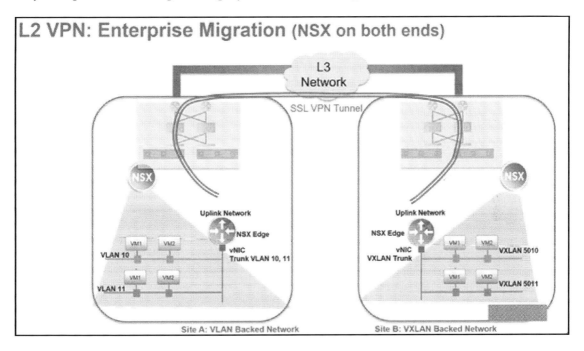

After the workload migration, it is possible to change the routing announcement to directly access on the greenfield environment:

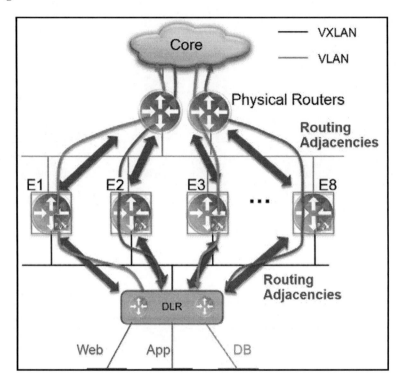

Greenfield routing

NSX for vSphere port and protocol requirements

The NSX for vSphere port and protocol requirements are as follows:

Source	Destination	Port	Protocol	Description
Client PC	NSX Manager	443	TCP	NSX Manager administrative interface
Client PC	NSX Manager	80	TCP	NSX Manager VIB access
ESXi Host	vCenter Server	80	TCP	ESXi host preparation

vCenter Server	ESXi Host	80	TCP	ESXi host preparation
ESXi Host	NSX Manager	5671	TCP	RabbitMQ
ESXi Host	NSX Controller	1234	TCP	User World Agent connection
NSX Controller	NSX Controller	2878, 2888, 3888	TCP	NSX Controller cluster - state sync
NSX Controller	NSX Controller	7777	TCP	Inter-controller RPC port
NSX Controller	NSX Controller	30865	TCP	NSX Controller cluster - state sync
NSX Controller	NTP Time Server	123	TCP	NTP client connection
NSX Controller	NTP Time Server	123	UDP	NTP client connection
NSX Manager	NSX Controller	443	TCP	NSX Controller to NSX Manager communication
NSX Manager	vCenter Server	443	TCP	vSphere web access
NSX Manager	vCenter Server	902	TCP	vSphere web access
NSX Manager	ESXi Host	443	TCP	Management and provisioning connection
NSX Manager	ESXi Host	902	TCP	Management and provisioning connection
NSX Manager	DNS Server	53	TCP	DNS client connection
NSX Manager	DNS Server	53	UDP	DNS client connection
NSX Manager	Syslog Server	514	TCP	Syslog connection
NSX Manager	Syslog Server	514	UDP	Syslog connection
NSX Manager	NTP Time Server	123	TCP	NTP client connection
vCenter Server	NSX Manager	80	TCP	Host preparation
NSX Manager	NTP Time Server	123	UDP	NTP client connection
REST Client	NSX Manager	443	TCP	NSX Manager REST API

VXLAN Tunnel End Point (VTEP)	VXLAN Tunnel End Point (VTEP)	8472	UDP	Transport network encapsulation between VTEPs
ESXi Host	ESXi Host	6999	UDP	ARP on VLAN LIFs
ESXi Host	NSX Manager	8301, 8302	UDP	DVS Sync
NSX Manager	ESXi Host	8301, 8302	UDP	DVS Sync

Refer to the following vSphere documentation for ESXi and vCenter Server requirements: `http://pubs.vmware.com/vsphere-60/topic/com.vmware.ICbase/PDF/vsphere-esxi-vcenter-server-60-installation-setup-guide.pdf`

Reference documents

For more information, see the following configuration and administration guides, white papers, and best practice documents:

- *VMware NSX for vSphere Documentation*:

  `https://www.vmware.com/support/pubs/nsx_pubs.html`

- *VMware NSX Installation Guide*:

  `http://pubs.vmware.com/NSX-62/topic/com.vmware.ICbase/PDF/nsx_62_install.pdf`

- *VMware NSX Upgrade Guide*:

  `http://pubs.vmware.com/NSX-62/topic/com.vmware.ICbase/PDF/nsx_62_upgrade.pdf`

- *VMware NSX Cross-vCenter Installation Guide*:

  `https://pubs.vmware.com/NSX-62/topic/com.vmware.ICbase/PDF/nsx_62_cross_vc_install.pdf`

- *VMware NSX Administration Guide*:

  ```
  http://pubs.vmware.com/NSX-62/topic/com.vmware.ICbase/PDF/nsx_62_
  admin.pdf
  ```

- *VMware NSX vSphere API Guide*:

  ```
  http://pubs.vmware.com/NSX-62/topic/com.vmware.ICbase/PDF/nsx_62_api.
  pdf
  ```

- *VMware NSX Command Line Interface Reference*:

  ```
  http://pubs.vmware.com/NSX-62/topic/com.vmware.ICbase/PDF/nsx_62_cli.
  pdf
  ```

- *VMware NSX for vSphere Network Virtualization Design Guide*:

  ```
  http://www.vmware.com/files/pdf/products/nsx/vmw-nsx-network-
  virtualization-design-guide.pdf
  ```

Summary

Network virtualization offers a functioning micro-segmentation solution using the distributed firewall functionality of VMware NSX for vSphere. This service delivers enhanced security protections to workload-workload traffic, either virtual-to-virtual or virtual to physical, and provides granular, dynamic control over security policies within the software-defined data center. This chapter includes the following modules:

- The micro-segmentation and security service provides assessment, technical validation of pre-requisites, design, deployment, and validation of NSX for vSphere micro-segmentation functionality. This includes L2-L4 **distributed firewalls** (**DFW**), the identity firewall, basic service composer, activity monitoring, and logging.
- The assessment, design, and integration of NSX for vSphere with next-generation firewall-VM Series for NSX and vCenter manager.
- The implementation of firewall policies, workload traffic, VM-to-VM traffic, redirection to L4-L7 deep packet inspection, and advanced firewall security protections in the existing NSX for vSphere micro-segmentation and security solution.

Application modelling for the micro-segmentation service provides a repeatable methodology for securing applications within the virtual infrastructure. This methodology is tailored to meet a customer's specific requirements, and has been proven through the analysis and implementation of micro-segmentations for a select number of predetermined applications in the customer environment.

This chapter relates to the VMware product VMware NSX. In the next chapter, we will learn more about security and compliance. We will dive into specific industry examples and Best Practices to harden the system as per the customer security policy to achieve Industry Specific Compliance and Certifications.

Dealing with Data Sovereignty

9

This chapter will give you a brief overview of sovereignty compliance strategies and how to use an encryption solution to secure data at all stages of your cloud journey, from storage to transit, sharing, and achieving data sovereignty. It will help you to select the right national cloud provider to store all the data within a country where that data is collected, so it is subject only to the laws of that particular country. It will also help you to ensure that data backup and secondary data centers for data recovery/disaster recovery purposes remain local as well.

- Ensuring the security of your data with a new network model
- Knowing where your data resides in a data center
- Industry-specific best practices and security certificates

We will learn about industry-specific security and compliance in a Cross-Cloud model, and follow best practices to harden databases, as per company security policies, to achieve business values with highly agile IT infrastructure.

Security

The hypervisor platform is, undoubtedly, a secure environment from its technical architecture point of view. The hypervisor has a small footprint of around 200 MB, and it also has APIs for monitoring, so you don't need third-party applications on the host. You can refer to the *VMware vSphere Hardening Guide* for more details on security configurations at `https://www.vmware.com/ca/en/security/hardening-guides`.

Securing ESXi hosts

To protect the ESXi hosts against unauthorized intrusion and misuse, consider the following options for improving infrastructure security:

- Limit user access:
    - To improve security, restrict user access to the management interface and enforce access security policies, such as setting up password restrictions.
    - The ESXi shell has privileged access to certain parts of the host, therefore provide only trusted users with ESXi shell login access.
    - Confirm that SSH access is disabled. This prevents remote access to the console of ESXi hosts.
- Use only VMware sources to upgrade or patch ESXi hosts. VMware does not support upgrading these packages from any source other than a VMware source. If a download or patch is used from another source, management interface security or functions might be compromised.
- Regularly check the VMware Security Center for any alerts that might impact the environment. VMware monitors all security alerts that could affect ESXi security and, if needed, issues a security patch.
- ESXi runs only essential services. A limited subset of vendors have hardware agents that can run on ESXi hosts. However, VMware does not recommend running any third-party agents on ESXi hosts.
- By default, all ports not specifically required for management access to the host are closed. Ports must be specifically opened if additional services are required.
- By default, weak ciphers are disabled and all communications from clients are secured by SSL. The exact algorithms used for securing the channel depend on the SSL handshake. Default certificates created on ESXi use SHA-1 with RSA encryption as the signature algorithm.
- Use a dedicated network vLAN or firewall for access to the ESXi host management interfaces. This prevents the chance of unauthorized parties from gaining access to the network.

Lockdown mode

To increase ESXi security, the hosts can be put in lockdown mode. In vSphere 6.0, lockdown mode has multiple settings and a user exception list. This allows for users and solutions to be excluded from the lockdown-mode settings. The following are the different configuration options available:

- **Disabled**: Lockdown mode is disabled.
- **Normal**: **Direct Console User Interface (DCUI)** is not blocked. Privileged user accounts can still log in to the ESXi host console and exit lockdown mode.
- **Strict**: DCUI is stopped and is only accessible through vCenter.

These settings provide more flexible access than the standard ESXi configuration normally allows. Strict mode dramatically reduces the manageability of the hosts because vSphere CLI commands cannot be executed from an administration server or script. In normal mode, the exception list provides an increased level of security, but specific users are allowed access to perform administrative functions, if required.

Securing vCenter Server

Consider the following when planning security for vCenter Server:

- Remove full administrative rights to vCenter Server from the local Windows administrator account and grant them to a special-purpose local vCenter Server administrator account.

  You can give full vSphere administrative rights only to specific administrators who really need them. You can restrict these rights to any group or members.

- You can define rules for logging in directly to the vCenter Server system. Users with defined tasks log in to the system with audited events.

- You must install vCenter Server using a service account rather than the local Windows system account. Using a service account enables Windows authentication for SQL Server with enhanced security. The service account must be an administrator on the local machine with all service rights.

- You have to give minimal access to a vCenter Server database user. The database users needs only rights specific to database access, along with some privileges required for installation and upgrades, which can be removed after the product is installed or upgraded.

- Connect vCenter and the ESXi hosts to a directory service. Create users and groups in the directory service to simplify user and group management, and to present a consistent user and group view to any interface managing the environment.
- Apply the principle of least privilege to users who have access to vCenter Server:
    - Enhances security by reducing the attack surface
    - Simplifies vCenter Server administration
- Do not add Windows special identity groups (such as everyone) to vCenter Server roles. Create specific Windows groups for specific vSphere management and assign the appropriate user permissions.
    - Membership is automatically calculated by Windows and is not static
    - Not using these groups reduces unplanned access issues
- Confirm that generic groups, such as the Windows administrators group, do not have permissions in vCenter. Create a specific Windows group for vCenter Server system administration. This reduces the risk of Windows administrators not trained in vSphere from gaining privileged access to the vCenter Server system.
- Configure additional administrators in vCenter **Single Sign-On (SSO)** users and groups, as appropriate, to allow multiple administrators access to the system in case an account is locked out.

Encryption and security certificates

ESXi and vCenter Server are well supported with standard X.509 version 3 certificates (you can get more details on these certificates at `https://tools.ietf.org/html/rfc6187`) to encrypt session data between components. By default, **VMware Certificate Authority (VMCA)** provisions vCenter Server components and ESXi hosts with signed certificates.

VMware virtual infrastructure use the following certificates by default:

- **ESXi certificates**: Used for SSL communication to and from the ESXi host. VMware CA delivers these certificates by default, and they are stored locally on each ESXi host.

- **Machine SSL certificates**: Used for communicating to and from vCenter Servers and Platform Service Controller instances. All communication goes through the reverse proxy, then a single certificate can be used. VMware CA provisions these certificates and they are stored in the **VMware Endpoint Certificate Store (VECS)**.
- **Solution user certificates**: Used by all solutions and services added to vCenter SSO for inter-component communication. VMware CA provisions these certificates and they are stored in VECS.
- **vCenter SSO signing certificate**: All certificates provisioned by VMCA have been signed by a root certificate. The root certificate is provisioned during installation of the Platform Services Controller and is stored on the local host file system. This can be changed as per requirement, but it should be managed by the vSphere Web Client.

Signed certificates are now used for the entire infrastructure and are automatically regenerated as needed for all solutions and for vCenter systems (where they are added to the Platform Services Controller domain). This solves many of the challenges that existed in previous releases. Note, however, that certificate operations are currently only administered through the command line.

If signed certificates are required, the vCenter SSO signing certificate can be replaced with an equivalent subordinate VMCA certificate from an external VMCA to allow it to function as a member of the certificate hierarchy in the environment.

For more details, see the *vSphere Security Certificates* section of the *vSphere Security* guide (`https://docs.vmware.com/en/VMware-vSphere/6.0/vsphere-esxi-vcenter-server-602-security-guide.pdf`).

Virtual network security considerations

The virtual networking layer includes virtual network adapters and virtual switches. ESXi relies on the virtual networking layer to support communications between virtual machines and their users, as well as communication with IP storage and other management traffic, such as vSphere vMotion.

In terms of communication, access to the network occurs in the same way as a physical host, only ESXi uses virtualized NICs and switches on the ESXi host. To provide external access, virtual switches are assigned a physical uplink on the ESXi host that has been connected to the appropriate networks.

The following characteristics apply to isolation in a virtualized network context:

- If a virtual machine does not share a virtual switch with any other virtual machine, it is completely isolated except through externally accessible means
- If no physical network adapter is configured for a virtual switch, virtual machines on that switch are completely isolated from any physical networks, but the virtual machines can still talk to one another
- If safeguards such as firewalls or antivirus are used to protect a virtual machine, the virtual machine is as secure as a physical machine

In addition to the built-in network security, the methods used to secure a virtual machine network depend on a variety of factors. Some of these factors include:

- The guest operating system that is installed.
- Whether the virtual machines operate in a trusted environment.
- The characteristics of the physical network.
- For example, ESXi supports IEEE 802.1q vLANs, which can be used to further protect the virtual machine network or storage configuration. However, if the physical switch does not support vLANs, the vLANs cannot be used to further enhance ESXi security.

The network can be one of the most vulnerable parts of any system. The virtual machine network requires as much protection as its physical counterpart. Virtual machine network security can be enhanced in several ways:

- Adding firewall protection to the virtual network by installing and configuring host-based firewalls on some or all of its virtual machines. However, because host-based firewalls can slow performance, security needs must be balanced against performance requirements before deciding to install host-based firewalls on virtual machines anywhere else in the virtual network.
- Keeping different virtual machine zones within a host on different network segments. If virtual machine zones on their own network segments are isolated, the risks of data leakage from one virtual machine zone to the next are minimized. Segmentation prevents various threats, including **Address Resolution Protocol** (**ARP**) spoofing, in which an attacker manipulates the ARP table to remap MAC and IP addresses, thereby gaining access to network traffic to and from a host. Attackers use ARP spoofing to generate man-in-the-middle attacks, perform DoS attacks, hijack the target system, and otherwise disrupt the virtual network.

- Planning segmentation carefully lowers the chances of packet transmissions between virtual machine zones, thereby preventing sniffing attacks that require sending network traffic to potential victims. Segmentation can be implemented by using either of two approaches, each of which has different benefits:
  - Use separate physical network adapters for virtual machine zones so that the zones are isolated. Maintaining separate physical network adapters for virtual machine zones is probably the most secure method and is less prone to misconfiguration after the initial segment creation.
  - Set up vLANs to help safeguard the network. vLANs provide almost all of the security benefits inherent in implementing physically-separate networks without the hardware overhead.

Network firewalls and vCenter Server

Firewalls provide basic protection for the network. A firewall is typically configured to protect vCenter Server so that there is a limited attack surface that can be exploited. This is most commonly accomplished by having vCenter on the same management network as the ESXi hosts, and configuring a firewall between the vCenter Server and the clients as an entry point for the system.

During normal operation, vCenter Server listens for data from its managed hosts and clients on designated ports. vCenter Server also assumes that its managed hosts listen for data from vCenter Server on designated ports. If a firewall is present between any of these elements, the necessary ports need to be opened to support permitted communication and data transfer.

Firewalls might also be included at a variety of other access points in the network, depending on how the network will be used and the level of security various devices require. Select the locations for firewalls, based on the security risks that have been identified for the network configuration in your environment. The following is a list of other locations where firewalls might commonly be deployed for ESXi implementations:

- Between the clients and vCenter Server.
- Between the clients and ESXi hosts if you are using the vSphere Client to connect directly.

- If firewalls are added between ESXi hosts, and if there is a plan to migrate virtual machines between the servers, perform cloning, or use vSphere vMotion, ports must also be opened in any firewall that separates the source host from the target hosts so that the source and targets can still communicate.
- Between the ESXi hosts and network storage, such as NFS or iSCSI storage. These ports can be configured according to the specifications of the network.

Adding more firewalls increases the complexity of administration of the networking elements. It is often best to secure the network with other means, such as vLANs, rather than creating an overly complicated firewall configuration.

Securing virtual machines with vLANs

vLANs are an IEEE standard networking scheme, with specific tagging methods, that allow routing of packets only to those ports that are part of the vLAN. When properly configured, vLANs provide a dependable means to protect a set of virtual machines from accidental or malicious intrusions.

vLANs allow a physical network to be segmented so that two machines in the network are unable to transmit packets back and forth unless they are part of the same vLAN. For example, accounting records and transactions are among a company's most sensitive internal information. In a company whose sales, shipping, and accounting employees all use virtual machines in the same physical network, one might protect the virtual machines for the accounting department by setting up vLANs.

Securing virtual switch ports

Virtual switches act in the same way as a physical switch in regard to the types of traffic that can be passed. As a result, both the standard virtual switch and vSphere Distributed Switch have security policies that can be configured to restrict different types of traffic.

Consider the following policies that are available with vSphere virtual switches:

- **Promiscuous mode**: The ability to allow a guest adapter to see all traffic passed on to a virtual switch.
- **MAC address changes**: The ability to accept or reject MAC address changes that have been made within the guest OS of a VM.

- **Forged transmits**: The ability to reject traffic that has different MAC addresses between the source and the frame.
- **Ingress traffic shaping**: Control or limit inbound traffic flow. This is only available for the vSphere Distributed Switch.
- **Egress traffic shaping**: Control or limit outgoing traffic flow.
- **vLANs**: Allow for traffic to be segmented into broadcast domains for security.
- **QoS**: Allow priority to be set for types of traffic. This is only available on the vSphere Distributed Switch.

Each of these policies can help to further secure the network configuration.

Securing iSCSI storage connectivity

If iSCSI storage is configured on a host, measures can be taken to minimize its security risks. Consider the following:

- Require that the host or initiator be authenticated by the iSCSI device or target whenever the host attempts to access data on the target **logical unit number (LUN)**. ESXi supports only CHAP key authentication for iSCSI.
- Verify that each iSCSI name is unique, and traffic is only allowed for expected initiators.
- Use segregated vLANs or dedicated storage-only switches for the iSCSI traffic, to prevent unauthorized snooping on that network.

Securing NFS storage connectivity

If NFS storage is configured on a host, measures can be taken to minimize the security risks associated with NFS. Consider the following actions that can be taken to safeguard NFS storage:

- Enable Kerberos with v4.1 NFS connectivity to encrypt traffic
- Use segregated vLANs or dedicated storage-only switches for the NFS traffic to prevent unauthorized snooping of that network

Virtual machine security considerations

Virtual machines are the containers in which applications and guest operating systems run. By design, all VMware virtual machines are isolated from one another. This isolation enables multiple virtual machines to run securely, while sharing hardware resources (CPU, memory, I/O), and provides their ability to access both hardware and to maintain uninterrupted performance.

Even a user with system administrator privileges on a virtual machine's guest operating system cannot breach this layer of isolation to access another virtual machine without privileges explicitly granted by the ESXi system administrator. As a result of this virtual machine isolation, if a guest operating system running in a virtual machine fails, other virtual machines on the same host continue to run. The guest operating system failure of one virtual machine has no effect on:

- The ability of users to access other virtual machines
- The ability of other operational virtual machines to access the resources they need
- The performance of other virtual machines

Virtual machines are similar to physical machines in that they are vulnerable to attack primarily through their network interfaces. To secure virtual machines, software should also be installed to protect the virtual machines from network vulnerabilities. Consider the following measures that can be taken to protect virtual machines from attacks:

- Confirm that antivirus, anti-spyware, intrusion detection, and firewalls are enabled for every virtual machine in the virtual infrastructure.
- Keep all security measures up to date, such as application of the latest security patches.
- Use a patch management tool to keep the virtual machine software and applications up to date.
- If the data center requires it, use smart card readers to access virtual machines with the vSphere Web Client remote console.
- Use vCenter Server roles to limit access to the virtual machine console windows.
- Create virtual machines from virtual machine templates that have been secured.
- We can protect virtual machines by configuring resource reservations and limits on the host. We can define that a specific virtual machine always receives at least 10% of the host's CPU resources through the detailed resource controls available in ESXi.

- Resource reservations and limits protect virtual machines from performance degradation and will help to achieve certain objectives from an application standpoint. If any virtual machine consumes excessive shared hardware resources on a host (such as being incapacitated by a **denial-of-service (DoS)** attack), a resource limit on that machine prohibits the attack from grabbing up so much of the hardware resources that the other virtual machines are also affected. Resource reservation on each of the virtual machines confirms that, in the event of high resource demands by the virtual machine targeted by the DoS attack, all the other virtual machines still have enough resources to operate.

Security design decisions

The following table lists the security storage design decisions for this architecture design:

Design decision	Design justification	Design implication
For this design, the customer has made the following decisions:		
ESXi hosts and vCenter Server are secured as defined in their respective logical designs.	Limiting user access and configuring appropriate security is a must for the virtualized environment.	None.
Lockdown mode will not be enabled.	ESXi already complies with internal security policies and therefore lockdown mode is not required.	None.
The default VMCA configuration will be used for the certificate infrastructure of the environment.	Added complexity to change to an internal VMCA certificate when signed certificates are already in place as a result of the VMCA.	Root certificate will need to be installed on the client.

Micro-segmentation and security design offers a functioning micro-segmentation solution using the distributed firewall functionality of VMware NSX for vSphere. This service delivers enhanced security protections for workload-workload traffic, either virtual-to-virtual or virtual-to-physical, and provides granular, dynamic control over security policies within the software-defined data center. This project includes the following modules:

- **Micro-segmentation and security**: This service provides assessment, technical validation of pre-requisites, design, deployment, and validation of NSX for vSphere micro-segmentation functionality. This includes L2-L4 stateful **distributed firewall (DFW)**, identity firewall, basic service composer, activity monitoring, and logging. This service includes a knowledge transfer session for the customer on the deployed solution.
- **PAN security**: Assessment, design, and integration of NSX for vSphere with **Palo Alto Networks (PAN)** next-generation firewall-VM Series for NSX, and Panorama manager. Implementation of PAN firewall policies, workload traffic, VM-to-VM traffic, redirection to L4 to L7 deep packet inspection, and advanced PAN firewall security protections in the existing NSX for vSphere micro-segmentation and security solutions.
- **Application modeling for micro-segmentation**: This service provides a repeatable methodology for securing applications within the virtual infrastructure. This methodology is tailored to meet a customer's specific requirements and is proven through the analysis and implementation of micro-segmentation for a select number of pre-determined applications in the customer environment.

The following are the activities included to achieve this:

- **Assess**: Gap identification between current and preferred end state
- **Design**: Solution design through a series of workshops and consultation
- **Deploy**: Deployment and validation of technology components
- **Validate**: Validation of detailed design
- **Knowledge transfer**: Knowledge transfer of the design, deployment, and operations procedures

Micro-segmentation – how to define security on east-west traffic

Specification	Description
Review solution requirements	We have to review requirements and use cases to define a customer's business and technology objectives. This should be combined with the components in the service checklist to customize functional design parameters. These design parameters are used to design the use cases.
Review and validate technical prerequisites	We have to configure vSphere with all pre-requisites for NSX components and physical network configurations (such as IP addressing, subnets, MTU, DMZ, auto-deploy, jumbo frames, and multicast), considering that they are designed to support the NSX micro-segmentation security services. Always follow VMware best practices guides for resolution.
Design sessions	Micro-segmentation and security design focuses on the following: • Virtual network architecture • Security architecture • Firewall policy • Data aggregation guidelines • Trust boundary topologies
Architecture design	• Development of architecture: • Virtual network diagrams • VMware NSX Edge firewall services • Workload network topology • Diagrams for NSX for vSphere components and management • Layer 3 Edge firewall operational requirements • Distribute firewall operational requirements • Firewall policy • Security group design • Service Composer use and interaction • Rules/policies for distributed firewall, Layer 3 Edge firewall, and identity firewall • Logging and monitoring • Define technical configuration parameters for solution components to implement the design

Deployment of NSX for vSphere Components	Pre-deployment assessment of the hardware and software requirements to determine whether the environment is ready and capable to start the NSX deployment.
NSX for vSphere Manager instance(s)	Installation, configuration, and validation of NSX for vSphere manager appliances, with registration to existing and configured VMware vCenter Server instances to protect workloads.
VMware ESXi hosts distributed firewall	Installation, configuration, and validation of distributed firewall ESXi kernel modules.
Edge firewall instance(s)	Installation, configuration, and validation of Layer 3 Edge firewall instances in either standalone or HA configuration.
Security groups	Security group definition and configuration.
Firewall rules configuration	Pack(s) of firewall rules configuration included. Each pack consists of up to ten (10) firewall rules, to be split between edge, distributed, and identity firewalls.
Configuration of micro-segmentation functional services	This service assesses, designs, and deploys the micro-segmentation solution using vCenter instance.
DFW	Configuration of stateful firewall functionality between tenant virtual machines within the same ESXi host or across different ESXi hosts using the DFW functionality
Activity monitoring	Configuration and demonstration of the ability to view activity on monitored virtual machines through the NSX for vSphere solution, and how this can be used to create application network flow models for future rule development and for troubleshooting and optimization
Identity firewall	Configuration for providing the capability to enforce security rules based on external directory service membership
Service composer	Define and apply security policies based on service profiles for NSX firewall rules
Logging and monitoring	Direct logging output to a pre-installed customer-designated syslog target such as VMware vRealize Log Insight

PAN security – integrating NSX with Palo Alto

Specification	Description
Requirements review	Requirements review and use case definition workshops to ascertain customer security policy goals and application security policy enforcement requirements. The result of these workshops is combined with the materials in the service checklist to establish functional design parameters for Palo Alto next-generation firewall integration.
Design review sessions	PANs integration with NSX design sessions facilitate drive key NSX for vSphere design decisions and security policy configuration parameters to support a customer's selected PANs and integrated NSX security use cases. This session includes review of customer security policy, compliance requirements, and VMware best practice recommendations on: • Application multi-tiering architecture • Firewall policy • Workload connectivity requirements • Security architecture-enterprise multizone security • Application threat protection
Integration of PANs next-generation firewall components	Pre-deployment review of integration requirements and determination of whether the NSX for vSphere environment is ready and capable to start the integration of a Palo Alto next-generation firewall
Panorama Manager	Installation and configuration of Panorama OVA on the designated cluster: • Registration of Panorama server with VMware NSX Manager Configuration of PANs installation package available to the NSX Manager by web browser: • Configuration of PANs licensing
VM-Series firewall	Installation of VM-Series for NSX firewall by way of NSX Manager

NSX firewall rule configuration	Pack(s) of firewall rules configuration included. Each pack consists of up to ten (10) firewall rules, to be split between edge, distributed, and identity firewalls. Configuration of guest VM traffic steering from NSX to the PAN service VM for introspection and threat prevention Confirm traffic flows through Panorama security platform Create Security Tags in NSX and confirm that these appear as dynamic groups in the Panorama interfaces Review Panorama user interfaces and integration with NSX platform Configuring and tuning security policy between the DFW and PANs VMs Create Security Tags in NSX and confirm these appear as dynamic groups in Panorama interfaces Confirmation of traffic steering from NSX to PANs service VMs Confirmation of PANs advanced threat protection for a guest VM
Security monitoring	Review of Panorama and NSX DFW user interface Monitoring security policy of guest VMs on Panorama Manager

Application modeling for micro-segmentation – protecting your apps from east-west traffic in a data center

Specification	Parameters	Description
Application profiling		Validate identified applications for micro-segmentation Understand and gather business requirements to understand application complexity Definition of simple, medium, and complex applications: Simple application: • One or two integration points with other systems • Relatively low risk Amount of VMs range: • **COTS**: < 20 VMs • **Custom applications**: < 10 VMs Medium application: • Application with multiple interdependencies • Three to four integration points • Moderate level of risk Amount of VMs range: • **COTS**: < 40 VMs • **Custom applications**: < 20 VMs Complex applications Applications with complex interdependencies More than five integration points High level of risk Amount of VMs range: • **COTS**: Custom range • **Custom applications**: Custom range
Analyze applications		Understand the selected application's network topology, configuration, architecture, and application integration points Review policies (for example, security based, firewall rules) to understand existing rules based on applications selected

Application security policy design		Definition and documentation of application specific security policy (per application)
Application security policy methodology		Definition and documentation of a repeatable process tailored to meet a customer's requirements for micro-segmentation of applications, incorporating business and risk objectives for securing application-specific network communications within the virtual data center. Creation of an overall workflow to show a repeatable process to implement an application-specific security policy.
Application security policy execution		Deploying the application-specific security policy via a deployed NSX environment.
Application security policy validation		Testing and validation of applied application-specific security policies.

VMware vRealize Configuration Manager architecture design

The VMware vRealize Configuration Manager architecture design was developed to support virtual infrastructure compliance and change management within the customer environment. The required platform being defined here will be used to assist a customer with configuration, change, and compliance of their virtual infrastructure, including the guest computing resources, as well as provide a tool for patching both Linux and Windows Server guest machines.

This chapter details the recommended implementation of a **vRealize Configuration Manager (VCM)** foundation architecture based on VMware recommended practices and specific customer requirements and goals. The document provides both logical and physical design considerations that encompass all VMware VCM-related infrastructure components, including requirements and specifications for virtual machines, networking and storage, and management. After this initial foundation architecture is successfully implemented, the architecture can be recreated within other environments and classifications to support further customer initiatives.

Backup and restore

While most configuration changes will be made via the vSphere Web Client, these changes are then written to the NSX Manager database. Backup system configuration is provided by the NSX Manager appliance interface, not via the vSphere Web Client.

It is critical that NSX Manager is backed up on a regular basis. Backups can be scheduled on an hourly, daily, or weekly basis, down to the minute. The backup data is saved to a remote location that the NSX Manager can access through FTP or SFTP. It is possible to exclude logs and flow data from backups.

FTP and SFTP are currently the only available options for backup of the NSX Manager. SFTP is recommended for increased security.

General use cases of customers

This design is targeted at the following use cases:

- **Change management**: This is the process for managing change in the project
- **Configuration management**: A configuration management process defines how configuration management will be done to those parameters which are configurable or, require formal change control, and the process for controlling changes
- **Patch management**: Ability to apply OS patches to guest machines:
    - Windows
    - Red Hat Linux
- **Guest OS compliance**: toolkits for Windows and Linux
- **Virtual infrastructure compliance**: vSphere hardening guides

vRealize Configuration Manager logical architecture overview

The following diagram depicts the entire logical architecture featuring all of the functionality possible within a VCM deployment. In most cases, customers will deploy an architecture design that matches the agreed upon use cases being driven by business requirements:

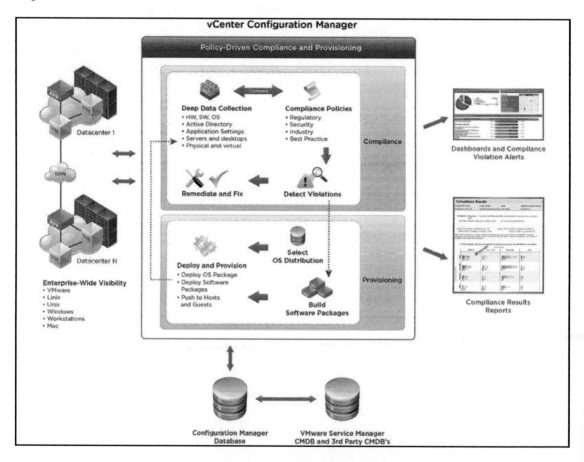

VCM logical architecture overview

VCM implements an agent-based model for compliance and change management data collections. For each vCenter server, VCM uses an intermediary managing agent to collect data via the vSphere VIM API. Collections to ESX classic hosts are via an agent proxy (not required for ESXi 5 and higher hosts). For Microsoft Active Directory compliance, an agent with the Active Directory extensions is deployed on each domain controller.

VCM platform

This section details the logical specifications of the VCM collectors and databases required for the customer's deployment. The overall design and deployment consists of three distinct phases. The first phase includes deploying an instance of VCM within the primary data center. It will be configured to meet the defined use cases for managing both primary and secondary data centers:

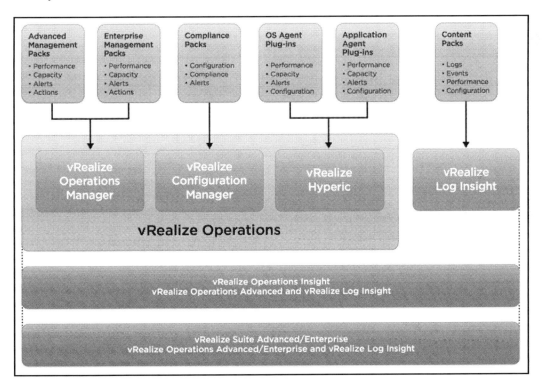

vRealize Components complement each other

The design is based on a two-tier VCM deployment supporting both primary and secondary data centers.

User access to VCM shall be configured to use HTTPS and basic authentication to the collector server. Managing agent machines will be utilized to act as a proxy for collecting virtual infrastructure data. A managing agent machine can be any supported Windows Server guest machine with minimum resources allocated and the VCM agent installed:

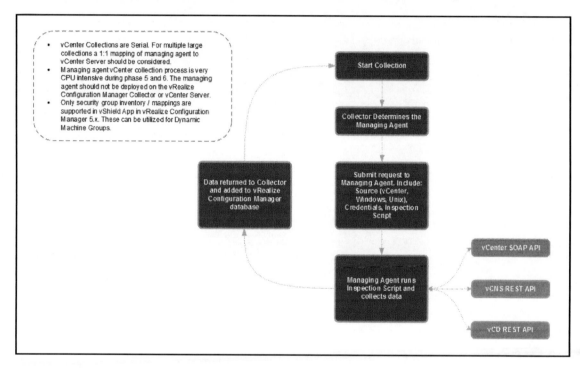

VCM managing agent logical architecture

The objects that were managed are brought under the management of this new VCM instance in a secondary data center. The first instance of VCM is left in place as preparation for the final phase III end-state configuration. The following diagram shows the workflow of Configuration Manager:

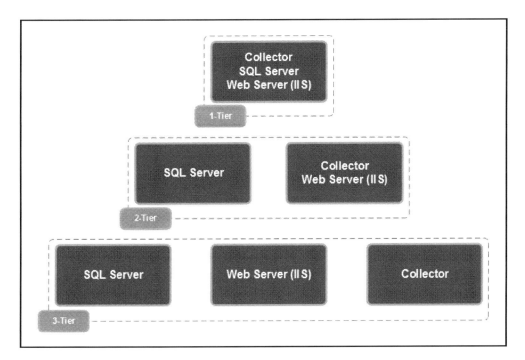

VCM possible deployments

The preceding diagram depicts the end-state configuration for the two instances of VCM deployed within primary and secondary data centers. As shown, the primary data center instance will manage a sandbox environment, and will be used for dev/test purposes by customers.

Summary

We have learned, in this chapter, how NSX Manager generates self-signed certificates for each of the hosts and controller nodes that are pushed to them over secure channels. A single CA-signed certificate will be installed for the NSX Manager to secure both the management interface and API endpoint on port 443. The vFabric RabbitMQ broker certificates, sent to the NSX Manager for communications with ESXi hosts, are uniquely generated on first boot.

NSX Manager instances on each site are configured to integrate with the vCenter SSO service associated with the vCenter Server instance to which they are bound. This facilitates the secure authentication of vCenter users within NSX for vSphere and any of the identity stores configured under vCenter, including LDAP, Active Directory, and NIS directories. The integration is set up through the NSX Manager user interface by supplying the address and port of the vCenter SSO server.

The NTP settings for the NSX Manager must be configured to ensure its time is in sync with the time of the vCenter SSO service. SSO authentication is highly time sensitive, so verify that the components involved are not subject to drift.

There are two ways to access and configure NSX Manager. The vCenter/vSphere web UI is the primary configuration interface for NSX. When NSX is deployed to vSphere, configuration extensions are installed and available within the vSphere web UI and vCenter. All NSX configuration including firewall policies, routing, and logical switching is configured there.

NSX for vSphere/vCenter uses **role-based access control (RBAC)** to grant permissions to users or groups, and to control access to resources and operations that users can perform. RBAC is a method of regulating access to configuration objects and rights within NSX based upon user or group membership. Roles are usually defined across administrative task boundaries or based upon the technical responsibility of the user or group.

We will next learn about how to apply compliance standards for different customers, evaluate the customer's internal compliance policies and processes, how to map customer policies and processes to acceptable risk, and finally, identify any potential gaps and challenges.

10
Designing Effective Compliance Regulations to Fix Violations

This chapter will help you in designing compliance regulations for multiple purposes. Compliance is no longer the domain of only legal, security, and compliance departments. With the move to the cloud and the rise of mobile technology, IT now plays an essential role in determining how to be compliant. Vertical markets have specific requirements in security and compliance. Also, it's not only IT that is dealing with compliance, it's also business divisions that are struggling with the requirements, and IT has to deliver by leveraging the best technology: VMware.

Security and compliance must be a shared responsibility between IT and its cloud service provider. In this chapter, we will cover the following topics:

- Assessing what compliance standards are relevant for your organization
- Evaluating the maturity of your own internal compliance policies and processes
- Mapping your policies and processes to acceptable risk
- Identifying any potential gaps and challenges

We have to analyze the number of applications, types of shared resources, and pertinent levels of regulations in both physical and virtual environments, and map them according to the **Content Security Policy (CSP)**'s security features and **Industry Specific Compliance**, such as ISO 14000, PCI DSS, HIPAA, and so on.

Best practices to follow for compliance regulations

Compliance regulations and internal auditors tend to focus on a core set of typical control objectives and control activities. Control objectives specify the actions that must be performed to be in compliance with the standard or requirement. Objectives state what needs to be done, but not how to do it. For example, an objective might state, "*All administrator actions on the financial production application will be reviewed on a daily basis and correlated with approved change requests.*"

Control activities are the set of actions that you implement in order to meet the control objective. Activities state how to accomplish objectives and describe exactly how actions are done on a periodic basis to meet the intent of the control objectives. For example, a control activity might be defined with the statement, "*Log all administrative activity on the production financial application and review the log daily. All actions in the log are matched with our change request system. If the log is not reviewed by 4 PM, there is an automatic escalation to management.*"

Any system, such as a server, an application, or a database, that falls under the jurisdiction of a compliance or audit regimen is said to be in-scope. If an application or database is in-scope, then the platform on which it runs is also in-scope. If an in-scope application or database is running in a **virtual machine** (**VM**), on a hypervisor, the hypervisor layer is also in-scope.

Although there are many different compliance and internal audit standards and best practices, they tend to have very similar sets of control objectives. When speaking about compliance in a virtual environment, the goal should be to implement control activities on the virtualization layer for the most common core controls. This best practice promotes consistency and scalability of your compliance control activities.

In this chapter, you will learn more about several categories of controls, along with some specific examples. We will explore a couple of these controls in more depth. The controls that are presented in this section are only a few examples out of the many controls that exist. Our objective is to give you an idea of how compliance controls are organized, represented, and implemented. Each published standard has its own set of specific, required controls that must be implemented in order to meet that standard's compliance requirements. In a later section, we will examine the tools that VMware provides to help you ensure that you are in compliance with a given standard.

Controls are the specific requirements that a site must implement and adhere to, in order to be in compliance with a given standard. Examples of control categories include the following:

Network controls might dictate how network isolation must be implemented or how network data is to be monitored. Change control and configuration management might specify processes to ensure that changes are tracked, and are made only by those who are authorized to make changes to the configuration. The access controls and roles category might include controls that require the use of role-based delegated administration for administrative staff. The *vulnerability management category* might include controls that specify when and where antivirus software must be deployed, or how patch management must be handled. Logging controls ensure that all changes or activities are logged so that you enforce accountability requirements.

We will examine some sample controls from each category and explain how you can use VMware functionality or features to implement the example controls:

Systems that are connected to networks are inherently vulnerable to being compromised through their network connections, so many compliance standards include network controls. There are features and technologies in VMware products that actually make it easier and more effective to implement network controls when compared to physical server and network deployments.

A standard might be required. For example, you segment your network traffic to separate different categories of data. In a physical network environment, you might use VLANs or multiple layer 3 subnets to implement a segmentation requirement. In a virtualized environment, you can leverage additional VMware functionality to implement a network segmentation control. For example, virtual switches contain port groups that you can use to specify security and other policies that apply to groups of VMs. VXLANs allow you to create logical, virtual networks that span layer 3 boundaries or that span multiple switches on a single layer 2 network. You can create multiple virtual switches to support your network segmentation policies and requirements.

Another network control might require strict isolation of your site's management network. You can use NSX to define network boundaries between your production and management networks or applications. Many standards include monitoring controls. In a VMware virtualized environment, you can easily implement a monitoring requirement with VMware App Traffic Monitor as well as with the industry standard SNMP and syslog capabilities.

Change control and configuration management controls specify how changes to the environment are performed. A standard might require that you have a defined process in place and that all changes are audited. System configurations must be consistent and managed centrally to prevent unauthorized changes that can lead to noncompliance after a system is accredited and deployed. VMware provides several options that you can use to ensure that your systems are configured correctly.

For change and configuration control, you have the option of using **vCenter Configuration Manager (VCM)**. VCM eliminates manual, error prone, and time consuming configuration management tasks. VCM can automatically and continuously detect and compare configuration changes to your site policies or compliance requirements.

It is important to harden your system configurations to reduce vulnerabilities and to maintain compliance. VMware publishes hardening guides that you can use to direct your hardening efforts. You can also use vSphere templates or clones to deploy new VMs from a preconfigured master VM that adheres to your compliance requirements. A third example control is a requirement to verify and monitor the integrity of files. As with other configuration change monitoring, you can use vCenter Configuration Manager to monitor your environment for inappropriate file modifications.

Access controls specify which administrative users can access and perform administrative tasks on your systems. Compliance requirements might dictate that you assign separate sets of administrative duties to different groups of administrators. This practice prevents any single administrator from having so much power or rights that the administrator can perform unauthorized actions without being detected. This practice is known as the separation of duties doctrine, or the two-person rule. VMware provides functionality known as role-based delegated administration, which you can use to assign administrative rights to different administrators. Role-based delegated administration is implemented through the use of permissions. A permission specifies who can perform which actions, and on which objects.

vSphere introduced a Single Sign-On service. All administrative access uses the Single Sign-On service, including the vSphere client and the vSphere web client, which is the new primary administrative interface in vSphere. You can use the vSphere web client to log in to a vCenter Server, for example, vCenter Server uses the vSphere Single Sign-On server to authenticate you. Once authenticated, you can access other administrative interfaces or utilities without having to authenticate again. Your client software presents your authenticated credentials to the new service so that you don't have to. The Single Sign-On service has extensive logging functionality that you can use as part of your compliance logging controls. Single Sign-On is enabled by default in vSphere.

Most compliance regimes require that you keep your systems updated with current patches in order to reduce vulnerabilities and risks associated with out-of-date software. VMware has two primary tools that you can use to keep your systems patched.

You can get more details on this from this link: `https://www.hhs.gov/hipaa/for-professionals/privacy/laws-regulations/index.html`

For payment card industry compliance and SOX with VMware, please refer to this link: `https://www.vmware.com/content/dam/digitalmarketing/vmware/en/pdf/solutions/vmware-payment-card-industry-solution-guide.pdf`, `https://blogs.vmware.com/security/tag/sox`.

VCM has the ability to automatically remediate out-of-compliance configurations and to assess the operating system patch status so that it can deploy updated patches as needed.

VMware Go is a browser-based management service that aims to ease and simplify the virtualization process for small- and medium-sized organizations. Although VMware Go has a number of features, from a compliance perspective, the patch management aspect is the most relevant. The VMware Go Pro version allows you to scan physical and virtual machines for missing patches for Microsoft operating systems as well as applications from a wide selection of software vendors. You can scan by machine name, domain name, or IP address range, and you can schedule automated patch scans and deployment. VMware Go Pro is able to export your patch deployment historical data into Excel, comma-separated value files, PDF, or other formats for analysis or reporting purposes.

Aside from keeping your systems upgraded and patched, you can use vShield Endpoint to manage antivirus and anti-malware policies for virtualized environments with the same management interfaces you use to secure physical environments. vShield Endpoint offloads antivirus and anti-malware agent processing to a dedicated secure virtual appliance that is delivered by VMware partners. vShield Endpoint is part of the vSphere platform. It consists of the hardened secure virtual appliance, which includes the partner vendor's antivirus software, a driver for virtual machines to offload file events, and the VMware Endpoint security loadable kernel module to link the first two components at the hypervisor layer.

Most compliance standards include a logging control that requires the system to be able to store information about specific events and administrative actions. System events include changes in state or configuration, error conditions, performance issues, and so on. Administrative tasks must also be logged and typically include every action taken by an administrative user. Many compliance standards require that the log data be stored so that it is inaccessible to the administrators who are being logged. This practice ensures that an administrator cannot perform unauthorized actions and then modify the logs to remove evidence of their illicit actions.

Logs are the foundation of effective logging, monitoring, and reporting. Logging entails collecting the required data and storing it in a secure, unalterable manner. Monitoring is the act of examining the collected data and can be performed by a compliance auditor, managers, or administrators themselves, depending on the objective. A reporting function allows you to create accurate, consistent, and verifiable reports about the events and actions taken on the audited system.

vSphere, vCenter, and NSX all have extensive logging capabilities. Keep in mind that although logging is an almost integral component of a compliance regime, logs are also useful to IT administrators for performance monitoring, troubleshooting, and resource or capacity planning purposes.

While logging is not usually a compliance activity on its own, it is often a key part of other logging activities and is consequently an integral component of most systems that are subject to compliance regulations. Effective logging functions ensure that all relevant events and tasks are recorded. Events are actions that occur in the system, while tasks are actions that are performed by the system administrators or users. In both cases, you need to know who, or what, did what to what. A comprehensive logging function fulfills that requirement.

With the notable exception of the Windows vCenter Server, most components of vSphere now utilize the industry standard syslog logging utility. Syslog originated in *Berkeley Unix* in the *1980*s and has since been adopted by a wide range of vendors in thousands of products. With syslog, you have fine grained control over the location of log files. Systems or applications that use syslog encapsulate each log message into a UDP datagram that is then sent to a syslog collector service. The syslog collector can be local on the vSphere host or it can be on a remote system. You can control the maximum size of your log files. You can also configure log file rotation policies so that individual log files do not grow too large to manage. vSphere uses *syslog* for all of its logging functions. Logs are sent to local files in the */var/log* directory on the host. These log files contain important information that you can use for both security and performance reasons. Now, we will list some of the information that you can find in the log files:

- You can find shell authentication successes and failures, which you can use to detect unauthorized access attempts
- You can also examine DHCP events including discovery, lease requests, and renewals
- vSphere patch and update installation logs are available
- Host management service is available including VM and host events, and communication with vSphere client and vCenter Server
- You can find VMkernel startup and kernel module loading information
- Management service initialization, watchdogs, scheduled tasks, and **Direct Console User Interface (DCUI)** use is also logged in these files
- USB device arbitration events are logged including VM pass through
- VMkernel core events are logged including device discovery, storage and networking driver events, and VM startups
- The warning and alert log contains summaries from other files

vSphere hosts can be managed directly as standalone hosts. However, most environments manage their hosts with vCenter Server. vSphere hosts that are managed by vCenter Server include additional logs. The *vpxa* process is vCenter Server's agent on the ESXi host. The associated vpxa logs have information about all of the communication that has occurred between vCenter Server and the vpxa agent on the host. vCenter Server manages all High-availability (HA) clusters. A **Fault Domain Manager** (FDM) service runs on the host if the ESXi host is part of the cluster. The FDM service captures additional logging information in its own log files on the ESXi host. FDM logs have information about both HA Master and HA Slave actions on each host. vCenter Server generates its own logs in addition to ESXi log files. vCenter Server uses syslog to process its log messages like all ESXi components. The master vCenter Server logs are in files called `vpxd.log`. The `vpxd.log` file has information about all vSphere client and web services connections. Internal tasks and events are also logged along with communications from vCenter Server to vpxa agents.

vCenter log profile metrics for all operations managed by the vCenter Server are kept in several log files, including `vpxd-profiler.log`, `profiler.log`, and `scoreboard.log`. Profiled metrics are used by the VPX Operational Dashboard, which you can view using a web browser at `https://vCenterName/vod/index.html`. The `cim-diag.log` and `vws.log` contain files **Common Information Model (CIM)** monitoring information, including communication between vCenter Server and the CIM, the interface of managed hosts. The drmdump log files contain information about actions designed and taken by the VMware Distributed Resource Scheduler. These logs are compressed and you can view vCenter Server logs with the vSphere client from the `Home > Administration > System Logs` screen.

The Edge capability of NSX provides a critical security function, so it's important that you collect and secure information about all activities and events that occur. Edge uses syslog to generate log messages, so the logs can be forwarded to a centralized logging server. You can enable or disable logging in Edge. You can also determine the level of logging to perform, and for which types of events. You define firewall and network address translation (NAT) logging at the rule level. VPN logging is managed based on the site-to-site connection name. The web load balancer function is managed at the pool level, including specific URLs or folders. DHCP logging is configured at the service level, including binding operations, such as DHCP releases or renewals. NSX Edge also collects statistics about the network traffic that it manages. Both the logs and network flow statistics are accessible through REST APIs. **REST** is the acronym for a web services architecture known as **Representational State Transfer**. Clients make requests for information from servers, which in turn provide the requested information to the client in the form of a representation of the requested resource. Because VMware Edge implements the REST APIs, third parties can easily integrate Edge logging and statistics management into their applications.

The following diagram illustrates **Log Insight** Integration with NSX through REST APIs:

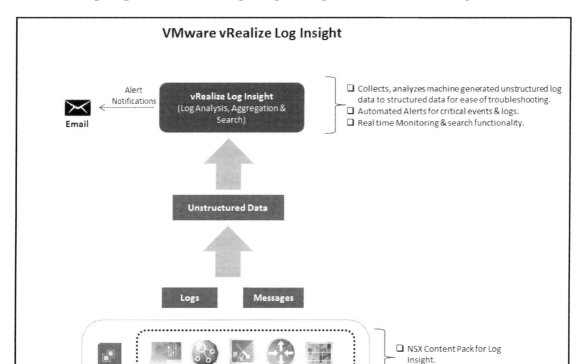

Centralized log collection of all NSX components

NSX manager manages VMware security products and provides for integration and management of third party security services. You use the manager to manage and deploy Edge virtual appliances, as well as to view logs and reports generated by the Edge appliances.

The Solution Guide for PCI is a comprehensive and detailed document that includes very specific mappings between the PCI controls and the designated solution that you use to implement or enforce the given control.

For example, you can address network controls and network logging requirements with VXLAN, distributed switch port groups, and NSX. Change control and configuration management solutions include vCenter Configuration Manager and NSX. You can use the refresh operation with VMware View linked clones to regularly reset virtual desktops back to a known, compliant configuration.

We can implement and enforce access controls and roles with the logging mechanisms that we discussed earlier, along with the role-based access control functions of vCenter, vCloud, and NSX.

We can use vCenter Configuration Manager and vShield Endpoint to address vulnerability management compliance controls:

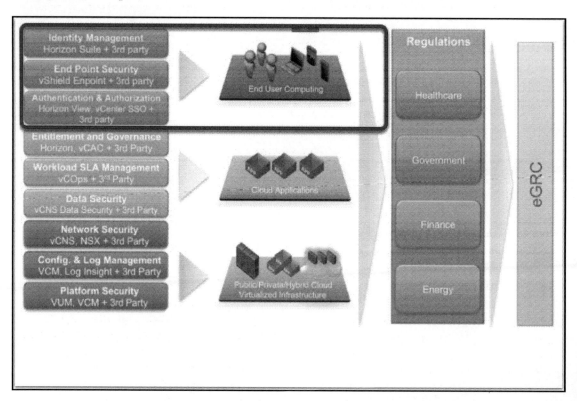

You can use VCM to manage nearly all of the components in your environment, including your VMware infrastructure, operational components, Active Directory, and security components, as well as applications. From a compliance perspective, VCM provides automated collection, assessment, change tracking, and remediation of your systems. This consistent, automated configuration management allows you to use policy driven configuration management to ensure initial and ongoing system compliance. VCM automates configuration and management tasks across virtual and physical servers, workstations, and desktops. VCM has a large number of features and functions, some of which are relevant to your compliance efforts. VCM features help you enforce your compliance requirements.

They help you to automatically detect and compare changes to your compliance policies to avoid configuration drift. You can manage continuous compliance with the out-of-the box templates and toolkits that are part of the product. Configuration change execution and monitoring can be centralized across VMware infrastructure and Windows, Linux, and Unix operating systems.

There is rigorous and continuous configuration data collection, configuration assessment, and change auditing, and unified reporting of configuration data and compliance assessment results in real-time scenarios.

Remediation of out-of-compliance configurations is automated, and vCM is a **Security Content Automation Protocol (SCAP)** 1.0 validated product. Information about SCAP is available at: `http://scap.nist.gov/revision/1.0`.

The VMware center for compliance and policy has released a set of free compliance checkers that you can use to perform an assessment of your systems. Each compliance checker performs a compliance check for a single standard. You can simultaneously assess a small number of hosts or virtual machines for compliance. The exact number of simultaneous assessments depends on the specific compliance checker. To use any of the available checkers, download and launch the selected checker on a Windows desktop. The compliance checkers use an intuitive, easy to use, web-based interface with little or no learning curve. Simply point the checker at a target environment (specific hosts or specific VMs) and execute a compliance assessment request. The compliance report provides a detailed rule-by-rule indication of passes or failures of the selected object or objects. For compliance violations, you are directed to a detailed knowledge base where you can find an explanation of the rule violation and advice on how to remediate the violation.

Three use cases for virtualization technology from a security perspective are as follows:

- It is common to be wary when you first consider running your business critical applications on virtual, rather than physical machines. In this module, we first examine how you can secure and protect business critical applications.
- The second use case that's of particular concern is a **virtual desktop infrastructure (VDI)** deployment. The desktop might contain sensitive or confidential organization data that must be protected. In addition, sending desktop display data across potentially unprotected public networks is a concern. We address these VDI-based security issues in the second half of this module.
- The third use case, cloud deployments, is discussed in a separate module later in this course.

Many organizations have virtualized portions of their physical IT infrastructure. Typically, organizations virtualize their less critical systems and applications first. This approach gives them time to gain experience with virtualization technology, concepts, and implementations, and time to train and certify their IT staff who will be managing the virtual infrastructure. In order to remain competitive, organizations must ultimately consider virtualizing their business critical applications as well. Successful organizations that want to remain competitive are moving toward **IT as a service (ITaaS)**. These organizations need to turn their IT infrastructure into a competitive advantage, which means they must leverage the same operational and capital expense savings from their business critical applications as their initial virtualization yielded when they consolidated their base IT infrastructure.

Business critical applications are known by several different terms, including *line-of-business applications,* or *Tier-One apps*. Generally speaking, business critical applications are those applications on which the success or failure of the business or organization rests.

In one real-world example, an automobile manufacturer virtualized their assembly line computer systems to achieve greater reliability and availability because they were experiencing regular stoppages caused by failures of the application on physical servers. When the application or server on which the application ran was down, the entire assembly line would be halted. The company calculated that each minute the application was down, it cost them roughly one million US dollars. Their assembly line application is a perfect example of a business critical application that requires the highest level of availability and robustness. These applications are directly related to business revenue. If the application is unavailable for infrastructure or security reasons, the business loses real money. For obvious reasons, upper level management is understandably wary of any changes to these business critical applications.

Likewise, many business critical applications are subject to regulatory compliance or audit controls, which add to their importance. A virtualization infrastructure that can support business critical applications must provide three essential capabilities. All three of these capabilities are directly or indirectly related to the security of your applications:

- The first capability is **Availability**. If an attacker or unscrupulous insider can make an application unavailable to the legitimate users, the attack succeeds and the business or organization suffers harm.
- The second essential capability of a business class virtualization infrastructure is **Security.** Applications and data must be secure so that both the business and its customers or clients have confidence in the business' controls. Security includes securing not just the application, but the guest operating system, as well as the host and infrastructure on which the application depends.
- Finally, the third capability is **Compliance.** When you virtualize business critical applications, the virtualization environment must be able to support the application's required compliance and audit controls in the same manner as a physical deployment.

We will examine each of these three capabilities in more detail.

The second essential infrastructure capability is security. The owners or managers who are responsible for business critical applications must have confidence in the security of the underlying systems on which their applications run. Management has familiarity and experience with running their applications on dedicated physical hardware, but virtualizing that hardware can be something's that unknown, especially where security is concerned. Securing virtual applications depends on securing both the virtual machines on which the applications run, as well as the networks to which the VMs and applications connect.

You can leverage VMware security products to ensure the security of your business critical applications. NSX provides firewall protection for groups of related virtual machines, such as those hosting your application, and its dependent services, such as supporting database systems.

We will examine each of these in more detail in the following sections.

Business critical applications typically have heightened security requirements, for business or compliance reasons. You can use NSX to create a mixed trust environment in which some applications or systems require different levels of security than others. There are three trust zones that are shown in this example: the DMZ, the Extranet zone, and the PCI zone, in which, payment-related business critical applications are deployed. All zones belong to the same Distributed Resource Cluster. By putting them all in the same cluster, you gain optimal utilization and consolidation from features such as VMware **Distributed Resource Schedule (DRS)** and VMware High Availability. The next diagram represents trust zone from on-premise cloud to public cloud:

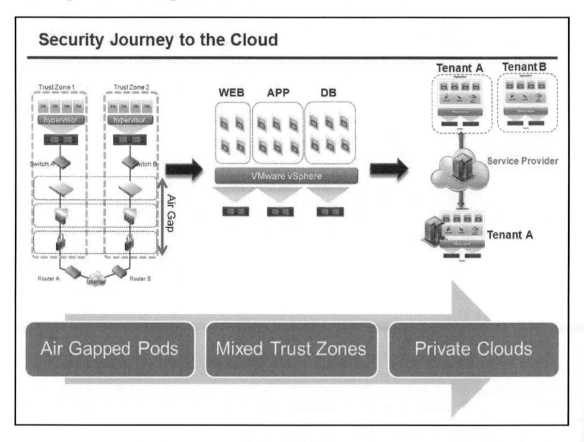

Mixed-trust environment

The PCI zone is used to enforce PCI compliance controls for payment-related systems. PCI standards mandate the network segmentation of servers that process credit card data from other systems in order to protect consumers. In a virtualized environment such as this one, virtual firewalls provide the required segmentation in a much more flexible and dynamic manner than a physical firewall deployment.

NSX adds additional functionality to an application to identify and protect sensitive business data on the systems you are protecting. NSX Edge is a virtual appliance-based firewall that is used to protect the perimeter of virtual data centers. Edge allows you to create firewalled environments based on function rather than on physical location and physical network devices.

With NSX, you can enable firewall policies between VMs that process credit card data and other untrusted networks and machines as required by the PCI data security standard:

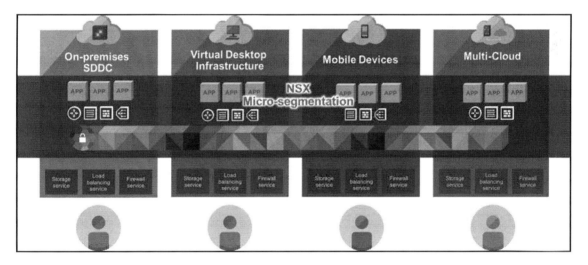

NSX micro-segmentation

Virtual machines that belong to different trust zones run on physical hosts and share the same physical network devices. A trust zone can be loosely defined as a network segment within which data flows relatively freely, whereas data flowing in and out of the trust zone is subject to stronger restrictions.

Examples of trust zones include:

- **Demilitarized zones (DMZs)**
- PCI cardholder data environments
- Site-specific zones, such as segmentation according to department and function
- Application-defined zones, such as the three tiers of a web application

Virtual technology does not have to significantly change the network topology. However, purely replicating a physical network with virtual machines can greatly limit the benefits of virtualization.

In physical environments, organizations can isolate their networks using physically separate networks or VLANs. In virtualized environments, administrators have fine grained control for implementing segmentation. You can group ports on a virtualized environment together in a port group. Each port group can have a separate VLAN ID.

Within a cloud infrastructure, users and consumers can create their own networks based on their organizational needs. These networks, called vApp networks, are based on port groups in vSphere.

VXLANs separate the VM network ID from its physical location using a layer 2 abstraction. VXLANs preserve isolation on the network level while at the same time, VMs can communicate across different locations.

Many business critical applications are multi-tiered apps, and you can use vCloud networking and security to provide support to layered, multi-tiered applications. For example, you might have VMs running a two-tiered application, where the web services and a **customer relationship management** (CRM) application are running on a frontend server, and the database is running on a backend server. You might also place the frontend servers in one cluster and the backend servers in another cluster.

You can use an app's firewall rules to provide security for business critical applications at different levels. These rules can be IP- or subnet-based, just like you would use on a traditional firewall. However, by leveraging container labels, such as data centers and clusters to create the firewall rules, your configuration is much simpler, less error-prone, and automatically adapts when VMs are added or removed from the environment.

You can leverage vSphere functionality in conjunction with Edge to create a variety of configurations to support your business critical application's security. As a general rule, you should implement security in layers, so that there is no single point of vulnerability. Application security is enhanced and enforced in layers throughout the vSphere or vCloud environment and can include a number of components.

For example, you can create a DMZ deployment to provide three-tiered application protection with vCloud Networking, Security, Edge, and vSphere High Availability. You can use different combinations of firewall rules and **network address translation (NAT)** configurations within various Edge security appliances to enforce varying protection levels for your virtual data centers. You capture your logging data from all of your Edge security appliances and use syslog's centralized collection functionality to secure the logs on a dedicated, hardened, logging server to protect against tampering. You can use the Edge health and performance monitoring and flow monitoring capabilities in conjunction with the vCenter Server performance monitoring charts to detect errors, performance bottlenecks, or clues about potential security issues. Using Edge and vCenter Server, you can greatly improve the security and reliability of your business critical application deployments.

When you deploy your business critical applications on physical, dedicated systems, the required compliance and audit control processes are well-known functions for most IT staff. When you virtualize the business critical applications that are subject to regulatory or legal compliance requirements, you must ensure the same level of compliance. We discussed the compliance and audit control features of vSphere infrastructure and vCloud products in a previous section.

Desktop operating systems and applications present unique security challenges, particularly in a physical deployment environment. Traditionally, data is exchanged between data center servers and clients through applications that are deployed in both locations as well as through the use of file sharing protocols. Client assets, user software, and user actions are only partially controlled because of the decentralized nature of physical desktop deployments. Data center assets are highly controlled, and no user software execution is allowed.

Some business critical applications are desktop-based, rather than server-based. That is, they run on Windows desktop operating systems, such as Windows 7. VMware View is a complete, feature rich virtual desktop infrastructure solution that supports the virtualization of Windows desktops.

With VMware View, you can standardize your user access method to your corporate Windows desktop sources. This standardization enables a centralized, scalable, top-down enforcement model that allows you to enforce your corporate security and compliance requirements for Windows desktops. Once the desktops are centralized and virtualized, you can centralize the management of your business critical applications. With this centralized management structure, you have the ability to entitle applications to specific groups of users, or to pools of desktops, based on your organization's defined use cases. That is, only those users who need access to a particular business application will actually be entitled to access that application. Both the entitlement, and the application itself, are managed centrally by the administrator, rather than by the Windows desktop owner.

When you convert your user desktops to virtual desktops with View, the data center boundary is effectively extended, and the client boundary is reduced, as shown in the following diagram. Rather than having only minimal control over the user desktops, with VMware View virtualized desktops, you identify and control 100% of your desktops. This approach allows you to ensure compliance with your corporate desktop policies and configurations. User controlled software runs as a parallel workload to data center servers where it can be centrally managed and secured.

VMware View is integrated with the vShield Endpoint antivirus virtual appliance solution. vShield Endpoint implements antivirus protection for desktop VMs through the use of an antivirus virtual appliance. The vShield Endpoint security VM uses the hypervisor kernel to inspect the VMs' data and network traffic. Antivirus software that is installed in the security virtual machine is applied to the data from outside of the protected VM Windows operating system, making it impossible for viruses or other malicious software to defeat the antivirus checks:

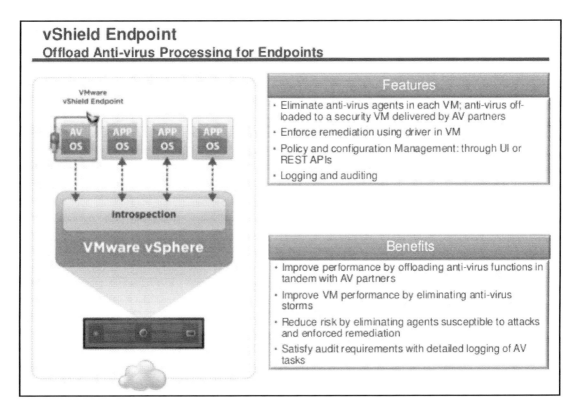

vShield Endpoint
Offload Anti-virus Processing for Endpoints

Features

- Eliminate anti-virus agents in each VM; anti-virus off-loaded to a security VM delivered by AV partners
- Enforce remediation using driver in VM
- Policy and configuration Management: through UI or REST APIs
- Logging and auditing

Benefits

- Improve performance by offloading anti-virus functions in tandem with AV partners
- Improve VM performance by eliminating anti-virus storms
- Reduce risk by eliminating agents susceptible to attacks and enforced remediation
- Satisfy audit requirements with detailed logging of AV tasks

vShield Endpoint Protection for Antivirus

You can use NSX Edge and apps to secure your View desktops. Use Edge to create protected zones that contain your VMware View components, including View clients and the Connection and Security Servers to which the users connect. In addition, the security zone contains the vSphere host clusters that serve as your View desktop sources, as well as your management VMs that provide services such as vCenter Server, or management applications such as the Splunk logging utility. You can use Edge firewall rules to allow or control access to shared resources, including vCenter Server, and the required network connections. An app can then be used to create enclaves of users and business critical applications within each security zone that you create for your View instance with Edge.

This practice isolates different sets of users from one another, even though they might be using and sharing the same View server components in the View deployment:

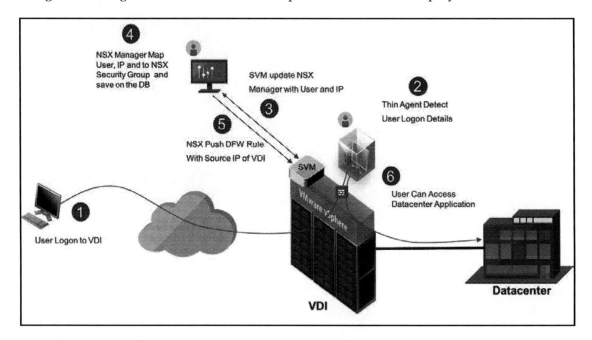

Protecting VDI Infrastructure

Your users might need to access their View desktops from insecure locations such as the internet, or through untrusted corporate partner connections. You should never deploy a View Connection Server in an insecure location where it is open to attack. A Connection Server must be a member of an Active Directory domain so that users can be authenticated. If you deploy a Connection Server in your internet DMZ and someone compromises the Windows server, your entire Active Directory structure might be exposed.

VMware View supports a specialized type of Connection Server called a Security Server. A View Security Server is never part of an Active Directory domain. You pair a Security Server on your DMZ with a Connection Server that is a member of the domain. Authentication requests are passed through your internal firewall from the Security Server to the Connection Server. This practice protects your internal user data and systems from unauthorized access.

As with View, all connections between View users, administrators, View servers, Connection Servers, and Security Servers, must be encrypted. In previous versions, encryption was optional for these connections. Encryption provides enhanced protection and confidentiality for your users data, which is particularly important when user's are using business-critical applications in their View desktops, as these applications often have access to proprietary or highly valuable organizational data.

The Payment Card Industry Data Security Standard contains over 250 control objectives. Managing compliance with these objectives is a significant effort for most organizations. When the cardholder data environment is contained within a virtualized infrastructure, the ability for an organization to be adequately prepared for a PCI compliance audit can be challenging.

To address this issue, a customer can get assistance by conducting a VMware PCI Readiness engagement. VMware's PCI Readiness service includes both a rapid assessment as well as dedicated time for VMware to work, with customers executing targeted remediation activities.

The end objective is for customers to have a reasonable expectation of satisfying their PCI auditors as far as the virtualized infrastructure is concerned.

The following objectives will be met through VMware's PCI Readiness service:

- To quickly understand the current security configurations of vSphere as well as the administrative access controls and roles assigned within the vSphere management platform within the deployed VMware environment
- To learn about current security best practices for protecting the hypervisor layer and management platform for the virtualized data center, specific to the customer's environment
- To understand how the current virtual data center architecture promotes data isolation and limits interactions across zones of trust through capabilities such as:
  - Virtual network separation, configuration, and infrastructure
  - Organization of guest virtual machines (VMs) on hosts with similar data classification levels
  - Analysis of virtual machine container configuration
  - Use of existing technologies to isolate traffic, and which are also provided for monitoring within hypervisor instances

To better understand the security challenges in the virtual data center and to develop a capability for ongoing research into current trends and threats for virtualization, a customer can deploy a vSphere environment on physical hosts. A server environment is virtualized, with guest operating systems such as Microsoft Windows, Linux, DOS, BeOS. Disaster recovery for the client environment is normally managed via a secondary data center. Technical recommendations to address specific security challenges facing organizations today within the virtual data center include:

- VMware hosts, who will be examined from a security configuration perspective, constituting a representative sample that a customer can apply to the environment as a whole
- Instances of VMware vCenter Server
- Instances of VMware update manager
- Network switch instances, either physical or virtual, as a representative sample for configuration review
- Security Zones, consisting of enterprise/internal, DMZ, and sensitive
- VMware vRealize Automation
- VMware vMotion design and configuration
- VMware Configuration Manager
- VMware NSX, with approximate instances and rules

The activities for this engagement are organized into the following phases:

1. Project planning
2. Data collection
3. Data analysis
4. Report generation and data integration

Data collection

VMware consultants will use three principal methods to gather environment data necessary to complete the engagement—documentation requests, technical data gathering, discussions with <CUSTOMER NAME>, and administrators/architects for both virtualization and security.

Typical documents requested for this project include, but are not limited to:

- Information security data classification policies/security requirements for in-scope security zones
- Firewall rules and configuration requirements
- Security hardening guidelines and templates for vCenter Servers, networking, hypervisors, and other in-scope VMware products
- Security operational procedures for the virtual environment

We will conduct technical data gathering using custom tools and scripts. In order for the scripts to be run, administrative access may be required. After documentation review and technical data gathering, we will perform an initial review to identify any gaps in the data gathering process. We will attempt to address any gaps and gather additional information with the <CUSTOMER NAME> personnel. These sessions often include, but are not limited to:

- Virtualization administrators
- Virtualization architects
- Active Directory administrators
- Security administrators
- Security architects
- Risk analysts

Data analysis

After completion of the data gathering phase, we will begin the data analysis phase. We will collate and correlate disparate results from data gathering elements to evaluate the current security posture at customer sites as it relates to the virtual environment.

We will review the results of technical data gathering against known hardening guides, customer's specifications, and security best practices specific to the customer's line of business. Areas to be examined include:

- Unprivileged user actions
- Virtual devices
- Virtual machine information flow
- Virtual machine management APIs
- ESXi host installation
- Host communications

- Logging
- Management
- Integration
- Monitoring
- Host console
- vNetwork (Virtual Networking)
- Network architecture
- Administrative roles and responsibilities
- System patch and revision levels

Any high risk vulnerabilities will immediately be brought to the attention of the customer's personnel for rapid remediation.

Report generation and data integration

After completing data analysis, we will create a report that contains a summary of project activities, all findings and recommendations, and a prioritized roadmap for remediation.

Deliverables include:

- A VMware Security Health check report that reviews current security posture, provides a gap analysis against current best practices/customer requirements, and establishes a prioritized roadmap for remediation
- Reviews key findings and next steps to effectively improve a customer's virtualization security posture
- A virtualization security workshop to review security settings, vCenter roles and responsibilities, security monitoring, intrusion detection, and logging forensics/techniques

Standard use cases

This also includes the plan and design of public clouds and connectivity to an existing vSphere production environment leveraging vCloud Hybrid Manager.

Network virtualization

The following list explains stretching the application networks using VXLAN:

- **L2 and L3 Networking functionality**:
    - L2 connectivity between virtual machines on the same Layer 2 network
    - (Optional) Configure Edge Gateway interfaces with the internet and Direct Connect (MPLS), dependent of design requirements
- **Routing functionality**:
    - L3 connectivity between network(s) and external networks using VMware NSX Edge routing functionality (static or dynamic)
    - High availability with equal cost multipath (ECMP) on NSX Edge Gateways

NSX Edge Gateway Firewall and Trust Groups

The following are the zero-trust principles throughout the micro-segmentation deployment:

- **Micro-segmentation using Trust Groups**: The Trust Group firewall is a hypervisor kernel embedded firewall that provides visibility and control for virtualized workloads and networks. Customers can create access control policies based on objects such as data centers and virtual machine names, and network constructs such as IP addresses or IP set addresses.
- **Edge-based firewalls**: The firewall within the Edge gateways helps customers meet key perimeter security requirements, such as building DMZs based on IP/VLAN constructs and tenant-to-tenant isolation in multi-tenant virtual data centers, as well as acting as a VPN endpoint. If required in the design of the target subset of five (5) tenant virtual machines, we will implement a rule base within the Edge firewall.

VMware vCloud Hybrid Manager

Installation of vCloud Hybrid Manager between one public cloud instance and a vCenter instance on a customer's premises is done to enable migration connectivity.

The scope of this activity entails the planning and design of VMware's Cross-Cloud Networking services in a new public cloud production instance:

- One vCloud organization per provider vDC
- Installation of the vCloud Hybrid manager to the vCenter instance

The services provided in this scope of work are organized in the following phases:

- **Phase 1**: Planning
- **Phase 2**: Kickoff
- **Phase 3**: Solution overview
- **Phase 4**: Assess
- **Phase 5**: Design

Phase 1 – Planning

We will discuss the following topics:

- Scope of work and objectives
- Business drivers

Phase 2 – Kickoff

- Describing the project goals, phases, and key dates
- Explaining the expected project results and deliverables
- Agreeing on communication and reporting processes
- Validating the project expectations and clarifying roles and responsibilities

Phase 3 – Solution overview

We will brief the customer on the high level capabilities of Cross-Cloud Advanced Networking features and services.

Phase 4 – Assess

We will ascertain the customer's technology goals and requirements. In addition to determining requirement, we also conduct a vSphere and physical network validation review. This review is performed to confirm vSphere and physical network parameters (such as IP addressing and subnets) that can significantly impact the connectivity between the onsite network environment and public cloud.

The goal of the workshops is for the customer team to do the following:

- Understand the network virtualization operating model
- Identify the impact and challenges of network virtualization and microsegmentation adoption in the Cloud

We will determine gaps between the current state, future state requirements, determined use case, and the scope of this **Statement of Work** (**SOW**), documenting the finalized requirements and use cases.

Phase 5 – Design

We will develop a network and security design for the Cloud environment based on the requirements and use cases from the Assess phase. To accomplish this objective, we will perform the following workshops and design documentation activities:

VMware network virtualization design to focus on the following:

- Virtual network architecture
- Workload connectivity requirements
- Infrastructure service delivery
- Security architecture
- Specific design components as applicable to selected use cases for the Cloud solution, including feature considerations such as:

    - Organizational networks
    - Logical routing
    - NSX Edge gateway services
    - Logical firewalls

- Develop the architecture design document, including:
- Network diagrams:
  - Organizational networks
  - Logical routing
  - NSX Edge gateway services
  - Layer 3 edge firewalls
  - Logical load balancer
- Workload network topology
- Virtualization diagrams for Cloud network components
- Security design:
  - Distributed firewall operational requirements

Conceptual design

vRealize Configuration Manager employs an agent-based model for compliance and change management data collections. Data collected from different sources is recorded in the Configuration Manager database where it is available for reporting and compliance checking. If any changes to a managed machine or virtual environment are initiated externally, they will only be reflected in Configuration Manager after the successful completion of a scheduled/manual data collection from a machine or virtual environment.

Logical design

vRealize Configuration Manager implements an agent-based model for compliance and change management data collections. For VMware vCenter Server, VMware vCloud Director, and VMware NSX Manager collections, Configuration Manager uses an intermediary managing agent to collect data through the use of the vSphere VIMAPI, vCloud REST API, and NSX Manager REST API:

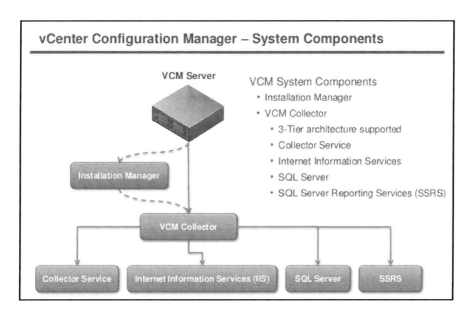

Configuration Manager Logical Architecture

vRealize Configuration Manager agents will be deployed on each managed system where required. When agents are deployed from the collector to managed systems, they are automatically licensed and trusted by vRealize Configuration Manager. If deployed manually, agents need to be added to the Configuration Manager console. Mutual authentication between vRealize Configuration Manager and Windows agents will be implemented. Agents will be configured to use TCP port 26542 to listen to the collection requests.

Three types of authentication are currently supported to protect user access to the Configuration Manager user interface:

- **Basic IIS Authentication**: To be used in any split deployment (two- or three-tier) if Kerberos cannot be used. Prefer HTTPS to plain HTTP because sensitive collection results, configuration data, and configured passwords travel across the network.
- **Windows/NTLM**: For single-tier deployment only with all components installed on the same server.
- **Kerberos**: Recommended for split deployments (two- or three-tier). If the Active Directory objects, modification is possible. This method is more secure than basic IIS authentication and provides single-sign on for all Configuration Manager components.

User access to vRealize Configuration Manager will be configured to use HTTPs and basic authentication to the collector server.

VMware vRealize Configuration Manager platform

This section details the logical specifications of the vRealize Configuration Manager collectors and databases required for a customer's deployment. The following diagram displays the vRealize Configuration Manager logical design for the virtual data center:

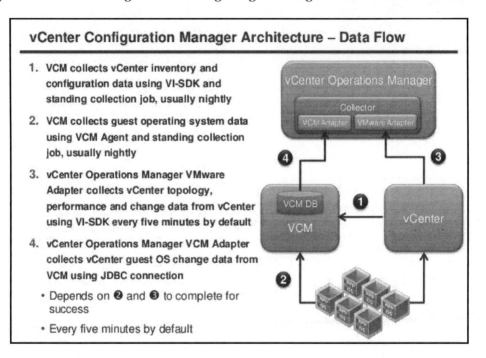

Configuration Manager DC logical design

The vRealize Configuration Manager collector deployed in the management cluster is responsible for compliance, audit, and change and configuration management reporting for all VMs running within the management cluster, as well as compliance and reporting against every ESXi 5.x host. The solution will be deployed in a two-tier configuration, where the collector and UI components will reside on one virtual machine, and the collector database service and SQL Server reporting services on a second virtual machine.

The vRealize Configuration Manager collectors deployed in each payload cluster will be independent, and be responsible only for guest operating systems compliance, auditing, changes, and configuration management within their cluster. Each of the resource cluster collectors will be deployed in an all-in-one configuration (single-tier) that includes a local SQL database.

vRealize Configuration Manager guest OS compliance

Windows machine collections are granular, and for the purposes of change and compliance, management will track individual registry values and file system settings. Although only out-of-the-box compliance templates will be used, copies of these can be made and modified to include additional attributes.

Security and compliance templates can be enforced on groups of machines so that they are compliant. Any changes made to a managed machine can be rolled back to their previous state if they are found to be not-compliant, or if they have been made without changes to authorization.

The following table contains the machine groups, compliance baseline templates, and a schedule for compliance comparison jobs.

Scheduling of compliance check for hosts and VMs:

Compliance template	Machine group	Frequency
VMware vCenter Configuration Manager Hardening—Host	VCM	Daily (06:00)
VMware vCenter Configuration Manager Hardening—VM	VCM	Daily (06:00)

Configuration Manager guest OS compliance:

Design decision	Design justification
The guest OS of the vCM Web/Collector server will be scanned for compliance	No other Windows or Linux servers other than the vCM Web/Collector server will be available for guest OS compliance scanning

Summary

The VMware Compliance Solution designs and implements a compliance solution using the capabilities of VMware products. The solution focuses on use cases addressed by VMware vRealize Configuration Manager. The primary focus is on configuration management, related patch management, compliance visualization, and reporting. The solution is delivered in phases, which include requirements gathering, architecture, design, implementation, solution validation, and outputs to review compliance.

For customers who want to automate configuration and compliance management across virtual and physical servers, this solution will help to increase efficiency by eliminating manual, error-prone, and time-consuming work. A desired outcome is to provide the correct communication, processes, and tools to help enable the critical success factors—visibility, accountability, measurement, and improvement—to work together and give IT control of the change management process. This service will cover self-service consumption of logical networking and security services provided through the integration of vCloud Automation Center and NSX. vCAC and NSX allows users to create complete application templates that combine compute, storage, networking, and security services in a blueprint for on-demand deployment.

In the next chapter, we will learn about how to optimize system sizing and best practices. We will discuss the key CapEx components and associated ongoing support costs.

11
Lower TCO and Greater ROI with Maximum Agility

This chapter focuses on how to achieve the goal of the cloud, which is to extend virtualization techniques across the entire data center to enable the abstraction, pooling (aggregating resources), and automation of all data center resources. This would allow a business to dynamically reallocate any part of the infrastructure for various workload requirements without forklifting hardware or rewiring.

In this chapter, we will cover the following topics:

- Operational readiness for the cloud
- Cost comparison methodology and approach
- Technical capabilities and business benefits of the SDDC stack

Operational readiness for the cloud

VMware has become a strategic asset for customers today, and supports them during their journey of building their **Software-Defined Data Center** (**SDDC**) based on VMware technology.

Financial transparency, process maturity, organizational setup, and technology implementation are critical factors for success at every stage of their journey towards delivering IT as a service.

VMware defines the following journey stages towards SDDC:

- **Phase 1-Cost Center**: IT operates as a Cost Center. The focus is to reduce costs through CapEx and OpEx savings by improving IT efficiency, which is done by standardizing and virtualizing the infrastructure.
- **Phase 2-Service Provider**: IT becomes a service provider by delivering secure, highly available, and resilient IT services that meet business demands and service level requirements.
- **Phase 3-Business Partner**: IT transforms to become a Business Partner by automating the delivery of the infrastructure and application, resulting in faster delivery times and more responsive IT, enabling business faster access to the market:

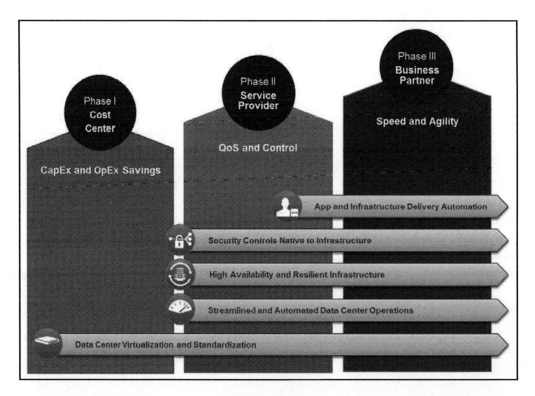

SDDC journey stages

The stages are shown in the preceding figure. SDDC journey stages are described in the following sections:

Phase 1 – Cost Center

In this phase, the focus is *virtualization* and *standardization* of compute, network, and storage layers of the data center, allowing IT to deliver up to 70% reduction in CapEx. This phase provides IT the ability to run traditional or new application types such as big data on this virtualized, standardized infrastructure, which is independent of the underlying hardware stack, and is easily extensible to the hybrid cloud.

There are three stages of capability maturity for data center virtualization and standardization (note that data center virtualization and standardization stretches across Phases 1 to 3):

- **Stage 1**: Compute virtualization, virtualization for business critical apps, big data application support
- **Stage 2**: Software-defined storage, network virtualization, extension to hybrid cloud, data center migration
- **Stage 3**: Management across hybrid, heterogeneous data centers

The following capabilities are crucial at Phase 1:

- **Financial model and measurement:** Awareness and understanding of the costs of assets and underlying infrastructure capacity
- **People and organization:**
    - Establishment and assignment of SDDC center of excellence and roles
    - Development and implementation of a training plan for the center of excellence staff
- **Process and control:**
    - IT processes are adapted for virtualization, but are largely manual, with ad hoc interprocess integration
    - Establishment of standard operating procedures for consistency in operations
    - Focus on limited, continuous improvement
- **Tools and technology:**
    - Compute virtualization
    - Network virtualization
    - Storage virtualization

- Online, self-service capability for development, testing, and UAT workload provisioning
- Some production business workloads run in the SDDC environment
- Operational tools defined for SDDC environments

Phase 2 – Service Provider

IT has transformed from traditional models and is focused on delivering business services within an SDDC environment. This represents a cultural shift within the organization. To be successful, it requires enhanced IT operational maturity, an optimized IT organizational structure, and supported SDDC management tools.

Phase 2 focuses on the following:

- Alignment and buy-in from key business stakeholders
- Creation of service governance, life cycle and service design, and development processes
- Providing service-based financial transparency
- Automating and integrating tools and technology in internal and external systems

Key capabilities for this phase include:

- **Financial model and measurement:**
    - Usage metering and cost showback or chargeback
    - Granular costing of underlying infrastructure assets
    - Educating IT customers about paying for services as an operating expense
    - Changing from project-based budgeting to demand-based budgeting
- **People and organization:**
    - Center of Excellence has been established with dedicated, experienced, and knowledgeable staff
    - Staffing levels have been reviewed and updated
    - Interfaces and involvement of extended team to the Center of Excellence

- **Process and control:**
    - Fully integrated IT operational processes are adapted for SDDC
    - Standard operating procedures are enhanced and automated where feasible
    - Agile-based service design and development processes are established
    - Service-level financial transparency
- **Tools and technology:**
    - Services are defined and offered through an online consumer portal for self-service access to the service catalog
    - Automated disaster recovery for SDDC
    - Blueprint and policy-driven service development and provisioning
    - Purpose-built management tools for proactive SDDC operations

Phase 3 – Business Partner

This is the final phase for a mature SDDC, when a highly efficient, scalable SDDC with hybrid cloud capability is available for an organization. IT is delivered as a service. There is automated, policy-driven governance and control across the SDDC environments, with zero-touch operations supported by predictive and self-healing operational tool capabilities. True application mobility and device-independent access is available. The SDDC environment is considered to be the de facto model within the organization.

IT has changed roles and has become a Business Partner by increasing the following:

- **Agility**, resulting in faster time to market
- **Efficiency**, resulting in reduced costs
- **Reliability**, resulting in a dramatically increased quality of service

There are three stages of capability maturity for this outcome, which are as follows:

- **Stage 1**: This is about automating the delivery of infrastructure across heterogeneous physical and virtual environments and being able to track the VM costs effectively
- **Stage 2**: Maturity enables capabilities for application and middleware automation so IT organizations can support business requests for applications such as exchange, Oracle, and middleware requests such as a **Platform as a Service (PaaS)** environment for faster development

- **Stage 3**: Maturity extends the capabilities for infrastructure, middleware, and application delivery automation to the hybrid cloud

The following are key capabilities for Phase 3:

- **Financial model and measurement**:
    - Usage-based pricing and chargeback for services provided to business customers
    - Service demand-based budgeting
    - Priced catalog of what the services offer
- **People and organization**:
    - The Center of Excellence manages all elements of infrastructure, end user, and application operations
- **Process and control**:
    - Optimized, integrated, and fully automated IT processes enhance business agility and efficiency
    - Continuous process, service, and performance improvement based on predictive capabilities
- **Tools and technology**:
    - Full hybrid capabilities
    - Automated infrastructure and application provisioning across multiple hardware platforms, hypervisors, and clouds
    - Tools that support single panes of glass management across SDDC and hybrid environments
    - Service-level disaster recovery
    - Tools that support automated corrective actions for self-healing

Contrasting approaches to building a private cloud

You can build a private cloud with existing specialized hardware, complex integration of missing SDDC software components, and with manual administration having lots of difficulties. This will also expose applications to risks, which can all negatively impact business performance and brand names.

We will discuss different approaches to solve this in the following topics.

VMware Cloud Foundation

VMware Cloud Foundation software establishes a unified SDDC platform for the hybrid cloud. In the context of the private cloud, customers can deploy VMware Cloud Foundation software on top qualified ready nodes from HPE, QCT, Fujitsu, and others in the future, with qualified networking.

VMware Cloud Foundation has been designed from the start to be the simplest path to an SDDC private cloud, enabling certified VMware partners or customers to build SDDC clouds based on VMware Cloud Foundation for use at the time of delivery or build:

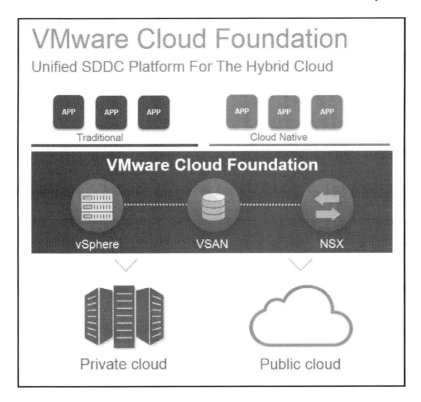

VMware Cloud Foundation overview

Once a VMware Cloud Foundation system is delivered, customers simply need to connect it to a network and, in a matter of hours, they have a complete SDDC cloud with compute, storage, networking, security, and management.

VMware Cloud Foundation integrates logical and physical compute, storage, and networking into a unified solution. It brings together VMware's compute, storage, and network virtualization into a natively integrated stack that combines Hyper-Converged software (vSphere plus Virtual SAN) with network virtualization (NSX):

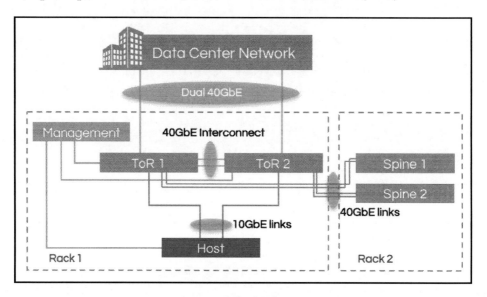

Network connectivity in data center

A typical deployment contains x86-based **Hyper-Converged (HC)** ready nodes with **Direct Attached Storage (DAS)**, **Top-of-Rack (ToR)** switches, a management switch, and **Power Distribution Units (PDU)**. The second rack contains **Spine** switches to interconnect racks in a highly resilient, scale-out, **Spine Leaf** architecture. The following list represents the major components of data center:

- **Networking:** Spine, Leaf, and management switches are provided by qualified hardware partners. VMware NSX provides network virtualization, load balancing, and security.
- **Management cluster:** The management cluster uses 3+ HC servers, and hosts the SDDC management software and necessary components.
- **Workload clusters:** The HC servers are ready nodes from qualified partners with virtualization and software-defined storage from VMware vSphere and VSAN.

The key difference from other partial SDDC architectures is that VMware Cloud Foundation virtualizes and abstracts every infrastructure layer—networking, compute, storage—using a natively integrated SDDC stack that embeds all layers as virtualized services directly within the vSphere hypervisor kernel.

VMware Cloud Foundation can be utilized for various use cases like Infrastructure as a Service (**IaaS**), private clouds, disaster recovery, or **Virtual Desktop Infrastructure** (**VDI**). VMware Cloud Foundation has powerful hybrid cloud capabilities to use in the public cloud as a service model.

VMware Cloud Foundation infrastructure management

SDDC Manager is responsible for policy-based resource allocation to specific virtual machines by automating cluster creation. It also has **REpresentational State Transfer** (**REST**)-based APIs to enable programmability for seamless operations with the existing data center management and monitoring tools.

The SDDC Manager provides:

- Automated, simplified, and rapid setup of the entire SDDC-based private cloud
- Automated lifecycle management of the entire SDDC platform including day 0 to day 2 processes such as bring-up, configuration, provisioning, and patching/upgrades
- Workload domain abstraction for isolating pools of resources into the private cloud capacity with different availability, performance, and security attributes
- Integrated management of servers/switches and virtualized resources from a single pane
- Operational simplicity and automation for health monitoring of both physical and virtual infrastructures
- Simplified IaaS and VDI service deployment and operations similar to a public cloud

As a result, the VMware Cloud Foundation solution significantly improves agility and reduces **total cost of ownership** (**TCO**), enabling a simpler and cheaper way to deliver an SDDC private cloud.

A traditional 3-tier architecture-based private cloud

We can build a private cloud using traditional 3-tier systems with various software products included in order to build a partially integrated SDDC solution. We have gone through various traditional 3-tier integrated systems or converged infrastructures as well as 3-tier **do-it-yourself (DIY)** reference architectures. *Figure 3* shows the basic approach to the rack design using a traditional 3-tier architecture:

- **Networking:** Spine and Leaf based on networking provided by industry leaders. Hardware-based load balancing and security was used when needed in lieu of software-based.
- **Management cluster:** A dedicated set of isolated servers forms a compute cluster, which is sized to host all dedicated management software for operating both the hardware and virtualization software infrastructure.
- **Compute cluster:** A dedicated set of servers reserved exclusively for hosting private cloud workloads. All servers were based on blade servers with necessary components.
- **Storage cluster:** External hybrid storage arrays and storage controllers were evaluated. The **storage area network (SAN)** was based on dedicated network components.

Each of the traditional 3-tier architecture-based systems that we evaluated supported a virtualized private cloud on top of their prebuilt or reference architecture-based systems. The vendors typically shipped VMware capable systems with pre-installed vSphere and vCenter components. The creation of an SDDC-like environment will require either a professional services engagement or significant customer-led customization, which will result in limited integration, automation, and lifecycle management capabilities:

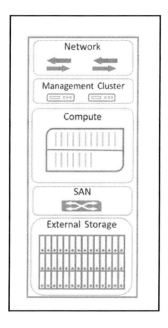

Traditional 3- tier architecture

A 3-tier system has an additional overhead for every component, since it comes with its own management software, while VMware solution has a single management interface for all components, as mentioned in the following table:

	VMware Cloud Foundation	**Traditional 3-Tier DIY or CI**
SOFTWARE		
Compute Virtualization	VMware vSphere Ent+	VMware vSphere Ent+
Network Virtualization or Software Defined Networking	VMware NSX Adv.	VMware NSX Adv. or Cisco ACI
Storage Virtualization	VMware vSAN Adv.	None
Software for Management		
Virtualization Management	vCenter (if needed)	vCenter (if needed)
Lifecycle Management	VMware SDDC Manager	Software products from multiple vendors

Infrastructure Management and Automation	VMware SDDC Manager	Individual element manager plus vCenter plug-ins
HARDWARE		
Network	Spine switches (second rack) Leaf switches (each rack) Management switch (each rack)	Spine switches Leaf switches Management switch
Security and Load Balancing	None	Physical firewalls and load balancers required with Cisco ACI
	(all within NSX)	
Storage Area Network	None (all within vSAN)	Independent FC SAN switches
Compute for Workloads	Modular scale-out HCI servers (qualified ready nodes)	Blade servers Blade chassis Additional components
Compute for Management Cluster	Modular scale-out HCI servers	Management cluster built with standard rackmount servers
Storage and Controllers	Modular scale-out HCI servers and within vSAN	External hybrid arrays and storage controllers

Cost comparison methodology and approach

The systems were configured and optimized for customers' use cases, where the quantitative hardware metrics could be considered and compared to reference architectures from different vendors for cost comparison analysis. Each 3-tier system was tuned to meet similar CPU, memory, and storage parameters so that comparative study was possible within the given reference architecture. This helped us to compare VM density in a fair way.

The following are the references used in this comparative approach:

- A single *42-U* rack deployment as infrastructure
- Use of a vendor's reference architecture
- Configuration of a solution with the same compute, storage, and networking resources to make the comparison relevant
- Consideration of key CapEx components with three years of ongoing support costs
- Leverage of VMware OpEx savings study and model for three years OpEx cost

All traditional 3-tier setups were configured on the same line as the VMware Cloud Foundation setup. Since no-one had a fully integrated SDDC software solution, we have integrated the missing SDDC software to make it a complete solution. The objective was to have all solutions more or less the same with the VM density per system rack.

The following table briefs you on the high-level configurations for each solution:

	System Configuration Comparison Matrix	
Component	VMware Cloud Foundation	Traditional 3-Tier DIY or CI
Cloud Platform	VMware Cloud Foundation	vSphere and additional SDDC software
Compute Platform	HCI rack mount servers (all nodes the same)	Blade servers (8/16 nodes per chassis)
Cores per CPU	12	12
Memory per node	384 GB	384 GB
CPU speed	2.6 GHZ	2.6 GHZ
Dedicated management nodes in solution	3 (from preceding HCI servers)	4 (isolated rack-mount servers)
Available compute nodes in solution	21	20
Storage technology	vSAN	External hybrid array, SAN switches, and storage controllers

SSD for caching	34 TB	35 TB
Raw storage capacity	230 TB	122 TB
Raw to effective capacity overhead estimate	50%	80%
Effective capacity	115 TB	125 TB

Assuming the preceding configurations, the VM density numbers were calculated based on the following formula, and outlined in the following table:

VM density calculation		
VMware Cloud Item Foundation		Traditional 3-Tier
Total CPU cores in solution	576	576
Dedicated cores for management	72	96
Compute cores available for customer VMs	504	480
Overcommit ratio	4.0	4.0
Available vCPUs	2,016	1,920
VM supported (based on 2vCPUs per VM)	1,008	960
Estimated memory available per VM (GB)	8.0	8.0
Estimated usable storage per VM (GB)	100	130

Hardware and software cost analysis

The approach used to calculate the cost metrics for each of these scenarios was to build solutions that matched the preceding characteristics. When possible, for the 3-tier systems, the hardware and software BOM structure exactly matched those provided by a vendor's own reference architecture. The list prices were obtained from vendor pricing tools, vendor reseller quotes, and pricing databases. Because of the constraints on building real systems based on real pricing, not every dimension in the area of compute/storage/memory ratios could be matched exactly. Instead of trying to force fit the ratio, it is left up to the readers to gauge the importance of each variable when comparing the scenarios.

The costs of the solutions were calculated in the following categories:

Hardware CapEx

For compute/server/networking, the actual prices of components were used based on current vendor pricing, and vendor reseller quotes for compute, storage, and networking resoucces. The cost of racks, cables, and installation were excluded, but it increased the cost for the traditional 3-tier DIY and **Converged Infrastructure (CI)**.

Hardware support

The actual maintenance pricing was used with a three-year quote, and then the support was extended on a per-year basis. It is likely that there is going to be a 5%–8% per year hardware support cost.

Software CapEx

All perpetual software components that are not bundled with the hardware vendor are included based on different criteria.

Common software components like costs of Windows software for the management cluster or client VM software were not included.

Software support

The annual software support gets included and calculated for three years.

Cost comparison results - upfront costs for hardware, software, and support

The following table summarizes the upfront cost attributes of each system for a private cloud:

Upfront costs for HW, SW, and support (list price)		
VMware Cloud traditional cost item foundation 3-Tier		
HW CapEx	$556,625	$1,854,227
SW CapEx	$647,040	$311,600
HW Support (3 Years)	$83,494	$445,014

SW Support (3 Years)	$485,280	$233,700
Total upfront cost	$1,772,439	$2,844,541
Savings using VMware Cloud Foundation	38%	

Our in-depth analysis indicates that using VMware Cloud Foundation results in a significant upfront cost saving over using traditional 3-tier systems. The costs of the server and networking hardware were significantly reduced by using a HC infrastructure, similar to what's used in large webscale service provider data centers. The resulting hardware cost savings help to offset the incremental SDDC software costs needed to provide storage and networking capability that leading 3-tier component vendors typically provide within hardware.

Comparing the key technical capabilities and business benefits

In this fast-paced global economy, companies must be able to perform with agility, flexibility, and speed. Building a private cloud infrastructure goes a long way in fulfilling that promise, but only if it is built to scale dynamically, and can evolve with the ever-changing business requirements.

With that in mind, the following key attributes were considered and evaluated with each of the contrasting private cloud deployments. As each attribute is described, we also contrast the capabilities of VMware Cloud Foundation versus several industry-leading traditional 3-tier CI and DIY systems.

SDDC Operations Capability Model:

1	Basic	In this state, basic operational processes and tools are adapted for core virtualization, but not for SDDC. Process objectives are defined, but activities are largely manually performed. Some are specialized roles for managing virtualized environments, while some are SDDC capabilities for self-service dev/test deployments. Basic operational controls are defined (monitoring, error notification).
2	Controlled	At this level, limited operational processes and tools are adapted for SDDC. Objectives for processes are documented. Organizational roles and responsibilities are defined. Limited automated integration with existing IT processes exists (change, configuration, and so forth).

3	Service-driven (min)	Here, there is complete operational control over processes and tools with a new SDDC operating model in place and established. The organization is service-driven, and offers services through the consumer portal for self-service access to the service catalog. There are clearly defined service design and development procedures. Detailed measurement coupled with benchmarking is what drives decisions. There is complete operational control and quality of service assurance. Established service-level financial transparency.
4	Business automation (target)	At this level, there are automated process management policies and operational controls in place. The organization's focus is toward business agility, and critical business services are offered through the cloud with complete operational control. Detailed measurements and metrics are automatically collected and presented to the user. An expanded SDDC operating model is established, supporting SDDC operations.
5	Optimized	At this level, operational control is automated and policy-driven. Automated self-healing operations to remediate errors and maintain quality of service are enabled. Real-time measurement and benchmarking drive decisions. The IT organization is focused on innovative initiatives, recognized as a partner to the business, and is directly adding significant positive value.

Integrated provisioning and life-cycle management

The goal of building an SDDC private cloud is to try to make the infrastructure as invisible as possible, and push as much of the work to a self-service portal as possible. In order to do that, it is critical that the provisioning of the infrastructure matches the workloads that have been deployed. In addition, it must easily adapt to various workloads, and keep the environment updated to the latest software versions, security updates, and patch levels. As the software and hardware go through various revisions over the life of the infrastructure, it is important to have tools that ensure compatibility at various levels. With that in mind, we considered the following attributes:

- Do infrastructure management tools seamlessly provision workload-specific domains with unique attributes customized for that workload domain?
- Do infrastructure management tools work across the entire SDDC stack by deploying the software and configuring the hardware at the same time?

- Do management tools ensure that the various components of the SDDC stack have been tested together?
- Is there a centralized tool for managing the patches and upgrades of all software components?
- How easy is it to cycle infrastructure and move to a new infrastructure?

Support experience

The quality of support is key, as companies seek to shift human resources currently dedicated to maintaining infrastructure to instead focus on business innovation. Support complexity is reduced by reducing the complexity of design, reducing the number of vendors involved, and providing integrated tools that work across the entire infrastructure. With that in mind, we considered the following attributes:

- Is there a clear process to follow when something is not working?
- Are vendors cooperating with each other throughout the support experience?
- Is there a single tool that can be used to diagnose tough technical issues?
- How solid is the relationship between your vendors of choice? Is it likely to remain that way in the future?

Comparison of the key technical and business value attributes

The following table measures and compares each scenario across the attributes we previously discussed:

Comparison matrix of key technical capabilities and business benefits:		
Vendor compared	**VMware Cloud Foundation SDDC**	**Traditional 3-Tier DIY or CI**
SCALABILITY		
Scalability granularity?	One additional HCI server or rack at a time.	Rack(s) at a time once initial footprint is exceeded
Full SDDC virtualization across network, storage, and compute?	Yes	No

TIME TO VALUE		
Time to size solution based on customization?	Low	Medium (CI) – High (DIY)
Completeness of integrated solution upon delivery?	High	Medium (CI) - Low (DIY)
INTEGRATED PROVISIONING AND LIFE-CYCLE MANAGEMENT		
Can update software components and apply security updates with one tool?	Yes	No
Can provision workload-specific clusters?	Yes	Yes (CI) - No (DIY)
Number of tools to manage software patching and upgrades?	One integrated tool	Typically three or more
Can cycle portions of infrastructure automatically?	Yes	No
SUPPORT EXPERIENCE		
One vendor to call initially?	Yes	Yes (CI) - No (DIY)
Centralized tool for troubleshooting and debugging?	Yes	No
Complexity in solving problems?	Low	Medium – High
Coordination between vendors in solving problems?	Yes	Yes (CI) - No (DIY)

The following are the technical capabilities of Cloud (SDDC) services deployed by the IT team:

Summary	The purpose of the SDDC solution is to provide the long-term vision that drives the planning and policies for deployment and consumption of SDDC services. These services are completely aligned and customized with current and future business objectives, and can be modified on demand without any cost or complexity.

Technical activities/capabilities	• Manages the entire life cycle of the cloud service offering, from strategic planning to tactical activities • Determines what services should be included in the overall portfolio, making sure that the service offering strategy aligns with the IT strategy • Proactively identifies potential SDDC service offerings based on demand information • Ensures the service portfolio is correctly represented in the self-service portal • Manages development and enhancement efforts on the SDDC service offering • Regularly monitors and reports on service-level attainment for their SDDC/Cloud service offering(s) • Responsible for service costs and financial models for SDDC service offering(s) • Performs capacity planning and develops operating budgets for SDDC/Cloud services • Provides ongoing leadership and technical expertise through appropriate team members to support the SDDC Infrastructure • Works with appropriate teams to translate SDDC business requirements into technical requirements and service design • Evaluates and implements IT procedures, operations, and equipment selection for maximum efficiency, cost containment, and uptime • Ensures conformance to SDDC/Cloud infrastructure standards and best practices • Point of responsibility for SDDC/Cloud infrastructure incidents, expansion, and capacity planning, and server and network equipment deployment and provisioning • Ensures Cloud infrastructure hardware and software is maintained and secured through proper security audits, back-ups, code releases and patches, and staff training • Ensures reports are generated on system performance and capacity, providing forecasting usage to assist in capacity planning and designing future infrastructure expansion and purchases • Oversees implementation of service methodologies including incident management, problem management, change management, and capacity management

Cloud admin activities	• Administers the SDDC service catalog, creates global blueprints, assigns compute resources, reservations, and policies to appropriate business groups • Works with an SDDC IT security compliance analyst to release services into production • Provisions new SDDC resources • Responsible for the workload migration process
Cloud admin activities	• Documents and maintains SDDC decision criteria for virtualization • Develops and maintains the model for capacity forecasting • Coordinates a resolution of issues around the application suitability for virtualization • Contributes to the development of the cloud resource forecast, and is responsible for the development and maintenance of the SDDC infrastructure forecast • Responsible for reviewing and analyzing capacity reports for the SDDC infrastructure • Initiates a request for new SDDC infrastructure components when a new capacity is required • Optimizes and balances SDDC infrastructure capacity • Monitors SDDC operations and services to ensure service quality is being delivered on a daily basis • Ensures that all routine maintenance tasks are completed on all operational infrastructures • Investigates, diagnoses, and takes prescribed actions on all operational events, alarms, and incidents • Supports the incident and problem resolution of issues related to SDDC/Cloud infrastructure capacity and performance
Cloud admin activities	• Installs, configures, and maintains network components • Provides technical support for network components • Improves quality of services • Adheres to network standards • Monitors and controls service levels of network suppliers • Ensures adequate vendor support is received • Adheres to maintenance contracts • Provides regular feedback on network performance, both in general and against specific service levels • Participates in network planning, design, development, deployment, and modification

Cloud admin tasks	• Defines and enforces controlled access to corporate security zones as required • Administers firewall processes to ensure data security • Installs, tests, and configures firewalls • Configures, supports, and evaluates security tools • Reviews network designs and evaluates compliance to applicable security standards • Conducts security audits and provides recommendations to mitigate risks • Ensures compliance to security standards and policy • Designs solutions, configures, or supports firewalls, content engines, intruder detection, or prevention systems • Configures and supports VPNs and enterprise gateway devices • Administers remote access infrastructure • Produces or updates remote access policy • Monitors system performance and executes approved preventative maintenance • Protects the network from malicious entities such as hackers, viruses, and spyware • Upgrades, manages, and maintains VPN concentrators, routers, and other network equipment
Cloud admin activities	• Designs and provisions storage to SDDC as required • Responds and provides technical support to storage failure, performance and capacity alerts, and event notifications • Executes installations and changes • Maintains storage environment by implementing approved upgrades as required • Monitors, escalates, and remediates storage alerts to identify potential incidents • Escalates and follows incidents with senior management and others to ensure capacity management, data storage integrity, and performance service level objectives are met
Cloud admin activities	• Ensures that current backup and recovery policies meet availability, BC/DR, and security requirements • Develops and manages a Data Retention Policy that is compliant with legal and regulatory requirements • Implements and administers backup and recovery packages and tools • Procures magnetic tapes, diskettes, cartridges, paper, microfiche, and all other media and devices when required • Establishes and maintains a clear physical identification system for media for easy identification • Monitors backup jobs and schedules to ensure these take place without error

Cloud admin activities	• Monitors SDDC infrastructure compliance to IT security and policies • Triggers remediation for IT non-compliance • Participates in service blueprints, VM templates, and system deployment testing and validation to ensure compliance to security policies, standards, and hardening guidelines • Develops security test plans as well as test scripts • Validates service functionality as well as service integration workflows from an IT security perspective
Cloud admin activities	• Operates and implements all operational infrastructure and procedures • Participates in incident and problem support activities when requested • Investigates, diagnoses, and takes prescribed actions on all operational events, alarms, and incidents • Monitors all operations and services to ensure service quality is being delivered on a daily basis • Maintains operational logs and journals on all events, warnings, alerts, and alarms, recording and classifying all messages; maintains all operational data collection procedures, mechanisms, and tools • Ensures that all routine maintenance tasks are completed on all operational infrastructures
Infrastructure management and monitoring activities	• Administers SDDC Infrastructure billing operations • Gathers cost and budget data when requested • Assembles budget, accounting, and charging reports • Assists in development and maintenance of SDDC Infrastructure cost models • Assists in developing cost/benefit cases for IT investments • Advises Management Team on the cost-effectiveness of SDDC and IT solutions • Assists with external audits when requested • Conducts ad hoc performance and IT financial studies on request • Analyzes and breaks down SDDC Infrastructures into cost components and categories • Communicates the impacts of planned IT investments

Application, middleware, and DB activities	**App** • Monitors the software application, documents, analyzes problems, and publishes maintenance schedule • Sets up administrator and service accounts • Maintains system documentation • Interacts with users, and evaluates vendor products • Provides advice and training to end users • Troubleshoots and resolves any reported problems • Provides application performance tuning • Maintains SLA, system availability, capacity management, and performance **DB** • Implements backup and recovery of databases and middleware • Administers users, profiles, files, indexes, tables, views, constraints, sequences, snapshots, stored procedures, and devices • Executes performance tuning, sizing of databases when necessary, in conjunction with changing management • Reporting and housekeeping on all databases' rollback, roll-forward routines, scripts, backup, and recovery routines **Middleware** • Sets up and maintains software according to defined procedures • Sets up and monitors status of services and processes • Installs bug fixes, vendor updates, and regulatory releases according to change and release management processes

Security policy as per organization's compliance metrics	• Develops and maintains the Information Security Policy, and ensuring appropriate authorization, commitment, and endorsement from senior IT and business management • Communicates and publicizes the Information Security Policy to all appropriate parties • Ensures that the Information Security Policy is enforced and adhered to • Identifies and classifies IT and information assets (Configuration Items), and the level of control and protection required • Assists with business impact analyses • Performs security risk analysis and risk management in conjunction with availability and IT service continuity management • Designs and implements of security controls and security plans • Develops and documents procedures for operating and maintaining security controls • Monitors and manages all security breaches and handling security incidents, taking remedial action to prevent recurrence wherever possible • Promotes education and awareness of security • Ensures all changes are assessed for impact on all security aspects, including the Information Security Policy and security controls, and attending Change Advisory Board meetings when appropriate • Performs security tests
Regulatory compliance activities	• Acts as one of the central interfaces with regulators, legal, internal audit, PMO, and other relevant technology/system teams/departments/organizations • Defines and implements appropriate controls to meet the preceding compliance requirements • Manages compliance programs within an organization in accordance with corporate policy and procedures • Audits and monitors compliance activities periodically in accordance with corporate guidelines • Monitors and reviews performance and compliance status of departments/organizations to compliance requirements • Ensures all gaps are addressed and completed timely

Disaster recovery activities	• Drives the development and implementation of the IT Disaster Recovery Plan • Performs business impact analyses for all existing and new IT services • Responsible for any IT elements relating to company Disaster Recovery/business continuity plans • Reports to IT and business senior management and stakeholders on the status of Disaster Recovery Plan and resource requirements • Schedules and coordinates the testing of the Disaster Recovery Plan periodically and ensures encountered issues are addressed and remediated • Co-ordinates and manages IT DR resources where required • Management of all third parties in relation to hardware and software support contracts • Undertakes regular reviews, at least annually, of the IT DR Plan to ensure that they accurately reflect the business needs • Attends Change Advisory Board meetings when appropriate

OpEx costs savings analysis

Converged infrastructure systems simplify upfront integration efforts and operations compared to the 3-tier traditional approach. Even then, it doesn't get the efficiency, scalability, and agility that customers need to compete and succeed in markets. CIOs used to take decisions by adapting public cloud apps or emerging data center appliances under market pressure in an attempt to run more efficiently. This approach will introduce further complexities like heterogeneity and vulnerabilities, which increase OpEx costs. VMware Cloud Foundation gives customers better options from the operational perspective, and also minimizes upfront CapEx.

IT teams running a virtualized data center based on the 3-tier architecture model are considered in this chapter. They used to do activities like planning and build-up, system configuration, provisioning capacity, life cycle management, and many more, such as back-up, monitoring, integration, application architecture, and so on.

We will consider a team of four IT engineers, and each engineer works 1,760 hours per year, so in total, the four-person team works 21,120 hours over three years. This four-person IT team has a network admin, storage admin, App and DB admin, and a cloud admin, along with a shared project manager resource, whose cost is excluded.

For example, **buildup and planning** occurs regularly due to data center growth and churn, but occurs less frequently than **life cycle management** or **other**:

IT labor activity	% of total labor hours per activity	Labor hours, three yrs, Traditional 3-tier	Source: VMware Cloud Foundation customers and industry analyst data. Scenario: four-person FTE team over three years. Annual hr/FTE: 1,760 hr. Labor rate: $75/hr. Note: These averages may differ across IT teams
Build-up and planning	10%	2,112	
Configuration	10%	2,073	
Provision capacity	17%	3,684	
Life cycle management	28%	5,859	
Other	35%	7,392	
Total	100%	21,120 hr	

Let's now consider VMware Cloud Foundation results in real data centers. VMware has deployed Cloud Foundation at several Fortune 500 companies worldwide that currently run virtualized data centers using traditional 3-tier architectures. We have reviewed and validated the findings that these companies reported back to VMware. The resident IT teams reported that, compared to their traditional 3-tier systems, VMware Cloud Foundation enabled more efficient data center operations, resulting in the average labor savings shown in the following table. Simply put, each IT team spent less time in the first four IT labor activity categories when using VMware Cloud Foundation technology compared to the time they spent on the same activities using their existing traditional 3-tier data centers. The percentage of hours saved is an average across all participating companies with each company saving more or less time than the average percentage. For example, on average, compared to their traditional 3-tier data centers, VMware Cloud Foundation enabled each IT team to spend only ~2% of the time usually spent on build-up and planning, only ~4% of the time usually spent on configuration, only ~20% of the time usually spent on provisioning capacity to Business Partners, and only ~13% of the time usually spent on life cycle management.

Furthermore, each IT team was delighted at the possibility of spending the freed up time (~58%) on long-delayed strategic activities and innovative high-value IT projects:

IT Labor Activity	Average % hours saved compared to Traditional 3-Tier	Source: VMware Cloud Foundation customer trials at global Fortune 500 companies. Note: Savings compared to traditional 3-tier architectures will be lower. The *other* category is unchanged until future VCF capabilities are announced. These are averages across many trial customers.
Build-up and planning	98.2%	
Configuration	96.3%	
Provision capacity	80.0%	
Life cycle management	87.5%	
Other	0.00%	

If we return to our four-person IT team that is running a virtualized data center based on a traditional 3-tier architecture, we can apply the average percentage of hours saved to each IT labor activity. As you can see, on average in our model, the four-person IT team can achieve a 58% total time saving over three years, or around $ 910,525. This four-person IT team can now spend that time on projects that deliver the efficiency and agility that its Business Partners have been demanding for a long time:

IT labor activity	# of labor hours (Traditional 3-tier)	Three-year labor cost Traditional 3-tier	% of hours saved compared to Traditional 3-tier	# of hours VMware Cloud Foundation	Three-year labor cost VMware Cloud Foundation
Build-up and planning	2,112	$158,400	98.2%	38	$2,880
Configuration	2,073	$155,439	96.3%	77	$5,784
Provision capacity	3,684	$276,336	80.0%	737	$55,267
Life cycle management	5,859	$439,424	87.5%	735	$55,143

| Other | 7,392 | $554,400 | 0.00% | 7392 | $554,400 |
| Total | 21,120 hrs | $1,584,000 | 57.5% | 8980 hrs | $673,475 |

In conclusion, VMware Cloud Foundation, on average, enables IT teams to spend 58% less time on routine IT labor activities, which is time that IT teams can instead spend on more impactful activities, such as system enhancements and application innovation, which make IT organizations more agile and efficient. Agile and efficient IT organizations have the capacity to respond rapidly to Business Partner demands, enabling them to capture market opportunities faster, and to run business operations more effectively.

 Total Cost of Ownership (TCO) Savings Comparison: CapEx and OpEx.

When looking at TCO savings over three years, the following graph gives an example of what can be saved when using VMware Cloud Foundation over alternative traditional 3-tier architectures.

The following graph and table combines all the costs associated with deploying both architectures:

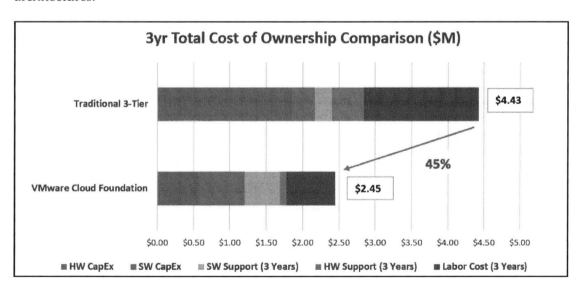

Three-year Total Cost of Ownership Comparison (TCO)		
	VMware Cloud Foundation	3-Tier System
HW CapEx	$556,625	$1,854,227
SW CapEx	$647,040	$311,600
HW Support (3 Years)	$83,494	$445,014
SW Support (3 Years)	$485,280	$233,700
Labor Cost (3 Years)	$675,572	$1,584,000
Three-year Total Cost of Ownership	$2,448,010	$4,428,541
Savings using VMware Cloud Foundation	45%	

Virtualization First Policy

In an effort to support the business objectives, IT has started server consolidation and virtualized every component in the data center. As IT continues its transformation journey towards an SDDC to become more agile and responsive to business needs, IT has decided to introduce the following policy.

All computing (Windows and Linux servers running on x86 platforms) and networking requests will be fulfilled with virtual machines and virtual networks instead of physical machines and physical network devices, unless there are exceptional requirements. The exception process requires data evidence to support the physical server and network request, and incurs additional delivery time and costs. IT will maintain a list of approved exceptions, and regularly publishes these to the businesses.

IT is introducing this directive because virtualizing is reducing costs while increasing service performance with faster project deliveries and higher availability. The list of benefits includes:

- Lower TCO
- Increased server utilization
- Reduced system build times from months to days
- No planned maintenance and downtime for server and storage
- Reduced downtime and recovery

- Improved availability and disaster recovery capability
- Hardware independence
- Ability to scale and make changes to systems and infrastructure programmatically

IT is committed to reducing capital and operational costs to the business while increasing capabilities and improving the stability and flexibility through an SDDC.

Summary

This chapter contains ideas on calculating real-world TCO for the presented solutions; however, differences in customer environments, skill sets, and related services will drive differences in TCO analyses. Furthermore, the supported business outcomes, and especially the automation level of the compared offerings, vary. You will need to conduct an analysis tailored to your own environment to develop TCO numbers consistent with your environment. Finally, the analysis presented in this paper is designed to raise awareness about how to evaluate solutions. The analysis is not about proving which solution is the best for specific circumstances. Each solution covered in this analysis has its own proven merits.

We will discuss VMware pricing and licensing in the next chapter. We will cover the subscription terms offered for Dedicated Cloud, Virtual Private Cloud, and Disaster Recovery, as well as answer the question *What are Advanced Networking Services?* and explain how to buy them.

12
VMware Pricing and Licensing for a Cross-Cloud Model

This chapter will help you to learn about the VMware Cloud Foundation pricing and licensing, as well as about VMware Cloud on AWS, which is very important for decisions based on total cost analysis. We will cover the following topics in this chapter:

- Transforming data centers with Cloud Foundation
- Cloud Foundation licensing with pricing and packaging
- VMware pricing and licensing in AWS Cloud
- VMWare's **Subscription Purchasing Program (SPP)**

Transforming a data center with Cloud Foundation

To build a private cloud, IT needs to:

- Modernize the infrastructure by virtualizing compute, storage, network, and security with a software-defined approach
- Automate the delivery and ongoing management of the virtualized infrastructure, enabling end users to consume it as a service

You can also procure Cloud Foundation as a software-only package from VMware and deploy it on supported hardware, as described in the *VMware Compatibility Guide*: http://vmware.com/go/cloudfoundation-vcg.

SDDC Manager fills a gap that in the past was not covered by any tools at all and for which customers had to write their own tools or scripts. SDDC Manager covers the automation of infrastructure-related tasks. It deploys and manages software components that in the past were mostly manual activities. SDDC Manager makes vCenter Servers more powerful, because it handles the tedious aspects of installation, patching, and maintaining them. This opens up new perspectives. In the past, customers liked to have as few vCenter Servers as possible to avoid management overhead. This brought in scalability issues in large environments. With Cloud Foundation, vCenter Servers can be used much more flexibly and much closer to actual use cases. This is especially powerful for multi-tenant environments where IT departments manage multiple vCenter Servers manually. SDDC Manager also provides the ability to orchestrate across VMware products, taking advantage of APIs exposed by vCenter, NSX Manager, and so on. You do not need to adjust your processes a lot to run NSX. The existing physical networking and switch configuration see little change. You can add the use of NSX incrementally. Your network administrators will gain much more flexibility by adopting the new capabilities NSX offers to do their work. Cloud Foundation drastically lowers the entry hurdle for NSX, because the set up and life cycle management of NSX is automated. In some cases, customers have used Cloud Foundation as a Trojan horse to establish NSX in their environment.

Use resource pools to secure capacity assignments, for example, for NSX Edge VMs, and apply resource pools best practices. Use a dedicated Workload Domain for VMs, which requires a dedicated ESXi host cluster. Use additional Workload Domains to scale out beyond a single cluster size. Use DRS affinity group/rules to create sub-cluster capacity to adhere to application licensing rules.

Cloud Foundation leverages automation to patch and upgrade vCenter Servers. Please consult the vCenter Server documentation and the documentation of your extensions, if extra manual steps are required before or after the upgrade. Then, follow these instructions. This is like your regular environment with the difference that the actual vCenter Server upgrade is automated so you have much less work to do. Churn alone is not the only reason you might want Cloud Foundation. In manufacturing, business risk mitigation is extremely important, because the economic damage can be disastrous when the IT services controlling production fail. Cloud Foundation mitigates risks drastically with its built-in automation and life cycle management capabilities. It is more than just an automated provisioning solution targeting churn of common repetitive tasks. It offers life cycle management for configuration, infrastructure provisioning, and updating/patching. Cloud Foundation is based on its own VMware Validated Design. It leverages the same BOM, and it is based on the same engineering validation processes as all other VMware Validated Designs. SDDC Manager delivers this automation experience for the compute, storage, and network infrastructure as an integrated solution that is pre-tested, validated, and has full product support.

The vRealize Suite has its strengths in workload and application automation, SDDC manager focuses on the infrastructure underneath. Hence, Cloud Foundation's SDDC Manager and **vRealize Automation (vRA)** are two different automation tools. They work on opposite ends of the spectrum, and together they complement each other by providing a full end-to-end SDDC solution.

SDDC Manager automates the deployment and configuration of vCenter Server instances, but it does not replace or duplicate functionality—you can still use vCenter the same way you are used to, SDDC Manager just makes it easier to manage the deployment, configuration, and life cycle of the VCs in the SDDC. SDDC Manager does bring-up and life cycle management of vCenter itself (along with other SDDC components). Making it a part of vCenter will create a catch-22 problem. SDDC Manager needs to have full control over all components it deploys. Multi-tenancy is typically provided by Cloud Management Platforms which reside on top of Cloud Foundation. You can also use Workload Domains to create isolated pools of infrastructure.

Cloud Foundation is for customers who have requirements for agility and flexibility, that are hard to achieve with traditional technologies. Once agility becomes a focus, software-defined storage and software-defined networking are the obvious options. Both are included in Cloud Foundation together with compute virtualization. No other software for the underlying virtualized compute, storage, or network infrastructure is required to be purchased. Workload Domains help organize the life cycle management of the infrastructure. They define the areas that are updated. Workload Domains are also designed for future improvements. They are designed to allow multiple types of workloads on the same infrastructure. Customers have confirmed that this flexibility actually helps speed up innovation a lot, especially when this covers photon or **VMware Integrated OpenStack (VIO)** workloads in the future. Apart from a few minutes in the wizard, no further effort is needed to manage Workload Domains. They translate SLA requirements to vSAN configuration settings.

You will want to automate recurring tasks via API calls. All APIs from VCF, built-in vSphere, vSAN, and NSX are transparent to allow full automation. SDDC Manager actions such as Workload Domain tasks, life cycle management, or hardware management do not occur as often and are handled via the user interface. Automated alerts and automated monitoring is done via vRealize Log Insight. Service providers have access to the SDDC Manager REST API to build their own user interfaces. You can manually integrate IP-based storage today. In the future, Cloud Foundation will support the automated consumption of external IP-attached array storage inside a workload domain. You can keep your existing storage if you wish and migrate to Cloud Foundation with vSAN as primary storage over time, when hardware refresh cycles are due.

Also check your business case for moving to vSAN sooner as the benefits of easier management and low ongoing costs might justify an earlier move.

Check your **Total Cost of Ownership (TCO)** and business case. For some smaller deployments, the CapEx investment is smaller than the OpEx savings. This is especially true if you have a shortage of skilled people. The automation provided by SDDC Manager will help a lot, and you also have lower risks.

You can layer the same DR components and capabilities that you currently use onto VCF to protect your virtualized infrastructure—for example, vSphere Replication and Site Recovery Manager or Dell EMC RecoverPoint® for VMs. VMware's SDDC Integration Architecture team is working on a paper describing BC/DR options for VCF. You can leverage existing technology and implement any vSphere-compatible backup/restore solution on top of Cloud Foundation.

You can keep your VxRail installation in parallel with Cloud Foundation and distribute your workloads across the systems. vRA can automate deployments on both systems and serves as a common interface. In addition, it is possible to migrate the VxRail workloads (VMs) into a Cloud Foundation workload domain, power down the hardware, and re-purpose it as a Cloud Foundation-supported node inside the Cloud Foundation installation—thus adding to the capacity in the Cloud Foundation installation. Dell EMC has two separate products—VxRail and VxRack SDDC (powered by VCF). VCF provides a high degree of automation for bring up and day 2 operations, including LCM. These are not available in VxRail. Also, VCF gives you a choice of supported hardware across multiple vendors—this is not possible with VxRail. The architecture at the base is the main differentiator between VCF and VxRail. VxRail is without NSX, which probably makes it suitable for ROBO environments, however VCF is a true enterprise-level SDDC product

VMware allows customers to accomplish this through Cloud Foundation and vRealize Suite. Cloud Foundation helps customers quickly and efficiently, and manages the cloud infrastructure foundation through SDDC Manager. SDDC Manager automates the life cycle management of the cloud infrastructure stack (from bring-up, to configuration, infrastructure provisioning, upgrades/patches, and so on), making it extremely simple for the cloud admin to build and maintain the cloud stack.

vRealize Suite plugs in on top of Cloud Foundation and provides the management layer that helps customers to efficiently manage their virtualized infrastructure and workloads, and offer them as a service. vRealize Suite also provides day 1 automation capabilities (self-service catalogue, automated workload provisioning, policy-based governance, API functionality) and day 2 operations capabilities (workload monitoring, troubleshooting, capacity management, business planning).

Cloud Foundation is the cloud infrastructure platform that delivers the software-defined foundation, whereas vRealize Suite is the Cloud Management Platform that automates the delivery and ongoing management of the cloud infrastructure to apps and VMs, using a service model approach. The two complement each other and are the key ingredients for building a VMware-based private/hybrid cloud.

Terms of Service (TOS) is applicable to all VMware cloud service offerings. It replaces the service-specific TOS as maintaining service-specific TOS is neither scalable nor market-standard.

TOS incorporates documentation applicable to the following:

- Service description (offering-specific)
- **Data Processing Addendum** (DPA) (universal; replaces Data Privacy Addendum)
- **Service level agreement** (SLA) (if any)
- Support policy
- VMware's standard form of ELA directs customers to the terms using the following URL:

      www.vmware.com/download/eula.html

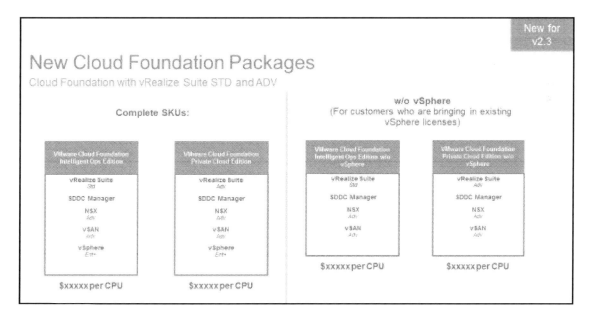

- Single set of terms governing VMware software and cloud services offerings
- Merges the software licensing terms from the **End User License Agreement (EULA)** and the cloud services terms from the TOS
- Reflects the same substance as the TOS, but presented differently
- Additional resource that is not intended to replace our separate universal EULA or TOS agreements
- A combined form that could simplify our ELA contracting process by reducing the number of separate documents needed:

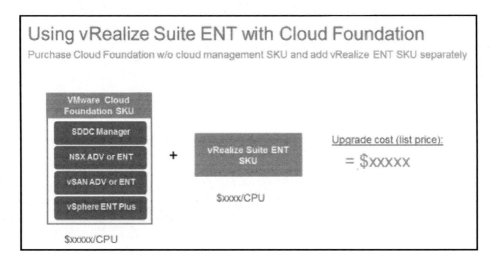

Today, VCF leverages the SDDC Manager to fully automate the deployment of the core SDDC components—compute, storage, and network virtualization—together with the vRealize Suite components, Log Insight, vRealize Operations, and vRA. Life cycle management of the vRealize Suite components is done the same way as in other DIY environments:

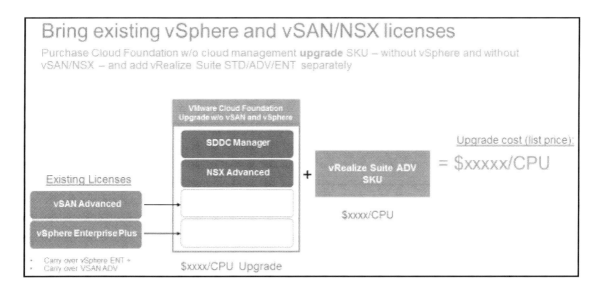

Cloud Foundation ensures a very prescriptive way of setting up the VMware software. This standardization is a core requirement for the advanced automation functionality provided by SDDC Manager. Cloud Foundation always deploys the whole stack. You can migrate your existing workload into the Cloud Foundation system and then re-purpose your existing infrastructure. If the existing infrastructure consists of vSAN ReadyNodes, that fulfill the Cloud Foundation requirements, you can use it as additional capacity after the migration. Also, remember that Cloud Foundation fits in perfectly as a deployment endpoint to your existing Cloud Management Platform such as vRA:

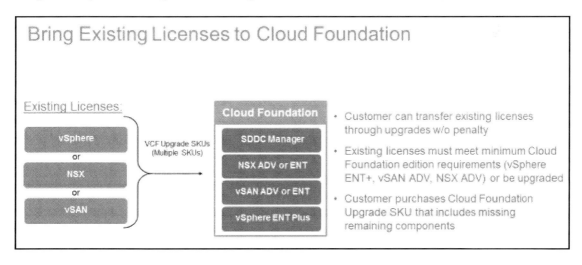

Clubbing existing Licenses with VCF

Through the standardized hardware and software architecture, you can now build heterogeneous workloads. VCF is built based on building blocks that can scale up and out, incrementally. Starting with a 1/3 rack, customers can scale up in as small of an increment as per server. Customers can similarly scale out across racks. The physical compute, storage, and network infrastructure becomes part of a single shared pool of virtual resources that is managed as one system, using the SDDC Manager. From this shared pool, customers can carve out separate pools of capacity called Workload Domains, each with its own set of specified CPU, memory, and storage requirements to support various workloads types such as VDI or business critical apps, such as Oracle DB. As new physical capacity is added, it will automatically be recognized by the SDDC Manager and be made available for consumption. Therefore, you are no longer bound by the physical constraints of a single physical server or rack.

The VMware Cloud Foundation with Horizon per CCU SKU is as follows:

Using Cloud Foundation with Horizon ENT (per CCU) in a mixed environment (VI and VDI workloads)

VMware Cloud Foundation

VI Workload Domain #1
10 nodes

VI Workload Domain #2
6 nodes

VDI Workload Domain
98 VDI seats

Management Workload Domain
4 nodes

Example of a mixed Cloud Foundation environment

Cloud Foundation (per CPU)
In this example:
- 8   CPU licenses – Management workload domain
- 20 CPU licenses – VI workload domain #1
- 12 CPU licenses – VI workload domain #2
- **40 CPU licenses – Total CPU licenses needed**

Cloud Foundation with Horizon ENT (per CCU)
- 5 packs of 10 seats – VDI workload domain

If customer has existing Horizon licenses, refer to next slide

- Perpetual licensing
- Per CCU licensing metric
- Sold in 10 or 100 packs

- VCF per CCU SKU: $713.40 per CCU
- Restricted to running VDI workloads only (complete VDI-only VCF instance or dedicated VDI workload domain in a mixed VCF instance)

Allows customers to convert existing Horizon (CCU) licenses into VMware Cloud Foundation with Horizon (CCU).

For customers looking to run Horizon environments on VMware Cloud Foundation per CPU, they can buy the Horizon add-on SKU:

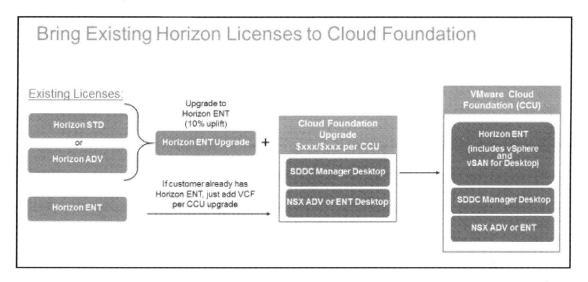

Using existing Horizon Licenses with Cloud Foundation

- Horizon ENT add-on SKU—per CCU licensing
- VMware Cloud Foundation with Horizon ENT (per CCU)
- 5 packs of 10 seats—VDI Workload Domain

Cloud Foundation runs any workload that runs on vSAN based infrastructures. Customers are using vSAN for all types of production workloads. Running applications on Cloud Foundation might require adjustments in how they are distributed across clusters. There are corner cases such as Microsoft Failover Clustering Instances where applications require specific hardware that is not possible on Cloud Foundation.

The following images show the VMware Cloud Foundation SKUs:

		VMware Cloud Foundation			
		Basic	Standard	Advanced	Enterprise
MANAGEMENT	Automated lifecycle management	●	●	●	●
		SDDC Manager	SDDC Manager	SDDC Manager	SDDC Manager
	BUSINESS includes Cloud Business Planning and showback			●	●
	BUSINESS includes Cloud Costing, Cloud Compare		●	●	●
	AUTOMATION includes App Provisioning			●	●
	AUTOMATION includes Infra Provisioning, Governance			●	●
	LOG INSIGHT includes Log analytics		●	●	●
	OPERATIONS includes Capacity planning, OS/app monitoring		●	●	●
			vRealize Suite STD	vRealize Suite ENT	vRealize Suite ENT
	NETWORK OPS includes AWS VPC, tags in M-Seg planning				●
	NETWORK OPS includes Flow Analysis, M-Seg Planning		●	●	●
			vRNI ADV	vRNI ADV	vRNI ENT

NETWORKING	VPN (IPSEC and SSL)				●
	Multi-Site NSX optimizations [3]				●
	Cross vCenter NSX [3]				●
	Automation of security policies with vRealize	●	●	●	●
	NSX Edge firewall, load balancing	●	●	●	●
	Distributed switching, routing and firewalling	●	●	●	●
		NSX ADV	NSX ADV	NSX ADV	NSX ENT
STORAGE	Data-at-rest Encryption				●
	Stretched Cluster with Local Failure Protection [3]				●
	Erasure coding (all-flash only)	●	●	●	●
	Deduplication and compression (all-flash only)	●	●	●	●
		vSAN ADV	vSAN ADV	vSAN ADV	vSAN ENT
COMPUTE	Distributed Resource Scheduler	●	●	●	●
	Cross-VC vMotion, and Long Distance vMotion	●	●	●	●
	High Availability, and fault tolerance	●	●	●	●
		vSphere ENT+	vSphere ENT+	vSphere ENT+	vSphere ENT+
	License Price (per CPU)	$XX,XXX	$XX,XXX	$XX,XXX	$XX,XXX
	Bundle discount	*0%*	*9.5%*	*12.6%*	*13.9%*
	SKU	CF-CPU-B1-C	CF-STD-C	CF-ADV-C	CF-ENT-C

Soft bundle structure components can be upgraded or renewed independently of each other, perpetual licensing, per CPU licensing metric, production SnS only:

1. Minimum licensing requirement for VCF is the Basic edition, that is, vSphere ENT+, vSAN ADV, NSX ADV, and SDDC Manager.
2. Please make sure you reach out to your VMware Sales specialist for help in building the right package for your requirements.

Part Number	Item Description	List Price (USD)
VMware Cloud Foundation – Core Editions		
CF-CPU-B1-C	VMware Cloud Foundation Basic (Per CPU)	$13,635.00
CF-STD-C	VMware Cloud Foundation Standard (Per CPU)	$16,995.00
CF-ADV-C	VMware Cloud Foundation Advanced (Per CPU)	$19,995.00
CF-ENT-C	VMware Cloud Foundation Enterprise (Per CPU)	$23,995.00
Upgrades from vSphere to VMware Cloud Foundation		
CF-CPU-B2-C	Upgrade: VMware vSphere 6 to VMware Cloud Foundation Basic for (Per CPU)	$10,145.00
CF-B1-VS6-STD-C	Upgrade: VMware vSphere 6 to VMware Cloud Foundation Standard (Per CPU)	$14,195.00
CF-B1-VS6-ADV-C	Upgrade: VMware vSphere 6 to VMware Cloud Foundation Advanced (Per CPU)	$17,555.00
CF-B1-VS6-ENT-C	Upgrade: VMware vSphere 6 to VMware Cloud Foundation Enterprise (Per CPU)	$21,850.00
Upgrades from vSphere + vSAN to VMware Cloud Foundation		
CF-B2-VS6-STD-C	Upgrade: (VMware vSphere 6 and VMware vSAN 6) to VMware Cloud Foundation Standard (Per CPU)	$10,375.00
CF-B2-VS6-ADV-C	Upgrade: (VMware vSphere 6 and VMware vSAN 6) to VMware Cloud Foundation Advanced (Per CPU)	$13,835.00
CF-B2-VS6-ENT-C	Upgrade: (VMware vSphere 6 and VMware vSAN 6) to VMware Cloud Foundation Enterprise (Per CPU)	$16,791.00

Upgrades from vSphere + NSX to VMware Cloud Foundation		
CF-B3-VS6-STD-C	Upgrade: (VMware vSphere 6 and VMware NSX) to VMware Cloud Foundation Standard (Per CPU)	$10,021.00
CF-B3-VS6-ADV-C	Upgrade: (VMware vSphere 6 and VMware NSX) to VMware Cloud Foundation Advanced (Per CPU)	$13,491.00
CF-B3-VS6-ENT-C	Upgrade: (VMware vSphere 6 and VMware NSX) to VMware Cloud Foundation Enterprise (Per CPU)	$15,592.00
Upgrades from vSphere + vRealize Suite (or vCloud Suite) to Cloud Foundation		
CF-B4-VS6-STD-C	Upgrade: (VMware vSphere 6 and vRealize Suite 2017) to VMware Cloud Foundation Standard (Per CPU)	$10,343.00
CF-B4-VS6-ADV-C	Upgrade: (VMware vSphere 6 and vRealize Suite 2017) to VMware Cloud Foundation Advanced (Per CPU)	$10,343.00
CF-B4-VS6-ENT-C	Upgrade: (VMware vSphere 6 and vRealize Suite 2017) to VMware Cloud Foundation Enterprise (Per CPU)	$14,716.00
SDDC Manager – Standalone SKU		
CF-SDDC-MAC-C	VMware SDDC Manager (Per CPU)	$1,535.00

Many hardware vendors are providing their own tools to manage hardware lifecycles. This can be a decision criteria when selecting hardware for Cloud Foundation. Pick the hardware vendor that has the best tools to manage their hardware lifecycle.

VMware pricing and licensing in AWS Cloud

The price of the service includes VMware's software, AWS' Cloud infrastructure, and support costs. Data transfer and IP are charged separately. Customers can choose on-demand (hourly) or subscription-based (one year or three year) options to consume the service.

Eligible customers may purchase VMware Cloud on AWS by purchasing either SPP credits or **Hybrid Purchasing Program (HPP)** credits and redeeming those credits on the service. Please refer to the following websites for more details on these credits:

- **SPP program guide**: `https://www.vmware.com/content/dam/digitalmarketing/vmware/en/pdf/solutions/vmware-spp-program-guide.pdf`
- **HPP program guide**: `https://cloud.vmware.com/vmc-aws/pricing`

All HPP and SPP funds will be subject to the terms and conditions of the HPP and SPP programs.

We expect pricing to be very attractive to customers. Customers will be able to leverage the benefit of overcommit provided by VMware to increase consolidation ratios on their VMware Cloud on an AWS host, and achieve comparable total cost of ownership versus native Cloud instances on a per-VM basis. Furthermore, the service will have a compelling value proposition that bundles the VMware software and full software lifecycle management, AWS-dedicated purpose-built cloud infrastructure, and technical support.

The high-level differences of VMware Cloud on AWS as compared to EC2 are:

- **Re-platforming**: VMware Cloud on AWS allows for a direct VM migration without transformation, conversion, or re-platforming efforts
- **Operating Systems (OS)**: VMware Cloud on AWS allows customers to run a wider variety of OS that are not supported on EC2
- **Custom sized VMs**: Such as 1 vCPU with 64 GB memory or whatever the customer may desire, can be deployed within a VMware Cloud on AWS SDDC
- **Compute**: VMware Cloud on AWS comes with built-in high availability
- **Networking**: The VMware NSX networking platform included with VMware Cloud on AWS supports capabilities that are not directly supported in EC2 (for example, multicast traffic, overlapping IPs and so on)
- **Storage**: VMware Cloud on AWS comes with the enterprise-class shared storage solution vSAN that is tightly integrated with vSphere
- **Over-subscription**: Customers may choose to significantly oversubscribe an ESXi host, which may be more economical than purchasing individual EC2 instances

VMware Cloud is an overall cloud strategy, including products, services, and so on. **VMware Cloud on AWS** is one of the offerings that we have in the VMware Cloud portfolio.

The VMware Cloud Services tools have been built to provide customers with an ability to consume cost analysis as a service. Functionality for Cost Insight is not yet equal to vRealize businesses, however, the entire set of VCS will get more integrated as time progresses.

Bare metal servers are dedicated servers running in the AWS-availability zones. They are also dedicated to the customer (that is, single tenant). The customer gets direct access to vCenter so they can deploy VMs however they would like. AWS services will not be available on NSX. All networking services are handled through NSX, but will tie into the VPC construct.

The key third-party solutions will be backup/recovery and configuration management. Other ISV ecosystem solutions include security (Palo Alto NetWorks, McAfee, Fortinet, and so on), cloud migration, costing (cloud physics, and so on), and DevOps (Puppet, Chef, and so on). Horizon Desktops will not be able to function on VMware Cloud on AWS when initially available and will require some adjustments made to the Horizon.

VIO will not be supported or functional on VMware Cloud on AWS. There will be no higher SLA supplementary support options available during the initial availability. vMotion support migration between instances on VMware Cloud on AWS will not be available during initial availability, this is something that will be evaluated in the future.

During initial availability and through the rest of this financial year, the selling motion is direct. However, there may be exceptions. Resell options are being evaluated. If a customer leverages native AWS services, there will be two different sets of billing for VMware and AWS. The native AWS services would be billed by AWS. The charges from VMware would include software, support, and the AWS hardware to run VMware Cloud on AWS.

We will be able to leverage AWS regulatory compliance certifications in future. We have a roadmap for regulatory compliance across IT, security, government, industry-specific regulations, and so on. vCenters include hybrid link mode support at initial availability. It will be 1:1, but we are expanding this in the future. Customers won't need an additional license for vRealize business for cloud, over and above the VRB they already have. They will not need an additional license for vRealize businesses above and beyond, unless they need to cover more CPUs/VMs. Customers can use their AD/DNS on-premises. Hybrid linked mode will help customers to do so. AWS won't be able to sell this service. VMware will sell, own, operate, and manage this service.

PSO is used to design and deploy, but now, since it's all automated to a standard design, any other service can be offered, such as customer readiness assessments, migration services, and transformation services, just to name a few. There will be a robust catalog of services.

A customer purchases the services from VMware direct. There is no requirement for a full SDDC on-premises to leverage VMware Cloud on AWS, but the additional NSX and vSAN components enhance the service. VMware on AWS licensing is not based on existing licensing models. We are largely mirroring AWS' model of on-demand, one year and three year subscriptions, with a simple and flexible packaging model that suits the needs of a cloud service. The management stack will sit on the initial four nodes that a customer spins up. It is a small percentage of resources on the initial cluster. It is controlled by a dedicated resource pool. Customers are responsible for figuring out connectivity to AWS data centers.

The VMware Cloud Services tools have been built to provide customers with an ability to consume cost analysis as a service. Functionality for cost insight is not yet equal to vRB, however, the entire set of VCS will get more integrated as time progresses.

Customers pay a basic fee for the SDDC core components in AWS Cloud and everything is included in the price that they pay for the service. There is an SLA (99,9999%) provided to the customer. The default SLA is 99.95. If the customer wants to add additional hosts, it takes minutes.

Summary

VMware provides a service level commitment in the SLA; the SLA provides 99.9% availability commitment. VMware warrants that the service offering will perform in accordance with the SLA. (TOS, section 9.1.) SLA credits are the sole and exclusive remedy for breach of the limited warranty and failure to meet the availability commitment. There is no negotiation with SLA, as VMware cannot assume additional liability beyond providing SLA credits.

There are four ways to purchase Cloud Foundation software:

- Directly from VMware
- From VMware channel partners
- As part of an integrated system from OEM vendors
- As a subscription service from a public cloud service provider

When purchasing a Cloud Foundation integrated system, the OEM partner will be the **single point of contact** (**SPOC**) for support of both hardware and software. When Cloud Foundation software is purchased from VMware separately from the qualified hardware, the support model will follow the standard practice of VMware products with VMware GSS delivering support for the Cloud Foundation software.

- **License keys delivery**: License keys provided as part of the VMware vCloud Air Network Program will be delivered to the License Administrator via the VMware License Portal.
- **Additional license keys**: Service providers requiring additional license keys to implement their solutions should contact their VMware approved aggregator or VMware business development manager. If there are any questions on the one-off ordering process, email VSPPReporting@vmware.com for assistance.

We will conclude this book with the economics of Cross-Cloud services in the next chapter.

13
The Economics of Cross-Cloud Services

This chapter is about how to do cost analysis of different cost categories, along with comparing them with existing competitive solutions on the market. It discusses ways to optimize the return on investment by minimizing costs and increasing opportunity for revenue streams. We will learn about the following topics:

- Total cost of ownership with cost categories
- OpEx cost saved with VMware Cloud Foundation
- Calculating cost-benefit per application compared to other solutions

The following model estimates the total cost of ownership of VMware Cloud Foundation versus other potential infrastructure solutions.

Total cost of ownership with cost categories

The cost categories are as follows:

TCO Cost Categories	Description
Hardware and software	This contains costs for hardware and software (only for capitalized software) used to deliver services. For example, server, SAN storage, network equipment, and optical cables. This also contains costs for non-capitalized software used to deliver services. For example, annual software license subscription, software upgrade, and so on. Note: In TNB's current expense accounts structure, it is not possible to split hardware and software expenses.
Maintenance	This contains costs for maintenance of software and hardware used for delivering services. This includes services contracts, equipment, tools, and materials.
Labor	This contains TNB staff related costs for delivering services. It will also include contractors and external labor costs, such as consultants.
Facilities	Facilities will include all data centers, office, utilities, furniture, and so on used by ICT staff or hosting ICT equipment and infrastructure.
Telecom	This includes costs of rental and services charged by telecommunications service providers, such as telecom lines.
Transport	Transport includes costs of fleet vehicles, maintenance, and operating costs.
Others	Costs that do not fall into the preceding categories are classified as Others. This includes advertising, legal, and so on.

In the following section, we have mapped customer's expense accounts to the previous cost categories:

Category	Item	BAU	CaaS	Explanation
CapEx (Server)	Physical server	294	30	Estimated 294 servers required from new projects.
	Physical server unit cost	MYR 18,000	MYR 43,000	Unit server cost with less specification = RM 18,000
				Unit server cost with better specification for virtualization = RM 43,000
	Physical server total cost	MYR 5,292,000	MYR 1,290,000	BAU (number of servers x unit cost) – 294 x 18,000 = 5,292,000
				BAU servers specs = 2 CPU with 6 Cores, 16 GB memory, SAN HBA, 2x 10 GB NIC, Redundant Power Supplies, 2 x 300 GB SAS disks
				CaaS (number of servers x unit cost) – 30 x 43,000 = 1,290,000
				CaaS servers specs 2 CPU with 12 Cores, 512 GB memory, 2 x SAN HBA, 2 x 10 GB NIC, Redundant Power Supplies, 2 x 300 GB SAS disks
	Server rack	20	2	
	Server rack unit cost	MYR 16,300	MYR 16,300	
	Total server rack cost	MYR 326,000	MYR 32,600	One rack can host 15 physical servers plus other equipment such as switches and UPS
				In BAU, number of racks needed is 20 and in CaaS, racks needed is only 2 with each rack costing RM 16,300
				In CaaS, cost of rack in BAU = 16 x RM 16,300 = RM 260,800
				Cost of rack in CaaS = 2 x RM 16,300 = RM 32,600

CapEx (Storage)	Shared storage (TB)	0	30	
	Storage cost (per TB)	MYR 29,000	MYR 29,000	
	Total storage cost	MYR 0	MYR 870,000	100 GB shared storage for each BAU server or a total of 29.4 TB needed in CaaS. 1 TB costs RM 29k so 29.4 TB x 29,000 = RM 870,000
CapEx (Professional service)	Professional service	MYR 0	MYR 1,350,000	To completely plan, design, and build a new CaaS platform by VMware, RM 1,350,000 is needed
CapEx (OS license)	Windows license	MYR 1,176,000	MYR 495,000	In BAU, RM 4,000 of Windows 2012 Standard licensing needed for each physical server RAC OR 294 x 4000 = RM 1,176,000
				In CaaS, RM 16,500 of Windows 2012 data center licensing needed for each host OR 30 x 16,500 = RM 495,000
CapEx (VMW license)	VMware license	MYR 0	MYR 1,980,000	60 CPU licenses for 30 hosts with 15 x vCloud Ent for Gold Environment, 45 x vCloud Adv for silver and bronze
OpEx (Power and cooling)	Commercial rate per kWh	MYR 0.36	MYR 0.36	
	Average physical server power usage per day (kWh)	10.80	10.80	
	Cooling power usage per physical server per day (kWh)	14.04	14.04	
	Total power and cooling per year cost	MYR 959,609	MYR 97,919	

OpEx (Labor)	Labor provisioning per server	MYR 2,500	MYR 2,500	
	Total labor provisioning	MYR 735,000	MYR 75,000	To provision each server requires RM 2,500. in BAU 294 x 7500 = RM 735,000. in CaaS, 30 x 7,500=RM 75,000
Business agility	Downtime cost per server	MYR 4,000	MYR 0	
	Total downtime cost and avoidance - vMotion/HA	MYR 1,176,000	MYR 0	Average cost of unplanned and planned downtime due to hardware failure and maintenance is RM 4,000 per server. the total cost is 294 x 4000 = RM 1,176,000. With HA features of virtualization, this can be completely avoided without affecting applications, so application owners and support personnel do not need to be on standby due to server or hardware maintenance
	Total	MYR 9,664,609	MYR 6,190,519	
	Savings	MYR 3,474,090		
	ROI	56%		

The table compares CapEx and OpEx savings between VMware Cloud Foundation and other solutions (based on default parameters).

Customers can input the environment data and the number of racks they want to deploy in the preceding chart, and the cost comparisons and productivity uplift will be automatically populated in the upcoming chart. Note that the software cost for VMware Cloud Foundation will be net incremental if customers input their current licenses under the *Existing Environment*.

- **Workloads parameters across solutions**: The parameters show the workload density, # nodes per rack, hardware and software support %, and so on. Customers can input the hardware and software support % in the yellow cells. No inputs are needed for other data (set as default and the same across solutions).

- **CapEx (Software)**: This illustrates the software BOM and component prices. All infrastructure solutions are configured with similar products to match VMware Cloud Foundation out-of-the-box capabilities. No inputs are needed. Once customers choose the editions and the type of workload they plan to deploy in the summary tab, the costs will be updated automatically.
- **CapEx (Hardware)**: This demonstrates the hardware BOM and specifications. Hardware across all other infrastructure solutions has been configured with similar specifications to create an apple-to-apple comparison. Once customers choose the vendor and workload type in the summary tab, the VMware Cloud Foundation hardware BOM will update automatically. Customers can input the hardware costs and specification. They can also input the dedupe ratio (for All-Flash) and utility rate (for hybrid) to calculate the usage storage.
- **OpEx**: This demonstrates the building blocks behind OpEx savings. No inputs needed. Once customers input the labor cost information in the summary tab, the costs will be populated automatically.

Here's a summary of cost analysis with other vendor solutions:

Software BOM	Metric	VMware Cloud Foundation			Traditional DIY			Nutanix			Microsoft CPS		
		Quant.	Price	Total Cost	Quant.	Price	Total Cost	Quant.	Price	Total Cost	Quant.	Price	Total Cost
- VMware Cloud Foundation	CPU	48	$9,985	$479,280									
- vSphere	CPU	48	$0	$0									
- VSAN	CPU	48	$3,995	$191,760									
- NSX	CPU	48	$4,495	$215,760									
- SDDC Manager	CPU	48	$1,495	$71,760									
- vRealize Suite	CPU	48	$0	$0									
- Horizon View add-on	CCU	4267	$375	$1,600,000									
- vCenter	Instance	2	$0	$0									
VMware Products (A La Carte)													
- vSphere	CPU				48	$3,495	$167,760	48	$3,495	$167,760			
- NSX	CPU				48	$4,495	$215,760	48	$4,495	$215,760			

Item	Unit	Qty	Cost	Total	Qty	Cost	Total	Qty	Cost	Total	Qty	Cost	Total
- vRealize Suite	*CPU*				*48*	*$0*	*$0*	*48*	*$0*	*$0*			
- vCenter	*Instance*				*2*	*$0*	*$0*	*2*	*$0*	*$0*			
- Horizon View (Include vSphere and VSAN)	*CCU*				*4267*	*$575*	*$2,453,333*	*4267*	*$575*	*$2,453,333*			
- Horizon NSX Add-on	*CCU*				*4267*	*$125*	*$533,333*	*4267*	*$125*	*$533,333*			
Nutanix Product													
- Pro License	*Server*							*24*	*$18,827*	*$451,853*			
Microsoft Product													
- Windows Server 2012 R2 Data center	*Annual*										*3*	*$154,400*	*$463,200*
- SW and HW Premier Mission Critical Support for the full appliance	*Annual*										*3*	*$50,000*	*$150,000*
- Citrix XenD	*CCU*										*2000*	*$450*	*$900,000*
SW	CPU	*48*	*$9,985*	*$479,280*	*48*	*$7,990*	*$383,520*	*48*	*$17,404*	*$835,373*	*48*	*$9,650*	*$463,200*
SW Support	CPU	*48*	*$7,489*	*$359,460*	*48*	*$5,993*	*$287,640*	*48*	*$5,993*	*$287,640*	*48*	*$0*	*$0*
Total Cost	CPU	*48*	*$17,474*	*$838,740*	*48*	*$13,983*	*$671,160*	*48*	*$23,396*	*$1,123,013*	*48*	*$9,650*	*$463,200*

OpEx cost saved with VMware Cloud Foundation compared to other solutions:

% of labor hours	# of hours (VMware Cloud Foundation)	VMware Cloud Foundation % Hours Saved Compared To:			
		Nutanix	Microsoft CPS	Traditional DIY	Existing Environment
10%	23	75.00%	50.00%	98.18%	98.18%
10%	46	75.00%	50.00%	96.28%	96.28%
17%	442	75.00%	50.00%	80.00%	80.00%
28%	441	75.00%	50.00%	87.45%	87.45%
35%	4435	0.00%	0.00%	0.00%	0.00%
100%	5388	34.7%	15.0%	57.5%	57.5%

Category of Cost	Cost of Labor				
	VMware Cloud Foundation	Nutanix	Microsoft CPS	Traditional DIY	Existing Environment
Build up and planning	$1,728	$6,912	$3,456	$95,040	$95,040
Configuration	$3,470	$13,881	$6,941	$93,264	$93,264
Provision Capacity	$33,160	$132,641	$66,321	$165,802	$165,802
Upgrade and Patching	$33,086	$132,344	$66,172	$263,655	$263,655
Other	$332,640	$332,640	$332,640	$332,640	$332,640
Total	$404,085	$618,419	$475,529	$950,400	$950,400

Workload parameters as per applications:

Parameters	VMware Cloud Foundation	Nutanix	Microsoft CPS	Traditional DIY	Existing Environment
Hybrid Storage:					
# of VMs per rack before overhead	1000	1000	1000	1000	1000
# of VDIs per rack	2000	2000	2000	2000	2000
Overhead on VM density	0%	0%	0%	0%	0%
All Flash Storage:					
# of VMs per rack before overhead	1600	1600	1000	1600	1600
# of VDIs per rack	4267	4267	2000	4267	4267
Overhead on VM density	0%	0%	0%	0%	0%
# of CPUs per server	2	2	2	2	2
# of servers per rack	24	24	24	24	24
# of CPUs per rack	48	48	48	48	48
SW support, as % of list price, per year	25.0%	25.0%	25.0%	25.0%	25.0%
HW support, as % of list price, per year	8.5%	8.5%	4.7%	8.5%	8.5%
VM density	33.3	33.3	20.8	33.3	33.3
# VMs per server	66.7	66.7	41.7	66.7	66.7

VDI density	88.9	88.9	41.7	88.9	88.9
# VDIs per server	177.8	177.8	83.3	177.8	177.8
# of servers required	9.0	9.0	14.4	9.0	9.0
# of servers to be purchased	9.0	9.0	15.0	9.0	9.0
# of racks required	0.38	0.38	0.60	0.38	0.38
# racks to be purchased	0.38	0.38	1.00	0.38	0.38

Manpower analysis with their working hours for precise OpEx cost:

Optional Input for Labor Breakdown					
Build-up and Planning		# of FTEs	# of weeks	# hours	
	Project manager	1	1	40	
	Networking specialist	2	2	160	
	Storage specialist	1	2	80	
	Server specialist	2	1	80	
	VM specialist	1	2	80	
	Total			440	
	VMware Cloud Foundation			8	
	% savings			98.18%	
Configuration		# of FTEs	# of weeks	# hours	
	Project manager	1	3	15	5 hrs/week
	Networking specialist x2	2	2	160	
	VM specialist	1	1	40	

		# of FTEs	# of weeks	# hours	
	Total			215	
	VMware Cloud Foundation			8	
	% saving			96.28%	
Provision Capacity		# of FTEs	# of weeks	# hours	
(Work domains)	VM specialist	1	1	40	
	Total		1	40	
	VMware Cloud Foundation			8	
	% savings			80.00%	
Upgrade and Patching		# of FTEs	# of weeks	# hours	
	Project manager	1	3	15	5 hrs/week
	VM specialist	1	NA	240	5 hrs/ESXi host
	Total			255	
	VMware Cloud Foundation			32	
	% savings			87.45%	
			# of hours	# of days	
	One rack		950	119	
	VMware Cloud Foundation		56	7	
			94.11%	17.0	

The service-based cost classification guidance—manufacturing customer:

Cost Type	Service Cost Element (Examples)	Service Manufacturing			CapEx/OpEx	Assumptions/Comments
		Direct Cost Components	Direct Cost Labor	Indirect Cost Overhead		
Computing Hardware	Server hardware: Chassis, blade, and compute resources	Yes		Yes	CapEx	Typically, most of the server-side hardware is classified as a fixed cost, because it is part of a long term investment (CapEx). Moreover, based on the component positioning and the service being costed-out, the cost element could be a direct cost to the service (for example, blade server cost to an SDDC environment), or an indirect cost, and part of the service overhead, such as the cost of a blade server allocated to a single VM while it is being shared with other VMs.
	Desktops/laptops, scanners, projectors, printers, and technical support tools	Yes			CapEx/OpEx	The client-side hardware could be on a fixed-cost basis (for the most part), and hence CapEx classified. However, it can also be part of some leased contract (per-desktop basis), and therefore it could be classified as a variable cost, and operational expenditure (OpEx). The desktop/laptop service cost elements represent direct cost to the overall Desktop as a Service, unless positioned otherwise.

Network	Switches, routers, circuits, network equipment, transport and access, cables, and fiber optic cables	Yes		Yes	CapEx	Generally, the majority of network components are classified as fixed capital expenses because they are expensive and used for years when supporting IT services. Similar to server hardware, these cost elements could be directly allocated (that is, traced) to a service, or could be classified as indirect overhead cost to an SDDC VM as a service for instance. A less-expensive approach could be deployed if the VMware SDDC virtual networking advantage (that is, NSX) is enabled, which lowers those fixed and CapEx costs along with some direct labor costs involved.
Storage	Storage related equipment (IBM, HDS, and EMC)	Yes		Yes	CapEx	Most of the storage investment is for long-term usage, and that's why it is seen as a fixed capital cost. Storage cost elements could be classified as direct cost components if they are allocated entirely for one service, but for the most part they are classified as indirect cost as part of the overhead to support a service, such as SDDC VM as a Service.
Appliances	Security, firewall, backup, network tools/tests, and so on	Yes		Yes	CapEx	Similar to Network

Software	Enterprise license agreements	Yes		Yes	CapEx/OpEx	If one time upfront payment, then CapEx. Otherwise (if annually paid), then OpEx. Also, if maintenance cost can be separated from software licenses cost, then also OpEx maintenance cost.
	Subscription basis (for example, pay-as-you-go)	Yes		Yes	OpEx	Pay-as-you-go software is typically classified as variable, but could be seen as fixed if the contract is for the full period. However, in all cases it is part of the operational expenses (OpEx), and no depreciation is considered. The same direct and indirect cost classification discussion applies as with the licensed enterprise agreement.
Facilities	Data center facilities, power, and cooling supplies	Yes		Yes	CapEx/OpEx	Data center facilities are all fixed cost assets, and are classified as capital expenses. If you are costing out the data center as a service, these costs are direct. However, if you are costing a service that is running out of this data center, these costs are classified as indirect costs.

Contracts	Maintenance and Support contracts	Yes		Yes	OpEx	Contracts are typically based on the type and scope of contracts. For example, some contracts are based on activities performed, which can be classified as variable, and others are based on flat rate and can be safely classified as fixed. These are typically seen as operational expenses, and are mostly considered indirect costs because they hold support terms for a lot of other services provided by a specific vendor. Contracts costs could be classified as direct cost if the entire contract can be allocated to a service.
Projects	ICT projects and process improvement	Yes		Yes	CapEx/OpEx	Depending on the project's context, purpose, structure, execution timeline, and fiscal year, some of its costs are classified as variable, others as fixed. Similarly, some of its phases might be classified as capital investments, while others are classified as operational expenditures. If a project affects one service, it can be entirely allocated to that service (direct cost). However, if a process improvement project is expected to improve all IT efficiency, its cost is classified as indirect cost to all IT services.

Labor	CIO and top IT leadership team				OpEx	Typically, the IT executive team cost is considered part of IT overhead, and therefore, it is one of those cost elements that should *not* be part of the service manufacturing cost calculation. These costs are seen as fixed because they don't change frequently over time, and are part of the operational expenditures.
	ICT staff (non-leadership)		Yes	Yes	OpEx	The service related roles costs are fixed costs because they don't frequently change over time, but could be classified as variable if their utilization based cost varies over periods. These costs are classified as direct costs (for example, a dedicated service admin) or indirect cost, such as a shared service administrator who manages 10 other services and whose cost allocation might be based on percentage of time spent, or utilization. These are typically operational costs.

	Hourly paid (for example, overtime or contracts)		Yes	Yes	OpEx	The hourly paid labor is a variable cost. However, if the laborers are supporting IT services, they are either direct or indirect costs depending on the scope of services or dedication level. These costs are typically operational.
Overhead	Office supplies, office rent, and so on				CapEx/OpEx	Follow finance department guidelines and policies.
Others	Training and professional development	Yes		Yes	OpEx	Follow finance department guidelines and policies.
	T and E	Yes		Yes	OpEx	Follow finance department guidelines and policies.
Fleet	Transport vehicles	Yes		Yes	CapEx	
	Fuel	Yes		Yes	OpEx	

Summary

VMware allows customers to continue their cloud journey through Cloud Foundation and vRealize Suite, where Cloud Foundation addresses the cloud infrastructure layer and vRealize Suite addresses the **Cloud Management Platform** (**CMP**) layer of a cloud stack.

Cloud Foundation helps customers quickly and efficiently stand-up and manage the cloud infrastructure foundation through SDDC Manager. SDDC Manager automates the lifecycle management of the cloud infrastructure stack (from bring-up, to configuration, infrastructure provisioning, upgrades/patches, and so on), making it extremely simple for the cloud admin to build and maintain the cloud stack.

Following are the important aspects of any cloud deployments:

- **Multi-tenant**: Multi-tenancy is an architecture in which a single instance of a software application serves multiple customers. Each customer is called a tenant. Tenants may be given the ability to customize some parts of the application, such as color of the **user interface (UI)** or business rules, but they cannot customize the application's code.
- **Operational Expenditure (OpEx)**: An operating expense, operating expenditure, operational expense, operational expenditure, or OPEX is an ongoing cost for running a product, business, or system. Its counterpart, a **capital expenditure (CapEx)**, is the cost of developing or providing non-consumable parts for the product or system. For example, the purchase of a photocopier involves CapEx, and the annual paper, toner, power, and maintenance costs represents OpEx. For larger systems such as businesses, OpEx may also include the cost of workers and facility expenses such as rent and utilities.
- **On-Premises/Off-Premises (OPOP)**: Cloud computing will simply become ubiquitous in its many forms and we are all going to end up with a hybrid model of cloud adoption—a veritable mashup of cloud services spanning the entire gamut of offerings that we already have today.

Cloud Foundation and vRealize Suite are hybrid cloud solutions that extend to public clouds. Cloud Foundation is offered via IBM Cloud. vRealize today, manages vCloud Air network clouds, AWS, and Azure (via professional services support) endpoints, and helps customers to get the benefits of Cross-Cloud services, across different platforms, in different locations.

Please browse the following reference for more documents and the latest updates:

```
https://www.vmware.com/in/products/cloud-foundation.html, https://www.vmware.
com/content/dam/digitalmarketing/vmware/en/pdf/products/cloud-foundation/
vmware-cloud-foundation-one-cloud-case-study.pdf
```

Other Books You May Enjoy

If you enjoyed this book, you may be interested in these other books by Packt:

Hybrid Cloud for Architects

Alok Shrivastwa

ISBN: 978-1-78862-351-3

- Learn the demographics and definitions of Hybrid Cloud
- Understand the different architecture and design of Hybrid Cloud
- Explore multi-cloud strategy and use it with your hybrid cloud
- Implement a Hybrid Cloud using CMP / Common API's
- Implement a Hybrid Cloud using Containers
- Overcome various challenges and issues while working with your Hybrid Cloud
- Understand how to monitor your Hybrid Cloud
- Discover the security implications in the Hybrid Cloud

VMware vSphere 6.5 Cookbook
Abhilash G B, Cedric Rajendran

ISBN: 978-1-78712-741-8

- Upgrade your existing vSphere environment or perform a fresh deployment
- Automate the deployment and management of large sets of ESXi hosts in your vSphere Environment
- Configure and manage FC, iSCSI, and NAS storage, and get more control over how storage resources are allocated and managed
- Configure vSphere networking by deploying host-wide and data center-wide switches in your vSphere environment
- Configure high availability on a host cluster and learn how to enable the fair distribution and utilization of compute resources
- Patch and upgrade the vSphere environment
- Handle certificate request generation and renew component certificates
- Monitor performance of a vSphere environment

Leave a review - let other readers know what you think

Please share your thoughts on this book with others by leaving a review on the site that you bought it from. If you purchased the book from Amazon, please leave us an honest review on this book's Amazon page. This is vital so that other potential readers can see and use your unbiased opinion to make purchasing decisions, we can understand what our customers think about our products, and our authors can see your feedback on the title that they have worked with Packt to create. It will only take a few minutes of your time, but is valuable to other potential customers, our authors, and Packt. Thank you!

Index

N

Printed in Great Britain
by Amazon